Christian Missionary Activity in the Early Middle Ages

Professor Richard E. Sullivan

Richard E. Sullivan

Christian Missionary Activity in the Early Middle Ages

VARIORUM

This edition copyright © 1994 by Richard E. Sullivan.

Published by VARIORUM
Ashgate Publishing Limited
Gower House, Croft Road,
Aldershot, Hampshire GU11 3HR
Great Britain

Ashgate Publishing Company
Old Post Road,
Brookfield, Vermont 05036
USA

ISBN 0-86078-402-9

British Library CIP data
Sullivan, Richard E.
Christian Missionary Activity in the Early Middle Ages
(Variorum Collected Studies Series; CS 431)
I. Sullivan, Richard E. II. Series
266.009

The paper used in this publication meets the minimum requirements of the
American National Standard for Information Sciences – Permanence
of Paper for Printed Library Materials, ANSI Z39.48-1984. ∞ ™

Printed by Galliard (Printers) Ltd
Great Yarmouth, Norfolk, Great Britain

COLLECTED STUDIES SERIES CS431

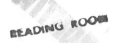

CONTENTS

This volume contains x + 265 pages

PUBLISHER'S NOTE

The articles in this volume, as in all others in the Collected Studies Series, have not been given a new, continuous pagination. In order to avoid confusion, and to facilitate their use where these same studies have been referred to elsewhere, the original pagination has been maintained wherever possible.

Each article has been given a Roman number in order of appearance, as listed in the Contents. This number is repeated on each page and quoted in the index entries.

PREFACE

I am grateful for the opportunity to draw together into a single collection the six essays that make up this volume. Their citation over the years by a variety of scholars suggests that they may still be useful to anyone interested in what was one of the crucial facets of the history of the early Middle Ages, namely, the spread of Christianity in the world inhabited by the heirs of the Roman Empire and of Greco-Roman civilization. Their appearance in a single volume will certainly make them more easily accessible.

The investigations from which these articles emerged were originally prompted by a sense of frustration. Even at the beginning of my education as an historian more than a half century ago I was fascinated by the spread of religion as a dimension of the changing historical scene. As my attention to that phenomenon became more sharply focused on the early Middle Ages—an era notable for the remarkable success of the adherents of Christianity and Islam in propagating their messages—I found myself hard pressed to understand what was involved in the processes through which one religion replaced another. The scholarly treatments which I read, especially those dealing with the spread of Christianity, were dominated by a triumphal tone, an unwavering assumption that the victory of Christianity was inevitable. That assumption, reflecting an interpretation of the historical process deeply rooted in the Judeo-Christian intellectual tradition, was sometimes glossed to suit modern sensibilities by adding the element of power to the formula: the inevitable was made more inevitable by the superior political, military, economic, and cultural resources of the victors. In short, the spread of Christianity during the early Middle Ages posed no real historical problem.

However, when I began to examine the surviving record that dealt with the spread of Christianity between about 500 and 900, it became obvious that there were many unanswered questions. What were the particular circumstances at any specific moment that provided the opportunity to win converts? Who took the initiative in the effort to advance Christianity? Who did the actual work of confronting those holding a different religion? What motivated missionary leaders and workers to undertake their formidable task? What resources were at their avail? What methods did they use to persuade non-Christians to accept Christianity? What was the nature of the encounter between missionaries and their target population? What was the consequence in the lives of converts of accepting a new religion? What difference did success in winning converts make in the world inhabited by the victors? Did any of these facets of missionary activity change with passing time? Somehow, explanatory paradigms that posited inevitability or that hinged on *Machtpolitik* were too constricted to embrace what the evidence said about the many sides of early medieval missionary activity.

The studies collected here attempted to expand the field of vision from which these issues were viewed. They sought to translate the dialogue involving religious expansion from the idiom of universal history to one that was particular and specific in terms of time, place, and circumstance. They sought to put the encounter between the adherents of different religious into a context that involved the full range of circumstances surrounding the lives of all of the protagonists. To the extent that my efforts in these directions bore any fruit, it became clear to me that the advance of Christianity was much more complex than previously investigators had allowed. The engagement of the adherents of different religions occurring in specific settings and unique circumstances unleashed forces that reverberated through the lives of all involved in ways that made a difference in the course of history. In fact, my ventures into early medieval missionary history left me convinced that no aspect of the history of that era can make any sense unless due attention is given to the complex events surrounding the encounters in which human relationships with the divine and the souls of men and women were at stake. Whether my essays sustain that conviction must remain for the reader to decide.

A great length of time has passed since the publication of the earliest essay in this collection (1953) and quite a few years since the latest (1979). In the interval scholars have continued to explore the history of the expansion of Christianity during the early Middle Ages, although perhaps not as intensively as the subject warrants. While the source base upon which ongoing research in early medieval missionary history has relied has not changed much during the last forty years, the way in which historians decode those sources has undergone considerable change. So also have the issues that inform modern historical inquiry. As a consequence, recent scholarship has enriched our understanding of the themes and issues treated in the essays presented here. As best I am able to assess the overall thrust of that scholarship and with due allowance for bias, there seems no reason to conclude that that enrichment has outdated the crucial findings reflected in the essays included here. In re-reading these studies I was struck by how they pre-figured many themes that have become central to contemporary approaches to religious expansion: cross-cultural interactions and their results; comparative approaches to historical movements; strategies and techniques of communication; the frontier phenomenon; *mentalités*; the conversion process; popular religion; ideology. That awareness has led me to hope that reading these essays as a collection might encourage a new generation of scholars informed by the latest focal points of historical inquiry to turn once again to the study of the impact of religion and all its cultural accoutrements on the lives of people of the early Middle Ages.

I gratefully acknowledge the assistance rendered me by the library staffs at the University of Illinois, Northeast Missouri Teachers College (now Northeast Missouri State University), and Michigan State University. Equally invaluable was the encouragement extended by fellow students and colleagues at these same institutions. I also wish to thank the copyright-holders who granted permission to reproduce these essays.

For the encouragement given long ago to join the then thinly populated ranks of those interested in the early Middle Ages and for the counsel they offered in guiding my first steps in that strange terrain, I am eternally in the debt of the late Edgar N. Johnson and of Charles E. Odegaard. To them I dedicate this volume.

East Lansing, Michigan   RICHARD E. SULLIVAN
March 1, 1993

I

CAROLINGIAN MISSIONARY THEORIES

The spectacular successes won by Christianity over paganism during the Carolingian period (c. 687-900) have usually been explained in terms of a victory gained by the use of forceful methods, a conclusion which is certainly substantiated in large part by the record of missionary affairs in the period. However, a note of caution should, perhaps, temper this generalization. Carolingian literature contains a considerable number of discussions of and allusions to the question of the best way to conduct missionary work. Often these theoretical considerations of missionary technique emphasize means other than force to gain converts. A description of these theories of missionary procedure might be useful in illuminating the rather obscure question of the methods employed by missionaries during the eighth and ninth centuries.

One problem that the Carolingian theorists on missionary method grappled with was that of finding a way to make pagans receptive to Christianity as a substitute for their existing religion. Carolingian writers developed two distinct concepts on this question. A small number argued that a concerted effort must be made to persuade the pagans by religious argument alone that Christianity was a superior religion with infinitely more to offer than the pagans' old religion. However, most Carolingians, prompted by a strong conviction that the spread of Christianity was divinely ordained and by a hatred of paganism, felt that pagans could rightly be coerced into accepting

* Mr. Sullivan is assistant professor of history in Michigan State University. The present article has been derived in part from material used for a doctoral dissertation at the University of Illinois.

Christianity, the most efficient form of coercion being some form of political pressure.

The concept of peaceful persuasion by argumentation on religious grounds was usually presented by eighth and ninth-century writers only in very broad terms. The papacy often counseled missionaries to confront their pagan audiences with Christian concepts couched in language suited to pagan mentality. Scripture was usually designated as the best source of material apt to convince pagans that Christianity was superior to paganism.[1] Nicholas I, writing to the newly converted Bulgar king, Boris, in 866 indicated the rationale which prompted the papacy to insist that conversions must be made by persuasion. He argued that conversion was a gift of God, brought about by enlightenment from on high. Any attempt to hasten the opening of the pagan's heart except by argument was fruitless and dangerous.[2] Missionary biographers repeatedly paid their respects to the idea of peaceful persuasion as a proper means of winning converts. Hardly a missionary biography is without a reference, usually in very generalized terms, to the efforts which the subject devoted to an attempt to persuade the pagans to give up their ancient religion.[3] Occasionally a biographer

---

[1] For examples, cf. *S. Bonifatii et Lulli Epistolae*, 12, 17, 20, 21, 24, 25, 26, 28, 42, 43, edited by Michael Tangl, *Die Briefe des heiligen Bonifatius und Lullus*, *Monumenta Germaniae Historica* (hereafter cited as *MGH*), Epistolae Selectae (Berlin, 1916), I, 17-18, 30-31, 34, 35-36, 41-47, 49-52, 67-69; *Epistolae selectae pontificum Romanorum Carolo Magno et Ludowico Pio regnantibus scriptae*, 11, edited by Karolus Hampe, *MGH,* Epistolae, V, 69-70; Migne, *PL*, CXVIII, 1035-1036; Rimbert, *Vita Anskarii*, c. 13, edited by G. Waitz, *MGH,* Scriptores rerum Germanicarum in usum scholarum (Hanover, 1884), p. 35. Hereafter Boniface's letters will be cited as Boniface, *Ep.*, ed. Tangl, with appropriate letter and page numbers. The following abbreviations will be used for the various series in the *MGH* : SS. for Scriptores; SS. rer. Merov. for Scriptores rerum Merovingicarum; SS. rer. Germ. for Scriptores rerum Germanicarum in usum scholarum; Ep. for Epistolae.

[2] Nicholas, *Ep.* 99, c. 41, edited by Ernestus Perels, *MGH,* Ep., VI, 582-583.

[3] For some typical examples of this aspect of missionary biographies, cf. Willibald, *Vita Bonifatii,* c. 5-6, in *Vitae sancti Bonifatii archiepiscopi Moguntini,* edited by Wilhelmus Levison, *MGH,* SS. rer. Germ. (Hanover and Leipzig, 1905), pp. 23-27; *Vita sancti Willehadi*, c. 2-5, edited by Albertus Poncelet, Acta Sanctorum, Nov., III, 843-845; Altfrid, *Vita s. Liudgeri*, Lib. I, *passim,* in *Die "Vitae sancti Liudgeri,"* edited by Wilhelm Diekamp, *Geschichtsquellen des Bisthums Münster* (Münster, 1881), IV, 3-53; Rimbert, *Vita Anskarii,* c. 7, 8, 11, 26-28, edited by Waitz, pp. 28, 30, 32-33, 55-59; Eigilis, *Vita sancti Sturmi,* c. 22-24, edited by Pertz, *MGH,* SS, II, 376-377; Alcuin, *Vita Willi-*

illustrated how he thought this should be done by putting words into the mouth of a missionary in the form of a sermon that a missionary was alleged to have delivered to a pagan audience.[4] These sample sermons dwelt especially on the great power of the Christian God, the inanity of pagan deities, and the beneficial rewards, both present and future, that would result from the acceptance of Christianity. The emphasis in these sermons tended to be on the material benefits that pagans would gain by accepting the Christian God, suggesting that Carolingian writers thought that pagans might most easily be moved by an argument that convinced them that a new religion would provide them a happier earthly existence.[5]

Occasionally writers of the Carolingian period sought to explain in greater detail what arguments they thought might be convincing. In 738 or 739 Gregory II addressed a letter to the Saxons, exhorting them to accept Christianity. Couching his arguments in the language of Scripture, he commanded the Saxons to abandon their "lying deities" and to accept the one God, who had made all things and who willed that all men would worship Him. He tried to convince the Saxons that they would be lacking in faith, grace, and eternal salvation unless they accepted the Christian God, although he made no attempt to explain these theological concepts to his untutored audience.[6] Nicholas I wrote a letter to Heric II of Denmark in 864 trying to hasten the king's conversion. The pope's letter concentrated primarily on explaining the omnipotence of the Christian God and the desirability of eternal salvation. He attempted to make Heric realize that only in the hereafter would man escape the miseries and disappointments of terrestial life and that only a belief in the Christian

---

brordi archiepiscopi Traiectensis, c. 9, 11, edited by W. Levison, MGH, SS. rer. Merov., VII, 124, 126; Venerabilis Baedae Historica Ecclesiastica Gentis Anglorum, V, c. 9-11, in Venerabilis Baedae Opera Historica, edited by Carolus Plummer (Oxford, 1898), I, 298-302.

[4] Alcuin, Vita Willibrordi, c. 11, edited by Levison, MGH, SS. rer. Merov., VII, 125; Vita Lebuini antiqua, c. 6, edited by A. Hofmeister, MGH, SS, XXX², 794; Ermoldus Nigellus, In honorem Hludowici Christianissimi caesaris augusti elegiacum carmen, Lib. IV, vv. 1911-1991, edited by Edmond Faral in Les classiques de l'histoire de France au moyen âge (Paris, 1932), XIV, 146, 148, 150.

[5] Rimbert, Vita Anskarii, c. 27, edited by Waitz, pp. 57-59, especially stresses material rewards.

[6] Boniface, Ep. 21, edited by Tangl, pp. 35-36.

God could assure salvation, the pagan gods being powerless to save a man.[7]

The most explicit example of the thinking on the problem of persuading a pagan to surrender to Christianity came from the pen of an Anglo-Saxon, Daniel, Bishop of Winchester and close friend of St. Boniface. In a letter to Boniface,[8] Daniel drew up an argument to be used against the pagans his friend was encountering in Germany. The bishop suggested that a missionary should begin by provoking the pagans to present their own version of the origins of the gods and goddesses. Then the missionary should assault the illogicality of their mythology, demonstrating in as many ways as possible the self-contradictions involved in a theory of divinity which rested upon the idea of gods being begotten through the intercourse of male and female and which centered around a worship of gods in the form of graven images. Daniel also advised Boniface to attack the pagans' belief that their gods brought them material benefits by pointing out the favorable position of Christians as compared to the pagans. Throughout his whole exposition on converting pagans, Daniel placed the emphasis on disputation as the surest means to shake the confidence of the pagans in their old religion. He believed that pagans could grasp the fine points involved in a discussion of the origins of gods, the creation of the universe, and the powers possessed by various deities. He was certain that Boniface could succeed best against the pagans by "touching them from the flank, so to speak, so that the pagans, thrown into confusion rather than angered, may be ashamed of their absurd ideas and may understand that their infamous ceremonies and fables are well known to us."[9] The crucial step for a missionary was to undermine the confidence of the pagans in their gods. Daniel counseled the avoidance of a positive statement of Christian teaching, except as a means of comparison with the absurdities of pagan belief; to present a positive case for Christianity would only antagonize the pagan mentality.

These discussions of the necessity and the means of persuading pagans to become Christians, however, must not be overemphasized, since they formed a small part of missionary theory. Most Carolingian writers assumed that a missionary would begin his work under con-

---

[7] Nicholas, *Ep.* 27, edited by Perels, *MGH*, Ep., VI, 293-294.

[8] Boniface, *Ep.* 23, edited by Tangl, pp. 38-41.

[9] *Ibid.*, p. 40.

ditions where large masses of pagans had been left no choice but to accept baptism; the missionary needed to concern himself very little with "persuasion." This attitude was well illustrated in the literature that grew out of the problem of converting the Avars in 796. When Alcuin addressed his letters to Charlemagne's court in 796 to plead for a sensible missionary policy in connection with the Avars, he made no protest against the fact that Charlemagne's armies would force the Avars to accept baptism. He was interested in what happened after the Avars had been made submissive.[10] A synod held on the Danube just prior to the campaign of 796 to lay plans for converting the Avars gave no attention to the question of persuading the Avars to become Christians. Its decisions were made on the assumption that Charlemagne's armies would create an audience for the missionaries.[11] A tract entitled *Ratio de cathecizandis rudibus,* probably composed as a guide for the priests who were to be sent to baptize the Avars and one of the fullest Carolingian discussions of the problem of instructing pagans, paid only passing attention to the question of convincing pagans to surrender their old religion. The tract was written on the assumption that priests would be dealing with pagans who already were willing to accept Christianity, and that the missionaries need not worry about disposing of stubborn adherents to paganism.[12] To these authors and many others of the age missionary work in the proper sense began after the pagans had been made to see the necessity of changing their old religion by someone other than the missionary.

Several Carolingian writers made it perfectly clear that they felt the most efficient way to bring pagans to the point where they would listen to Christian teaching was the use of political force, arguing openly that it was justifiable and praiseworthy to initiate the conversion process by the use of the sword. The author who wrote that Charlemagne "preached with the iron tongue"[13] intended his statement as praise. Paganism deserved no better treatment than ruthless suppression. In the same spirit Alcuin advised one of Charle-

---

[10] Alcuin, *Ep.* 99, 107, 110-113, edited by Ernestus Dümmler, *MGH,* Ep., IV, 143-144, 153-154, 156-166.

[11] *Concilia aevi karolini,* I, 20, edited by Albertus Werminghoff, *MGH,* Leges, Sectio III, Tomus II¹, 172-176.

[12] *Ratio de cathecizandis rudibus,* edited by Joseph Michael Heer, *Ein karolingischer Missions-Katechismus* (Freiburg im Breisgau, 1911), pp. 77-88.

[13] *Translatio sancti Liborii,* c. 5, edited by G. Pertz, *MGH,* SS, IV, 151.

magne's sons "to be terrible against pagans."[14] An Irish pilgrim named Clement summed up the attitude of the era very well when he wrote the following to Tassilo, Duke of Bavaria, after the latter had won a military victory over the Avars in 772:

The Lord our Almighty God will fight with you and for you. They the enemy are pagans and gentiles who do not believe in your God, but adore idols and images of demons. Concerning such gods the prophet Jeremias said: "Let the gods who did not make heaven and earth perish from the earth and from under the earth." And let it be likewise to those who make them and who adore idols; let them disappear and flee from the face of the Lord; let them be terrified and dispersed and perish from the sight of Christians.[15]

Pope Hadrian I proclaimed Charlemagne worthy of the highest praise for bringing the Saxons into the Christian fold by conquest, and he publicized papal approval of this admirable deed by announcing the observation of a fast to give thanks for the marvelous success.[16] Einhard praised Charlemagne's persistence in pursuing the Saxon wars until the pagans were ready to surrender their religion.[17] Even Alcuin, who complained that "the whole miserable people of the Saxons lost the effect of the sacrament of baptism because this people never had the foundations of the faith in their hearts,"[18] did not blame the failure of the Saxon mission on the fact that the opening for Christianity had been created by force. His contention was that the Saxons were not handled properly once they had arrived at the point where they were willing to accept the faith. He was always ready to approve stern measures as a way of bringing pagans to the baptismal font and to praise those who used such measures.[19]

---

[14] Alcuin, *Ep.* 119, edited by Dümmler, *MGH*, Ep., IV, 174.

[15] *Episolae variorum Carolo magno regnante scriptae*, 1, edited by Dümmler, *MGH*, Ep., IV, 796. For comparable examples, cf. Boniface, *Ep.* 120, edited by Tangl, p. 256; Angilbertus, *De conversione Saxonum carmen*, vv. 24-27, 37-46, 48, 56-62, edited by Ernestus Dümmler, *MGH*, Poetae latini aevi carolini, I, 380-381.

[16] *Codex carolinus*, 76, edited by Wilhelmus Gundlach, *MGH*, Ep., III, 607-608.

[17] Einhard, *Vita Karoli Magni imperatoris*, c. 7, edited by Louis Halphen, *Les classiques de l'histoire de France au moyen âge* (2 ed., Paris, 1938), pp. 24-26.

[18] Alcuin, *Ep.* 113, edited by Dümmler, *MGH*, Ep., IV, 164.

[19] Cf. especially, *ibid.*, 110, p. 157. Also, *ibid.*, 7, 41, 98, 178, 185, pp. 31-33, 84-85, 142, 294, 310-311 for expression of similar ideas.

However, the use of force to convince pagans that they must accept Christianity was only a preliminary step in the Carolingian concept of missionary method. The literature dealing with missionary procedures reveals a keen concern about the most suitable manner in which to handle pagans who had been brought to the point where they had no choice but to accept Christianity. The theorists almost universally accepted the idea that pagans, regardless of how they had been made ready to accept the Christian faith, had to receive instruction in the rudiments of that belief before they could be baptized. Such instruction was thought necessary in order to make them realize the importance of their conversion and thus to guarantee their firmness in the new faith.

During the early phase of the Carolingian period when Anglo-Saxon missionaries dominated the scene most discussions of missionary procedures made little reference to the need for instructing pagans before baptizing them. The practices followed by the Anglo-Saxons indicate that they needed no reminders that pagans should be instructed prior to baptism. The Anglo-Saxon concept of missionary method, strongly influenced by Irish ideas, centered around the actual meeting of missionary and pagan for the purpose of presenting Christian ideas to the pagans.[20] It was only when the Carolingian rulers turned to forceful methods that writers sought to develop arguments justifying and urging pre-baptismal instruction. Alcuin was the leading spokesman in this cause. Moved by his realization of the failure of the Saxon mission and by the prospect that the Avars might be driven to the same reaction, he wrote Arn of Salzburg in 796 to urge the following approach to the conversion of pagans:

Our Lord Jesus Christ ordered his disciples, saying "Go, teach all peoples, baptizing them in the name of the Father, the Son, and the Holy Spirit, teaching them to follow all that I have ordered you." He said to teach first and then baptize. First, He ordered them to teach the catholic faith; after the faith had been accepted, He ordered them to baptize in the name of the Holy Trinity. Then having imbued them with the faith and washed them with holy baptism, He ordered them to instruct in Gospel precepts.[21]

In other letters Alcuin tried to buttress this argument, always emphasizing the pressing need to find a substitute for forced baptism.

[20] For a discussion of Anglo-Saxon missionary method cf. my article, "The Carolingian Missionary and the Pagan," *Speculum*, XXVIII (October, 1953), 705-740.
[21] Alcuin, *Ep.* 113, edited by Dümmler, *MGH*, Ep., IV, 164.

He argued that rigorous impositions, like the tithe, only repelled the "infantile and avaricious minds" of the pagans. True conversion came only when the rational mind that existed in each pagan had been affected as a result of being confronted with the basic tenets of the faith.[22] The missionary must be content to wait for God to enlighten each pagan before administering baptism, bearing the onerous and discouraging burden of presenting Christian beliefs to pagans as a service in God's cause.[23]

Important as it was to try to persuade some elements of Carolingian society that more care must be taken to instruct pagans, this was a rather useless move unless some attempt was made to define what ought to be taught. A considerable amount of attention was given to this aspect of the education of pagans. This question did not assume specific form until the debacle in Saxony brought the problem to the front as a crucial issue in Carolingian royal policy. Prior to that most writers on missionary procedure assumed that missionaries knew what to teach to unbaptized pagans ready to accept Christianity. Most of the saints' lives extolling the missionary work of the Anglo-Saxons begin with a panegyric on the extensive knowledge about the faith which the missionaries possessed prior to their encounters with pagans. These saints were pictured as being so learned in theology that there were few who could add anything to their knowledge.[24] Under such conditions there was little use in trying to instruct them on what they should teach pagans. Apparently continental society accepted this estimate of Anglo-Saxon missionaries. Gregory II was willing to accept Boniface as a co-worker in spreading the faith because he felt that the latter had been "from childhood a student of sacred literature" and, therefore, was especially suited for instructing pagans.[25] The only specific idea that emerges from most of the writing concerned with Anglo-Saxon missionaries was the

---

[22] *Ibid.*, 110, p. 158.

[23] *Ibid.*, 111, pp. 159-162.

[24] For examples of this, cf. Willibald, *Vita Bonifatii*, c. 1-3, edited by Levison, pp. 4-13, *Vita Burchardi*, c. 2, edited by O. Holder-Egger, *MGH*, SS, XV, 48; Nun of Heidenheim, *Vita Wynnebaldi*, c. 1-2, edited by Holder-Egger, *MGH*, SS, XV, 106-107; Nun of Heidenheim, *Vita Willibaldi episcopi Eichstentensis*, c. 2, edited by Holder-Egger, *MGH*, SS, XV, 89; Lambert of Hersfeld, *Vita Lulli*, c. 1, edited by Holder-Egger, *MGH*, SS, XV, 135-136; *Vita Willehadi*, c. 1, edited by Poncelet, *Acta Sanctorum*, Nov., III, 842; Alcuin, *Vita Willibrordi*, c. 2-4, edited by Levison, *MGH*, SS. rer. Merov., VII, 117-119.

[25] Boniface, *Ep.* 12, edited by Tangl, p. 17.

conviction that Scripture was the basic source for the ideas that were fitted for pagan instruction.[26] It was assumed that a skilled missionary would be able to extract from Scripture the kind of material that was fitted for the pagan mentality prior to baptism.

However, the Saxon disaster, as has been noted, led to a serious concern over finding a means to impress upon the pagans a deeper, more comprehensive appreciation of Christianity. Perhaps realizing that little consideration had been given to the problem of selecting materials suited for pagan instruction, several writers of the late eighth and early ninth centuries attempted to clarify this issue. And here Alcuin again served as the leading spokesman. Reminding Charlemagne that Paul, "the preacher of the whole world, with Christ speaking to him, signified that the new conversion of peoples to the faith ought to be fed on pleasant precepts just as the age of infancy is nurtured on milk, lest the fragile mind vomit what it has drunk on account of the difficult precepts,"[27] Alcuin tried to define a body of doctrines which summed up the essence of the faith, yet was fitted to the mental ability of the pagans. He stated:

First a man ought to be instructed concerning the immortality of the soul and concerning future life and concerning the retribution of good and evil men and the eternal reward for each kind. After that each ought to be taught for what sins and crimes he will suffer eternal punishment with the devil and for what good deeds and works he will enjoy eternal glory with Christ. Then a belief in the Holy Trinity ought to be diligently taught and the coming into the world of our Lord Jesus Christ, Son of God, for the salvation of the human race ought to be expounded. The newly-won mind ought to be made firm concerning the mystery of His passion, the truth of the resurrection, the glory of the ascension into heaven, His future coming to judge all people, and the eternity of the punishment upon evil doers and the prize for the good. And then the man, strengthened and prepared in the faith, ought to be baptized.[28]

Alcuin argued that three general features of the faith would have a special appeal to the pagans, viz., the idea of eternal retribution for good or evil conduct, the way in which man earns his punishment or

[26] For examples illustrating the importance attached to the use of Scripture in missionary instruction, cf. *ibid.,* 12, 30, 43, 76, pp. 18, 54, 68, 159; Eigilis, *Vita Sturmi,* c. 2, edited by Pertz, *MGH,* SS, II, 366; Liudger, *Vita Gregorii,* c. 8, edited by Holder-Egger, *MGH,* SS, XV, 73.

[27] Alcuin, *Ep.* 110, edited by Dümmler, *MGH,* Ep., IV, 157.

[28] *Ibid.* pp. 158-159.

I

reward, and the story of Christ and His relation to sinful mankind. As a more complete exposition of his ideas and as a guide for their application, Alcuin directed anyone interested—presumably those who would engage in teaching the Avars—to St. Augustine's *De cate-chizandis rudibus*.

If one turns to Augustine's work, expecting to find, as Alcuin says, "that order which ought to be followed in instructing a man of adult age,"[29] he will encounter certain difficulties. Augustine's manual was written to serve as a guide for the first phase of a well-defined procedure governing the admittance of pagans to the Christian fold. This procedure required that a candidate first account for his motives for wanting to be a Christian and give formal recognition to certain basic elements of the faith which were presented to him by an instructor. Thereupon the pagan became a catechumen and received more extensive instruction.[30] Augustine wrote his tract only with the first step in mind, since it was not intended to serve as a guide for teaching catechumens through the whole period of instruction that would conclude with baptism. Since the early system of initiating pagans into the Church had almost entirely dropped out of use by the end of the eighth century, there is no reason to believe that Alcuin proposed to use the work for the exact purpose for which it was written. Moreover, St. Augustine made it clear that he was writing with an audience that had some education, and in this respect Alcuin's prospective pupils could hardly qualify.[31]

In spite of this difficulty, Augustine's work was still suited for Alcuin's purpose. Augustine was concerned with making a pagan realize that conversion involved the acceptance of the fundamental

[29] *Ibid.*, p. 159.

[30] For a description of the early institution of the catechumenate and its subsequent transformation, cf. L. Duchesne, *Origines du culte chrétien* (5 ed., Paris, 1920), pp. 309-360; G. Bareille, "Catéchuménat" in *Dictionnaire de théologie catholique,* edited by A. Vacant and E. Mangenot (Paris, 1902, ff), II, 1968-1987; P. de Puniet, "Catéchuménat" in *Dictionnaire d'archéologie chrétienne et de liturgie,* edited by Fernand Cabrol and H. Leclercq (Paris, 1907, ff), II², 2579-2621.

[31] For statements indicating Augustine's purpose, cf. *S. Aureli Augustini Hipponiensis episcopi de catechizandis rudibus liber unus,* c. 1, 26, tr. with introduction and commentary by Joseph Patrick Christopher [The Catholic University of America, Patristic Studies, Vol. VIII] (Washington, 1926), pp. 14, 112-114. For the kind of audience Augustine had in mind, cf. especially, *ibid.,* c. 8, 9, 16, pp. 38, 42, 68

ideas of the Christian faith and that conversion on any other than purely religious grounds was invalid. His tract sought to outline these basic ideas in a way that a pagan could grasp before he proceeded to a fuller study of the new religion. In short, Augustine was intent upon defining the minimum religious knowledge that a potential convert must have before being accepted into the Christian community. Alcuin was in quest of the same thing—a guide to be used in presenting the barest essentials of Christian doctrine to the pagan Avars. By examining the content of Augustine's work as it related to the rudiments of the faith, one can discover what Alcuin thought should be taught to pagans in order to prepare them for baptism.

St. Augustine approached his problem in two ways. First, he outlined the most fundamental concepts which an instructor must present to a candidate for baptism.[32] Then he supplied a sample discourse illustrating the presentation of these concepts in an interesting and comprehensible manner.[33] God's ways toward man should first be impressed upon potential converts. This end could be accomplished by presenting a summary of Old Testament history with emphasis on man's sinfulness,[34] and by retelling the story of Christ as presented in the New Testament with emphasis on God's love for man.[35] From this review of the scriptural account of the history of creation the pagan would learn the basic teachings of Christianity: the hope of salvation, the last judgment, and the promise of rewards for the good and of horrible punishments for the wicked.[36] The pagan would learn that only eternal life mattered and that only the Christian God could grant it—on His own terms. Finally, the pagan would learn of the evils and temptations of the world, including especially those involving any sort of idolatrous practice.[37] In Alcuin's opinion this was the milk upon which the tender minds of pagans ought to be nourished. Prior to baptism the pagan must be convinced that the Christian God is the all-powerful Creator, that He has a special concern for man, that He sent His Son as a

[32] *Ibid.*, 3-15, pp. 22-68.

[33] *Ibid.*, c. 16-26, pp. 68-114.

[34] *Ibid.*, c. 3, 16-21, pp. 22-24, 68-94, gives a summary of this material as it might be presented in lecture form.

[35] *Ibid.*, c. 4, 6, 22-24, pp. 26-30, 32-34, 94-104, summarizes the story of Christ in suitable lecture form.

[36] *Ibid.*, c. 7, pp. 34-36.

[37] *Ibid.*, c. 7, pp. 34-38.

Redeemer, that Christ instituted a church through which God could be reached, and that God provided eternal joy for those who lived a good life. If these ideas were properly presented to a pagan they might bring about a fundamental change of heart, and no pagan could be baptized until he knew and accepted these ideas.

Further evidence revealing what the Carolingian era thought should be taught to pagans prior to their baptism is contained in the *Ratio de cathecizandis rudibus,* probably written about the same time Alcuin was concerning himself with the conversion of the Avars. This work, composed as a guide for missionaries, dealt directly with the problem of instructing pagans who had expressed a willingness to accept Christianity, but who knew nothing about the new religion.[38] The author advised missionaries to take special pains to test the pagan's motives for desiring to become a Christian. Prior to any instruction the prospective convert must realize that the only acceptable reason for conversion was a desire to gain eternal life; the acceptance of Christianity in order to secure a temporal reward was not justifiable and must be discouraged. In order to establish this point in the mind of the pagan, the author developed an argument which hinged upon the concept that every man—including the pagan—was endowed with an immortal soul which eventually would be brought to account before God. The only way to save that soul was to give up the love of the mortal world for the love of God, to believe that in the soul alone resided the only real worth of human nature and that a certain pattern of conduct would insure a happy future for that soul. Having established the idea that no pagan could escape accounting for his soul, the author of the tract advised the missionary to show the pagan what God demands of him. Drawing from the Decalogue, the author argued that the pagan must be shown that he had to cease to worship idols, to commit murder or adultery, to bear false witness, to engage in incantations, auguries, or sacrifices of a pagan nature, and to worship in any other place except a church dedicated to the one God. The pagan must be exhorted to love God and his neighbor if he expects to gain salvation. Once this general argument had been developed, the author of the tract urged the missionary to devote special attention to certain important elements contained in it. A long section was devoted to God's intolerance of the worship of idols while another lengthy discussion treated

[38] *Ratio de cathecizandis rudibus,* c. 1, edited by Heer, p. 77.

the real nature of the Christian God. The pagan must be shown that God is all-powerful, merciful, just, good, wise, the source of all that man possesses, the creator of all; He is the ultimate that anyone could expect in divinity. It was especially important that the missionary compare the Christian God with the pagan gods in order to demonstrate the inferiority of the latter. The whole discussion was designed to turn the pagan's mind to the worship of a deity whose ability to act knew no limits, whether it be for the benefit of those who obey and worship that deity or for the condemnation of those who spurn that god.[39]

Ermoldus Nigellus in his poem in honor of Louis the Pious presented another version of what the Carolingian age considered the proper material for teaching pagans who were being prepared for baptism. In describing the preparations made prior to sending Ebo of Rheims to Denmark for missionary work in 823, Ermoldus had Louis deliver to Ebo a set of instructions on how to proceed once he had arrived among the pagan Danes. Louis urged that Ebo portray the Christian God as a mighty ruler in heaven, the creator of all things, including man. He was then to recount the story of man in paradise, his fall, the sinful generations that followed the fall, the deluge, and the emergence of a new horde of sinners. Then the missionary must explain God's decision to send His Son to redeem man, the Incarnation, and the death of Christ. The pagans must be made to understand that Christ provided for eternal salvation by instituting baptism, through which sinful man was regenerated and without which there could be no hope for eternal happiness. Moreover, the pagans must have it impressed on them that God demanded to be worshipped alone; they must abandon their worship of idols fashioned by human hands. Ebo was told to explain to the pagans the folly of a reasonable man worshipping such gods and the extent to which the worship of idols endangers the hope of salvation. As a final piece of advice, Louis instructed Ebo to rely on the Old and the New Testaments as infallible guides for his teaching.[40]

Almost all Carolingian writers on missionary affairs rejoiced when pagans had finally been baptized, which was unquestionably the high-point of the struggle against paganism. However, these theorists did

---

[39] These arguments are developed in *ibid.*, c. 1-6, pp. 77-88.

[40] Ermoldus Nigellus, *In Honorem Hludowici . . . carmen,* Lib. IV, vv. 1911-1991, edited by Faral, pp. 146, 148, 150.

I

not consider that the task of conversion was finished once pagans had been baptized. Several writers felt that the instruction which had been begun prior to baptism had to be continued in some fashion thereafter. Almost everyone who expressed an opinion on missionary problems assumed that a long and laborious effort would have to be expended on new converts before the conversion process could be considered concluded.[41] The evidence pertaining to this further stage of missionary work does not contain a concise statement of the procedure or the material by which a new convert's religious life might be improved. The nature of the problem made any kind of instruction fitting. Faced with a horde of new Christians who admittedly had not been fully schooled in the Christian religion, the Church could quite logically sanction any kind of instruction that would bring converts up to the religious standards customary throughout western Christendom. Although the usual approach to the instruction of new converts was vague and extremely general, two lines of activity received rather considerable discussion and might, therefore, be accepted as the chief concerns of Carolingian missionary writers when they contemplated the staggering task of enlightening those who had recently left paganism. On one hand, rather extensive attention was given to the transmission of a fuller knowledge of doctrinal matters and their ethical implications; on the other, even greater concern was shown for the proper instruction of new converts in matters of liturgy and ecclesiastical discipline.

Carolingian writers who concerned themselves with increasing the newly baptized converts' knowledge of the faith were usually inclined to concentrate on a few basic tenets of the new religion. They advocated that missionaries further analyze and explain religious ideas to which the new converts had been introduced prior to baptism. The most thorough example of a Carolingian discussion of a doctrinal and ethical instruction for new converts is contained in a tract entitled *De singulis libris canonicis scarapsus,* written by Pirmin.

[41] For examples illustrating the concern held by theorists on the problem of post-baptismal instruction, cf. Boniface, *Ep.* 24, 26, 28, 45, 51, 68, 87, edited by Tangl, pp. 41-43, 47, 51-52, 73-74, 92, 141, 200; Alcuin, *Ep.* 110, edited by Dümmler, *MGH,* Ep., IV, 159; *Concilia acvi karolini* I, 20, edited by Werminghoff, p. 175; Nicholas, *Ep.* 99, edited by Perels, *MGH,* Ep., VI, 566-600; Eigilis, *Vita Sturmi,* c. 3, edited by Pertz, *MGH,* SS, II, 366-367; Nun of Heidenheim, *Vita Wynnebaldi,* c. 5-7, edited by Holder-Egger, *MGH,* SS, XV, 110-112.

The author spent several years in the first quarter of the eighth century attempting to improve religious life in Bavaria and Alemannia, where the population was nominally Christian but was far from adequately versed in a knowledge of the faith. His tract was intended as a handbook to guide priests who were trying to correct this situation.[42]

Pirmin devoted the first section of his work to a summary of the history of mankind with special emphasis on man's fall and God's provision for his salvation. Obviously, this was intended to refresh the memories of the new Christians on doctrinal matters, since Pirmin closed the discussion by asking his audience to recall the vows taken at the time of baptism and repeated the Apostles' Creed as the best expression of the fundamentals of the faith. Pirmin implied that any attempt to instill a deeper understanding of the faith in the minds of new converts must begin only after the converts had grasped the meaning of the Christian interpretation of history, and after they had understood the basic doctrines set forth in the Creed. Post-baptismal instruction ought to begin by a thorough review of the material that should have been learned before baptism.[43]

Pirmin then came to the real point of his tract. "A Christian who has the name but does not do the deeds will not be glorified by Christ. He is a Christian who imitates and follows Christ in all things. . . .It is fitting for us, brothers, who have been baptized and have perceived the mandates of God to take care as the Holy Spirit warns in the Holy Scripture, that is, to look away from evil and to do good."[44] The author listed and explained in detail the chief sins through which Christians transgress God's commands, and attempted to elucidate

---

[42] For the details of Pirmin's career cf. the two *Vitae*, edited by Carolus de Smedt, *Acta Sanctorum*, Nov., II, 34-47; *Herimanni Augiensis Chronicon*, a. 724, 727, edited by G. Pertz, *MGH*, SS, V, 98; Walafrid Strabo, *Visio Wettini*, vv. 27-37, edited by Ernestus Dümmler, *MGH*, Poetae latini aevi carolini, II, 304-305; Hrabanus Maurus, *Carmina*, lxviii, edited by Ernestus Dümmler, *MGH*, Poetae latini aevi carolini, II, 224-225; cf. also Kohler and Hauck, "Pirmin" in *Realencyklopädie für protestantische Theologie und Kirche*, 3 ed., edited by Albert Hauck (Leipzig, 1896-1913), XV, 409-412; Carolus de Smedt, "Commentarius Praevius de sancto Pirmino Episcopo," *Acta Sanctorum*, Nov., II, 2-33; and the articles by G. Jecker, G. Schreiber, and E. Christmann in *Archiv für mittelrheinische Kirchengeschichte*, V (1953), 9-101.

[43] Pirmin, *De singulis libris canonicis scarapsus*, Migne, *PL*, LXXXIX, 1031-1035.

[44] *Ibid.*, 1036.

the nature of certain general and abstract sins, like cupidity, vain-glory, and pride. He also expanded his discussion to such matters as violations of marriage regulations, perjury, murder, usury, theft, and perversion of justice. He placed an unusually heavy emphasis on the sinfulness of engaging in pagan practices, taking care to supply a list of forbidden practices. This preoccupation with sin suggests that Carolingian missionary theorists felt that an explanation of the nature of sin must be given an important place in the education of new converts.[45]

Turning his attention to more constructive advice, Pirmin proceeded to list Christian duties whereby new converts could obtain positive credit in the eyes of their new God. Among the requirements which he especially stressed were the payment of ecclesiastical dues and tithes, worship on holy days, proper conduct in church, frequent reception of the Eucharist after confession to a priest, and the performance of charitable works. Taken as a whole, this passage emphasizes the necessity of impressing upon converts the idea of good works, as well as instructing them in the specific duties expected of them.[46] However, as if he were concerned lest his audience be alarmed in the face of their newly acquired burdens, Pirmin closed with a discourse on the glories of the celestial kingdom and the terrors of hell. He insisted that new converts understand perfectly that their new religion involved a *quid pro quo* arrangement and did not consist of a series of onerous burdens. Here, as throughout the tract, Pirmin revealed an undercurrent of anxiety that his audience had not yet fully grasped the otherworldly point of view which he considered vital to Christian life. He wanted to make certain that this concept be made a part of the outlook of his charges.[47]

Although Pirmin's work, which could be supplemented by scraps of evidence gleaned from missionary biographies, suggests that Carolingian writers thought that post-baptismal instruction ought to be limited to a few basic theological concepts, it ought to be noted that in the last half of the ninth century western writers showed a keen concern over guarding the "orthodoxy" of the doctrines taught to new converts. This element was injected into western missionary affairs as a result of the competition that arose between western and eastern missionaries in the conversion of the Bulgars, the Moravians, and certain Slavic groups in southeastern Europe. The papacy was the

---

[45] *Ibid.*, 1036-1041.   [46] *Ibid.*, 1042-1044.   [47] *Ibid.*, 1044-1050.

leading spokesman of the West on this problem. Nicholas I and John VIII constantly warned Boris of Bulgaria of the danger involved in permitting Greek "error" to spread among his subjects, and of the danger Boris ran of damning his own soul by associating with the Greeks.[48] Hadrian II and John VIII expended a great deal of effort assuring the world that the Greek missionaries, Cyril and Methodius, were orthodox and defending these missionaries against charges of error in doctrine. John's stout defense of Methodius leaves the impression that Rome felt that one of the gravest problems facing a missionary in a newly converted land was that of transmitting a sound body of Christian doctrine.[49] The whole body of papal writing relative to the question of doctrinal orthodoxy touched only a few topics—the *filioque* question, the nature of clerical life, and the propriety of utilizing unique liturgical practices. The importance which the papacy attached to the controversy demonstrates, however, that the West felt that newly won Christians must be instructed with great care in doctrinal matters before the conversion process could be completed.

An even greater amount of attention was given by Carolingian writers on missionary affairs to the problem of instituting practices of worship and discipline among new converts. This theme is so ever-present in missionary discussions that one is forced to conclude that the Carolingian age was far more concerned with the outward behavior of new Christians than with their appreciation of the subtleties of Christian doctrine. Here, too, the popes supply the bulk of evidence revealing Carolingian attitudes toward the question of educating new converts to conduct themselves according to Christian rules. Especially revealing are the letters of several popes of the first half of the eighth century to Boniface and a long set of instruc-

---

[48] Cf. Nicholas, *Ep.* 99-100, edited by Perels, *MGH*, Ep., VI, 566-609; *Liber pontificalis*, edited by L. Duchesne (Paris, 1886-1892), II, 164-165; John VIII, *Fragmenta Registri, 7, 37*, edited by Ericus Caspar, *MGH*, Ep., VII, 277-278, 294-295; John VIII, *Registrum, 66, 182, 192, 193, 298, 308, ibid.,* pp. 58-60, 146, 153-154, 158-159, 260 266-267.

[49] For the activities of Hadrian and John VIII in this connection, cf. *Vie de Méthode,* c. 8-13, in F. Dvornik, *Les légendes de Constantin et de Méthode vues de Byzance* (Prague, 1933), pp. 387-391; John VIII, *Fragmenta Registri,* 15-16, 20-23, edited by Caspar, *MGH*, Ep., VII, 281, 283-286; John VIII, *Registrum, 200-201, 255, 276, ibid.,* 160-161, 222-224, 243-244; *Vita s. Clementis Bulgarorum archiepiscopi,* c. 5-6, Migne, *PG*, CXXVI, 1201-1208.

I

tions despatched by Nicholas I in 866 to Boris of Bulgaria. It must be noted that in both of these cases the papal directives were provoked by a request for guidance from the actual missionary scene. Thus, these papal writings are not exactly theoretical considerations of what should be done in missionary areas to perfect the practices of worship and the conduct of daily life among converts. However, the very fact that information would be sought at Rome, where there was probably only a limited knowledge of actual conditions in the missionary field, suggests that the Carolingian era was aware of the existence of a broad concept of treating Christians whose pattern of conduct was not completely satisfactory, and that the papacy was best fitted to interpret it in specific cases.

A review of papal writings[50] on this score shows that missionary theorists were concerned throughout the Carolingian period with a definite group of liturgical and disciplinary questions. Missionaries were to strive to end all traces of paganism, including those which tended to slip into religious practice under the guise of Christian worship. The worship of old gods, respect for old shrines, trust in omens, reliance on lots, resort to pagan healing practices, the continued use of ancient insignia and pagan incantations, to mention only a few of the chief items discussed, were all to be extirpated from the lives of new converts. The missionaries were expected to impose on the converts new marriage practices; it was held to be especially important that the Christian usages concerning the degree of blood relationship be respected and that adultery and sexual promiscuity be prohibited. The converts should be taught to respect the sanctity of churches and the privileges of the clergy, and they should learn how to dress for church and how to act when they were in attendance of ceremonies. They should likewise become acquainted with the liturgy, taught how to pray, how to assist at Mass, and how and when to receive the sacraments. Furthermore, they were to be acquainted with the whole idea of doing outward penance for their sins according to existing penitential practices, and to learn to accept the responsibility for supporting the Church financially. Obviously, these are the basic rudiments of an outward practice of

[50] The following paragraphs are based chiefly on Boniface, *Ep.* 24, 26, 28, 50-51, 80, 86-87, edited by Tangl, pp. 41-43, 44-47, 49-52, 80-92, 172-180, 191-201; and Nicholas, *Ep.* 99, edited by Perels, *MGH,* Ep., VI, 566-600. Pirmin's tract, *De singulis libris canonicis scarapsus,* Migne, *PL,* LXXXIX, 1029-1050, touches on almost exactly the same ideas and thus corroborates these letters.

Christianity; one may suspect that Carolingian writers of missionary practice felt that new converts could not be considered Christians until they had begun to conduct their outward lives within the framework of these fundamental practices. The real task of post-baptismal missionary labors was to aim for success on this level; to get the large numbers of converts to observe these bare essentials of Christian practice was a major undertaking, success in which would mark a real accomplishment and a long stride toward Christianization of ex-pagans.

There are hints in the papal letters, however, that missionaries were expected to begin to inculcate into the minds of recent converts ideas about how their new religion must affect their daily living in a more extensive way. Nicholas I expressed this concept more clearly than any other writer on missionary affairs. In his letter to King Boris he repeatedly expressed the idea that Boris and his people must learn to conduct their political life on a new plane. It was un-Christian, e.g., to treat slaves and fugitives as the Bulgars were accustomed to treat them, and Bulgar concepts of justice should be tempered by Christian ideas of mercy and charity. Familiar usages in war and diplomacy were to be abandoned for a new pattern of conduct. Nicholas sent his representatives into Bulgaria armed with a law code that would serve as a guide to the Christianization of the political life of the Bulgars. Behind all his remarks was the assumption that a convert must begin rather soon after his baptism to transform all has habits to fit Christian concepts of behavior. The Carolingian era was not entirely content to dismiss new converts with only a superficial acquaintance with the Christian ethic; missionaries were expected in due time to transform the new Christian's conduct and moral outlook completely.

A slightly different, and probably complementary, glimpse into Carolingian ideas on post-baptismal instruction in the realm of moral precepts can also be gleaned from the saints' lives. These biographies almost invariably contain a section devoted to the good deeds and the miracles performed by the missionaries. The accounts were always set in a definite context: the biographer tried to make the point that the good deeds of his subject exercised a tremendous influence on the new converts, teaching them by example a great deal about the ideal Christian way of life. Whether most of these accounts are reliable is extremely doubtful, but they do supply an excellent picture of what the author and his readers thought an ideal missionary would

I

try to do among his newly baptized followers as a means of improv-ing the quality of religious life of new Christians.

The missionaries—as reflected in the idealized descriptions of their personal relationships with their new charges—were expected to educate the converts in a relatively few but highly important ethical concepts. The typical missionary was always quick to lead his flock to think of God in times of crisis, thus conditioning each convert to trust completely in divine power to guard him from danger and to become a creature of abiding faith under all circumstances. Most of the missionaries even came back from the grave to aid their former charges and convince them that they had intercessors before God, thereby further encouraging a complete trust in God. The saints' lives are full of accounts of missionaries aiding the sick. These incidents reflect the Carolingian idea that new converts must be taught the virtue of mercy. The missionaries were pictured in the saints' lives as giving freely to the poor; by these acts they were teaching charity, without which no man could be a Christian in the Carolingian age. The saints were seen to bring comfort to those who were full of terror, to console the criminals, to answer violence with forgiveness, to demonstrate their faith by standing fearless in the face of death and danger, and to support the weak against the strong. They ever-lastingly demonstrate their contempt for the flesh and the material world by undergoing extreme hardships and deprivation. In short, Carolingian missionary thought seems to have assumed that as soon as possible after baptism attempts should be made to inspire the new convert to practice mercy, charity, trust in God, justice, and forgive-ness, especially wherever these virtues might alleviate the lot of the unfortunate in their society.[51]

Although post-baptismal instruction in doctrinal, ethical, and liturgi-cal matters was vital to successful missionary work, Carolingian society always presumed that one more step was also absolutely

---

[51] For examples of this, cf. Rimbert, *Vita Anskarii,* c. 35-39, edited by Waitz, pp. 66-74; Liudger, *Vita Gregorii,* c. 13, edited by Holder-Egger, *MGH,* SS, XV, 77-78; Rudolph of Fulda, *Vita Leobae,* c. 13-16, ed. by Holder-Egger, *MGH,* SS, XV, 127-129; Lupus, *Vita Wigberti,* c. 13, ff, edited by Holder-Egger, *MGH,* XV, 41-42; *Vita Willehadi,* c. 9-11, edited by Poncelet, *Acta Sanctorum,* Nov., III, 845-846; *Vitae Pirminii, passim,* edited by de Smedt, *Acta Sanctorum,* Nov., II, 34-47; Alcuin, *Vita Willibrordi,* c. 14-31, edited by Levison, *MGH,* SS. rer. Merov., VII, 127-138; Altfrid, *Vita Liudgeri,* Lib. I, c. 25-32; Lib. II, *passim,* edited by Diekamp, pp. 30-53.

necessary. Seldom did anyone say much about the need to institute a definite ecclesiastical organization in newly converted areas. Nonetheless, the actions of nearly every missionary and of nearly all agencies even remotely connected with missionary work demonstrate clearly that no one would have thought a missionary venture concluded until an ecclesiastical organization had been completed.

The present study has no space for a lengthy examination of the establishment of an organization in all the lands won over to Christianity during the Carolingian period. Suffice it to say that the record strongly suggests that missionary work was seldom undertaken without the eventual organization of converts in mind. The search for missionary priests went on incessantly, and almost always this search was for priests to serve among those who already had become Christians.[52] Bishoprics were created at the earliest possible moment and capable men were sought out to occupy the new sees, as a study of the careers of St. Boniface and St. Methodius, or of the history of the Archbishoprics of Hamburg and Salzburg would illustrate.[53]

[52] For typical examples of the attention given to recruiting missionary priests, cf. Boniface, *Ep.* 42, 80, edited by Tangl, pp. 67, 178, Willibald, *Vita Bonifatii,* c. 6, edited by Levison, p. 34; Rudolph of Fulda, *Vita Leobae,* c. 9-10, edited by Holder-Egger, *MGH, SS,* XV, 125; Lupus, *Vita Wigberti,* c. 2, edited by Holder-Egger, *MGH, SS,* XV, 39; Nun of Heidenheim, *Vita Wynnebaldi,* c. 4, edited by Holder-Egger, *MGH, SS,* XV, 109; Liudger, *Vita Gregorii,* c. 2, 8, edited by Holder-Egger, *MGH, SS,* XV, 67-68, 73; Nun of Heidenheim, *Vita Willibaldi,* c. 5, ed. Holder-Egger, *MGH, SS,* XV, 104; Eigilis, *Vita Sturmi,* c. 2, edited by Pertz, *MGH,* II, 366, Alcuin, *Vita Willibrordi,* c. 9, edited by Levison, *MGH, SS.* rer. Merov., VII, 124; Rimbert, *Vita Anskarii,* c. 7-9, 12, 14-15, edited by Waitz, pp. 27, 30-31, 33-34, 36-37; *Liber pontificalis,* edited by Duchesne, II, 164-165, 185; Anastasius Bibliothecarius, *Epistolae sive Praefationes,* 5, edited by E. Perels and G. Laehr, *MGH,* Ep., VII, 412; *De conversione Bag. et Carant. libellus,* c. 1-14, edited by Wattenbach, *MGH, SS,* XI, 1-14; Altfrid, *Vita Liudgeri,* Lib. I, c. 22, edited by Diekamp, pp. 25-27; *Vita Willehadi,* c. 5, edited by Poncelet, *Acta Sanctorum,* Nov., III, 843-844; Alcuin, *Ep.* 111, edited by Dümmler, *MGH,* Ep., IV, 159-162.

[53] For Boniface the essential sources are *Ep.* 12, 16, 18, 28, 44-45, 50-53, edited by Tangl, pp. 17-18, 28-29, 31-33, 50, 70-74, 80-95; Willibald, *Vita Bonifatii,* c. 5, ff, edited by Levison, pp. 18, ff. Cf. Theodor Schieffer, *Winifred-Bonifatius und die christliche Grundlegung Europas* (Freiburg, 1954); Joseph Lortz, *Bonifatius und die Grundlegung des Abendlandes* (Wiesbaden, 1954); *Sankt Bonifatius. Gedenkgabe zum zwölfhundertsten Todestag,* hrsg. von der Stadt Fulda in Verbindung mit den Diözesen Fulda und Mainz (Fulda, 1954); Maurice Coens, "S. Boniface et sa mission historique d'apres quelques auteurs recents," *Analecta Bollandiana,* LXXIII (1955), 462-495; J. Gottschalk, "Die

The actions of laymen show that the pressure to organize converted lands was not merely an ecclesiastical aim.[54] Missionary biographers almost invariably ascribed to their heroes the attainment of an episcopal office, treating this advance as if it were a necessary part of missionary work, and not a reward for good work. A typical manifestation of this spirit emerged in those cases where a missionary refused to accept a promotion to an established diocese, but then accepted a missionary see out of a realization that his mission would not be fulfilled until the hierarchy had been completed.[55] No one had to write a tract urging the Christian world of the eighth and ninth centuries to pay heed to the problem of organization; everyone assumed that this was an integral part of missionary work.

The creation of an episcopal structure marked in Carolingian thought the culmination of missionary effort, beyond which no special

---

Bonifatius-Literatur von 1923-1950," *Studien und Mitteilungen zur Geschichte des Benediktiner-Ordens*, LXII (1950), 237-246, for recent considerations of Boniface's work in organizing Europe. For Methodius, cf. *Vie de Méthode*, c. 5-12, edited by Dvornik, pp. 385-390; John VIII, *Registrum*, 200-201, 255, 276, edited by Caspar, *MGH*, Ep., VII, 160-161, 222-224, 243-244; John VIII, *Fragmenta Registri*, 15-16, 20-23, edited by Caspar, *MGH*, Ep., VII, 280-281, 283-286; *Vita s. Clementis*, c. 7-10, Migne, *PG*, CXXVI, 1208-1213. Helpful in dealing with Methodius' career are two books by F. Dvornik, *Les slaves, Byzance et Rome au IX* siècle* (Paris, 1926), and *Les légendes de Constantin et de Méthode vues de Byzance* (Prague, 1933). For the missionary role of Hamburg, cf. especially, Rimbert, *Vita Anskarii*, edited by Waitz, *passim;* Migne, *PL*, CXVIII, 1035-1036; CXIX, 876-879, 962; Nicholas, *Ep.* 26, edited by Perels, *MGH*, Ep., VI, 291-292; Stephen, *Epistolae passim collectae, quotquot ad res Germanicas spectant*, 2, 5, edited by G. Laehr, *MGH*, 358-359, 364-365; Formosus, *Ep.* 1-3, edited by Laehr, *MGH*, Ep., VII, 366-370; Adam of Bremen, *Gesta Hamburgensis Ecclesiae Pontificum*, c. 1-53, Migne, *PL*, CXLVI, 457-495. For Salzburg, cf. *De conversione Bag. et Carant. libellus*, edited by Wattenbach, *MGH*, SS, XI, 1-14; Alcuin, *Ep.* 107, 112-113, edited by Dümmler, *MGH*, Ep., IV, 153-154, 162-166; *MGH, Diplomata Karolinorum*, I, 211, edited by Engilbertus Mühlbacher, pp. 282-283.

[54] For Pepin of Heristal and Utrecht, cf. Alcuin, *Vita Willibrordi*, c. 7, edited by Levison, *MGH*, SS. rer. Merov., VII, 122; Bede, *Hist. eccl.*, V, c. 11, edited by Plummer, pp. 301-305. For Charlemagne and Louis and the Saxon bishoprics, cf. the sources cited by H. Wiedemann, *Die Sachsenbekehrung* (Münster i. W., 1932), and Albert Hauck, *Kirchengeschichte Deutschlands* (3 and 4 ed., Leipzig, 1887-1920), II, 399-424, 696-700. For Louis the Pious and Louis the German and Hamburg, and for Charlemagne and Salzburg, cf. the sources cited in note 53, above.

[55] *Vita secunda s. Liudgeri*, Lib. I, c. 17, edited by Diekamp, p. 62.

thought needed to be given to the question of the progress of Christianity in newly converted areas. The above investigations leave no doubt that missionary problems evoked considerable thought during the Carolingian period. Probably the ideas expressed by the theorists were never applied fully in the conduct of missionary work, and a study of the missionary record of the Carolingian period would certainly reveal some major aberrations. The frequent recurrence of most of the ideas, however, compels one to accept the wide currency of definite principles of good missionary practice in the Carolingian period. [Missionary work was not, at least in theory, merely a matter of brutally compelling pagans to accept the new religion. Many figures were deeply aware of the significant transformation that needed to be worked out to bring about a true conversion from paganism to Christianity and were intent on discovering the means necessary to bring about that transformation.] It would be surprising if at least some of these ideas did not influence the conduct of the missionaries themselves and of those who lent their support to missionary efforts.

II

THE CAROLINGIAN MISSIONARY AND THE PAGAN*

A SINGLE ideal gave shape and meaning to much of Carolingian history. Men of that era were convinced that the City of God on earth was necessary, desirable, and attainable.[1] They were confident that there could be built a world inhabited by Christian peoples, living in peace with one another on the basis of Christian ethics, believing in and worshipping one God, and organized into one state and one church. However, the Carolingians were beset by a variety of problems in their attempt to achieve the ideal Christian society. One of these problems arose from the fact that the Christian world of the eighth and ninth centuries was an island surrounded by a sea of aggressive, belligerent non-Christians, who threatened at every moment to destroy God's kingdom on earth.[2] This challenge inspired a vigorous effort to bring part of these outsiders into the Christian fold, where they not only would gain eternal salvation but also would cease obstructing the consummation of God's will relative to His earthly children. The result was one of the more significant chapters in the history of the expansion of Christianity, a missionary effort that made considerable additions both to the population and to the area of Christendom.

Carolingian missionary activity has been extensively studied from a variety of approaches. One problem, however, has caused considerable difficulty and has usually been by-passed or summarily dismissed in these studies. Very little has been done to describe the methods used by Carolingian missionaries to compel the pagans to abandon their ancient religions and subscribe to Christianity. What happened when Carolingian missionary and pagan met thus remains vague and shadowy.[3] Perhaps such need not be the case. A re-examination of the main sources which relate to Carolingian missionary activity supplies evidence for presenting a more definite and concise picture of this particular aspect of Carolingian history.

From a Carolingian missionary's point of view the task of converting the pagans consisted of winning their consent to submit to baptism as a sign of the acceptance of Christianity. It is in the period between the first contact established by the missionary with the pagans and the performance of the baptismal rite

---

* This article is drawn largely from research done in connection with the preparation of a doctoral dissertation in the Department of History at the University of Illinois.

[1] For a typical expression of this ideal see Agobard, *Epistolae, #3* (ed. E. Dümmler, *MGH, Epistolae,* v, 158–159).

[2] Louis Halphen, *Les Barbares des grandes invasions aux conquêtes turques du XIᵉ siècle,* third ed. (Paris, 1936), pp. 191–209, 234–309, gives a good picture of the tenuous position of Christiantiy at this moment.

[3] A typical attitude toward the exact nature of Carolingian missionary method is expressed by Josef Schmidlin, 'Die frümittelalterliche Missionsmethode,' *Zeitschrift für Missionswissenshaft,* vii (1917), 177: 'Was wir an Literatur und Quellen darüber besitzen, ist trotz der scheinbaren Fülle und Zugänglichheit des Materials nicht viel: die mittelalterlichen Lebensbeschreibungen und Chroniken, so zahlreich und redselig sie sonst sind, gehen Kaum auf diese Innenseite des Christianisierungsprozesses ein, so dass wir uns mit einigen wenigen Bruchstücken behelfen müssen, die mehr den Charakter von Überesten tragen. . . . '

that the most obscure phase of Carolingian missionary method arises. By way of introduction to a description of this crucial period in the process of converting pagans it is necessary to note certain steps that preceded it and had an important bearing on it. Carolingian missionary activity almost invariably was inaugurated by the establishment of permanent missionary posts in pagan areas.[4] A small group of volunteers, organized and equipped at various places and by various people within the Christian world, moved into the pagan world and selected a suitable location from which to begin its real work. Every effort was immediately turned to the task of making this center self-sufficient economically. Land was acquired. This land was cleared, crops were planted, herds were acquired, and an adequate labor force was gathered. Very quickly buildings were constructed so that living quarters would be available and religious needs would be supplied. Although none of this was achieved without a great deal of hardship and frequent disappointment, a thriving center was operating in the midst of the pagan world amazingly soon after missionaries first decided to enter a certain area.

Having supplied their own needs, the missionaries assumed the offensive in the task of carrying their religion to the pagans. The first problem they faced was that of contacting the pagans. Their strategy was dictated by several conditions. It has already been noted that the missionaries were forced to establish themselves at certain fixed spots in order to support themselves. As a result they were concentrated at a few locations scattered sparsely over the missionary areas. The pagan world was almost completely lacking in large centers of population. None of the small villages in which the pagans lived was large enough to serve as an adequate missionary center. Finally, the missionary parties were much too small to permit the assignment of a missionary to each of the numerous pagan villages.[5]

[4] No attempt has been made to document these remarks concerning the initial establishment of missionary posts in the pagan world. The problem is worthy of a separate study. It might be said in passing, however, that more information can be found concerning this first step than about any other aspect of missionary work.

[5] The sources do not permit any generalization concerning the exact size of the missionary groups. Some information exists, however, to suggest that they were usually small. When Willibrord left England for missionary duty in Frisia, his party was made up of twelve monks; see Alcuin, *Vita Willibrordi*, c. 5 (ed. W. Levison, *MGH, Scriptores rerum Merovingicarum*, VII, 120; this series of *MGH* will be cited hereafter as *SS. rerum Merov.*); Bede, *Historia ecclesiastica gentis Anglorum*, v, c. 9 (ed. Carolus Plummer, *Venerabilis Baedae Opera Historica* [Oxford, 1896] I, 299; this work will be cited hereafter as Bede, *Hist. eccl.*, ed. C. Plummer, I, with appropriate book, chapter, and page number). Paul Willem Finsterwalder, 'Wege und Ziele der irischen und angelsächsischen Mission in fränkischen Reich,' *Zeitschrift für Kirchengeschichte*, XLVII, N.F., x (1928), 215, points out that twelve was the customary number among Irish missionary parties. Boniface took two or three companions with him on his first missionary expedition to Frisia; see Willibald, *Vita Bonifatii*, c. 4 (ed. Wilhelmus Levison, *Vitae sancti Bonifatii archiepiscopi Moguntini* in *MGH, Scriptores rerum Germanicarum in usum scholarum* [Hanover and Leipzig, 1905], pp. 15–16; this series of *MGH* will be cited hereafter as *SS. rer. Germ. in usum schol.*). Boniface apparently traveled in Hesse with one companion, a young monk named Gregory; see Liudger, *Vita Gregorii*, c. 2 (ed. O. Holder-Egger, *MGH, Scriptores*, xv, 67–69; this series of *MGH* will be cited hereafter as *SS.*). When Charlemagne sent Willehad into Saxony in 780, the missionary apparently was accompanied by a group of aides; see *Vita Willehadi*, c. 6 (ed. Albertus Poncelet, *Act Sanctorum*, November, III, 844; this collection will be cited hereafter as *AASS*);

Faced with these conditions, the missionaries followed the practice of circulating from one settled place to another in order to contact the pagans. Starting from their permanent centers, they traveled over wide stretches of the countryside. There are numerous examples of this kind of operation. Boniface's first move when he came to Hesse in 722 was to build the monastery of Amöneberg. Then, 'a congregation of servants of God having been collected,'[6] he proceeded to free many pagans from the captivity of the devil by preaching. The description of his destruction of the sacred oak tree at Geismar indicates that Boniface's presence at a pagan center usually attracted a crowd of pagans who turned out to listen to his preaching.[7] Boniface followed almost the same procedure in Thuringia, where he established a monastery at Ohrdruf and then spread the faith throughout the land.[8] Alcuin, the biographer of the Frisian missionary, Willibrord, says that after Willibrord had been established at Utrecht in 696, he began to sow the seed of the true faith far and wide; his success could be judged by the number of Christians living in the castles, towns, and villages all over southern Frisia.[9] Alcuin then describes several of Willibrord's numerous travels through the towns and villages of Frisia.[10] The churches at several places in Frisia retained for centuries a memory of Willibrord's presence, thus bearing out Alcuin's picture of the missionary's travels.[11] When Willibald, an Anglo-Saxon attracted to Germany by the fame of Boniface, was established as bishop of Eichstätt in 741, he was confronted with many pagan remnants in his diocese. He therefore established a monastery in connection with his episcopal see; using it as a center, he and his disciples covered the surrounding countryside, preaching and strengthening the faith.[12] His brother, Wynnebald, finding the same situation in the region surrounding his new monastery at Heidenheim near Eichstätt, likewise used his

---

this section lists the names of several 'disciples' of Willehad, all of whom were killed by the Saxons in 782. Virgil, bishop of Salzburg, sent groups of two or three priests into Carinthia during the early stages of the conversion of the Slavs in this area; see *De conversione Bagoariorum et Carantanorum libellus*, c. 5 (ed. W. Wattenbach, *MGH, SS.*, XI, 8–9). The largest missionary party on record seems to have been the ill-fated group that Boniface led into Frisia in 753. Two different accounts list the number that died with Boniface as fifty and fifty-three; see *E martyrologio Fuldense* (ed. W. Levison, *MGH, SS. rer. Germ. in usum schol.* [Hanover and Leipzig, 1905], p. 60); *Baedae continuatio, a.* 754 (ed. Carolus Plummer, *op. cit.*, I, 362).

[6] Willibald, *Vita Bonifatii*, c. 6 (ed. W. Levison, *MGH, SS. rer. Germ. in usum schol.*, p. 27): 'collecta servorum Dei congregatione. . . . '

[7] *Ibid.*, c. 6, pp. 30–32.

[8] *Ibid.*, c. 6, pp. 33–34. In one of his letters Boniface excuses himself for not having fulfilled a request made by an English abbess, Bugga, on the grounds that his constant travels prevented him; see *Bonifatii et Lulli Epistolae*, #27 (*Die Briefe des heiligen Bonifatius und Lullus*, ed. Michael Tangl, *MGH, Epistolae Selectae*, I [Berlin, 1916], p. 48), cited hereafter as Boniface, *Ep.* (ed. M. Tangl, *MGH, Epistolae Selectae*, I).

[9] Alcuin, *Vita Willibrordi*, c. 8 (ed. W. Levison, *MGH, SS. rerum Merov.*, VII, 123).

[10] *Ibid.*, c. 14–22, pp. 127–133.

[11] Gabriël H. Verbist, *Saint Willibrord, apôtre des Pays-Bas et fondateur d'Echternach* (Université de Louvain, *Recueil de travaux publiés par les membres des conférences d'histoire et de philologie*, 2e sér., 49e fasc. [Louvain, 1939]), *passim*, gives numerous cases where Willibrord seems to have a special connection with a Frisian church.

[12] Nun of Heidenheim, *Vita Willibaldi*, c. 6 (ed. O. Holder-Egger, *MGH, SS.*, XV, 105–106).

monastery as a center from which to go forth to destroy paganism.[13] 'By sowing the holy word far and wide among the people he won not a small number of them to God.'[14] Liudger's missionary work in Frisia and Saxony during the 770's and 780's carried him through numerous areas in these lands.[15] The first missionary work in Carinthia involved sending out missionary parties from the episcopal see at Salzburg, the monks returning periodically to the center from which they had been sent.[16]

Even in the case of the conversion of the Saxons, where there is very little evidence upon which to base the details of missionary method,[17] there are hints that missionaries traveled from certain central locations in order to contact the pagans. When Willehad was sent to Saxony by Charlemagne in 780, he was assigned to a definite locale. His biography indicates that he traveled all over that area, preaching, building churches, and baptizing pagans.[18] In 782 he was driven out of Saxony and was unable to return until 785. Two years later he was designated a bishop,[19] and in 789 he was able to dedicate an episcopal see at Bremen.[20] Since he selected this particular location in the area assigned to him as the site of his episcopal see, it seems likely that it had served as a center from which Willehad had conducted his missionary labors during the years preceding 789. Virtually the same development occurred at Münster. A certain abbot named Bernrad first worked as a missionary in that area.[21] When he died, Liudger, already an experienced missionary as a result of his work in Frisia, took his place. Liudger con-

---

[13] Nun of Heidenheim, *Vita Wynnebaldi*, c. 7 (ed. O. Holder-Egger, *MGH, SS.*, xv, 111–112).

[14] *Ibid.*, c. 7, p. 112: 'Et sic longe lateque per populos sacra seminando non parvum Domino populum adquesivit. . . . '

[15] Altfrid, *Vita sancti Liudgeri*, Lib. i, c. 25–29 (*Die Vitae sancti Liudgeri*, ed. Wilhelm Diekamp, *Geschichtsquellen des Bisthums Münster*, iv [Münster, 1881], pp. 30–35), cited hereafter as Altfrid, *Vita Liudgeri* (ed. W. Diekamp, iv, with correct page).

[16] *De conversione Bagoariorum et Carantanorum libellus*, c. 4–5 (ed. W. Wattenbach, *MGH, SS.*, xi, 7–8). See also Albert Hauck, *Kirchengeschichte Deutschlands*, 2nd ed. (Leipzig, 1900), ii, 457–464; Sigmund Riezler, *Geschichte Baierns*, 2nd ed. (Stuttgart and Gotha, 1927), i¹, 298–324; Matthew Spinka, *A History of Christianity in the Balkans* (Chicago [1933]), pp. 14–16.

[17] As general guides for the Christianization of the Saxons see especially H. Wiedemann, *Die Sachsenbekehrung* (*Veröffentlichungen des international Instituts für missionswissenschaftliche Forschungen: Missionswissenschaftliche Studien*, ed. J. Schmidlin, neue Reihe, v [Münster i. W., 1932]); Hauck, *Kirchengeschichte Deutschlands*, ii, 360–413; Hans von Schubert, *Geschichte der christlichen Kirche im Frühmittelalter: Ein Handbuch* (Tübingen, 1921); Kenneth Scott Latourette, *The Thousand Years of Uncertainty, A.D. 500–A.D. 1500* (New York and London, 1938), pp. 102–106; Louis Halphen, 'La conquête de la Saxe' in *Études critiques sur l'histoire de Charlemagne* (Paris, 1921), pp. 145–218; Sigurd Abel, *Jahrbücher des fränkischen Reiches unter Karl dem Grossen*, i (2. Aufl., bearb. von Bernhard Simson [Leipzig, 1888]); ii (fortgesetzt von Berhard Simson [Leipzig, 1883]); Émile Amann, *L'époque carolingienne* (*Histoire de l'église depuis les origines jusqu'à nos jours*, publiée sous la direction de Augustin Fliche et Victor Martin, vi [Paris, 1937]), pp. 188–190.

[18] *Vita Willehadi*, c. 5 (ed. A. Poncelet, *AASS*, Nov., iii, 844): 'ad pagum qui dicitur Wigmodia . . . ac pertransiens cunctam in circuitu diocesim, multos ad fidem Christi euvangelizando convertit. . . . '

[19] *Ibid.*, c. 6–8, pp. 844–845.

[20] *Ibid.*, c. 9, p. 845.

[21] *Vita secunda s. Liudgeri*, Lib. i, c. 17 (*Die Vitae sancti Liudgeri*, ed. Wilhelm Diekamp, *Geschichtsquellen des Bisthums Münster*, iv [Münster, 1881], p. 62).

structed a monastery at Münster and from that point carried on his missionary work.[22] When he was made bishop sometime between 802 and 805, he chose Münster as his episcopal see.[23] Paderborn had a similar history. It was an important point in several of Charlemagne's military campaigns,[24] and as early as 777 a church was built there.[25] In that year it was the scene of a mass baptism of the Saxons,[26] a fact which suggests it was a religious as well as a military center. In 799 or shortly thereafter it was made the seat of a new bishopric.[27] The same thing which happened at Bremen, Münster, and Paderborn may well have been repeated at several other locations in Saxony, including Hildesheim, Verden, Osnäbruch, Halberstadt, and Minden.[28] All of these sites where bishoprics later developed appear to have been missionary centers during the early phases of the conversion of Saxony.

Although contacting the pagans involved almost constant travel through the pagan areas, it would be wrong to visualize the typical Carolingian missionary as being completely on his own. Everything indicates that he remained in close contact with the missionary center for his area and had his activities directed and supervised from this center. The activities of Willibrord in Frisia, of Willehad and Liudger in Saxony, and of Willibald and Wynnebald in Nordgau seem to indicate that missionaries never wandered too far from their missionary centers. In at least two other cases — both involving missionary activity at a rather great distance from missionary centers — there is evidence of provision for a periodic return of missionaries to their centers. Albericus, who was bishop of Utrecht after 775, sent Liudger on a missionary assignment to the church at Dockum, built in northern Frisia at the site of Boniface's martyrdom. However, provisions were made for the missionary's periodic return to Utrecht in order to carry on his ascetic life.[29] Virgil of Salzburg sent out groups of two or three priests and clerics to proselytize in Carinthia. The repetition of names in the list of missionary personnel utilized for this undertaking suggests that some were sent on two or three different occasions and that a system of rotation was established at Salzburg, thus allowing missionary personnel to return to the seat of authority at Salzburg.[30]

[22] Altfrid, *Vita Liudgeri*, Lib. I, c. 23 (ed. W. Diekamp, pp. 27–29).

[23] *Ibid.*, c. 23, pp. 28–29.

[24] *Annales regni Francorum*, a. 777, 783, 785, 799 (ed. Fredericus Kurze, *MGH, SS. rer. Germ. in usum schol.* [Hanover, 1895], pp. 48, 64, 68, 106). A. Kleinclausz, *Charlemagne* (Paris [1934]), p. 38, calls Paderborn the capital of the march which was created south of the Lippe river as a result of the campaigns.

[25] *Annales Maximiniani*, a. 777 (ed. G. Waitz, *MGH, SS.*, XIII, 21); *Annales Sangallenses Baluzii*, a. 777 (ed. G. Pertz, *MGH, SS.*, I, 63); *Annales Petaviani*, a. 777 (ed. G. Pertz, *MGH, SS.*, I, 16).

[26] *Annales regni Francorum*, a. 777 (ed. F. Kurze, *MGH, SS. rer. Germ. in usum schol.*, p. 48).

[27] *Translatio sancti Liborii*, c. 2–5 (ed. G. Pertz, *MGH, SS.*, IV, 149–151).

[28] Wiedemann, *Die Sachsenbekehrung*, pp. 67–79, presents detailed evidence for thinking that all of these centers in Saxony were actually missionary centers very early during the conversion period.

[29] Altfrid, *Vita Liudgeri*, Lib. I, c. 17 (ed. W. Diekamp, p. 21).

[30] *De conversione Bagoariorum et Carantanorum libellus*, c. 5 (ed. W. Wattenbach, *MGH, SS.*, XI, 8–9): 'Qui tunc misit eis Heimonem presbyterum et Reginbaldum presbyterum atque Maioranum diaconum cum aliis clericis. Et non multo post misit iterum ibidem eundem Heimonem et Dupliterum ac Maioranum presbyteros et alios clericos cum eis. Iterumque misit eis Gozharium presbyterum,

That missionaries did remain in close contact with certain centers in their areas is further supported by the concern that was obviously felt in the Carolingian period for adequate supervision of missionaries. Possibly in an attempt to avoid the problems left behind by the free-lance Irish missionaries of earlier centuries,[31] special effort was usually exerted to place some ecclesiastical figure in charge of all missionary activities in any area. In some cases the abbot of a missionary monastery retained control over missionary activity in a certain region. Gregory, the abbot of the monastery at Utrecht from about 755 to 775, seems to have controlled missionary work in Frisia during all this time; for instance, he commissioned Lebuin to convert the pagans along the Yssel river, dividing Frisia from Saxony.[32] Sturmi, the abbot of Fulda, assumed leadership of the missionary work being done in southern Saxony about 776.[33] Wynnebald, abbot of Heidenheim, directed the conversion of those pagans still left in northern Bavaria.[34] More generally bishops or archbishops were created to manage missionary work. There seems to have been little reason for the elevation of Willibrord to the rank of archbishop in 695 with pagan Frisia as his province[35] except that he was thereby in a better position to coordinate and regulate missionary work. The same motive apparently dictated the intricate maneuvering connected with the foundation of the archbishopric of Hamburg in 832 as a preliminary to the conversion of the Scandinavians.[36] Each of Boniface's successive steps up the hierarchical ladder was intended at least partially as a measure to allow him to retain the direction of missionary activity over a constantly enlarging missionary field. When he left Rome in 719, he was granted special papal recognition as a missionary priest; this recognition was intended as a measure to insure his leadership over those who joined him.[37] After his success in winning converts, he returned to Rome in 722 and was made a bishop. Although he had no see, he enjoyed all the powers of a regular bishop and was thus in a better position to regulate the missionary work in Hesse and Thuringia.[38] In 731 he became an archbishop with power to consecrate bish-

---

Maioranum et Erchanbertum. Post eos Reginbaldum et Reginharium presbyteros. Ac deinde Maiora num et Augustinum presbyteros. Iterumque Reginbaldum et Gundharium. Et hoc sub Virgilio factum est episcopo.'

[31] For suggestions of the weaknesses of the Celtic missionary efforts see E. de Moreau, 'Les missions médiévales,' in Baron Descamps, *Histoire générale comparée des missions* (Paris, 1932), pp. 141–299; J. H. A. Ebrard, *Die iroschottische Missionskirche des sechsten, siebenten und achten Jahrhunderts* (Gutersloh, 1873); Louis Gougaud, *Les chrétientés celtiques*, 2nd ed. (Paris, 1911); Finsterwalder, 'Wege und Ziele der irischen und angelsächsischen Mission in fränkischen Reich,' *Zeitschrift für Kirchengeschichte*, XLVII, N.F., X (1928), 203–226.

[32] *Vita Lebuini antiqua*, c. 3 (ed. A. Hofmeister, *MGH, SS*, XXX², 792).

[33] Eigilis, *Vita Sturmi*, c. 22–23 (ed. G. Pertz, *MGH, SS.*, II, 376).

[34] Nun of Heidenheim, *Vita Wynnebaldi*, c. 7 (ed. O. Holder-Egger, *MGH, SS.*, XV, 111–112).

[35] Alcuin, *Vita Willibrordi*, c. 6–8 (ed. W. Levison, *MGH, SS. rerum Merov.*, VII, 121–123); Bede, *Hist. eccl.*, V, c. 11 (ed. C. Plummer, I, 302–303).

[36] *Vita Anskarii auctore Rimberto*, c. 12–14 (ed. G. Waitz, *MGH, SS. rer. Germ. in usum schol.* [Hanover, 1884], pp. 33–36; cited hereafter as Rimbert, *Vita Anskarii*, ed. G. Waitz, *MGH, SS. rer. Germ. in usum schol.*, with appropriate chapter and page).

[37] Boniface, *Ep.*, #12 (ed. M. Tangl, *MGH, Epistolae Selectae*, I, 17–18).

[38] *Ibid.*, #18, pp. 31–33, gives a definite statement of the powers which Boniface was to exercise. *Ibid.*, #17, pp. 29–31, gives a clear statement of the importance attached to the promotion. Willibald,

ops. He still had no fixed see or province; the advantage gained from his elevation was that he could better recruit workers for his missionary task and could begin to solidify the gains he had already made.[39] Both Willehad and Liudger are said to have exercised episcopal powers, especially that of ordaining priests, before either was actually elevated to the episcopal office.[40] One must conclude that they had been appointed to some kind of authority as a part of their missionary assignments in Saxony. The confusing picture of abbots of Benedictine monasteries sending monks and priests to do missionary work far from their monastic cells, of bishops wandering over wide areas without fixed sees, of archbishops holding office in pagan lands which possessed neither priests nor bishops, and of bishops building missionary monasteries in connection with their episcopal sees assumes meaning only when one sees that almost any means was utilized in the Carolingian period to provide direction and control over missionary efforts. The care exerted to provide missionary leadership was more than mere form; the leaders actually maintained control over missionary work. Boniface's letters are full of evidence which shows how closely he kept in touch with the religious problems in the missionary areas under his jurisdiction.[41] Both Willibald and Wynnebald likewise exercised close supervision over the destruction of paganism in northern Bavaria.[42] The missionaries who were murdered in northwestern Saxony in 782 were designated as the 'disciples' of Willehad,[43] indicating that he kept them advised on affairs relating to the conversion of the Saxons.

By a zealous pursuit of the strategy of circulation through pagan areas from fixed centers, the missionaries were able to come into personal contact with the pagans in the vicinity of the missionary centers. The missionaries' task at this point involved undermining the pagan religion to the extent that the pagan was willing to accept Christianity. Although the exact content of pagan belief in the eighth and ninth centuries is difficult to ascertain, certain broad ideas and practices emerge and must be introduced into a discussion of missionary method in order to describe the mode of attack adopted by the missionaries.[44] The pagan

---

Vita Bonifatii, c. 6 (ed. W. Levison, *MGH, SS. rer. Germ. in usum schol.*, pp. 26–36), supplies evidence of the effectiveness of the move in Hesse and Thuringia.

[39] Boniface, *Ep.*, #28 (ed. M. Tangl, *MGH, Epistolae Selectae*, I, 49–50).

[40] *Vita Willehadi*, c. 5 (ed. A. Poncelet, *AASS*, Nov., III, 844); Altfrid, *Vita Liudgeri*, Lib. I, c. 23 (ed. W. Diekamp, p. 28).

[41] See especially Boniface, *Ep.*, #26, 28 (ed. M. Tangl, *MGH, Epistolae Selectae*, I, 44–47, 49–52).

[42] Nun of Heidenheim, *Vita Willibaldi*, c. 6 (ed. O. Holder-Egger, *MGH, SS.*, XV, 105–106); Nun of Heidenheim, *Vita Wynnebaldi*, c. 7 (ed. O. Holder-Egger, *MGH, SS.*, XV, 111–112).

[43] *Vita Willehadi*, c. 6 (ed. A. Poncelet, *AASS*, Nov., III, 844): 'discipulos ipsius. . . . '

[44] This section dealing with pagan religion is largely based on the following works: P. D. Chantepie de la Saussaye, *The Religion of the Teutons*, tr. from the Dutch by Bert J. Vos (*Handbooks of the History of Religions*, ed. Morris Jastrow, III [Boston and London, 1902]; Eugen Mogk, 'Mythologie' in *Grundriss der germanischen Philologie*, ed. Hermann Paul (2nd ed., Strassburg, 1900), III, 230–406; Lubor Niederle, *Manuel d'antiquité slave* (Paris, 1926), II, 126–168. For descriptions of the Frisian religion of the eighth century, see Karl Freiherr von Richthofen, *Untersuchungen über friesische Rechtsgeschichte* (Berlin, 1880–1886), II, 412–494; Verbist, *Saint Willibrord*, pp. 61–67; Josef Jung-Diefenbach, *Die Friesenbekehrung bis zum Martertode des hl. Bonifatius* (*Veröffentlichungen des internationalen Instuts für missionswissenschaftliche Forschungen: Missionswissenschaftliche Studien*, ed. J. Schmidlin, Neue Reihe, I, Post Mödling bei Wien, 1931), pp. 48, ff. For the Saxons see Widemann, *Die Sachsen-*

religions were polytheistic. A rather elaborate mythology explaining the origins of the gods and of the world had been developed. Some kind of hierarchy of gods had been evolved; at the top of this hierarchy were a few all-powerful deities who were rather far removed from the affairs of human life. To fill the gap between the activities of the great gods and the affairs of everyday life, the pagans inhabited the world about them with a variety of elves, spirits, departed souls, witches, and demons, each of which had some particular sphere in which it exercised influence over men. However, the real strength of paganism did not rest on the peculiar character of its deities or on the rigid exclusiveness of its pantheon. The tenacity with which the pagans held to their ancient gods stemmed from their reliance upon the gods for aid in the conduct of every phase of human life. Pagan religion was most fundamentally grounded on the firm conviction that the gods possessed the power necessary to control and determine the entire course of human affairs. An elaborate system of worship had developed for the purpose of placating the angry spirits of the gods, of currying their favor toward any human undertaking, and of divining the probable reaction of the gods to any proposed action. This complete dependence upon the gods for the resolution of the problems facing man in his earthly existence engendered in the pagans a reluctance to break with the traditional religious system out of fear that the gods would retaliate and that life would go awry without their help. The pagans were primarily concerned with this world and its rewards. A mystical, otherworldly religion, based upon sacrifice, suffering, and good works for the sake of reward in the next world was foreign to the pagan mind. Morality in the Christian sense had little appeal to the pagans.

In spite of the obvious disparity of religious viewpoint between the Christian missionary and the pagan, the missionaries attacked with vigor the problem of convincing the pagan to surrender his religion and accept Christianity. To gain this end the Carolingian missionary used several arguments and inducements, which taken together best explain his success in gaining the pagan's consent to accept baptism.

The explanation of the nature of Christianity was one such means. The presentation of the main tenets of Christianity was achieved either by individual instruction of the pagans or by preaching to large numbers. Individual instruction found only limited application during the Carolingian period,[45] due chiefly to the limited number of missionaries. The few instances which can be found to prove the employment of personal instruction are almost all confined to cases involving kings or princes. The accounts of Willibrord's appeals to Radbod, king of the Frisians, and Ongendus, king of the Danes, show the missionary taking pains to explain the nature of Christianity to these kings.[46] Wulfram, the late seventh

---

bekehrung, pp. 5–15; Hauck, *Kirchengeschichte Deutschlands*, II, 361–364; Ludwig Schmidt, *Geschichte der deutschen Stämme bis zum Ausgang der Völkerwanderung: Die Westgermanen*, 2nd ed. (Munich, 1938), I, 67–70.

[45] Josef Schmidlin, 'Die Schule in der Mission,' *Zeitschrift für Missionswissenschaft*, XXVII (1937), 19–31; Laurenz Kilger, 'Zur Geschichte des Missionsschulwesens,' *Zeitschrift für Missionswissenschaft*, XIII (1923), 198–210.

[46] Alcuin, *Vita Willibrordi*, c. 9 (ed. W. Levison, *MGH, SS. rerum Merov.*, VII 123–124).

century bishop of Sens who is alleged to have resigned his episcopal see in order to attempt to convert the Frisians, also tried to persuade Radbod to be a Christian by describing for him the nature of the Christian faith.[47] When Boruth, the duke of the Slavs in Carinthia, agreed to permit the conversion of his son and nephew, these two young men were sent to a monastery for an education leading to conversion.[48] Anskar spent a great deal of time informing King Horic of Denmark as to the nature of Christianity in an attempt to convert him.[49] However, there is evidence that a few lesser figures in pagan society were singled out for individual instruction. Willehad educated the children of several nobles while he performed his missionary work around Dockum in northern Frisia.[50] Willibrord brought back from Denmark thirty Danish boys whom he intended to instruct in the faith at his monastery at Utrecht.[51] Willibrord also instructed two members of the important Wurssing family during the early period of Frisian missionary work.[52] Anskar collected a group of pupils around him after he had accompanied King Harald back to Denmark in 826; since he purchased some of then, it would seem that his pupils were of an inferior status socially.[53]

Since individualized instruction was of limited utility to missionaries, preaching was the chief means of presenting the basic points of Christianity to the pagans.[54] There is hardly an account dealing with missionary activity which does not make reference to preaching the word of God or sowing the seeds of the faith as an important part of missionary method. Unfortunately, there is little detailed evidence which throws light upon the manner or the content of the preaching used in connection with the conversion of the pagans. Only a few indirect references provide information upon which an evaluation of missionary preaching can be built.

As to the manner of preaching to the pagans, it has already been suggested that the missionaries appeared in village after village in order to contact the pagans. Once in the villages the missionaries perhaps requested that the pagans listen to what they had to say. Anskar even found in Sweden 'many who were well disposed towards the missionary and who willingly listened to the teaching of the Lord.'[55] Occasionally the missionaries forced themselves upon a group of pagans

---

[47] *Vita Vulframni*, c. 6–9 (ed. W. Levison, *MGH, SS. rerum Merov.*, v, 665–668).

[48] *De conversione Bagoariorum et Carantanorum libellus*, c. 4 (ed. W. Wattenbach, *MGH, SS.*, xi, 7).

[49] Rimbert, *Vita Anskarii*, c. 24 (ed. G. Waitz, *MGH, SS. rer. Germ. in usum schol.*, pp. 52–53).

[50] *Vita Willehadi*, c. 2 (ed. A. Poncelet, *AASS*, Nov., iii, 843): 'Nam et plurimi nobilium infantes suos ipsi ad erudiendum ibidem tradierunt.'

[51] Alcuin, *Vita Willibrordi*, c. 9 (ed. W. Levison, *MGH, SS. rerum Merov.*, vii, 124).

[52] Altfrid, *Vita Liudgeri*, Lib. i, c. 5. (ed W. Diekamp, p. 10).

[53] Rimbert, *Vita Anskarii*, c. 8 (ed. G. Waitz, *MGH, SS. rer. Germ. in usum schol.*, p. 30).

[54] The best discussions of missionary preaching are Wilhelm Konen, *Die Heidenpredigt in der Germanenbekehrung* (Düsseldorf, 1909); Hermann Lau, *Die angelsächsische Missionsweise im Zeitalter des Bonifaz* (Kiel, 1909), pp. 39–54; Hauck, *Kirchengeschichte Deutschlands*, i, 477–481; M. Schian, 'Geschichte der christlichen Predigt,' *Realencyklopädie für protestantische Theologie und Kirche*, ed. Albert Hauck (Leipzig, 1904), xv, 639–659.

[55] Rimbert, *Vita Anskarii*, c. 11 (ed. G. Waitz, *MGH, SS. rer. Germ. in usum schol.*, p. 32): 'Plures quoque erant, qui eorum legationi favebant et doctrinam Domini libenter audiebant.'

who had congregated for some other purpose. Lebuin, for instance, arose unannounced in the midst of an assembly of Saxon nobles and preached on the benefits of Christianity.[56] Missionaries occasionally secured the aid of some of the pagans or of the newly-won Christians in congregating an audience. The king of Sweden assisted Anskar by calling an assembly to listen to the Christian case.[57] The missionaries may have used some spectacular means of attracting pagan attention. One can imagine the effect on the pagans when Liudger appeared on the sacred island of Heligoland, which the Frisians had dedicated to one of their deities, Fosite, displaying a cross and praying aloud to his God[58] or the curiosity aroused when the Ewalds, two of the early missionaries in Saxony, set up their portable altar and conducted mass in the pagan villages.[59]

Once the pagans had been assembled, the missionaries addressed them in the pagans' native language.[60] Language differences were occasionally a cause for concern among missionaries, since it was imperative to find preachers who could communicate with the pagans. One of Boniface's earliest disciples was a young Frankish nobleman, Gregory, who evinced a great interest in the Anglo-Saxon's work and desired to serve him. Before giving his consent to Gregory's desire, Boniface tested the young man. He was well satisfied with Gregory's ability to read Latin. But then the great missionary asked the young man to transpose what he had just read into the native tongue. Obviously he wanted to make sure that Gregory could perform this feat before allowing him to join in missionary work.[61] A Saxon baptismal formula dating from the Carolingian period shows that Christian terminology had found its way into the Saxon language.[62] This suggests that some attempt had been made to discuss Christianity in the native tongues. The affinity between the languages of some of the missionaries and of the pagans suggests that in many cases missionaries could have spoken to the pagans without great difficulty.[63] The Anglo-Saxon missionaries could have learned rather easily either Frisian or Saxon, since all of these languages were closely related. The Frankish tongue, however, was not so closely related to the languages of the main pagan groups; thus missionaries of Frankish origin may have encountered difficulty in either Frisia or Saxony. Such difficulty is indicated by the fact that sometime after 785 the Frisians in the extreme northeastern part of Frisia indicated a willingness to accept Christianity; they requested Charlemagne to pro-

[56] *Vita Lebuini antiqua*, c. 6 (ed. A. Hofmeister, *MGH, S.S*, xxx², 793–794). For the plausibility of this account see A. Hofmeister, 'Die Jahresversammlung der alten Sachsen zu Marklo,' *Historische Zeitschrift*, cxviii (3. Folge, xxii [1917]), 189–221; Wilh. Kentzler, 'Über die Glaubwürdigkeit der Vita Lebuini und die Volksversammlung der Sachsen zu Marklo' and 'Entgegung' by S. Abel, *Forschungen zur deutschen Geschichte*, vi (1866), 343–356.

[57] Rimbert, *Vita Anskarii*, c. 26–27 (ed. G. Waitz, *MGH, SS. rer. Germ. in usum schol.*, pp. 55–59).

[58] Altfrid, *Vita Liudgeri*, Lib. i, c. 22 (ed. W. Diekamp, p. 26).

[59] Bede, *Hist. eccl.*, v, c. 10 (ed. C. Plummer, i, 200).

[60] See Konen, *Die Heidenpredigt in der Germanenbekehrung*, pp. 20–23.

[61] Liudger, *Vita Gregorii*, c. 2 (ed. O. Holder-Egger, *MGH, SS.*, xv, 67–68).

[62] *Interrogationes et responsiones baptismales* (ed. A. Boretius, *MGH, Capitularia regum Francorum*, i, #107, p. 222). Hauck, *Kirchengeschichte Deutschlands*, ii, 468, makes note of the same sort of evidence in the Slavic languages.

[63] See E. Prokosch, *A Comparative Germanic Grammar* (Philadelphia, 1939), pp. 21–34.

vide them with a teacher whose speech they could understand. Charlemagne sent Liudger, who was a native Frisian.[64] Apparently a Frank would not have been satisfactory. Some Franks, however, were able to overcome the language barrier. The above mentioned Gregory, although a native Frank, was a leading missionary figure in Frisia for a long period.[65] The Slavic language was even more difficult. Sturmi, the founder of Fulda, could converse with the Slavs he met in Thuringia only by means of an interpreter.[66] Possibly the Bavarian priests and monks who converted the Slavs and Avars on the southeastern border of the Frankish state also utilized interpreters. There is no evidence that any of them had learned the Slavic tongues. The success of their work strongly suggests, however, that priests had been found who could preach to the Slavs and the Avars in their languages.

A lack of valid sources complicates any attempt to discuss the content of missionary preaching designed to win converts. In a few instances the sources present sermons which allegedly were delivered to pagan audiences, but in every case these sermons are the creations of authors writing long after the occurrence of the incident described.[67] Thus they are of limited value. Only by indirection do the sources throw any light on the content of missionary sermons. The conclusions that can be drawn from this evidence must be tentative and qualified.

Some sermons to the pagans apparently attempted to inform the pagans concerning the Christian version of the origin and development of the universe and of man. Daniel, bishop of Winchester, in a letter of advice written to Boniface after the latter had begun his missionary labors on the continent, devotes almost his whole attention to the proper way to present this theme to the pagans.[68] When Louis the Pious deputed Ebo, archbishop of Reims, to carry Christianity to Denmark, he advised the archbishop to be certain to explain the creation of the world and of man, the fall of man, the deluge, and the coming of Christ the Redeemer.[69] Perhaps the best example of the content of such an explanation of the Christian version of history is contained in a tract compiled by the bishop-abbot

[64] *Vita secunda s. Liudgeri*, Lib. I, c. 16 (ed. W. Diekamp, *Geschichtsquellen des Bisthums Münster*, IV, 61–62). For Liudger's Frisian origin, see Altfrid, *Vita Liudgeri*, Lib. I, c. 1–8 (ed. W. Diekamp, pp. 6–13).

[65] Liudgeri, *Vita Gregorii*, c. 1 (ed. O. Holder-Egger, *MGH, SS.*, XV, 66).

[66] Eigilis, *Vita Sturmi*, c. 7 (ed. G. Pertz, *MGH, SS.*, II, 369): 'ibi magnam Sclavorum multitudinem reperit. . . . Unus autem ex illis qui erat ipsorum interpres, interrogavit eum quo tenderet? Cui ille respondit, in superiorem partem eremi se fore iturum.'

[67] Two such sermons that should be noted are the one which Willibrord allegedly delivered to Radbod (Alcuin, *Vita Willibrordi*, c. 11, ed. W. Levison, *MGH, SS. rerum Merov.*, VII, 125) and Lebuin's sermon to the Saxons at Marklo (*Vita Lebuini antiqua*, c. 6, ed. A. Hofmeister, *MGH, SS.*, XXX², 794; Hucbald, *Vita Sancti Lebuini*, c. 12–13, Migne, *PL*, CXXXII, 888–890). Willibrord is said to have delivered his sermon to Radbod before 714; Alcuin probably wrote his work between 785 and 797. The *Vita Antiqua Lebuini* was probably written a century after Lebuin's activity; see Hofmeister's introduction to the *Vita, MGH, SS.*, XXX², 790–791. Hucbald's *Vita Lebuini* was written early in the tenth century; see Max Manitius, *Geschichte der lateinischen Literatur des Mittelalters*, IX. Band, 2 Abt., 1. Teil (Munich, 1911), pp. 588–594.

[68] Boniface, *Ep.*, #23 (ed. M. Tangl, *MGH, Epistolae Selectae*, I, 38–41).

[69] Ermoldus Nigellus, *In honorem Hludowici carmen*, Lib. IV, v. 1911–1945 (ed. et trad. Edmond Faral, *Les Classiques de l'Histoire de France au Moyen Age*, publiés sous la direction de Louis Halphen, XIV [Paris, 1932], pp. 146, 148).

Pirmin, who labored in Alemannia in the early eighth century attempting to wipe out the last traces of paganism. Pirmin's tract was compiled as a kind of handbook to be used by priests to instruct Alemannians whose faith was shaky and whose knowledge of Christianity was extremely vague and confused. The first part of the tract is taken up with an account of the whole epic of the world, cast in terms of the sinfulness of man, God's efforts to save him, and the final redemption of man through the coming of Christ. Obviously, this part of the handbook could be very conveniently used by priests as a source for sermons. Pirmin might well have known how to appeal to the pagan mind in a sermon, since he had worked most of his life trying to extirpate pagan ideas among the Alemannians.[70] The chief source of the Christian version of history was the Bible, which was used widely in missionary work. Boniface on different occasions requested copies of certain books of the Bible from England.[71] and he was murdered in Frisia with a Bible in his hand.[72] Lebuin carried a Bible when he appeared at Marklo to argue the case for Christianity before the Saxon nobles.[73] Pope Gregory II especially instructed Boniface to use the Old and the New Testaments in converting the pagans.[74] Gregory, Boniface's disciple, secured 'many volumes of holy scripture,' when he accompanied his master to Rome in 722.[75] Thus it seems highly possible that many sermons to the pagans consisted of vulgarized versions of Biblical accounts of the origins of the world and of man. The mythology of the pagans was given a Christian counterpart by a well-chosen selection of Bible stories delivered as sermons.[76]

A comparison between the Christian God and the pagan gods was certainly a theme for sermons. Missionary literature is filled with statements of the necessity of impressing upon the pagans the superiority of the Christian God. Especially did the missionary advisers, like Alcuin and Daniel of Winchester, stress the importance of convincing the pagans that the Christian God was omnipotent, all-good, just, and merciful.[77] Undoubtedly the missionaries themselves likewise undertook to present these qualities of the Christian God to the pagans. Willehad, for instance, sought 'to persuade the Saxons to take notice of the one true God.'[78]

---

[70] For Pirmin's account of Christian history, see Pirmin, *De singulis libris canonicis scarapsus* (Migne, *PL*, LXXXIX, 1029-1035). For the detials of Pirmin's career see the two *Vitae* (ed. Carolus de Smedt, *AASS*, Nov., II, 34-47); *Herimanni Augiensis Chronicon*, a. 724, 727 (ed. G. Pertz, *MGH*, *SS.*, V, 98); Walafrid Strabo, *Visio Wettini*, ll. 27-37 (ed. E. Dümmler, *MGH*, *Portae latini aevi carolini*, II, 304-305); Hrabanus Maurus, *Carmina*, #lxviii (ed. E. Dümmler, *MGH*, *Poetae latini aevi carolini*, II, 224-225). See also Carolus de Smedt, 'Commentarius Praevius de sancto Pirminio episcopi' (*AASS*, Nov., II, 2-33).

[71] Boniface, *Ep.*, #34, 63 (ed. M. Tangl, *MGH*, *Epistolae Selectae*, I, 58-59, 128-132).

[72] *Vita altera Bonifatii*, c. 14 (ed. W. Levison, *MGH*, *SS. rer. Germ. in usum schol.*, p. 72).

[73] *Vita Lebuini antiqua*, c. 6 (ed. A. Hofmeister, *MGH*, *SS.*, xxx², 794).

[74] Boniface, *Ep.*, #12 (ed. M. Tangl, *MGH*, *Epistolae Selectae*, I, 18).

[75] Liudger, *Vita Gregorii*, c. 8 (ed. O. Holder-Egger, *MGH*, *SS.*, xv, 73): 'plura volumina sanctarum Scripturarum . . . illic acquisivit. . . . '

[76] See Konen, *Die Heidenpredigt in der Germanenbekehrung*, pp. 24-25, for the use of Scripture as a basis for explaining the Christian view of history.

[77] See especially Alcuin, *Epistolae*, #110 (ed. E. Dümmler, *MGH*, *Epistolae*, IV, 157-159); Boniface, *Ep.*, #23 (ed. M. Tangl, *MGH*, *Epistolae Selectae*, I, 38-41).

Possibly more effective than discourses on the attributes of the Christian God were sermons picturing His power to grant earthly rewards to the pagans. Daniel of Winchester advised Boniface to point out to the pagans how much better off in worldly possessions the Christians were than the pagans.[79] Lebuin was alleged to have told the Saxons at Marklo that they would receive greater benefits than they had ever known before if they would accept the Christian God.[80] There are suggestions that the most popular mode of comparison between the Christian God and the pagan deities was that of villification of the pagan gods. Willehad pointed out to the pagans the stupidity of seeking help from gods made from stones.[81] Again Daniel of Winchester's letter to Boniface sums up the spirit of such attacks.[82] He advised Boniface to chide the pagans on the retreat of their gods before the victorious Christian God. The pagans should be shown how silly it is to worship gods who need the king of things human beings offer them. The incongruity of gods being begotten by other gods in the manner of human beings was to be stressed. All of these suggestions might allow one to conclude that the following passage from Willibrord's alleged sermon to Radbod is a fair example of the manner in which the Christian God was presented to the pagans in a missionary sermon: 'It is not God that you worship, but the devil, who has deceived you, O King, into the vilest error, so that he might deliver your soul to eternal flames. For there is no God except the one God who created the heavens, the earth, and the sea and everything which is in them.'[83] And Hucbald's version of Lebuin's sermon to the Saxons also seems to supply a specimen of the attack aimed at the pagan gods by missionary preachers: 'The statues which you believe to be gods and which, deceived by the devil, you worship, are only gold or brass or stone or wood. They do not live; they do not move; they do not think. They are the work of men. Not one of them could be of help to itself or to anyone else.'[84]

Still another theme of missionary sermons was an attack on pagan forms of worship. This whole topic was probably very near to the missionary's mind, since so much effort was devoted during the Carolingian period to the problem of extirpating the last remnants of pagan practices throughout Christendom. Boniface's letters illustrate the concern felt by a missionary on this subject.[85]

[78] *Vita Willehadi,* c. 3 (ed. A. Poncelet, *AASS*, Nov., III, 843): 'coepit . . . persuadere ut, relicta supersticione idolorum, unius veri Dei notitiam susciperent. . . . '

[79] Boniface, *Ep.,* #23 (ed. M. Tangl, *MGH, Epistolae Selectae,* I, 40).

[80] Hucbald, *Vita sancti Lebwini,* c. 12 (Migne, *PL,* CXXXII, 889).

[81] *Vita Willehadi,* c. 3 (ed. A. Poncelet, *AASS,* Nov., III, 843).

[82] Boniface, *Ep.,* #23 (ed. M. Tangl, *MGH, Epistolae Selectae,* I, 38–41.

[83] Alcuin, *Vita Willibrordi,* c. 11 (ed. W. Levison, *MGH. SS. rerum Merov.,* VII, 125): 'Non est Deus, quem colis, sed diabolus, qui te pessimo errore, o rex, deceptum habet, ut animam tuam aeternis tradat flammis. Non est enim Deus nisi unus, qui creavit caelum et terram, mare et omnia, quae in eis sunt. . . . '

[84] Hucbald, *Vita sancti Lebwini,* c. 12 (Migne, *PL,* CXXXII, 889): 'Simulacra quae deos esse putatis, quosque a diabolo decepti venerando colitis, aurum vel argentum, aes, lapis, aut lignum sunt; non vivunt, non moventur, neque sentiunt. Opera enim hominum sunt, nec cuiquam alii, nec sibi possunt auxiliari.'

[85] Boniface, *Ep.,* #26, 28, 32, 50, 51 (ed. M. Tangl, *MGH, Epistolae Selectae,* I, 44–47, 49–52, 55–56, 80–92).

Other evidence suggests that this feeling of repugnance for pagan practices of worship found warm expression in missionary sermons. Willehad is said to have argued with the Frisians 'that it was silly and vain to seek help from stones and to hope for the solace of help from deaf and mute images.'[86] Sturmi and his priests also demanded that the Saxons destroy the temples and groves where they worshipped.[87] The tenor of such attacks on the pagan cults seems to be summarized in a poetic description of Louis the Pious' instructions to Archbishop Ebo as to how to present the Christian case to the pagan Danes:

They ought to give up their vain ways. It is a sin for a man who possesses reason to render worship to metal statues. How can Jupiter or Neptune or any of the gods which they worship or the images which they shape with their hands aid them? These miserable people practice a useless cult. They address their prayers to deaf and mute gods. They sacrifice to demons what ought to be given to God. It is evil to try to placate our God with the blood of beasts; He loves the holy prayers of men much more. Enough time has been given to these evil errors; the time has come to cut away the condemned religions.[88]

Apparently some Carolingian missionary sermons were also built around an attempt to explain the major theological concepts of the Christian faith. However all evidence suggests that this theme for sermons was not so popular as was an attack upon the pagan gods and the pagan forms of worship or as was an exhaltation of the power of the Christian God. It is not difficult to appreciate the reluctance on the part of missionaries to undertake a thorough exposition of Christian theology to their pagan audiences. The pagans could hardly have been fitted for an understanding of any comprehensive study of Christian theology in the early stages of their conversion. The time which elapsed in most cases between the arrival of missionaries in pagan areas and the first baptisms was too brief to allow an adequate presentation of the positive aspects of the Christian religion. Missionaries were content to wait until after baptism to try to instruct the pagans in Christian theology. Alcuin was undoubtedly reflecting the neglect of this phase of missionary preaching when, just prior to the campaign of 796 against the Avars, he wrote a series of letters charging that the failure of missionary efforts in Saxony was due to hasty baptism of the pagans who knew nothing about the faith.[89] In

---

[86] *Vita Willehadi*, c. 3 (ed. A. Poncelet, *AASS*, Nov., iii, 843); 'dicens insanum esse et vanum a lapidibus auxilium petere, et a simulacris mutis et surdis subsidii sperare solatium.'

[87] Eigilis, *Vita Sturmi*, c. 22 (ed. G. Pertz, *MGH*, *SS.*, ii, 376).

[88] Ermoldus Nigellus, *In honorem Hludowici caramen*, Lib. iv, vv. 1947–1957 (ed. E. Faral, *Les Classiques de l'Histoire de France au Moyen Age*, p. 148):

    'Linquere vana decet; sculptis servire metallis
      Heu scelus est homini, qui ratione veget.
    Juppiter aut Neptunus eos, vel quemque sequuntur,
      Quid juvat, aut manibus sculpta metalla suis?
    Vana colunt miseri; surdis mutisque precantur
      Daemonibusque litant debita danda Deo.
    Non pecudum placare Deum fas sanguine nostrum;
      Pluris amat hominis vota benigna pius.
    Jam satis errori tempus tribuere profano,
      Cultibus inlicitis cedere tempus adest.'

[89] Alcuin, *Ep.* #110–113 (ed. Dümmler, *MGH*, *Epistolae*, iv, 156–166).

spite of the rather convincing proof that doctrinal matters were neglected in sermons, there is some evidence to suggest that occasionally a missionary introduced such matters into his sermons. It has already been pointed out how the idea of a single deity was preached to the pagans.[90] Other theological concepts which appear to have been developed in sermons include ideas on immortality,[91] the Christian version of heaven and hell,[92] sin,[93] the nature of baptism,[94] and the Trinity.[95] However, it is impossible to find evidence which indicates that the sermons did more than merely touch on a few general aspects of Christian dogma.[96] One must

[90] See above, pp. 716–717.

[91] For example, Altfrid, *Vita Liudgeri*, Lib. I, c. 30 (ed. W. Diekamp, p. 36).

[92] For a description of the Christian version of heaven and hell, such as might have found its way into missionary preaching, see Boniface, *Ep.*, #10 (ed. M. Tangl, *MGH, Epistolae Selectae*, I, 7–15), where hell is especially well described in such passages as the following: 'Inter ea referebat se quasi in inferioribus in hoc mundo vidisse igneos puteos horrendam eructantes flammam plurimos et erumpente tetra terribilis flamma ignis volitasse et miserorum hominum spiritus in similitudine nigrarum avium per flammam plorantes et uluantes et verbis et voce humana stridentes et lugentes propria merita et presens supplicium consedisse paululum herentes in marginibus puteorum et iterum heiulantes cecidisse in puteos' (*ibid.*, p. 13).

[93] See Alcuin, *Vita Willibrordi*, c. 11 (ed. W. Levison, *MGH, SS. rerum Merov.*, VII, 125); Hucbald, *Vita sancti Lebwini*, c. 12 (Migne, *PL*, CXXXII, 888–889).

[94] *Vita Willehadi*, c. 3 (ed. A. Poncelet, *AASS*, Nov., III, 843): 'per sacri baptismatis ablutionem peccatorum suorum veniam promerei potuissent. . . .' Paulinus of Aquileia's discussion of the synod held on the Danube prior to the campaign against the Avars in 796 indicates that missionary priests were instructed to teach the pagans that baptism would put away all sins; *Concilia aevi karolini*, I, #20 (ed. A. Werminghoff, *MGH, Leges*, Sectio III, T. II¹, 174): 'quia per id peccata dimmitantur et regeneratus novus homo. . . .'

[95] The words of the baptismal vow taken by the pagans suggests that pagans had been instructed in the nature of the Trinity; see *Interrogationes et responsiones baptismales* (ed. A. Boretius, *MGH, Capitularia*, I, #107, p. 222): 'gelobistu in got alemehtigan fadaer? ec gelobo in got alamehtigan fadaer. gelobistu in crist godes suno? ec gelobo in crist gotes suno. gelobuist in halogan gast? ec gelobo in halogan gast.'

[96] One is tempted to introduce into this search for evidence describing the content of missionary preaching the material compiled by two figures who were deeply concerned with Carolingian missionary affairs. One was Alcuin, who became so concerned over missionary procedure at the time of the attack on the Avars in 796 that he wrote a series of letters trying to influence the decisions being made concerning the conversion of the Avars. In one of these letters (Alcuin, *Ep.*, #110, ed. E. Dümmler, *MGH, Epistolae*, IV, 157–159), he briefly outlines what he thinks ought to be taught to the pagans. Then he refers his readers to a tract by St Augustine, entitled *De catechezandis rudibus* (Migne, *PL*, XL, 309–348), for more specific information. An examination of Augustine's tract reveals a rather elaborate description of what pagans should be taught. The second source which contains evidence of the content of missionary preaching is a tract entitled *Ratio de cathecizandis rudibus* (ed. Joseph Michael Heer, *Ein karolingischer Missions-Katechismus* [Freiburg im Breisgau, 1911], pp. 77–88), which, in the opinion of the editor, was compiled at the time of the conversion of the Avars. It also presents a detailed description of what priests should teach their pagan audiences. However, there is absolutely no proof that either of these documents had any bearing on actual missionary preaching. Heer insists that the *Ratio de cathecizandis rudibus* was a handbook used by missionaries in the Avar territory (*ibid.*, pp. 42–49). But his only basis of proof is that its content squares with the decisions reached by an ecclesiastical synod held in 796, prior to the invasion of the territory of the Avars (see *Concilia aevi karolini*, I, #20, ed. A. Werminghoff, *MGH, Leges*, Sectio III, T. II¹, 172–176). Since it cannot be demonstrated that either of these discussions of what *ought* to be preached was ever used by missionaries, it hardly seems permissible to cite either of them as evidence of what missionaries actually preached to their pagan auditors.

conclude that missionary preachers did not concern themselves very seriously with an exposition of the main tenets of the faith.

How many pagans were influenced by the missionaries' attempts to explain the nature of the faith and to show its superiority over paganism through the means of preaching and instruction is impossible to judge. In general, it might be safe to conclude that this approach to the pagan was not sufficient in itself. No matter how great a preacher and teacher a Carolingian missionary was, he had to use additional arguments and inducements to win over the pagans, who were only slightly impressed by argument alone.[97]

As a supplement to preaching and instruction the missionaries of the eighth and ninth centuries relied heavily on the actual destruction of the objects which the pagans worshipped. Among the missionaries who resorted to this measure in order to impress the pagans can be included Willibrord, Boniface, Sturmi, Liudger, and Willehad, all of whom are praised in the literature of the age for having destroyed the hateful objects of pagan worship.[98] The Carolingian kings permitted their armies to indulge in the destruction of pagan temples. Charles Martel's forces burned numerous Frisian temples during a campaign in 734.[99] Charlemagne personally directed the destruction and looting of the Irminsul, a temple in Saxony, during the campaign of 772.[100] Such attacks were not always the product of the heat of battle or of sudden inspiration to a particular missionary; they were very often adopted as a part of general missionary policy. Albericus, bishop of Utrecht and consequently director of missionary activity in Frisia, ordered Liudger and other missionary priests to carry out a general program of destruction of pagan centers of worship in Frisia.[101] Liudger was also directed by Charlemagne to go to Heligoland to destroy the pagan temple there.[102] Carolingian rulers were exhorted again and again to root out paganism with the sword, destroying every sign and symbol of the worship of pagan gods.[103] Obviously missionaries and statesmen alike felt that this mode of attack helped immeasurably in winning converts.

The intention of these attacks on pagan objects of worship is quite obvious.

---

[97] Konen, *Die Heidenpredigt in der Germanenbekehrung*, pp. 10–13.

[98] Alcuin, *Vita Willibrordi*, c. 10, 14 (ed. W. Levison, *MGH, SS. rerum Merov.*, VII, 124–125, 128); Willibald, *Vita Bonifatii*, c. 6, 8 (ed. W. Levison, *MGH, SS. rer. Germ. in usum schol.*, pp. 31–32, 47); Eigilis, *Vita Sturmi*, c. 22 (ed. G. Pertz, *MGH, SS.*, II, 376); Altfrid, *Vita Liudgeri*, Lib. I, c. 16, 22 (ed. W. Diekamp. pp. 20, 26); *Vita Willehadi*, c. 4 (ed. A. Poncelet, *AASS*, Nov., III, 843).

[99] *Chronicarum quae dicuntur Fredegarii Scholastici Libri IV cum Continuationibus*, c. 17 (ed. Bruno Krusch, *MGH, SS. rerum Merov.*, II, 176).

[100] *Annales regni Francorum*, a. 772 (ed. F. Kurze, *MGH, SS. rer. Germ. in usum schol.*, p. 34).

[101] Altfrid, *Vita Liudgeri*, Lib. I, c. 16 (ed. W. Diekamp, p. 20).

[102] *Ibid.*, c. 22, pp. 25–26.

[103] For typical examples see *Translatio sancti Liborii*, c. 5 (ed. G. Pertz, *MGH, SS.*, IV, 151); *Epistolae variorum Carolo Magno regnante scriptae*, #1 (ed. E. Dümmler, *MGH, Epistolae*, IV, 496); *Codex Carolinus*, #76 (ed. W. Gundlach, *MGH, Epistolae*, III, 607–608); Einhard, *Vita Karoli magni imperatoris*, c. 7 (ed. L. Halphen, *Les Classiques de l'Histoire de France au Moyen Age*, 2nd ed. [Paris, 1938], pp. 24–26); *De Pippini regis victoria Avarica*, v. 6–12 (ed. E. Dümmler, *MGH, Poetae latini aevi carolini*, I, 116–117); Alcuin, *Ep.*, #110, 111, 113, 178 (ed. E. Dümmler, *MGH, Epistolae*, IV, 157, 161, 164, 294).

The pagan religions held a powerful grasp on their adherents primarily because the pagans feared to displease their gods by interrupting the traditional pattern of worship. Sacrilege would in the thinking of the pagans result immediately in divine retaliation against the guilty party and his society. The carefully staged destruction of venerated objects thus served the missionaries as a dramatic means of convincing the pagans of the powerlessness of their gods to avenge the Christian violators. These acts gave final proof both to the Christian arguments of the superiority of the Christian God, who revealed His might by allowing the missionaries to attack the pagan religion, and of the stupidity of worshipping the pagan gods, who demonstrated their incapacity by permitting these desecrations. The value of bold assaults on objects sacred to the pagans is suggested by the following description of Willibrord's activity on the island of Heligoland, which the Frisians honored as hallowed ground:

While the pious preacher of the word of God was on his way from Denmark, he came to a certain island between the borders of the Frisians and the Danes. The inhabitants of the land called this island Fositeland for a certain one of their gods named Fosite; a temple of this god had been built there. The place was held in so great veneration by the pagans that not one of the pagans dared to kill any of the animals which pastured there or anything else. Neither did any of them attempt to take water from the spring which ran there except in silence. When this man of God was cast on the shores of this place by a tempest, he remained there several days, so that a fit time for sailing might come when the wind subsided. But putting little stock in the silly worship of that place or the fierce mind of the king who was accustomed to condemn violators of the holy places with a cruel death, he baptized in the name of the Holy Trinity three men in the spring and ordered that the animals which pastured in that land be slaughtered for food by his followers. When the pagans saw that, they thought that the gods would be made furious or that the violators would suffer a sudden death. But when they observed that the violators suffered no evil, they were terrified and hastened to King Radbod with the story of what they had seen.[104]

The pagans might indeed find it difficult to continue their adherence to their old gods after such a demonstration of weakness.

The assault against paganism was not confined to religious grounds alone. Some evidence suggests that the missionaries could effectively utilize the promise of earthly rewards as an inducement to the pagan to surrender his ancient religion

[104] Alcuin, *Vita Willibrordi*, c. 10 (ed. W. Levison, *MGH, SS. rerum Merov.*, VII, 124–125): 'Et dum pius verbi Dei praedicator iter agebat, pervenit in confinio Fresonum et Daenorum ad quandam insulam, quae a quodam deo suo Fositae ab accolis terrae Fositesland appellabatur, quia in ea eiusdem dei fana fuere constructa. Qui locus a paganis in tanta veneratione habebatur, ut nihil in ea vel animalium ibi pascentium vel aliarum quarumlibet rerum quisquam gentilium tangere audebat nec etiam a fonte, qui ibi ebulliebat, aquam haurire nisi tacens praesummebat. Quo cum vir Dei tempestate iactatus est, mansit ibidem aliquot dies, quousque, sepositis tempestatibus, oportunum navigandi tempus adveniret. Sed parvi pendens stultam loci illius relegionem vel ferocissimum regis animum, qui violatores sacrorum illium atrocissima morte damnare solebat, igitur tres homines in eo fonte cum invocatione sanctae Trinitatis baptizavit, sed et animalia in ea terra pascentia in cibaria suis mactare praecepit. Quod pagani intuentes, arbitrabantur, eos vel in furorem verti vel etiam veloci morte perire. Quos cum nihil mali cernebant pati, stupore perterriti, regi tamen Rabbodo quod videbant factum retulerunt.' See Willibald, *Vita Bonifatii*, c. 6 (ed. W. Levison, *MGH, SS. rer. Germ. in usum schol.*, p. 31), for a similar account, describing Boniface's bold destruction of the sacred oak at Geismar.

in favor of Christianity. Two conditions helped create this opportunity for the Carolingian missionary. First, the pagan, by virtue of his religious tradition, was particularly susceptible to this appeal. He was a creature who thought of religion in terms of earthly rewards; his respect for a deity seems often to have been based on how much material benefit could be derived from the worship of that god. Second, the missionaries were backed by secular rulers who were willing to provide such rewards for those who would accept Christianity. This fortunate coincidence of pagan susceptibility and Frankish willingness to supply the necessary material support gave the missionaries a powerful tool of persuasion. The scanty information concerning missionary method suggests they made the most of it. Occasionally they might practice this form of bribery directly, winning a pagan convert by the actual grant of a reward of some kind. More often they presented their religion to a pagan audience which was well aware that acceptance of Christianity would result in material gain not from the missionary himself but from the missionary's strongest supporter, the Frankish ruler. Whatever may have been the exact nature of the transaction, there can be little doubt that Christianity was made more attractive to the materialistic pagan because of the rewards that might accrue from its acceptance.

An understanding of the fashion in which the promise of material rewards was used to win converts takes one into Carolingian politics. There repeatedly arose two separate political situations which offered the missionary his opportunity to entice the pagan with a promise of material gain. The first situation emerged as a result of the clash between Frankish and pagan military forces. In the course of these struggles the Franks almost invariably destroyed the existing political systems in the pagan world. The resultant confusion permitted accession to power and wealth to those pagans who were willing to recognize Frankish dominion and to cooperate with the Franks in establishing and maintaining order. The Frankish rulers were apparently anxious to find pro-Frankish elements in the conquered pagan areas. They usually made it obvious that they would reward those who accepted their overlordship. However, the rewards to be gained as a result of adherence to the Franks were always made contingent upon the acceptance of Christianity, which was apparently viewed by the Frankish rulers as an open sign of political submission. Two cases serve to illustrate the pursuit of this policy and its results from a missionary point of view. One of Pepin of Heristal's major tasks during his career as mayor of the palace was the establishment of permanent rule over those areas in southern Frisia which he had won by conquest.[105] Bede notes that in pursuit of this policy, Pepin 'rewarded with many benefits those who wished to receive the faith.'[106] One can hardly doubt that these rewards went to those Frisians who were for Pepin's cause politically as well as religiously. Charlemagne likewise rewarded the Saxons for supporting the Frankish cause and accepting Christianity. As early as 775 some Saxon nobles, like

---

[105] Gustav Richter, *Annalen des fränkischen Reichs im Zeitalter der Merovinger* (Halle, 1873), pp. 177–178; Schmidt, *Geschichte der deutschen Stämme*, II, 79.

[106] Bede, *Hist. eccl.*, V. c. 10 (ed. C. Plummer, I, 299): 'multisque eos, qui fidem suscipere uellent, beneficiis adtollens. . . .'

Hessi, the chieftan of the Ostphalians, and Bruno, the leader of the Angrarians, surrendered to the Franks.[107] Hessi, and undoubtedly many others, accepted Christianity at this time or shortly thereafter.[108] Among the means used by Charlemagne to achieve political surrender, and presumably religious submission, was the granting of gifts.[109] One author says that Charlemagne 'converted from pagan rites to the Christian religion a certain noble, Hessi, along with many others, to all of whom he gave countships and rewarded them with great honors, since he found them faithful to him in all things.'[110] Another source provides evidence that in 782 Charlemagne was able to appoint counts from among the native leaders, thus proving to the Saxons that there was an advantage to be gained from supporting the Franks.[111] Careful examination of the events of the Saxon wars shows that the Saxons almost never united in revolt against the Franks, but that a party within Saxony always remained loyal to the conquerors.[112] That loyalty must surely have been bolstered by the prospect of reward from the Carolingian kings.

From the missionary's point of view the effect of this policy on the pagan world is not difficult to imagine. Realizing that a new day had dawned as a result of Frankish might and that a splendid advantage could be gained by capitalizing on the Frankish anxiety to find a following in pagan lands, at least a faction of the pagans might have been quite willing to surrender to the new masters to gain the advantage usually accompanying such a surrender. That the Franks required them to become Christians did not deter the pagans long; the new God was obviously giving them the kind of material reward they expected but were not just then getting from their old gods, who had permitted the servant of the Christian God to crush them in battle. Thus was created a climate of opinion that was definitely favorable to the missionary. He could often plead his case before an audience, the members of which realized that by permitting themselves to be baptized they were taking an important step in gaining the rewards given by the Franks to their adherents.

---

[107] *Annales regni Francorum*, a. 775 (ed. F. Kurze, *MGH, SS. rer. Germ. in usum schol.*, pp. 40, 42).

[108] *Vita Liutbirgae*, c. 1 (ed. G. Pertz, *MGH, SS.* iv, 158), indicates that Hessi became a Christian very early in the period of the Saxon conversion. Possibly he was among those baptized in 776; see *Annales regni Francorum*, a. 776 (ed. F. Kurze, *MGH, SS. rer. Germ. in usum schol.*, p. 46).

[109] Eigilis, *Vita Sturmi*, c. 22 (ed. G. Pertz, *MGH, SS.*, ii, 376), says that Charlemagne converted the Saxons, 'partim etiam muneribus.' Eigilis clearly indicates that this method was employed before the death of Sturmi, which occurred in 779. Writing in 790, Alcuin, *Ep.*, #7 (ed. E. Dümmler, *MGH, Episotlae*, iv, 32), confirms the use of this method, saying ' . . . Saxones et omnes Frisonum populi, instante rege Karolo, alios premiis et alios minis sollicitante, ad fidem Christi conversi sunt.' See Wiedemann, *Die Sachsenbekehrung*, pp. 35–38.

[110] *Vita Liutbirgae*, c. 1 (ed. G. Pertz, *MGH, SS.*, iv, 158): 'ex paganico ritu christianae religioni subiugavit, quendam inter primores et nobilissimos gentis illius, nomine Hessi, cum aliis quam plurimis, quibus comitatum dederat, magnis etiam sustentavit honoribus, quia fidelem sibi in cunctis repererat.'

[111] *Annales Mosellani*, a. 782 (ed. Cl. I. M. Lappenberg, *MGH, SS.*, xvi, 497): 'Habuit Karlus rex conventum magnum exercitus sui in Saxonia ad Lippiabrunnen et constituit super eam comites ex nobilissimis Saxonum genere.' See also *Annales Laureshamenses*, a. 782 (ed. G. Pertz, *MGH, SS.*, i, 32).

[112] Halphen, 'La conquête de la Saxe' in *Études critiques sur l'histoire de Charlemagne*, p. 146, *passim*.

A second political situation in the pagan world created a further opportunity for the utilization of the prospect of material gain and political advantage as an inducement for the pagans to accept baptism. Since the Franks so clearly surpassed any of the pagan states in power, it became a regular practice for political factions within those pagan areas not yet conquered by the Franks to seek Frankish support for their particular cause. The Frankish rulers and those who represented them usually required a renunciation of paganism as a condition for granting support. The terms upon which such compacts were built are well represented by the demands made by Louis the Pious on King Harald of Denmark, who had been driven out of his kingdom and had sought Frankish aid so that he might be restored:

He came to the most serene emperor Louis, requesting that he be considered worthy to receive his help so that he would be able to regain his kingdom. Louis kept him with him for some time and urged him through personal persuasions and those of others to accept the Christian faith, because thus there would be more friendship between them and because the Christian people would more promptly and willingly come to his aid if both peoples worshipped the same God.[113]

One must suppose that similar conditions were laid down by Pepin of Heristal when, prior to 695, the Frisian noble Wurssing fled Radbod's kingdom and sought refuge in Francia. At least it is certain that Wurssing and his family became Christians prior to their restoration in Frisia.[114] Before the Slavic prince Boruth, faced with the problem of turning back the Avars, was able to receive the aid of the duke of Bavaria, he was required to allow his heir to be given a Christian education.[115] The Avar leaders who sought the aid of Charlemagne in 805 in order to protect their political interests likewise accepted baptism.[116] This evidence suggests that the pagan world was well aware that Frankish support was most likely to be forthcoming to the supporters of Christianity. Thus there always existed factions among the pagans who might be inclined to look with favor upon the Christian missionaries representing not only a new religion but also the political might of the Franks, whose assistance could be valuable in gaining local political ends. Here again the missionary's task would be eased by the fact that the prospect of material gain to be acquired by accepting Christianity opened ears that might otherwise have been deaf.

Unfortunately, it is impossible to produce detailed evidence to establish how extensively the missionaries used the prospect of material rewards as an enticement to gain a hearing for their religion. The political maneuvering involved in

---

[113] Rimbert, *Vita Anskarii*, c. 7 (ed. G. Waitz, *MGH, SS. rer. Germ. in usum schol.*, p. 26): 'Qui serenissimum adiit imperatorem Hludowicum, postulans, ut eius auxilio uti mereretur, quo regnum suum denuo evindicare valeret. Qui eum secum detentum tam per se quam per alios ad suscipiendam christianitatem cohortatus, quod scilicet inter eos ita maior familiaritas esse posset, populusque christianus ipsi ac suis promptiori voluntate in adiutorium sic veniret, si uterque unum coleret Deum. . . . '

[114] Altfrid, *Vita Liudgeri*, Lib. I, c. 2. (ed. W. Diekamp, p. 7).

[115] *De conversione Bagoariorum et Carantanorum libellus*, c. 4 (ed. W. Wattenbach, *MGH, SS.*, xi, 7).

[116] *Annales regni Francorum*, a. 805 (ed. F. Kurze, *MGH, SS. rer. Germ. in usum schol.*, p. 119–120).

these matters was conducted on the level of state policy. The gifts, offices, and advances in power granted to the pagans who had accepted the faith were made by the Frankish rulers. Only indirectly can the missionary be connected with the process. The fact that Pepin of Heristal's policy of granting benefits to those Frisians who accepted the Christian religion was carried out at exactly the same time that Willibrord, who had Pepin's backing was carrying on missionary work in in Frisia, suggests that Willibrord had a part in the transactions. And that the Wurssings, one of the families Christianized and benefited by this policy, became leading supporters of Willibrord during the period following the defeat of Radbod by Charles Martel further indicates that the missionary was a party in the dealings between the Frankish crown and the Frisian family.[117] It seems more than a coincidence that Charlemagne began to reward and promote Saxon nobles like Hessi at the very moment when Sturmi was engaged in missionary work in Saxony; the abbot of Fulda or some of his monks may well have been instrumental in negotiating the arrangements leading to the conversion and to the granting of rewards to Hessi. There can be little doubt that the missionaries in Carinthia were closely associated with the political arrangements that kept pro-Frankish, pro-Christian princes in power. The missionaries won their first converts when Boruth had to seek the assistance of the duke of Bavaria in order to hold power. The price which he paid for this support was that of sending his son and nephew to the monastery at Chiemsee for a Christian education. Perhaps the clergy at this frontier monastery had been instrumental in gaining Bavarian support for Boruth. Boruth's son and nephew, now Christianized, became princes in Carinthia. The nephew, Chotimir, who became prince with the special blessing of Pepin I, was accompanied to his realm by a priest from Chiemsee. Perhaps this priest was a representative of the Bavarian backers of Chotimir. Virgil, bishop of Salzburg, seems to have been important in maintaining connections between the Slavic prince and his supporters. Chotimir visited Virgil every year. Even more significant seems to be the fact that Virgil sent a steady stream of missionaries into Chotimir's pagan realm. These missionaries undoubtedly made every use of the fact that they represented the powers which placed and maintained the present prince in his office. This argument seems to have been efficacious; before long Virgil had to send a bishop into Carinthia, apparently to begin solidifying the gains made by the missionaries. This happy arrangement depended, however, on the continued support given Chotimir by the Bavarians and the Franks. Eventually Chotimir's rule was threatened by rebellion. Virgil, no doubt appreciating the true nature of the Christians' position, sent more priests into Carinthia to save the situation, that is, to try to maintain Chotimir in power. The prince died in about 769 and a reaction set in against his faction. The result was that there was not a priest in Carinthia for several years. Missionary effort ended miserably, probably because the missionaries could no longer entice converts by offering them rewards from the hands of the Bavarians and Franks. New missionary efforts did not begin until 772, when Duke Tassilo of Bavaria again succeeded in installing a pro-Bavarian and pro-Christian prince in power in Carin-

---

[117] Altfrid, *Vita Liudgeri*, Lib. i, c. 1–5 (ed. W. Diekamp, pp. 6–10).

thia. The new prince immediately appealed to Virgil for missionaries. No doubt he wanted his Slavs to be converted; perhaps he also felt that missionaries could help keep him in power by using the promise of rewards to win his Slavic subjects over to Christianity and, consequently, to his political cause.[118]

Perhaps these cases do not supply sufficient evidence to conclude that the missionaries often attempted to win converts by promising material rewards. Yet in each case the evidence points strongly to the fact that missionaries often pursued the practice of Ebo of Reims, who during the 820's went frequently to his missionary territory in Denmark, where 'in order to win souls he distributed much money and added many to the Christian religion . . .'[119] or the practice of Anskar, who frequently visited the Danish king, Horic, and 'tried to conciliate him with gifts . . . in order that he might gain permission to preach in his kingdom.'[120] At least it can be demonstrated that the prospect of political advancement and of material rewards brought many pagan leaders to the baptismal font. Whatever the part played by the missionaries in this process, it would appear that the material advantage to be gained by accepting Christianity worked in favor of the missionary and was thus one of the important means used in the missionary attack on paganism.

The missionaries possessed a powerful means of attracting the pagans through the medium of the civilization which the Christians carried with them. There is no necessity to argue the relative merits of Christian and pagan cultures at this point.[121] Suffice it to say that everything indicates that the pagans were impressed by the civilization that the missionaries possessed and that the missionaries knew this very important fact. Daniel of Winchester indicated that the pagans were vulnerable on this point when he advised Boniface to stress the point that the Christians possessed material advantages completely unknown to the pagan world.[122] Boniface apparently knew from experience that the English bishop's advice was sound when dealing with the 'barbarians.' On one occasion he wrote to an English abbess requesting that she 'make a copy written in gold of the epistle of [his] master, St Peter the Apostle, to impress honor and reverence for the sacred scriptures visibly upon the carnally minded to whom [he] preached.'[123] When Anskar began his first missionary journey to Denmark in the company of King Harald, he and his companions were not well-treated by the Danes until

---

[118] *De conversione Bagorariorum et Carantanorum libellus*, c. 4–5 (ed. W. Wattenbach, *MGH, SS.*, XI, 7–9).

[119] Rimbert, *Vita Anskarii*, c. 13 (ed. G. Waitz, *MGH, SS. rer. Germ. in usum schol.*, p. 35): ' . . . pro lucrandis animabus multa . . . dispensavit ac plurimos religioni christianorum adiunxit. . . . '

[120] *Ibid.*, c. 24, p. 52: ' . . . muneribus eum . . . conciliare studuit, ut sua licentia praedicationis officio in regno eius frui valeret.'

[121] Much of the recent literature concerning the Christianization of the Germans has been devoted to arguing the question whether Christianity destroyed a thriving Germanic culture and replaced it with an inferior one. See Laurenz Kilger, 'Bekehrungsmotive in der Germanenmission,' *Zeitschrift für Missionswissenschaft*, XXVII (1937), 1–19, for a list of some of the more important of these works and forceful criticism of their approach.

[122] Boniface, *Ep.*, #23 (ed. M. Tangl, *MGH, Epistolae Selectae*, I, 40).

[123] *Ibid.*, #35, p. 60: 'ut mihi cum auro conscribas epistolas domini mei sancti Petri apostoli ad honorem et reverentiam sanctarum scripturarum ante oculos carnalium in predicando. . . . '

the party reached Cologne, where Anskar was presented with a good boat by Bishop Hadebald. 'When Harald saw it, he decided to remain with them [the missionaries] in it. . . . This began to promote an increase of friendship and goodwill among them. . . .'[124] Here is excellent evidence that the pagans were impressed by the obvious superiority which the Christians possessed in the material realm. The missionaries did not have to rely on only ornate books and good boats to prove the superiority of their civilization; all about them they created living proof of their superiority.[125] The construction of new monasteries at Fritzlar, Amöneberg, Werden, Heidenheim, Ohrdruf, and Fulda called for the clearing of land that had previously been useless.[126] New buildings, including stone structures,[127] began to grace a countryside that had previously been forest.[128] The monks at Fritzlar planted a vineyard.[129] A stream was diverted at Fulda in order to supply the monastery with water.[130] A mill was built at Heidenheim and was made available to the residents of the area.[131] The part of metal working was practiced at Fulda.[132] Thriving schools were begun at Fulda, Fritzlar, Utrecht, and Ohrdruf.[133] Even more impressive was the fact that the Christian establishments in pagan areas quickly grew wealthy; some of them, like Fulda, became the dominant economic institutions in the area.[134] It is difficult to believe that the pagans were not as impressed by these innovations as they were by Boniface's book. They must have been powerfully attracted to the way of life which the Christians represented. This certainly would have inclined them to listen to the preaching and teaching of the possessors of such a magnificent material civilization.

The conduct of the missionaries in their relations with the pagans may have offered still another means whereby the Christians could induce the pagans to abandon their religion. Any attempt to evaluate the effect of the personalities and the habits of life of the missionaries on the pagans is seriously complicated

---

[124] Rimbert, *Vita Anskarii*, c. 7 (ed. G. Waitz, *MGH, SS. rer. Germ. in usum schol.*, p. 29): 'Hanc itaque praedictus Herioldus conspiciens, elegit ipse in eadem navi cum illis manere . . . ; sicque inter eos familiaritas coepit et benivolentia crescere. . . .'

[125] Flaskamp, 'Die Missionsmethod des hl. Bonifatius,' *Zeitschrift für Missionswissenschaft*, xv (1925), 89–93, supplies a good picture of this aspect of missionary life.

[126] For typical accounts describing the building of monasteries see Nun of Heidenheim, *Vita Wynnebaldi*, c. 7, ff. (ed. O. Holder-Egger, *MGH, SS.*, xv, 111, ff.), Eigilis, *Vita Sturmi*, c. 13 (ed. G. Pertz, *MGH, SS.*, ii, 370–371); *Vita secunda s. Liudgeri*, Lib. i, c. 28–30 (ed. W. Diekamp, *Geschichtsquellen des Bisthums Münster*, iv, 74–78).

[127] Nun of Heidenheim, *Vita Wynnebaldi*, c. 11 (ed. O. Holder-Egger, *MGH, SS.*, xv, 115).

[128] For example, Eigilis, *Vita Sturmi*, c. 20 (ed. G. Pertz, *MGH, SS.*, ii, 375): 'Sturmi . . . coepit . . . ministeria illorum monastica constituere, templum, id est ecclesiam, quod tunc habebant, ornare, et domos omnes monasterii recentibus columnis et grandibus trabidus novisque tectorum structuris corroboravit.' Also *Vita Willehadi*, c. 9 (ed. A. Poncelet, *AASS*, Nov., iii, 845).

[129] Lupus, *Vita Wigberti*, c. 9 (ed. O. Holder-Egger, *MGH, SS.*, xv, 41).

[130] Eigilis, *Vita Sturmi*, c. 20 (ed. G. Pertz, *MGH, SS.*, ii, 375).

[131] Nun of Heidenheim, *Vita Wynnebaldi*, c. 12 (ed. O. Holder-Egger, *MGH, SS.*, xv, 115).

[132] Eigilis, *Vita Sturmi*, c. 20 (ed. G. Pertz, *MGH, SS.*, ii, 375).

[133] Liudger, *Vita Gregorii*, c. 11 (ed. O. Holder-Egger, *MGH, SS.*, xv, 75–76); Lupus, *Vita Wigberti*, c. 5, 6 (ed. O. Holder-Egger, *MGH, SS.*, xv, 39–40).

[134] Eigilis, *Vita Sturmi*, c. 14 (ed. G. Pertz, *MGH, SS.*, ii, 372). See also, Liudger, *Vita Gregorii*, c. 5 (ed. O. Holder-Egger, *MGH, SS.*, xv, 72).

by the fact that the sources generally obscure the nature of the personal relationship which was established between missionaries and pagans. This is especially true of the saints' lives, which invariably laud the missionaries for their practice of Christian virtue. Seldom do the real men emerge from behind the idealized pictures presented by hagiography. However, a hint is sometimes dropped which suggests that the conduct of the missionaries might have attracted and impressed the pagans. Even if one disregards the accolades presented by the authors of the saints' lives, he can find sufficient evidence to prove that the missionaries generally conducted themselves admirably. They seem to have kept themselves above many of the factional struggles which tore the Carolingian church.[135] They made a serious effort to live the type of life which the age considered ideal; this was especially true in the monastic houses established by the missionaries.[136] They were among the most serious supporters of the attempts to regenerate morally the Frankish clergy and church.[137] They were zealous in their pursuit of learning, even while they were engaged in missionary work.[138] Their virtues may well have impressed the pagans, although one need not believe that these virtues inevitably put paganism to flight, as some contemporary accounts would have it.

The decency and the moral uprightness of the missionary probably had a direct effect upon the lives of the pagans. The sources, and especially the saints' lives, repeatedly imply that the missionaries sought to impress the pagans with their mercy, their charity, their patience, their courage, their industry, and their steadfast devotion to the Christian way of life. Willibrord is said to have provided for the welfare of beggars during his missionary days in Frisia.[139] Boniface and Gregory stood firm in the face of poverty and war in Thuringia, choosing to help the people in every way they could rather than to flee to safer territory.[140] After he became abbot of the monastery at Utrecht, the same Gregory used the money which

---

[135] Only occasionally is there evidence that the clergy working in the missionary field was involved in any serious quarrels. One such instance is the dispute between Lul and Sturmi; Eigilis, *Vita Sturmi*, c. 16–19 (ed. O. Holder-Egger, *MGH, SS.*, xv, 373–375). Boniface, of course, met violent resistance in his reforming efforts and thus became involved in ecclesiastical politics; but in this capacity he can hardly be considered a missionary.

[136] For instance, Sturmi made a special trip to Monte Cassino to find at first hand the manner in which a Benedictine house ought to be set up (*ibid.*, c. 14, pp. 371–372). Liudger made a similar trip to Italy for the same reason; see Altfrid, *Vita Liudgeri*, Lib. i, c. 21 (ed. W. Diekamp, p. 25).

[137] Boniface is preeminent in this respect; see Hauck, *Kirchengeschichte Deutschlands*, i, 515–551, for his activity as a reformer. The bishops whom he placed in the missionary field were also supporters of the reform movement.

[138] The schools established in connection with missionary work are indications of the interest which missionaries took in learning. Boniface, *Ep.*, #9, 27, 30, 34, 63, 76, 91, 96, 103 (ed. M. Tangl, *MGH, Epistolae Selectae*, i, 4–7, 47–49, 54, 58–59, 128–132, 158–159, 206–208, 216–217, 225–227), all indicate Boniface's avid interest in learning. Liudger's education, as described in Altfrid, *Vita Liudgeri*, Lib. i, c. 1–9 (ed. W. Diekamp, pp. 13–17), illustrates the serious attempts made in the missionary areas to perfect the education of priests and monks, and gives proof of Altfrid's statement that 'Erat sanctus Liudgerus in scripturis sacris non mediocriter eruditus. . . . Discipulis etiam suis mane diebus singulis tradere per se lectiones non neglexit. . . . ' (*ibid.*, c. 30, p. 35).

[139] Alcuin, *Vita Willibrordi*, c. 17 (ed. W. Levison, *MGH, SS. rerum Merov.*, vii, 129–130).

[140] Liudger, *Vita Gregorii*, c. 2 (ed. O. Holder-Egger, *MGH, SS.*, xv, 69–70).

he possessed to aid paupers;[141] some of them might well have been pagan paupers, since Gregory was deeply concerned with missionary activity in his role as abbot of the monastery at Utrecht. Liudger often invited paupers as well as rich men to eat with him during his many travels in pagan Frisia and Saxony.[142] He was reputed to have shown mercy toward a criminal who was about to be hanged.[143] Willibrord stayed the hand of some of his followers who wished to strike down the pagan who tried to murder him at the pagan temple on Walcheren island.[144] Admittedly these incidents are bound up with legends and with the fancy of the authors of the saintly biographies. Yet they may rest on some kernel of truth which would permit one to conclude that by such actions the missionaries established closer ties with the pagans and thus eased the way toward successful conversion of the pagans.

Still another reflection of the impression made by the missionary personalities on the pagans can be gleaned from a close scrutiny of the miracles that became connected with the missionaries during or soon after their labors among the pagans.[145] An examination of the miracles described by the hagiographers reveals that the great bulk of them center around such activities as granting aid to the aged, treating the sick, relieving the burdens of the poverty-stricken, and helping the oppressed. This vein of consistency in the legends of miracle working might well indicate that the missionaries did bend their efforts toward such good works among the pagans, that actual deeds of charity and mercy lay behind what later became legends of miracles. Even during their lives missionaries might have been viewed as 'miracle men' because of their steadfast devotion to their task and their willingness to offer their services to those pagans who needed assistance. The great numbers of pagans or newly won Christians who were alleged to have flocked to the tombs of dead missionaries in search of assistance[146] or who sought refuge in missionary churches during troubled times[147] suggest that the missionaries very early had found a place in the hearts of those they were trying to convert. This personal bond, based solely on the conduct of the missionaries, could well have helped to lead the pagans to conversion.

A final factor which served the missionaries in their attempts to convert the pagans was the power of the Frankish state. The Carolingian author who suggested that Carolingian missionary success was due primarily to the sword of the

---

[141] *Ibid.*, c. 12, p. 76.

[142] Altfrid, *Vita Liudgeri*, Lib. I, c. 30 (ed. W. Diekamp, p. 36).

[143] *Vita secunda s. Liudgeri*, Lib. I, c. 27 (ed. W. Diekamp, *Geschichtsquellen des Bisthums Münster*, IV, 72–73).

[144] Alcuin, *Vita Willibrordi*, c. 14 (ed. W. Levison, *MGH, SS. rerum Merov.*, VII, 128).

[145] Accounts of miracles are connected with virtually all of the saints' lives. Those included in *ibid.*, c. 14–22, pp. 127–133; Altfrid, *Vita Liudgeri*, Lib. I, c. 25–29 (ed. W. Diekamp, pp. 30–35), are especially illustrative.

[146] See especially, *ibid.*, Lib. II, *passim*, pp. 39–53; Lupus, *Vita Wigberti*, c. 26–30 (ed. O. Holder-Egger, *MGH, SS.*, XV, 43); Rudolph of Fulda, *Vita Leobae*, c. 22–23 (ed. O. Holder-Egger, *SS.*, XV, 130–131).

[147] For instance, the account told by Rudolph of Fulda, *Vita Leobae*, c. 14 (*MGH, SS.*, XV, 128), of how the people around Bischofsheim sought refuge in the church during a great storm.

king was perhaps hasty in his generalization.[148] However, he was no doubt correct in implying that the state did everything in its power to aid the spread of Christianity and the men who proselytized among the pagans. In this connection it is important to remember that missionary activity during the Carolingian period was confined almost wholly to territory which was at least nominally part of the Frankish kingdom. The serious attempts to convert the Frisians, Saxons, Slavs, and Avars were undertaken only after these people had been subjected to Frankish conquest. Consequently, the pagans in these areas were considered subjects of the Frankish king and were obliged to defer to his dictates. When the missionaries approached the pagans, they could conceivably represent themselves as agents of the Frankish state and use the power of the Frankish state as a means of buttressing the case for their religion.

The Frankish rulers often sought to strengthen the hand of the missionaries by granting to them the special protection of the crown. The missionaries, of course, already enjoyed the ordinary protection against violators of any kind which the Frankish kings preferred to all clergymen and to the church as an organization. Very often the missionary was able to furnish more specific proof that he had the backing of the king and that the king's pagan subjects would suffer punishment for any overt action against the person or the work of the missionary. Boniface, for instance, bore with him to Hesse in 723 a letter from Charles Martel, commanding that the missionary 'was to be left in peace and protected as a man under royal guardianship and protection.'[149] Willibrord was likewise graced with royal protection prohibiting any interference with his missionary preaching. Pepin of Heristal first extended that protection in the period immediately after he had driven Radbod out of southern Frisia in 690.[150] He continued the assistance at later dates. For instance, in 695 when it was necessary to begin the organization of the church in Frisia, Pepin was instrumental in securing the *pallium* for Willibrord from Rome.[151] Upon Willibrord's return Pepin presented him with several properties in Utrecht.[152] In 780 Willehad was sent into the Saxon province of Wigmodia, 'where with the backing of royal authority he would build churches, present the lessons of holy preaching to the people, and announce to all the people

---

[148] *Translatio sancti Liborii*, c. 5 (ed. G. Pertz, *MGH, SS.*, IV, 151): 'Quem [Karolum] arbitror nostrum iure apostolum nominari; quibus ut ianuam fidei aperiret, ferrea quodammodo lingua praedicavit.'

[149] Boniface, *Ep.*, #22 (ed. M. Tangl, *MGH, Epistolae Selectae*, I, 37): 'sub nostro mundeburdio et defensione quietus vel conservatus esse. . . . '

[150] Bede, *Hist. eccl.*, v, c. 10 (ed. C. Plummer, I, 299): 'ipse quoque imperiali auctoritate iuuans, ne qui praedicantibus quicquam molestiae inferret.'

[151] Both Alcuin, *Vita Willibrordi*, c. 6 (ed. W. Levison, *MGH, SS. rerum Merov.*, VII, 121), and Bede, *Hist. eccl.*, v, c. 11 (ed. C. Plummer, I, 302–303), make Pepin's part clear.

[152] Bede, *op. cit.*, p. 303; Boniface, *Ep.*, #109 (ed. M. Tangl, *MGH, Epistolae Selectae*, I, 235–236). Alcuin, *Vita Willibrordi*, c. 13 (ed. W. Levison, *MGH, SS., rerum Merov.*, VII, 127), says that Utrecht was not granted to Willibrord until the period of Charles Martel; Bede and Boniface must be counted as the better witnesses. A charter of Pepin I dated 23 May 753 throws some light on the nature of the grant made in 696; see *MGH, Diplomati Karolinorum*, I, #4 (ed. E. Mühlbacher, pp. 6–7). See also Verbist, *Saint Willibrord*, pp. 98–101; Hermann Nottarp, *Die Bistumserrichtung in Deutschlands im achten Jahrhundert (Kirchenrechtliche Abhandlungen*, ed. Ulrich Stutz, 96. Heft [Stuttgart, 1920]), pp. 9–17.

there the way to eternal salvation.'[153] Before Ebo, archbishop of Reims, went to Denmark on a missionary mission in 823, elaborate steps were taken by Louis the Pious to support him. An assembly was held; it agreed to send Ebo to Rome to secure papal authority for the missionary project. As a result Pope Pascal designated Ebo as a papal legate for northern Europe, thus providing the missionary with at least the outward marks of authority to aid him in his dealings with the pagan Danes. Almost the same measures were taken to aid Anskar in his missionary work in Scandinavia.[154] The missionary could usually proceed to his task with the assurance that the Frankish rulers would attempt whenever possible to protect his person and to punish anyone who attempted to destroy his work. The pagan was undoubtedly aware of the risk involved in any overt act against the Christians. His resistance to the advances of the missionaries might have been tempered by his realization that any injury to the missionaries was apt to bring down the wrath of the Frankish kings, whom most pagans respected at least as their conquerors.

The missionaries could also confront the pagans with the fact that, in terms of the laws laid down by the conquerors, pagan religions were illegal and subject to certain penalties. Even prior to the Carolingian period the church, with the backing of the state, had developed a tradition of legislation against paganism and of provision for punishment for those who engaged in the interdicted practices.[155] This type of religious legislation was continued throughout the Carolingian period. Sometimes the legislation was designed to put an end to pagan remnants still being practiced by Christians, the prohibition being stated in general terms.[156] In other cases the list of interdicted pagan practices was made more comprehensive and more specific. One list, the *Indiculus superstitionum et paganiarum*, which cannot be dated definitely but which was certainly a regulation enjoying the force of law, included thirty separate pagan practices all of which were outlawed.[157] Occasionally, the penalty for violation of these provisions was specifically stated, as in a capitulary published by Carlomann after the synod of Leptines held in 743.[158] All of this legislation was intended, of course, to aid in the final extirpation of pagan traces remaining within Christendom. Nonetheless, the provisions of these capitularies and of the decrees of ecclesiastical synods provided a

---

[153] *Vita Willehadi*, c. 5 (ed. A. Poncelet, *AASS*, Nov., III, 844): 'quo inibi auctoritate regali et ecclesias instrueret, et populis doctrinam sanctae praedicationis inpenderet, atque viam salutis aeternae libere cunctis illic habitantibus nunciaret.'

[154] *Epistolae Selectae Pontificium Romanorum Carolo Magno et Ludovico Pio regnantibus scriptae*, #11 (ed. K. Hampe, *MGH, Epistolae*, v, 68–70); Rimbert, *Vita Anskarii*, c. 13 (ed. G. Waitz, *MGH, SS. rer. Germ. in usum schol.*, pp. 34–35).

[155] See Carlo de Clercq, *La Législation religieuse franque de Clovis à Charlemagne: Étude sur les actes de conciles et de capitulaires, les statuts diocésains et les règles monastiques, 507–814* (Université de Louvain, *Recueil de travaux publiés par les membres de Conférences d'Histoire et de Philologie*, 2ᵉ sér., 38ᵉ fasc. [Louvain and Paris, 1936]), p. 102, for an excellent summary of this tradition.

[156] For examples of legislation against pagan practices issued during the Carolingian period, see *MGH, Capitularia*, I (ed. A Boretius), #10, c. 5, p. 25; #11, c. 4, p. 28; #12, c. 6, p. 30; #19, c. 6, 7, 14, pp. 45–46; #22, c. 65, pp. 58–59, #23, c. 20, 26, 34, p. 64; #33, c. 25, p. 96; #112, c. 15, p. 228.

[157] *Ibid.*, #108, c. 1–30, p. 223.

[158] *Ibid.*, #11, c. 4, p. 28: 'Decrevimus quoque, quod et pater meus ante praecipiebat, ut qui paganas observationes in aliqua re fecerit, multetur et damnetur quindecim solidis.'

rather specific statement of what the pagans were required to forsake and the penalties attached to a refusal. Even more important, this legislation let the pagans know that the Frankish crown looked upon their religions as illegal and subject to punishment.

The Carolingian rulers did not always leave the missionaries with only that kind of legal support which rested on a body of legislation conceived to eradicate a few isolated pagan practices mixed in with Christianity. They occasionally made a full scale assault on organized paganism through the instrumentality of the law, apparently intending to ease the burden of those charged with Christianizing the pagans. The most important example of this policy was the *Capitulatio de partibus Saxoniae*, which attempted to use the police power of the Frankish state to compel the Saxons to reject paganism and accept Christianity. The law stated that the Saxons must refrain from any violence to the person of the missionaries or to the churches which the missionaries had established.[159] Certain pagan practices, including human sacrifices, disrespect for Christian fast days, cremation of the dead, the continued adoration of pagan deities at the customary temples or holy places, and all kinds of divination were made punishable by death or by heavy fines.[160] The Saxons were required to present themselves for baptism, thereby signifying that they had become Christians.[161] Furthermore, they were specifically ordered to support the new religion by granting land to the church and by paying specified dues.[162] By the terms of the law the missionary was thus given tremendous aid. He could theoretically call upon the civil power to compel the Saxons to answer for refusal to give up paganism and to accept Christianity. Definite standards were established by which the missionaries could distinguish the pagan Saxon from the Christian Saxon. The severe penalties imposed for resistance to the dictates of the state — and its missionary agents — were obviously intended to frighten the Saxons into compliance, thus insuring a speedier and easier conversion.

The value to the missionaries of the backing given by the Frankish kings is difficult to estimate. Many factors suggest that the missionary could not rely completely on the Frankish state and its power in winning converts. The utility of these legal strictures against paganism depended directly upon the ability of the Frankish government to enforce its regulations. If the missionary was to exercise any advantage over the pagan by virtue of Carolingian legislation against paganism, he needed to be backed by an operating administrative machinery in the area where he worked. In view of the political situation which existed with pagan areas, it seems doubtful that the missionary could very often depend upon any immediate help from the state in converting pagans. Occasionally a Frankish army might be at hand to insure the enforcement of the laws against paganism and to speed up the work of destroying it. On several occasions Saxons were baptized in the presence of — and probably under compulsion of — a Frankish

---

[159] *Ibid.*, #26, c. 1–3, 5, p. 68.
[160] *Ibid.*, c. 4, 6, 7, 9, 21–23, pp. 68–69.
[161] *Ibid.*, c. 8, 19, p. 69.
[162] *Ibid.*, c. 15–17, p. 69.

army.[163] The missionaries who began work among the Avars in 796 were backed by armies.[164] The Franks, however, were not able to provide permanent occupation forces for conquered lands. Their armies dissolved at the end of every campaign. Moreover, the military commitments of the Franks were too great to allow them to concentrate their military forces in one area for more than a short time. Thus any missionary who depended upon the army to win converts was faced with the unpleasant prospect of remaining within pagan areas after the army departed. Once the armies had left, the authority of the Franks was extremely tenuous. The numerous rebellions which attended the conquest of the Frisians, Saxons, and Avars supply excellent proof of the difficulty the Franks had in establishing their rule permanently in a conquered area. The counts who were charged with the governance of newly-conquered areas were virtually powerless to stay the hand of rebellion. The only recourse left to the rulers was to proceed with another conquest and to exact new promises of obedience, thus wearing the pagans into submission. The exercise of Frankish authority in any systematic and permanent fashion depended not so much upon the ability of the Franks to conquer a land and rule it themselves as upon their success in winning in the pagan area a following which would willingly accept Frankish dominion and could thus be entrusted with the responsibility of governing in the name of the Franks. A factor in building up this following was the conversion of the pagans to Christianity. Seen in proper perspective, the work of the missionaries went hand in hand with political penetration; Christianization was a necessary step leading to political domination. In the early stage of the process of conversion the state was no more able to compel the conversion of a pagan than it was able to enforce a recognition of Frankish political domination. The missionary could not invariably rely on the enforcement of thoses laws and regulations by which the state guaranteed his protection and outlawed paganism.

Even though the support of the state might be a doubtful quantity in the work of a particular missionary in a particular area at a specific moment, one cannot wholly discount the importance of the support tendered by the state to missionary undertakings. The best proof of the aid rendered the missionaries is supplied by a missionary himself. Boniface openly admitted that he would have failed in his efforts without the backing of the Frankish state.[165] He probably meant that, although he might not have had at his immediate disposal the force necessary to protect his person or to punish the recalcitrant pagan, he could depend on the fact that the pagan's attitude was tempered by his realization that he might eventually be held accountable by the Frankish government for any harm to the missionary or any resistance to the missionary program. The Caro-

---

[163] *Annales regni Francorum*, a. 776, 780 (ed. F. Kurze, *MGH, SS. rer. Germ. in usum schol.*, pp. 46, 56).

[164] Alcuin, *Epistolae*, #107 (ed. E. Dümmler, *MGH, Epistolae*, IV, 153).

[165] Boniface, *Ep.*, #63 (ed. M. Tangl, *MGH, Epistolae Selectae*, I, 130): 'Sine patrocinio principis Francorum nec populum ecclesiae regere nec presbiteros vel clericos, monachos vel ancillas Dei defendere possum nec ipsos paganorum ritus et sacrilegia idolorum in Germania sine illius mandato et timore prohibere valeo.' The value of the aid of rulers is further indicated by the number of times Boniface requested such help; see *ibid.*, 20, 22, 93, 107, pp. 33–34, 36–38, 212–214, 232–233.

lingian rulers pursued their policy of conquest and subjugation with stubborn persistence. Resistance to Christianity eventually brought down the might of the Franks on the pagans, no matter how shadowy that power might seem in any particular locality of the missionary area. Carolingian missionaries could always remind the pagans of the power of their supporters. The close connection between the missionaries and the Carolingian state and the definite stand which the Carolingians had taken against paganism must have made many pagans weigh carefully the consequences of resistance. The missionaries undoubtedly played upon this uneasiness in the minds of the pagans. The threat which the missionary Lebuin allegedly made to the Saxons sums up the use which the missionaries could make of the support which the state promised them: 'If you are not willing to become adherents of God . . . there is a king in the neighboring land who will enter your land, conquer and devastate it. He will wear you out with many wars, drive you into exile, or even kill you, and give your property to whomever he wishes. You and your posterity will be his subjects.'[166]

The missionaries' armory of weapons against the pagans has now been described, and it is obvious that the weapons were numerous. The missionaries sought to convince the pagan by argument that Christianity was superior. They often relied upon bold attacks upon objects sacred to the pagans in order to provide clear proof that the pagan gods were completely powerless before the Almighty Christian God. They held out the promise that material rewards of various kinds might come to those who accepted baptism. Consciously and unconsciously they paraded the material aspects of Christian civilization before the eyes of the pagans. They sought to impress the pagans by exemplary conduct, often beneficial to the pagans. They came to the pagan world as representatives of the supreme political power of the Franks.

The success of these appeals and inducements depended upon how the pagan reacted, for few converts could be won unless the pagan gave his consent. To complete the study of the missionary and the pagan in the Carolingian period it is necessary to take account of the pagan side of the conversion process. This task is fraught with even more problems than that of describing the actions of the missionaries, for the pagan left no substantial evidence by which to judge adequately his reaction to the appeals of the missionaries.

The sources supply positive evidence of only one kind of pagan reaction: resistance to the appeals of the missionaries. This resistance took several forms. Often it consisted of arguments against Christianity. Daniel of Winchester's letter of advice to Boniface witnesses the ability of at least some of the pagans to present an argument in favor of their religion.[167] Radbod and Ongendus presumably listened to Willibrord; their refusal to accept the religion for which he pleaded

---

[166] *Vita Lebuini antiqua*, c. 6 (ed. A. Hofmeister, *MGH, SS.*, xxx², 794) 'Quodsi eius non vultis fieri, tunc mandat haec vobis: Praeparatus est in vicina terra rex quidam, qui vestram terram ingredietur, praedabit vastabitque, variis vos bellis fatigabit, in exilium adducet, exhereditabit vel occidet, hereditates vestras quibus voluerit tradet; eique postea subditi eritis ac posteris eius.'

[167] Boniface, *Ep.*, #23 (ed. M. Tangl, *MGH, Epistolae Selectae*, i, 38–41).

suggests that they disputed with him on the merits of the competing religions.[168] Radbod is alleged to have argued with Wulfram concerning the superior merits of the pagan Valhalla, peopled by departed warriors, over the Christian heaven, filled with paupers.[169] Boniface pointed out to Ethelbald, king of Mercia, that the pagans were quick to remind him that the English people, and especially the king, were 'scorning lawful marriage and living in wanton adultery like the people of Sodom.'[170] The missionary himself admitted what the pagans were obviously pointing out to him, namely, that pagan marriage practices were superior to those of the Christians.[171] He wrote an English priest, Herefrid, that he 'suffered from the disgrace of his people whether it be told by Christians or by pagans that the English race reject the usages of other peoples and the apostolic commands — nay, the ordinancy of God — and refuse to hold one wife, basely defiling and mixing up everything with their adulterous lusts, like whinnying horses and braying asses.'[172] On another occasion he wrote to Pope Zacharias telling him that a report had come to him indicating that on the first of January certain groups engaged in a huge parade in the very neighborhood of St Peter's church in Rome, conducting themselves in a pagan fashion. Boniface reminded the pope that such reports circulating among ignorant people were a cause of reproach and a hindrance to him in his preaching.[173] His remarks all indicate that the pagans and semi-Christian peoples among whom he was working were seeking to refute his claims about the character of Christianity and the superior life of its adherents.

The pagans often resorted to more violent forms of reaction. There were several cases where the pagans in a small locality drove the missionaries away. One or two of these cases provide a rather specific description of such reaction. After Willehad had spent some time working around Dockum in northern Frisia just prior to 780, he decided to seek a new scene of operation. Thus he moved across the Lauwers river into completely pagan territory. There he began to preach to the pagans, but his preaching immediately caused great anger among them. Some of them began to claim with great excitement that the missionary must be killed immediately for his attacks on the pagan gods. However, the more level-headed element of the population convinced the agitators that lots must be cast in order to determine the will of the gods in the matter of disposing of the intruder. The missionary was finally allowed to leave unharmed because the lot of death would

---

[168] Alcuin, *Vita Willibrordi*, c. 9–11 (ed. W. Levison, *MGH, SS. rerum Merov.*, VII, 123–126).

[169] *Vita Vulframni*, c. 9 (ed. W. Levison, *MGH, SS. rerum Merov.*, V, 668).

[170] Boniface, *Ep.*, #73 (ed. M. Tangl, *MGH, Epistolae Selectae*, I, 151): 'spretis legalibus conubiis adulterando et luxoriando ad instar Sodomitane gentis. . . . '

[171] *Ibid.*, #73, p. 150.

[172] *Ibid.*, #74, p. 156: 'Obprobrium namque generis nostri patimur sive a christianis sive a paganis dicentibus, quod gens Anglorum spreto more ceterarum gentium et despecto apostolico praecepto, immo Die constitutione legitimas uxores dedignentur habere et hinnientium equorum consuetudine vel rudentum asinorum more luxoriando et adulterando omnia turpiter fedet et confundat.' Translation from *The Letters of Saint Boniface*, tr. Ephraim Emerton (New York: Columbia University Press, 1940), p. 131.

[173] Boniface, *Ep.*, #50 (ed. M. Tangl, *MGH, Epistolae Selectae*, I, 84–85).

not fall against him.[174] Shortly thereafter Willehad entered Saxon territory. Here his preaching and admirable habits of life won him a following. But his adherents soon involved the missionary in difficulty; the new converts insisted on destroying pagan temples. Their enthusiasm aroused the pagan element to anger. Only a miracle — and a hasty retreat — saved the lives of Willehad and his associates.[175] Boniface was not so fortunate in northern Frisia. He too succeeded in winning a following. In the midst of his successes, however, he was attacked and murdered by a hostile element of the population.[176] The Ewald brothers also ran afoul of a faction which was afraid of the success the missionaries might enjoy. To avoid such a threat the pagans murdered the brothers.[177] From these incidents it appears that missionaries could almost always count on winning some converts in any locality. These successes usually gave rise to a pagan party which began to agitate against the Christians, producing arguments that the gods were angry and that their honor must be avenged either by murdering the missionaries or by driving them away. If the pagan party were the stronger, then the missionaries suffered death or were driven away. Flight almost always resulted in the destruction of the work which had been done. Most of the new converts reverted to their old religion, although one of Anskar's converts in Sweden retained her faith for many years without the services of a priest or of the church.[178]

In some cases pagan reaction to Christianity took the form of large-scale attacks embracing wide areas. The basic cause of such attacks was not usually religious. Pagan peoples often took arms to resist the Franks or to throw off Frankish domination. Nonetheless, Christianity always suffered, since it was a symbol of Frankish power. The various Saxon and Frisian attacks on the Franks and on Christianity illustrate the nature of this type of pagan reaction. In most cases the priests working in areas where pagans took to arms were dealt with harshly unless they fled. Some of Willehad's companions were killed for instance, in the Saxon rebellion of 782, although Willehad himself escaped.[179] The beginnings of such uprisings were usually marked by a general exodus of priests from missionary areas. Willibrord and his missionary group fled to Echternach when the Frisians attacked in 715.[180] Liudger hastily left Frisia in 784 when the Frisians joined the Saxon uprising.[181] Besides driving out the missionary priests, the pagans likewise destroyed the churches that had been built. The Saxons even made forays across the Frankish border for this purpose. In 774, for instance, they attempted to destroy the church at Fritzlar but were miraculously foiled. They at least had the pleasure of stabling their horses in the church.[182] The pagans

---

[174] *Vita Willehadi*, c. 3 (ed. A. Poncelet, *AASS*, Nov., III, 843).

[175] *Ibid.*, c. 4, p. 843.

[176] Willibald, *Vita Bonifatii*, c. 8 (ed. W. Levison, *MGH, SS. rer. Germ. in usum schol.*, pp. 47-51).

[177] Bede, *Hist. eccl.*, v, c. 10 (ed. Plummer, I, 299-300).

[178] Rimbert, *Vita Anskarii*, c. 20 (ed. G. Waitz, *MGH, SS. rer. Germ. in usum schol.*, pp. 44-45).

[179] *Vita Willehadi*, c. 6 (ed. A. Poncelet, *AASS*, Nov., III, 844).

[180] Willibald, *Vita Bonifatii*, c. 4 (ed. W. Levison, *MGH, SS. rer. Germ. in usum schol.*, pp. 16-18).

[181] Altfrid, *Vita Liudgeri*, Lib. I, c. 21 (ed. W. Keikamp, pp. 24-25).

[182] *Annales regni Francorum*, a. 773 (ed. F. Kurze, *MGH, SS. rer. Germ. in usum schol.*, pp. 36, 38); Lupus, *Vita Wigberti*, c. 13-22 (ed. O. Holder-Egger, *MGH, SS.*, xv, 41-42).

also made an effort to wipe out Christianity by compelling the converts to re-
nounce their new religion. This explains why Pope Hadrian advised Charlemagne
to show special leniency toward those Saxons who had been forced to surrender
Christianity during the war-torn years between 782 and 785.[183] A Saxon, writing
to Louis the Pious about 815, recounts how his father and his uncle, both Christians and faithful servants of Charlemagne, were forced to give up their property
because they refused to abjure Christianity during a Saxon rebellion.[184] Generally speaking, the wide-spread uprisings in the pagan world were disastrous to
the work of missionaries. No doubt, the missionaries sought to do everything possible to prevent such reactions to Christianity, knowing full well that the work of
a long period could easily be destroyed by one such onslaught. That fear is nowhere better revealed than in a letter which Boniface wrote in 752 to Abbot
Fulrad of St Denis. The missionary was preparing to depart from eastern Francia
for a new missionary undertaking in Frisia. He begged Fulrad to intercede with
King Pepin for the care and protection of the newly established churches along
the Saxon border, which Boniface felt might be destroyed in a moment if the
Saxons fell upon them, thus wiping out thirty years of constant labor.[185]

The spectacular accounts of pagan resistance must not, however, veil the more
important fact that in the long run the most usual reaction of the pagans to the
appeal of the missionaries was the acceptance of Christianity. Again and again
the sources make note that the missionary's work ended with 'the baptism of the
pagan.' It is virtually impossible to add much to this bald statement. The sources
provide almost no evidence of why the pagan listened to the missionary, of why
Christianity appealed to the pagan, of how he reached the decision to accept
conversion. One only knows his general reaction — he was converted.

A few isolated incidents remain, however, which help to explain certain aspects
of the otherwise inscrutable remark that great numbers of pagans surrendered
to the missionaries. It would seem that the decision to become Christian was
made by large groups in any locality. Possibly the pagans joined together in a
body to deliberate the course to be taken when the missionaries appeared and began to argue their case. The pagans who drove Willehad out of northern Frisia
congregated in a public assembly to cast lots to discover the will of the gods.[186]
The Saxons who presented themselves for baptism at Paderborn in 776 had apparently deliberated about the acceptance of the Frankish peace terms and had
decided to show their good faith by accepting baptism.[187] Occasionally the general
population referred this decision to the ruler. The residents of Heligoland turned
Willibrord over to Radbod, their king; apparently they were willing to abide by
his decision.[188] Of very great importance to the success of missionary work was

---

[183] *Codex Carolinus,* #76 (ed. W. Gundlach, *MGH, Epistolae,* iii, 607–608).

[184] *Epistolae variorum inde a morte Caroli Magni usque ad divisionem imperii collectae,* #2 (ed. E.
Dümmler, *MGH, Epistolae,* v, 301).

[185] Boniface, *Ep.,* #93 (ed. M. Tangl, *MGH, Epistolae Selectae,* i, 212–214).

[186] *Vita Willehadi,* c. 3 (ed. A. Poncelet, *AASS,* Nov., iii, 843).

[187] *Annales regni Francorum, a.* 776 (ed. F. Kurze, *MGH, SS. rer. Germ. in usum schol.,* p. 46).

[188] Alcuin, *Vita Willibrordi,* c. 10 (ed. W. Levison, *MGH, SS. rerum Merov.,* vii, 125).

the conversion of the ruling class in pagan society. [The Ewalds were murdered because the residents in one village feared that a favorable reception of the missionaries by their local ruler would result in the conversion of the whole district.[189] The faction which so feared the Ewalds apparently would have had no choice in the matter of conversion if the local leader decided to accept the faith. Thus when a Saxon noble like Hessi accepted the faith, one can assume that many of his subordinates likewise decided to become Christians. The influence of the nobility in the conversion process is revealed by the account describing the conversion of the Frisian noble, Wurssing.[190] Wurssing was an important figure in Frisian society, a judge who enjoyed fame as a dispenser of justice to all people as a helper of the poor and oppressed. He, along with many others, became victims of the tyranny of King Radbod, being deprived of his property and forced to flee to Francia. There he, his wife, his son, and a small following were converted. Eventually another son and three daughters were educated as Christians. One of the sons later returned to Frisia before the death of Radbod; presumably he remained a Christian. After the death of Radbod, Charles Martel sent Wurssing back to Frisia, giving him a liberal reward and ordering him to 'take up the cause of strengthening the faith.'[191] Wurssing settled near Utrecht where he and his sons became invaluable aides to Willibrord. Especially significant was the fact that Wurssing was 'acceptable to all the people.'[192] Large numbers of Frisians apparently accepted the faith because of the example of this honorable man or in order to enjoy his favor. Some evidence of the importance of Wurssing's conversion is revealed by a further study of the activity of his family. Another Frisian noble, Nothrad, and his wife, Adelburga, had likewise accepted the new faith, possibly at the same time as Wurssing. Adelburga had been instrumental in the conversion of her brothers, Willibraht and Thiadabraht. One of them, Willibraht, eventually became a clergyman, the first Frisian to accept a clerical office. Nothrad and Adelburga had a daughter, Liafburg, who miraculously escaped death at the hands of her pagan grandmother, who attempted to comply with pagan custom by killing the daughter of a household that had no sons. Liafburg was eventually married to the son of Wurssing and became the mother of Liudger and Hildigrim, both important figures in later missionary history. Thus Christianized nobles not only aided in the conversion of a nation by influencing the lower classes, but also exerted themselves to win recruits for the native clergy and to crush paganism within their own families. That they were able to bring pressure to bear upon the society in which they held a dominant position is illustrated by the activity of the Christian count in Carinthia, who refused to allow pagans to eat with him and his Christian companions, but ordered their food to be served to

---

[189] Bede, *Hist. eccl.*, v, c. 10 (ed. Plummer, I, 300).

[190] The following account of the Wurssing family is found in Altfrid, *Vita Liudgeri*, Lib. I, c. 1–7 (ed. W. Diekamp, pp. 6–12). See also Alexander Grieve, *Willibrord, Missionary in the Netherlands, 690–739, including a Translation of the Vita Willibrordi by Alcuin of York* (Westminister, England, 1932), pp. 69–73.

[191] Altfrid, *Vita Liudgeri*, Lib. I, c. 4 (ed. W. Diekamp, p. 9): 'et direxit eum ad patriam suam causa fidei roborandae.'

[192] *Ibid.*, c. 4, p. 9: 'acceptabilis universae plebi. . . .'

them along with the dogs, which, he said, were no worse than pagans.[193] Other bits of evidence suggesst that the Saxon nobles who befriended Lebuin,[194] Boniface's friends in Hesse and Thuringia,[195] the Carinthian prince, Cacatius,[196] the Swedish prefect, Herigar,[197] all contributed the same valuable services to their new religion as did Wurssing in Frisia and the count Boruth in Carinthia.

It might be erroneous to conclude that the decision to accept Christianity was entirely a decision imposed by the upper levels of pagan society on the mass of the pagan population. A few hints indicate that perhaps the whole pagan population could become enthusiastic about the new faith, especially if the coming of Christianity happened to coincide with some good fortune to the pagan group. One of the earliest missionaries to Frisia was the Anglo-Saxon, Wilfrid, who spent the winter of 678–679 preaching in Frisia. His biographer says that he was successful in winning converts chiefly because the catch of fish and the crops were good that year.[198] The pagan Frisians apparently saw in the new God powers excelling those of their ancient gods, a fact that made Christianity exceedingly attractive. Even more illustrative of the same pagan reaction is an account arising from Anskar's activities in Sweden. When he made his second visit to Sweden in 852 he asked permission of King Olaf to carry on his work. The king refused permission until he could put the question to an assembly of Swedish nobles. When the question was finally brought before the assembly, great confusion and discord arose.

In the midst of the noise and confusion one of the older men amongst them said: 'Listen to me, O king and people. Concerning the worship of this God it is well known to many of us that He can afford great help to those who place their hope in Him. For many of us have often proved this to be the case on several occasions when in perils by sea and in other crises. Why, then, do we reject that which we know to be necessary and serviceable. . . . Consider carefully, O people, and do not cast away that which will be to your advantage. For, since we cannot be sure that our gods will be favorably disposed, it is good for us to have the help of this God who is always, and under all circumstances, able and willing to aid those who cry to Him.' When he had finished speaking all the people unanimously decided that the priests should remain with them. . . .[199]

---

[193] *De conversione Bagoariorum et Carantorum libellus*, c. 7 (ed. W. Wattenbach, *MGH, SS.*, xi, 9).

[194] *Vita Lebuini antiqua*, c. 3 (ed. A. Hofmeister, *MGH, SS.*, xxx², 792).

[195] Willibald, *Vita Bonifatii*, c. 6 (ed. W. Levison, *MGH, SS. rer. Germ. in usum schol.*, pp. 26–27); Otloh, *Vita Bonifatii*, Lib. i, c. 24 (ed. W. Levison, *op. cit.*, p. 137).

[196] *De conversione Bagoariorum et Carantorum libellus*, c. 4–5 (ed. W. Wattenbach, *MGH, SS.*, xi, 7–9).

[197] Rimbert, *Vita Anskarii*, c. 11, 19 (ed. G. Waitz, *MGH, SS. rer. Germ. in usum schol.*, pp. 32–33, 39–44).

[198] Eddius Stephanus, *The Life of Bishop Wilfrid*, c. 26 (text, translation, and notes by Bertram Colgrave [Cambridge, England, 1927], p. 52).

[199] Rimbert, *Vita Anskarii*, c. 27 (ed. G. Waitz, *MGH, SS. rer. Germ. in usum schol.*, p. 58): ' . . . consurgens unus, qui erat senior natu, in medio plebis, dixit: "Audite me, rex et populi. De cultura istius dei pluribus nostrum bene iam est cognitum, quod in se sperantibus magnum possit praestare subsidium. Nam multi nostrum iam saepius et in marinis periculis et in variis necessitatibus hoc probaverunt. Quare ergo abicimus, quod necessarium nobis et utile scimus? . . . Attendite, populi, consilium vestrum et nolite abicere utilitatem vestram. Nobis enim, quando nostros propitios habere non possumus deos, bonum est huius dei gratiam habere qui semper in omnibus potest et vult ad se

One would not want to conclude, however, that these vague instances of pagan reaction to the missionary's appeal fully explain why and how so many were converted. One can assume other pagan reactions. Perhaps fear of the Franks caused them to bend before the missionaries. Perhaps Christianity as presented by the missionaries seemed not too much different than their old religions; the new religion had a mythology, a God who gave men rewards, a ritual, temples. Perhaps the pagans had lost faith in their ancient gods and were seeking for new ones. Perhaps the relatively magnificent civilization represented by the missionaries lulled them into submission. None of these possible pagan reactions can be demonstrated. Thus it seems best to admit the impossibility of describing adequately the pagan reaction to Carolingian missionaries and to be content with the generalized statement that many pagans accepted baptism as a result of the work of Carolingian missionaries.

Once the pagan had been baptized, the missionary's work was by no means finished. The pagan had still to be taught the real nature of Christianity. The new converts had to be organized into the structure of the Carolingian church. Often these tasks required decades of labor and are themselves worthy of a lengthy description. However, in the eyes of the Carolingian missionary the most important step in the conversion process was completed when the pagan was raised from the baptismal font. Thus this study of the missionary and the pagan can be brought to a close. Perhaps the main lines of the encounter of the missionary and the pagan can be seen a little more clearly, thus throwing a better light on a rather vague facet of Carolingian history.

---

clamantibus auxiliari." Hoc ergo ita perorante, omnis multitudo populi unanimis effecta, elegit, ut secum et sacerdotes essent. . . . ' Perhaps one of the benefits to which the elder referred was the fact that Birka, where the assembly was held, was saved from destruction some years previously when the pagan population rendered service to the Christian God after their own gods had failed them miserably; see *ibid.*, c. 19, pp. 39–44. That the decision taken by the Swedes at Birka was wise was perhaps demonstrated when shortly thereafter they were again saved from military defeat by worshipping the Christian God; see *ibid.*, c. 30, pp. 60–63.

III

The Papacy and Missionary Activity in the
Early Middle Ages

THE era in Western European history extending from 590 to about 900 perhaps had no more prominent feature than the gains won by missionaries for the Christian faith. Beginning with the pontificate of Gregory the Great the Christian frontier was pushed steadily forward until new barbarian invasions, the collapse of the Carolingian empire, and the secularization of the church temporarily interrupted this progress at the end of the ninth century. These gains were made in the face of great odds. Gregory the Great, writing to the Emperor Maurice in 595, dramatically posed the following picture of the task facing the Christian world: "Behold, all things in Europe are given over to the rights of barbarians. Cities are destroyed; castles are torn down; provinces are without people. No farmers inhabit the land. The worshippers of idols rage and domineer in the murder of the faithful. And still priests who ought to throw themselves weeping onto the pavement and the cinders, seek vain names for themselves and glory in new and profane words."[1] Gregory did not live to witness great burdens heaped upon Christendom by the Moslems, the Avars, the Saxons, the Norsemen, the Bulgars, and the Magyars, all of whom sought and often succeeded in circumscribing the Christian realm. Neither did he witness an internal collapse of the western political and ecclesiastical structure so serious that one of his successors, John VIII (872-882), was forced to beg the rulers of the West to assist in protecting Rome herself against invasions by the infidel Saracens and their Christian allies.[2] Nor did Gregory see the gradual bifurcation of what he seemed to think of as a single church into an eastern and a western church during the three centuries which followed his pontificate, creating a near schism which sometimes impeded missionary work.[3] These developments only highlight the magnitude of the achievement of the missionaries of the early Middle Ages.

The labor required to extend the Christian frontier during this era was shared by many groups. Among those was the papacy. In view of the repeated appearance of the papacy in the missionary record, certain questions arise, each having a bearing on missionary history and on the history of the papacy. How extensive was the papal contribution to the struggle against paganism? What was the exact nature of the papal contribution to the conversion of pagans? How

---

[1] *Gregorii I papae Registrum Epistolarum*, V, 37; ed. Paulus Ewald and Ludowicus M. Hartmann, MGH, Epistolae, I, 322: Ecce cuncta in Europae partibus barbarorum iuri sunt tradita, destructae urbes, eversa castra, depopulatae provinciae; nullus terram cultor inhabitat; saeviunt et dominantur cotidie in nece fidelium cultores idolorum; et tamen sacerdotes, qui in pavimento et cinere flentes iacere debuerunt; vanitatis sibi nomina expetunt et novis ac profanis vocabulis gloriantur. This collection will be cited hereafter as Gregory, *Reg.*, MGH, Ep., with appropriate volume, letter, and page numbers. The following abbreviations will be employed for other series in MGH: SS. for Scriptores; SS. rer. Merov. for Scriptores rerum Merovingicarum; SS. rer. Germ. in usum schol. for Scriptores rerum Germanicarum in usum scholarum.

[2] For examples of the way in which John VIII presented his plight see *Iohannis VIII. Papae Registrum* #1, 8, 22, 27, 31, 32, 33, 36, 56, 150, 193, 205, 263, 278; ed. Ericus Caspar, MGH, Ep. VII, 1-2, 7-8, 19-21, 25-26, 29-30, 31-32, 32-33, 35-36, 51-52, 126-127, 154-155, 164-165, 232-233, 245. This work will be cited hereafter as John VIII. *Ep.*; ed. Caspar, MGH, Ep. VII, with appropriate letter and page numbers.

[3] Louis Bréhier and René Aigrain, *Grégoire le Grand, les états barbares et la conquête arabe* (590-757) in *Histoire de l'église depuis les origines jusqu'à nos jours* V, ed. Augustin Fliche and Victor Martin (Paris, 1947), and Emile Amann, *L'Epoque carolingienne* in Fliche and Martin, *op. cit.*, VI (Paris, 1947), passim, for an account of the widening breach between Rome and Constantinople.

Reprinted from *Mediaeval Studies*, 17 (1955), 46-106, by permission of the publisher. © 1955 by the Pontifical Institute of Mediaeval Studies, Toronto.

did the papacy rank as a missionary agency when measured alongside other missionary agencies? Was there a continuity of papal missionary policy? This paper will attempt to shed some light on these questions by bringing together a record of papal missionary effort from 590 to 900 and by trying to evaluate the papal contribution to the total missionary effort of the era.

This study will be retracing familiar ground in the case of a few popes especially prominent in missionary history. It is the opinion of the writer that there has been an inclination to allow these well-studied cases to characterize papal missionary activity over the whole of the early Middle Ages. Such cases need to be set in proper perspective with the missionary activities of popes not so well-known and with the whole missionary effort of the period. Only by undertaking a complete account of papal missionary activity with an emphasis on the exact nature of the papal contribution can it be hoped that a more balanced version of the missionary role of the papacy may emerge.

I.

The missionary activity of Gregory the Great, perhaps the first pope to dispatch missionaries from Rome for the purpose of converting pagans,[4] makes the opening of his pontificate in 590 a significant point at which to begin a study of the papacy and missionary work. Gregory's part in the conversion of pagans, and especially the English nations, was so great that it remained a model for successful missionary ventures throughout most of the period under consideration. He himself sensed that his efforts were epoch making; in his *Moralia* he wrote as follows of the conversion of England: "By the shining miracles of His preachers has God brought to the faith even the extremities of the earth . . . Lo! the tongues of Britain, which before could only utter barbarous sounds, have lately learned to make the alleluia of the Hebrews resound in praise of God. Lo! the ocean, formerly so turbulent, lies calm and submissive at the feet of the saints, and its wild movements, which earthly princes could not control by the sword, are spellbound with the fear of God by a few simple words from the mouth of the priests; and he who, when an unbeliever, never dreaded troops of fighting men, now that he believes fears the tongues of the meek."[5] He wrote with pride to Queen Bertha of Kent that the news of the conversion of England was important enough to be heard as far away as Constantinople.[6] Some of the products of the conversion of England remembered well Gregory's contribution to the Christianization of their native land. Bede justified the introduction of a biographical sketch of Gregory into his *Ecclesiastical History of the English People* on the grounds that the English were the seal of the pope's apostleship, an honor that no other people could claim.[7] Boniface tried to secure copies of Gregory's letters of advice to the English mission to serve as guides for his own work in Germany.[8] Alcuin often referred to Gregory as "our teacher"

[4] Kenneth Scott Latourette, *The Thousand Years of Uncertainty: A.D. 500-A.D. 1500* in *A History of the Expansion of Christianity* II (New York and London, 1938-1945). p. 61; Johannes Haller, *Das Papsttums. Idee und Wirklichkeit* I, verbesserte und erganzte Ausgabe (Urach und Stuttgart, 1950), p. 364.

[5] *Sancti Gregorii Magni Moralium Libri* XXVII, 11; PL 76, 411: . . . quia emicantibus praedicatorum miraculis, ad fidem etiam terminos mundi perduxit . . . . ecce a lingua Britanniae, quae nil aliud noverat, quam barbarum frendere, jam dudum in divinis laudibus Hebraeum coepit Allelula resonare. Ecce quondam tumidus, jam substratus sanctorum pedibus servit Oceanus, ejusque

barbaros motus, quos terreni principes edomare ferro nequiverant, hos pro divina formidine sacerdotum ora simplicibus verbis ligant; et qui catervas pugnantium infidelis nequaquam metuerat, jam nunc fidelis humilium linguas timet.

[6] Gregory, *Reg.* XI, 35; MGH, Ep. II, 304-305.

[7] *Venerabilis Baedae Historica Ecclesiastica Gentis Anglorum* II, 1 in *Venerabilis Baedae Opera Historica* I, ed. Carolus Plummer (Oxford, 1896), p. 73. This work will be cited hereafter as Bede, *Hist. eccl.,* with appropriate book, chapter, and page numbers.

[8] *S. Bonifatii et Lulli Epistolae* #33, 54, 75 in *Die Briefe des heiligen Bonifatius und*

and "our preacher."[9] Gregory's instructions to the English mission were referred to so often in succeeding ages that they assumed the force of canon law.[10] It would be difficult to find a modern historian who did not fully acknowledge the importance of Gregory's missionary work.[11] These testimonials demonstrate that Gregory played a decisive role in the missionary history of his day and thus introduced the papacy as a vital agency in missionary work for a long time thereafter.

Although the English mission was the culmination of Gregory's missionary activities, he had attacked the problem of winning converts and had developed missionary techniques prior to the sending of a mission to England. His correspondence shows his awareness of several non-Christian elements in the realm under his sway and his sense of responsibility for converting them.

One troublesome situation that Gregory sought to correct was the persistence of pagan practices among those who were nominally Christian. Gregory's usual solution for this condition was to call the matter to the attention of those responsible for the spiritual life of such pagans, to reprimand them for their negligence, and to order them to destroy the remnants of paganism immediately. Bishops were most often the targets of papal reproofs. On several occasions Gregory wrote to bishops that he had heard that the worship of idols existed in their sees. He always ordered them to end this situation immediately, usually warning them that their own souls were in jeopardy because of their laxness.[12] Sometimes the pope suggested ways to fight against paganism. Venantius, bishop of Luna, was sternly warned in 599 to correct a situation reported by the *magister militum* of that city, who discovered that there were many in the city who desired to be ordained priests and deacons while at the same time the people living there were in need of the services of clergymen to recall them from infidelity and pagan worship. The bishop's duty was clear—he must provide more clergymen.[13] However, Gregory did not rest the matter with recalling the episcopate to its duty. He likewise asked lay rulers to end pagan practices. For instance, in September, 597, he wrote to Queen Brunehilda of the Franks in this fashion: "We likewise beg this, that you ought to restrain under the moderation of discipline certain of your subjects so that they will not worship idols, that they will not continue the worship of trees, and that they will not make sacrilegious sacrifices with the heads of animals, for it has come to us that many Christians frequent the churches . . . and do not cease to worship demons."[14] Occasionally Gregory requested a secular ruler to join hands with the bishops to discourage or destroy paganism.[15] His usual inducement to spur princes to action was the solemn promise of the pope himself that those who aided in this task would gain both praise in this world and eternal benefits in the

Lullus; ed. Michael Tangl, MGH, Epistolae Selectae I (Berlin, 1916), pp. 57, 96-97, 158, to be cited hereafter as Boniface, *Ep.;* ed. Tangl, with appropriate letter and page numbers.

[9] Alcuin, *Ep.* #124, 125, 128, 279; ed. Ernestus Dümmler, MGH, Ep. IV, 182, 184, 189, 436.

[10] See, for example, a letter of Pope Leo III in *Epistolae selectae pontificum Romanorum Carolo Magno et Ludowico Pio regnantibus scriptae* #5; ed. Karolus Hampe, MGH, Ep. V, 62; Hrabanus Maurus, *Ep.* #29, 31; ed. Ernestus Dümmler, MGH, Ep. V, 444-448, 455-462; Amalarius, *Ep.* #6; ed. Ernestus Dümmler, MGH, Ep. V, 251.

[11] For some typical examples see Erich Caspar, *Geschichte des Papsttums von den Anfängen bis zur Höhe der Weltherrschaft* II (Tübingen, 1930-1933), pp. 505-506, 668;

Gustave Schnürer, *L'église et la civilisation au moyen âge* I, tr. G. Castella (Paris, 1933-1938), pp. 365-414.

[12] For examples see Gregory, *Reg.* III, 59; VIII, 1, 19; MGH, Ep. I, 218-219; II, 1-2, 21.

[13] Gregory, *Reg.* IX, 102; MGH, Ep. II, 110. For another example of Gregory's concern over providing enough clergy to wipe out pagan remains see Gregory, *Reg.* IV, 29; MGH, Ep. I, 263.

[14] Gregory, *Reg.* VIII, 4; MGH, Ep. II, 7: Hoc quoque pariter hortamur, ut et ceteros subiectos vestros sub disciplinae debeatis moderatione restringere, ut idolis non immolent, cultores arborum non existant, de animalium capitibus sacrificia sacrilega non exhibeant, quia pervenit ad nos, quod multi Christianorum et ad ecclesias occurrant et . . . a culturis daemonum non abscedant.

[15] Gregory, *Reg.* XI, 12; MGH, Ep. II, 273.

hereafter. Gregory even laid some of the responsibility for ending pagan practices on Christian landholders. In May, 594, he addressed a letter to *nobilibus ac possessoribus in Sardinia insula consistentibus*.[16] After speaking of how saddened he was to hear that many peasants (*rusticos*) in those parts were given to idolatry, he severely called the landholders to their duty. Since the serfs were given into their charge to work the land, the nobles owed them something in return, namely, the guidance which would lead them to eternal salvation. Cautioning the nobles that the end of the world and the day of judgment were at hand, the pope asked them to lead their charges to the true faith. He added, perhaps as a fillip to entice the nobles of Sardinia to do some noteworthy act, that he would like to hear by letter from any who had won converts.

Gregory was also aware that the religious state of the Lombards was not satisfactory. Aside from their Arianism, many of them remained pagan. He made this situation his concern. In this matter Gregory was faced with a complicated situation. Hard political reality demanded that he do nothing to give the Lombards an excuse to attack Rome. His broad policy of peaceful relations with them likewise dictated that he avoid religious strife.[17] Nonetheless, he could not refrain entirely from trying to convert the Lombards, whether they were Arians or still pagans. Again he relied on the bishops of Italy to bear the burden. The death of the Lombard king Autharith, an avowed enemy of the Roman church, prompted the pope early in 591 to address a letter to all Italian bishops exhorting them to try to get the Lombards to accept the orthodox faith.[18] In September of the same year he advised the bishop of Narni, a city in Lombard hands, to persuade both Lombards and Romans to abandon paganism and heresy and to accept the true faith. He thought the moment opportune because a plague had struck the city; it was obviously divine punishment for the errant ways of the populace, the only escape from which was the acceptance of the true faith.[19] Gregory himself tried to influence the Lombard court through Queen Theolinda, a Bavarian princess who was orthodox[20]—an effort that Gregory perhaps felt was rewarded when Theolinda's young son, Adoloald, was baptized in the orthodox faith in 603.[21]

Gregory was concerned with pagan threats more remote from Rome than the cases cited above. He was troubled over the Avar-Slav assault on the Balkan peninsula. His interest in this area was not so much a missionary one; rather, his chief efforts were bent toward saving the ecclesiastical structure there and toward protecting displaced clergymen. For example, in 591 he wrote to all of the bishops of Illyricum ordering them to receive and sustain any bishop who had been driven out of his see by the barbarian invasions.[22] The next year Gregory himself tried to provide for one such bishop. He wrote to John, bishop of Lissus, a city near Durazzo, ordering him to fill a vacant see in Calabria until his own city could be freed from its barbarian invaders.[23] Gregory also offered his encouragement to the civil authorities in these troubled areas. His order to the bishops of Illyricum, cited above, was a confirmation of an imperial order. In March, 592, he wrote a congratulatory letter to the praetorian prefect of Illyricum, who had recovered the province from the barbarians.[24] Even farther from Rome Gregory demonstrated an interest in winning new converts. In 593 he wrote a letter to Domitian, the metropolitan of Armenia, declaring his disappointment

[16] Gregory, *Reg.* IV, 23; MGH, *Ep.* I, 257-258.

[17] For a review of papal relations with the Lombards in this period see Caspar, *Geschichte des Papsttums* II, pp. 471-478; Bréhier and Aigrain, *Grégoire le Grand, les états barbares et la conquête arabe* (590-757), pp. 48-54.

[18] Gregory, *Reg.* I, 17; MGH, *Ep.* I, 23.

[19] Gregory, *Reg.* II, 4; MGH, *Ep.* I, 103.

[20] Gregory, *Reg.* IV, 4, 33; IX, 67; XIV, 12; MGH, *Ep.* I, 236, 268-269; II, 87-88, 430-432.

[21] Gregory, *Reg.* XIV, 12; MGH, *Ep.* II, 431.

[22] Gregory, *Reg.* I, 43; MGH, *Ep.* I, 69-70.

[23] Gregory, *Reg.* II, 37; MGH, *Ep.* I, 132-133.

[24] Gregory, *Reg.* II, 23; MGH, *Ep.* I, 120-121.

that the bishop's efforts to convert the emperor of Persia had failed, but consoling that ambitious bishop with assurances that his efforts were praiseworthy.[25]

Whereas Gregory's efforts to win new converts in the above cases were chiefly in the form of exhortations, reprimands, reminders, and words of encouragement, his activities were more direct and more positive in at least two other cases, namely, in connection with the Jews and with a Sardinian tribe, the Barbaricini. With respect to the Jews Gregory adopted a policy of permitting their existence in Christendom on the basis of Roman law and of using his influence to prevent infringements on their rights.[26] For instance, he repeatedly forbade all attempts to interfere with Jewish religious practices, making himself available to hear the complaints of any Jewish individual or community that had been wronged.[27] He occasionally ordered Christians to make restitution to Jewish groups for interference with their rights.[28] He insisted that the Christian clergy refrain from forceful conversion of the Jews.[29] Gregory was equally insistent that the Jews confine their activities within legal bounds. He sought to prevent them from holding Christian slaves, gaining slaves by illegal means, leading Christians into sacrilege, taking revenge on converted Jews, or attempting to gain privileged status by bribery.[30]

This rather narrow legalism was constantly tempered by Gregory's anxiety to convert as many Jews as possible. To achieve this end he pleaded with his bishops to encourage with blandishments, admonitions, and persuasion the Jews in their dioceses to accept Christianity. He warned the bishops to avoid any compulsion, lest harshness and asperity harden the Jews against the true faith and lest those forced into baptism merely give lip-service to Christianity while retaining their old superstitions.[31] While encouraging the clergy to bend every effort to persuade the Jews to accept Christianity, Gregory himself sought actively to gain the attention of potential Jewish converts. He was apparently willing to listen to the problems of the Jews,[32] perhaps hoping to influence them personally by giving them an audience. He made it clear that Jews in slavery could gain their freedom by accepting Christianity and he insisted that various authorities see to it that such a reward was made possible.[33] He ordered the overseers of the papal patrimony to relieve the Jewish serfs of a part of their financial burden in return for accepting Christianity,[34] even offering in one case to write letters himself making such promises.[35] He personally ordered special subsidies for newly converted Jews.[36] He granted a man and his wife, who was formerly a Jewess, a special letter of protection against anyone who might do the new convert harm.[37] He ruled that the canonical rules of baptism be modified in order to accommodate Jewish converts. In this same case he even directed the local authorities to furnish the baptismal garb for those Jews who could not afford it themselves.[38] These acts of accommodation suggest that Gregory was convinced that the papacy had a vital role in encouraging the spread of Christianity. Its task was to incite those already Christian to present the teachings of Christianity to potential converts in an orderly, peaceful, non-provocative fashion, while the pope's own task was to use his power and prestige to encourage,

[25] Gregory, *Reg.* III, 62; MGH, Ep. I, 223.
[26] Gregory, *Reg.* II, 6; VIII, 25; IX, 38, 40; MGH, Ep. I, 105; II, 27, 67, 68, for cases in which Gregory speaks of respecting the rights of Jews.
[27] Gregory, *Reg.* I, 34; II, 6; IX, 195; XIII 15; MGH, Ep. I, 47-48, 105; II, 183-184, 383.
[28] See note 26, above.
[29] Gregory, *Reg.* I, 45; MGH, Ep. I, 71-72.
[30] For examples of Gregory's strictures to keep the Jews within the law see Gregory, *Reg.* II, 6; III, 37; IV, 9, 21; VI, 30; VII, 21; IX, 104, 213, 215, 228; MGH, Ep. I, 105, 195, 241-242, 255-256, 408, 464; II, 111-112, 199-200, 203, 223.
[31] Gregory, *Reg.* I, 34, 45; VIII, 23; MGH, Ep. I, 47-48, 71-72; II, 24-25.
[32] Gregory, *Reg.* I, 34, 45; II, 6; VIII, 25; IX, 38, 40; XIII, 15; MGH, Ep. I, 47-48, 71-72, 105; II, 27, 67, 68, 383.
[33] Gregory, *Reg.* IV, 9; VI, 29-30; MGH, Ep. I, 241-242, 407-408.
[34] Gregory, *Reg.* II, 38; MGH, Ep. I, 134.
[35] Gregory, *Reg.* V, 7; MGH, Ep. I, 288.
[36] Gregory, *Reg.* IV, 31; MGH, Ep. I, 267.
[37] Gregory, *Reg.* I, 69; MGH, Ep. I, 89.
[38] Gregory, *Reg.* VIII, 23; MGH, Ep. II, 24-25.

reward, and protect those about to accept baptism and to make every concession possible to ease their transition from their former religion to Christianity.

The Barbaricini, pagans living in the mountainous regions of Sardinia, provided Gregory with the problem of dealing directly with paganism on a larger scale than has been noted previously.[39] His personal intervention in this situation was prompted by the glaring neglect of these pagans by the local clergy and by the fact that the duke of Sardinia had inflicted a military defeat on them in 594. To capitalize on this situation Gregory sent an Italian bishop and a monk to Sardinia to bestir the Sardinian clergy into action and to discover and correct the sources of laxness. Their reports back to Rome on the conditions they found led Gregory to try to support their efforts. In May, 594, he dispatched four letters to Sardinia. One was a stinging rebuke to Januarius, bishop of Cagliari and principal clergyman in Sardinia, upbraiding him for his neglect in allowing paganism to exist in any area under his jurisdiction. In a slightly veiled threat Gregory promised that he would punish any Sardinian bishop in whose diocese he found a pagan. Gregory also wrote a letter to the landholders, ordering them to assume the responsibility for instructing their serfs and seeing to it that they were baptized. He also requested them to lend every possible assistance to his legates. A third letter was sent to Zaborda, the duke of Sicily, praising him for having subdued the Barbaricini and having exacted from them a peace treaty wherein they promised to become Christians. He exhorted the duke to complete what he had started by aiding in the conversion of his recent foes. Any efforts in that direction would glorify the duke in the eyes of both earthly princes and the heavenly King. Finally, Gregory wrote a letter to Hospito, the prince of the Barbaricini. Speaking in moderate language, the pope pointed out the folly of paganism and asked the prince to receive and aid the Italian clergymen who had come to convert his people. Gregory also asked Hospito to do whatever he could to make his subjects receive baptism. Gregory sent the blessings of St. Peter to Hospito as an inducement.

Gregory's efforts of 594 were not as successful as he had hoped. In June, 595, he took further action by writing to the Empress Constantina to report that the venality of the civil judges in Sardinia was impeding the work of his missions. In return for bribes these judges were freeing from penalty those guilty of pagan practices while exacting from new converts the price they had been paying previously to worship their pagan gods. Obviously the imperial government was expected to end these abuses. Still later, in October, 600, Gregory sent a letter to the *praeses* of Sardinia, Spesindeus, asking him to aid the local bishop in gaining converts. What the eventual fate of the Barbaricini was is not recorded; perhaps the lack of further information is proof of their conversion. Whatever the case, Gregory had taken the lead in trying to convert them. He had bent every effort to effect cooperation among his legates, especially charged to win converts, the local clergy, the civil authorities, the leader of the pagans, and the Christian landholders. Against such a combination paganism stood little chance. He advocated a method of gaining converts. The clergy, the landlords, and the civil authorities were encouraged to use persuasion and instruction on the pagans. The prince of those to be converted was asked to use his influence and his example in order to impress his subjects. Judicial proceedings were to be instituted against those who refused to be won by persuasion. Gregory himself was ready to use political sanctions against anyone who impeded the process. Apparently no other party except the papacy was interested or able to take the trouble to win even so small a victory for the faith.

The various attempts to win converts outlined above, most of which preceded

---

[39] The following material relative to the Barbaricini is based on Gregory, *Reg.* IV, 23, 25, 26, 27; V, 38; XI, 12; MGH, Ep. I, 257-258, 260-262, 324; II, 273.

the opening of the English mission, suggest that the latter undertaking was not nearly so unique as has sometimes been suggested. Gregory's activity prior to 596 indicates that he not only had an interest in missionary work but also had a rather broad concept of missionary technique. Nonetheless, his connection with the English mission marks his ultimate missionary achievement. To conceive of converting a people in a situation where his usual weapons—an ecclesiastical organization, a Christian majority, a civil administration that the pope could at least influence to some degree and that was unquestionably pro-Christian— were all lacking required a large amount of innovation and marked a new departure in papal policy.

Gregory alone must be credited with the inauguration of the English mission and with entrusting the task to competent hands. No other agency had concerned itself with English paganism. Gregory complained, for instance, that the neighboring clergy had shown no interest.[40] Nor was there any convenient solution at hand for attacking the situation in England, as is obvious from the considerable thought given by Gregory to the problem of starting the conversion of England. However fanciful may be the story of his encounter with the Angle slaves in Rome and his consequent decision to try to convert them, it may be entirely possible that Gregory himself thought of going to England.[41] After that plan, if it ever existed, came to nothing, his next scheme centered around creating a troop of native clergymen, recruited from the continental slave markets and educated in Rome, to return to England as missionaries. In 595 he ordered Candidus, the rector of the papal patrimony in Gaul, to purchase English boys, baptize them, and transport them to Rome, where they were to be placed in monasteries so that they might be used in the service of God.[42] In the meantime he may have thought of trying to inspire the Gallic and Celtic clergy to act in England, as has been suggested above. Finally he decided to select monks in Italy for converting the English.[43] That choice was a propitious one; Gregory put his hands on a potent weapon in the Benedictine order, fired as it was with desire for the service of God, flexible enough in its organization to meet unusual situations, and disciplined enough to accomplish any task put to it by some guiding authority. Perhaps it is not amiss to say that Gregory performed no greater service for early medieval missionary activity than to encourage the Benedictine order to participate.[44]

Once having chosen a force for the actual missionary work, Gregory threw his efforts into getting his missionary party to its destination. This task was a relatively simple one, although a party of nearly forty monks was involved.[45] Apparently Gregory assumed that a group of monks, traveling under a papal commission, would be able to find suitable hospitality along the way to England without his making any special arrangements, since his correspondence contains

[40] Gregory, *Reg.* VI, 49, 57; MGH, Ep. I, 423-424, 431-432. It is difficult from the text to decide just who was meant by Gregory when he wrote that England was being neglected by neighboring clergy (sacerdotes e vicino, p. 423; sacerdotes qui in vicino sunt, p. 431). The editors of Gregory's correspondence state that the reference is to the clergy of Ireland; see *ibid.*, p. 423, note 2. However, a little farther on in each of these letters Gregory asks the Frankish royalty that his missionaries be permitted to recruit the aid of priests in Frankish territory. He uses exactly the same phrase, *e vicino*, in designating whence these clergymen are to be recruited. This leads me to believe that he felt that both the Frankish and the Irish clergy had been negligent.
[41] Bede, *Hist. eccl.* II, 1, pp. 79-80; "The

Oldest Life of Pope St. Gregory the Great by a monk of Whitby," 9-10, in Charles W. Jones, *Saints' Lives and Chronicles in Early England* (Ithaca, N.Y., 1947), pp. 103-104; Paul the Deacon, *Vita s. Gregorii magni,* 17-20; PL 75, 49-51; John the Deacon, *Vita s. Gregorii magni* I, 21-24; PL 75, 71-72.
[42] Gregory, *Reg.* VI, 10; MGH, Ep. I, 388-389.
[43] John the Deacon, *Vita s. Gregorii magni* II, 33; PL 75, 99.
[44] Schnürer, *L'église et la civilisation au moyen âge* I, 365-414, gives a good characterization of the significance of the union of papacy and Benedictine monasticism in missionary efforts.
[45] Bede, *Hist. eccl.* I, 25, p. 45, supplies this figure.

53

no record of his having written any special letters to accompany Augustine and his companions when they left Rome the first time.[46] This assumption was sound, since the mission was well received by Protasius, bishop of Aix, Stephen, abbot of Lerins, and Arigius, patricius of Gaul.[47] But then there occurred an unforeseen development: a loss of heart within the mission, which was "seized by a sudden fear, and began to think of returning home, rather than to proceed to a barbarous, fierce, and unbelieving people, whose language they did not know."[48] Probably the missionaries heard stories of the magnitude of their task from those they met in Gaul which made it seem more serious than they had thought when they left Rome. Augustine returned to Rome. Gregory then acted firmly to save the mission. He put into Augustine's hands a strong rejoinder to the missionaries concerning their duty in the sight of God; one can assume he had spoken as firmly to Augustine in person. He called upon the missionaries as Benedictine monks to obey their abbot. And he spoke encouragingly of the favor that God would bestow on such a good work and of the eternal rewards the monks would gain for their efforts. This letter apparently convinced the party that it should proceed. As a further aid to the mission and perhaps as a demonstration of the importance he attached to the task, Gregory sent with Augustine special letters of commendation to important bishops along the route and to the Frankish rulers through whose territories the mission had to pass.[49] The pope called upon all of these personages to provide the material needs of the monks. Of the bishops he asked, in addition, that they offer their solace and their prayers. The Frankish rulers were called upon to protect the missionaries and to aid them in recruiting helpers for their task. These measures insured the arrival of the mission in England in May, 597. At least some indication that Gregory's letters had been important can be seen in a later papal letter written to Queen Brunehilda, one of those to whom a letter of commendation had been sent in 596, praising her for the help she had given to the mission as it passed through her territory.[50]

Unfortunately, the record is rather sparse concerning any further contributions on Gregory's part to the initial missionary venture in England. Nonetheless, there are certain hints that some thought had been given to the manner in which the missionaries were to proceed once they were in England and that Gregory was a party to these plans. Gregory himself wrote to Pelagius, bishop of Tours, and Serenus, bishop of Marseilles, that he had instructed Augustine, then on his way to England, to reveal to them more fully the affair in which the missionary was engaged.[51] This suggests some rather definite plans. Gregory had ordered Augustine to take interpreters from Frankish territories, again an intimation that plans had been made for dealing with the pagans.[52] Gregory had instructed Augustine to go to Arles for episcopal consecration in the event that he enjoyed success in England.[53] Implicit in such an order are certain

[46] For instance, Gregory began a letter to Pelagius of Tours and Serenus of Marseilles, to whom he was commending Augustine, as follows: Licet apud sacerdotes habentes Deo placitam caritatem religiosi viri nullius commendatione indigeant . . . . (Gregory, *Reg.* VI, 50; MGH, Ep. I, 425).
[47] Gregory, *Reg.* VI, 53, 54, 56; MGH, Ep. I, 428-431, thanks each of these dignitaries for their kindness to the missionaries.
[48] Bede, *Hist. eccl.* I, 23, p. 42: . . . perculsi timore inerti, redire domum potius, quam barbaram, feram, incredulamque gentem, cuius ne linguam quidem nossent. See also Gregory, *Reg.* VI, 50a; MGH, Ep. I, 426; in this letter, addressed to the missionary party, Gregory orders: Nec labor vos ergo itineris nec maledicorum hominum linguae deter-

reant. . . .
[49] Gregory, *Reg.* VI, 49, 50, 51, 52, 53, 54, 56, 57; MGH, Ep. I, 423-432. Bede, *Hist. eccl.* I, 24, pp. 43-44, adds Atherius of Lyons (whom he mistakenly designates as bishop of Arles) to this list.
[50] Gregory, *Reg.* VIII, 4; MGH, Ep. II, 6.
[51] Gregory, *Reg.* VI, 50; MGH, Ep. I, 425: Cui [i.e., Augustine] etiam ut promptiores ad suffragandum possitis existere, causam vobis iniunximus suptiliter indicare. . . . Bede, *Hist. eccl.* I, 24, pp. 43-44, says the same letter was sent to Atherius of Lyons.
[52] Bede, *Hist. eccl.* I, 25, p. 45: Acceperunt autem, praecipiente beato papa Gregorio, de gente Francorum interpretes.
[53] Gregory, *Reg.* VIII, 29; MGH, Ep. II, 30: Gregory, writing to Eulogius, bishop of

considerations that must have been discussed prior to Augustine's departure: the organization of converts won, matters of discipline, the administration of property that might be acquired, the recruiting and ordination of native clergy, and the possibility of extending the missionary work to wider areas in England. When Augustine first arrived in England he was equipped with certain liturgical items which were used to make an impression on Ethelbert, including a silver cross and an image of Christ painted on a board.[54] It is fair to assume that these articles had been brought from Rome at Gregory's behest, since in 601 the pope sent more objects of this order to aid in missionary work.[55] To carry these items on the long trip from Rome suggests that plans had been made for their use. Bede says that Augustine wrote a letter in 597 to Gregory to gain "a solution of some doubts that occurred to him."[56] The implication of this remark is that Gregory and Augustine had already discussed some of the problems in question at an earlier date, before Augustine left Rome. At one point in his responses to Augustine's questions Gregory says that he thought he had already answered Augustine, but that he supposed Augustine desired to be confirmed in the papal opinion.[57] The referral of missionary problems to Rome in itself suggests that Gregory had invited, if not ordered, such a procedure before the missionaries left Rome for England.

None of these pieces of evidence permits any certainty, but they lead one to the conclusion that Gregory had defined a regular program of action for his mission before it left Rome and that this program was followed. The appeal made directly to Ethelbert for permission to preach, the immediate organization of a monastic community at Canterbury, the careful attention given by the missionaries to their own personal conduct, the insistence that no compulsion be used to win converts, even after Ethelbert had been converted, the patient preaching to anyone that would listen, the rapid repair or building of churches— all cardinal features of the early success of the mission in England—may well have been the result of Gregory's instructions to his departing missionaries in 596. Just as he arranged for their safe passage to England, so also it is entirely possible that he was in large part responsible for their initial activities in that pagan land.

However true it may be that Gregory was responsible for the major portion of the program of Augustine's group, nothing can hide the fact that its success depended upon its reception in England and especially upon the attitude of Ethelbert. Gregory must have been aware of this fact, which meant that many matters were left undecided in 596, contingent upon the reception of Augustine in England. Thus there arose more opportunities for Gregory to act decisively in the conversion of the English.

Augustine enjoyed great success during his first years in England.[58] Not only was the king of Kent converted, but so also were large numbers of his subjects. Augustine felt encouraged enough to go to Arles to receive consecration as a bishop. Upon his return to England, he apparently was faced with problems that he could not dispose of himself nor could he rely upon his friend Ethelbert for their solution. Once again Gregory was called upon to contribute to the mission. In 597 two members of Augustine's mission presented themselves to the pope with a series of requests dealing with the future conduct of the mission.

Alexandria, says of Augustine: Qui data a me licentia a Germaniarum episcopis factus. . . . See also Bede, *Hist. eccl.* I, 27, p. 48.
[54] Bede, *Hist. eccl.* I, 25, pp. 45-46.
[55] *Ibid.*, I, 29, p. 63.
[56] *Ibid.*, I, 27, p. 48: simul et de eis, quae necessariae uidebantur, quaestionibus eius consulta flagitans.

[57] Gregory, *Reg.* XI, 56a; MGH, *Ep.* II, 338: Hoc non ambigo fraternitatem tuam esse requisitam, cui iam et responsum reddidisse te arbitror. Sed hoc quod ipse dicere et sentire potuisti, credo, quia mea apud te volueris responsione firmari.
[58] Bede, *Hist. eccl.* I, 25-27, pp. 44-48, describes the success of the mission.

Gregory's responses to this appeal were of fundamental importance in shaping the future development of Christianity in England.

One thing that Augustine needed was more missionary personnel.[59] His original party of forty did not suffice for the proper care of the increasing flock of converts and for the new churches that were being built. Gregory answered this request by sending a new group of missionaries from Rome in 601, including Mellitus, Justus, Paulinus, and Rufinianus;[60] the first three were to perform notable services in furthering the progress of Christianity in England. These reinforcements were given the usual papal letters of commendation to insure their passage to England.[61] It is difficult to imagine where else Augustine could have acquired such valuable aid than from Rome; again the pope had performed a vital missionary service.

Augustine also needed a variety of religious items to dedicate his new churches properly, to institute suitable religious service, and to educate those whom he had converted. When Gregory sent the new mission to England in 601, he also sent "by them whatever was necessary for the worship and services of the church, namely, sacred vessels and cloths for the altars, ornaments for the churches, and vestments for the priests and clerks, as well as relics of the holy apostles and martyrs and many books."[62]

The English mission was also uncertain as to how to proceed with the organization of the new church. Augustine transmitted several distinct problems to Rome with his legates in 597 and requested that Gregory order a procedure to be followed.[63] He was troubled about the kind of life the missionary party should follow, a problem apparently complicated by his own elevation to the episcopate, by the need to put his monks in charge of scattered churches, and by the entrance of certain recent converts into clerical life. Augustine asked for specific information about the disposition of church income, an issue that was perhaps new to a recently consecrated bishop and a recently converted king. He reminded the pope that he had no fixed see. New bishops might soon be needed; the matter of canonical ordinations was especially difficult, since Augustine was the only bishop in Kent. Augustine was also in doubt about his position relative to the Frankish and Celtic episcopacy.

Gregory resolved most of these problems on organizational matters in two letters which he sent to England in 601. The first, written on June 22,[64] prescribed a definite plan for the ecclesiastical organization of all England. Augustine was elevated to metropolitan rank, awarded the pallium, and assigned a see to be located at London. He was ordered to create twelve new bishops in his province as the opportunity presented itself. He was also directed to send a bishop to York as soon as possible so that another province with twelve suffragans could be erected there. Both new archbishops and their successors were to receive the pallium from Rome. The matter of supremacy was disposed of by authorizing Augustine to enjoy that position as long as he lived. Thereafter, whichever of the two archbishops was consecrated first was to be supreme.

In the second letter, written in July, 601,[65] Gregory made further provisions concerning the ecclesiastical organization of England and Augustine's position in it. The pope ordered that the English missionaries continue to follow a communal

---

[59] Gregory, *Reg.* XI, 41; MGH, Ep. II, 315; Bede, *Hist. eccl.* I, 29, p. 63.
[60] Bede, *Hist. eccl.* I, 29, p. 63.
[61] Gregory, *Reg.* XI, 34, 38, 40, 41, 42, 47, 48, 50, 51; MGH, Ep. II, 303, 311, 314-316, 319-321, 322, 324.
[62] Bede, *Hist. eccl.* I, 29, p. 63: et per eos generaliter uniuersa, quae ad cultum erant ac ministerium ecclesiae necessaria, uasa uidelicet sacra, et uestimenta altarium, ornamenta quoque ecclesiarum, et sacer-

dotalia uel clericilia indumenta, sanctorum etiam apostolorum ac martyrum reliquias, nec non et codices plurimos.
[63] Gregory, *Reg.* XI, 56a; MGH. Ep. II, 332-343, contains Gregory's answers and also gives the exact questions asked by Augustine.
[64] Gregory, *Reg.* XI, 39; MGH, Ep. II, 312-313.
[65] Gregory, *Reg.* XI, 56a; MGH, Ep. II, 332-343.

life. He also made special provisions for the maintenance and discipline of married members of the minor orders of the clergy, a body undoubtedly consisting of native converts who were now serving the new church. He instructed Augustine to make the traditional disposition of church income, that is, an equal division among the bishop and his household, the clergy, charitable activities, and the repair of churches. Augustine was given permission to consecrate new bishops without other bishops being present, as was required by canon law. He was also ordered to assume authority over all bishops in Britain. However, Gregory pointed out that the English archbishop had no rights over the Gallic bishops. These orders and directions permitted Augustine to begin the organization of his new converts. In 604 Justus was made bishop of Rochester and Mellitus bishop of London, the latter see being in the kingdom of the East Saxons and not suited for Augustine's metropolitan see.[66] However, Augustine failed to make any progress in establishing his authority over the bishops in the Celtic parts of the British Isles,[67] thereby falling short of Gregory's intentions. Nonetheless, the papal initiative was largely responsible for the first definite steps in organizing the church in England.

While disposing of these problems Gregory also sent letters to both Ethelbert and Bertha of Kent.[68] There is no definite evidence that any difficulty had arisen between the rulers and Augustine. As a matter of fact, Gregory did Bertha the high honor of comparing her to Helen, the mother of Constantine, for the aid she had given his mission. Bede says that Ethelbert was always helpful in advancing the cause of the mission.[69] However, the tone of both letters hints that Augustine felt that the rulers could do more and had asked the pope to attempt to induce them to greater activity. The letter to Bertha stressed especially her responsibiliy to spur her husband to greater efforts for the faith. Gregory gently rebuked her for not having converted her husband sooner. He especially pleaded with her to aid Augustine and his workers. In his letter to Ethelbert the pope charged the king with more specific duties. After duly praising his conversion, Gregory recommended a definite program of action for the king to pursue in the future: "Therefore, glorious son, take care with a sollicitous mind of the grace you have divinely received. Hasten to extend the Christian faith among the people subjected to you. Multiply the zeal of your righteousness for their conversion. Suppress the worship of idols. Overthrow the temples. Edify the manners of your subjects by great cleanness of life by exhorting, terrifying, soothing, correcting, and illustrating by the example of good works, so that you will find your rewarder in heaven whose name and reputation you have spread on earth."[70] After inciting Ethelbert to emulate the example of Constantine, Gregory asked him to cooperate completely with Augustine and to follow the archbishop's orders in all things. Gregory thus charged the king with a major role in extirpating paganism and inducing his newly converted subjects to live a Christian life. Such aid would certainly have been of major importance to the still relatively small number of missionaries in Kent. Moreover, the whole letter takes on deeper significance when one notes that Ethelbert was addressed as "king of the Angles," that is, the ruler of all the inhabitants of England, and when one remembers that at the same moment Gregory had provided Augustine with a plan for organizing all England into an

---

[66] Bede, *Hist. eccl.* II, 3, p. 85.
[67] *Ibid.*, II, 2, pp. 81-85, for Augustine's dealings with the Celtic clergy.
[68] Gregory, *Reg.* XI, 35, 37; MGH, Ep. II, 304-305, 308-310.
[69] Bede, *Hist. eccl.* I, 25-26, pp. 44-47.
[70] Gregory, *Reg.* XI, 37; MGH, Ep. II, 308-309; Et, ideo, gloriose fili, eam quam accepisti divinitus gratiam sollicita mente custodi, christianam fidem in populis tibi subditis extendere festina, zelum rectitudinis tuae in eorum conversione multiplica, idolorum cultus insequere, fanorum aedificia everte, subditorum mores in magna vitae munditia exhortando, terrendo, blandiendo, corrigendo et boni operis exampla monstrando aedifica, ut illum retributorem invenias in caelo, cuius nomen atque cognitionem dilataveris in terra.

episcopal structure. Gregory was mustering the resources to spread missionary work beyond Kent, and was relying heavily upon Ethelbert to assist in that operation. Perhaps Augustine had not yet been able to persuade the king to throw his full efforts into the task of completing the conversion of the whole population of England.

One final situation had developed during the early stages of the English mission with which Augustine and his fellow workers could not cope and which required papal guidance. When Laurentius and Peter came to Rome in 597, they brought with them an appeal to Gregory for instruction on a series of matters concerning the discipline of new converts. The missionaries had discovered that their knowledge of ecclesiastical regulations did not fit the cases that they had to deal with among their new converts. Gregory obliged them by supplying rather copious instructions in two letters sent to England in 601.[71] Throughout these letters he modified strict canonical regulations in order to fit the situation among those recently made Christians.

On problems of discipline the pope insisted on conformity to accepted norms as a general principle, but advised that too great severity be avoided. For those who stole from churches, he advised punishment tempered by charity. He ordered rather strict adherence to canonical regulations on marriages, although he permitted those who had contracted prohibited unions prior to their conversion to continue in these marriages: "For in this time the holy church corrects some things through fervor, tolerates other things through meekness, connives at still others through discretion. She thus carries on and connives so that she may often overcome the evil which works against her."[72] In matters of marriage Gregory stood on a single principle—only those that knowingly committed error should be punished. Otherwise, the task of the missionaries was to act charitably while trying to enlighten. Gregory also tried to lay down for the missionaries certain acceptable practices relative to sexual relations and childbirth, especially as these matters had a bearing on attendance at church services and reception of the sacraments. He was especially eager to caution his missionaries against too great reliance on Old Testament rules as final guides in these matters, perhaps feeling that their monastic way of life would make them too hard on the pagans.

Gregory was especially sollicitous to encourage the development of a ritual that would satisfy those who had recently left paganism. His emphasis on this matter suggests that he felt that an adequate ritual was absolutely necessary to insure the allegiance of the new converts to Christianity. He advised Augustine to use whatever of the Roman and Gallic rites that he found most suitable. Even more significant was the papal injunction to the missionaries not to attempt to cut away all remnants of pagan ritual immediately but rather to permit certain ancient practices under a Christian guise. Temples ought not be destroyed; they should be converted into churches by purifying them with holy water, constructing altars, and depositing relics. Gregory virtually sanctioned the sacrifice of animals in honor of the Christian God, thus permitting the new converts to continue one of their most ancient practices. He encouraged the missionaries to permit the performance of various other pagan rituals in honor of the saints, thus sanctioning a degree of polytheism for worshippers who had long been accustomed to dealing with a multitude of deities.

How thoroughly the English missionaries followed papal advice in matters of discipline and ritual is nearly impossible to determine. Perhaps it is safe to suggest that Gregory's instructions were followed since the missionaries had

---

[71] The following is based on Gregory, *Reg.* XI, 56, 56a; MGH, Ep. II, 331-343.
[72] Gregory, *Reg.* XI, 56a; MGH, Ep. II, 336: In hoc enim tempore sancta ecclesia quaedam per fervorem corrigit, quaedam per mansuetudinem tolerat, quaedam per considerationem dissimulat atque ita portat et dissimulat, ut saepe malum quod adversatur portando et dissimulando compescat.

sought his guidance. If such were the case, one must again credit Gregory with a major role in carrying through the mission to England. Once the missionaries had harvested the fruits of the first enthusiasm for Christianity, they faced the more difficult and perhaps more important task of imposing on the converts a Christian standard of morals and mode of worship. The papacy was ready with common-sense advice on specific problems. More significantly Rome counseled a general strategy in dealing with disciplinary problems—a program of moderation, patient instruction, tolerance, and progress by easy stages.

Less than three years after Gregory sent new missionaries and a whole set of new plans for further progress to the English mission, he died. A brief review of his efforts will show that he contributed decisively to missionary success in England at two crucial stages—at its beginning and at the moment when many conversions had offered a real hope for a magnificent victory over paganism, but when organization and discipline were necessary to seal the victory. Those contributions would certainly permit one to say that the papal role in missionary work had been great. Still it would be amiss to overlook one more role that Gregory played in the greatest missionary effort of his era. His persuasions and exhortations gave urgency and importance to missionary work. His letters are filled with references to what must have been a powerful idea in his age, namely, that any assistance to missionary activity was worthy of special notice in the sight of God. This assurance, vouched for by the pope's own word, was extended to the monks who set out for England but faltered in Provence. It was promised to Frankish bishops and Frankish kings for whatever they might do for missionaries. It was proffered to English royalty for their assistance. No one could doubt that he was helping in a good work of major proportions after he had received such papal assurances. Gregory's exaltation of missionary work did not stop at promises of eternal reward. He never forgot the earthly ambitions of men. He assured kings that their earthly fame would grow as they assisted in spreading the faith. He permitted them to think that they were performing a service to God's cause as great as that of Constantine or of the fabled Helen. On other occasions he highlighted the sanctity of missionary work by stern reminders that failure might have tragic results. For instance, in a somewhat inexplicable letter to Augustine in 601,[73] he cautioned his emissary against too great pride and contentiousness, lest these sins undo his work as a missionary. He chided Queen Bertha and his own missionary party with the ignominy of failing a great work once undertaken. In effect, Gregory manufactured a zeal for missionary work in Western European circles that had not yet developed that zeal to any great degree—the established episcopate, Benedictine monastic circles, royal houses. This psychological factor, which perhaps no one except the pope could have created at this particular moment, was certainly a key element in the progress of the Christian frontier in Gregory's day and in years that followed his pontificate.

II.

The passing of Gregory marked a decline in papal missionary activity. The next century of missionary history shows nothing comparable to his vigorous, decisive actions in beginning the conversion of England and in ending pagan remains in the already Christianized world. One is tempted to think that the retreat of the papacy from its position of missionary leadership was due primarily to the fact that for a long time the papal office lacked a personality as great as Gregory. Certainly there was no lack of opportunity for a continuation or repetition of Gregory's kind of leadership. Only Kent and Essex in England had been touched by Rome's missionaries in 604. The continental Christian world was surrounded by Germanic paganism. Slavic hordes were in the process of

[73] Gregory, *Reg.* XI, 36; MGH, Ep. II, 305-308.

occupying the Balkan area. However, other factors undoubtedly explained papal inactivity in the missionary history of the seventh century. The troubled relationship between papacy and Byzantine Empire and between papacy and Lombards consumed the major share of papal energy. The almost negligible role that the papacy was able to take in the affairs of the Frankish national church shut the See of Rome off from any real chance to consider missionary schemes in the Germanic world. Perhaps another Gregory would have circumvented these difficulties. But the seventh century produced no pope capable of matching his efforts, and so the papal missionary record was not impressive.

Almost all papal missionary activity in the seventh century was limited to England. Even there papal policy was dilatory and indecisive, confined largely to approving gains made by other agencies and to offering encouragement to those involved in missionary work. On only one occasion did the papacy inaugurate a new mission after the fashion of Gregory. In 634 Honorius I (625-638) sent Birinus to England, the latter "having promised in his presence that he would sow the seed of the holy faith in the inner regions beyond English parts, where no teacher had gone before."[1] Birinus was consecrated by Asterius, archbishop of Milan, upon papal orders. He decided to labor among the pagan West Saxons. He succeeded well enough to become bishop of Dorchester. However, Rome had nothing further to do with its agent. Christianity progressed among the West Saxons under the auspices of King Cenwalh, who had refused to accept Christianity from Birinus but had later been converted while a refugee in East Anglia; the king probably became a Christian for political reasons. Irish and Gallic influences were much greater among the West Saxons than was Roman influence during this critical period. Other than this one case the progress of Christianity in seventh-century England resulted from the initiative of kings, and especially the Northumbrian house, of Irish monks, and of Gallic clergymen.[2] Rome played only a minor role in this development.

Perhaps the failure of the papacy to continue to exercise leadership in the conversion of England resulted from the policy laid down by Gregory. He had envisioned a spread of Christianity from Kent, as was evident both in his elaborate scheme of episcopal organization of 601 and in his charge to Ethelbert, "king of the Angles." Gregory probably hoped to enlist the missionary services of the Irish by putting Ireland under the authority of the archbishop of Canterbury.[3] The papal plan was based on the political hegemony enjoyed by Kent at the beginning of the seventh century. That situation was not permanent. As a result the Kentish religious establishment was overshadowed along with Kentish political power. The seventh-century papacy made little attempt to adapt its policy to the changing environment in England.

The missionary activities of Gregory's successors were very largely tied to the Kentish church. Several seventh-century popes made some attempt to encourage and promote the Kentish establishment. They usually took care to send the pallium to the bishop chosen for the see at Canterbury, thus insuring each archbishop the proper dignity to spread the faith and investing each with the power to create suffragans.[4] Both Boniface IV (608-615) and Honorius I sent letters of encouragement to archbishops Mellitus, Justus, and Honorius.[5] Boniface IV's letter to Justus was filled with praise for his work and with assurances

[1] Bede, *Hist. eccl.* III, 7, p. 139: promittens quidem se illo praesente in intimis ultra Anglorum partibus, quo nullus doctor praecessisset, sanctae fidei semina esse sparsurum. The following is based on *ibid.*, pp. 139-141.
[2] The essential source is Bede, *Hist. eccl.* II-IV, *passim*, pp. 73-280. See also R. H. Hodgkin, *A History of the Anglo-Saxons* I (Oxford, 1935), pp. 268-302; William Hunt,

The English Church from its Foundation to the Norman Conquest (597-1066) (London, 1912), pp. 76-116; Bréhier and Aigrain, *Grégoire le Grand, les états barbares et la conquête arabe (590-757)*, pp. 289-316.
[3] Gregory, *Reg.* XI, 37, 39, 56a; MGH, Ep. II, 308-310, 312-313, 331-343.
[4] Bede, *Hist. eccl.* II, 8, 17, 18, pp. 95-97, 118, 120-122.
[5] *Ibid.*, II, 7, 8, 13, pp. 93-97, 120-122.

that his reward would be great in heaven. Honorius I, in a letter of almost the same kind to Honorius of Canterbury, especially encouraged the archbishop to be zealous in following the guidance of Gregory the Great and to be eager in strengthening the faith of new converts. In 610 Boniface IV received Mellitus, then bishop of London, who had come to Rome from England "about the necessary affairs of the English church." Mellitus was permitted to take a place at an episcopal synod held in Rome during his stay. Upon his return to England he carried with him the decrees of that synod so that they might be observed there. The missionary clergy was thus still relying on Rome for the settlement of difficult problems. Boniface also sent back with Mellitus letters to the archbishop Laurentius and his clergy, to King Ethelbert, and to the English people; very likely these letters contained orders to abide by papal decretals as well as answers to the problems which provoked Mellitus' journey.[6] Bede credits both Honorius I and John IV (640-642) with attempts to end the difficulties dividing the Roman clergy in England and the Celtic church.[7] Such a move certainly had missionary implications. Apparently the papacy had not abandoned Gregory's policy of bringing the Celtic church under the sway of Rome through the Roman-inspired organization in Kent. However, this meager collection of cases where the papacy in any way played a part in ecclesiastical life in Kent over a period of nearly fifty years, stretching from the death of Augustine (609?) to the death of Honorius of Canterbury (653), is not in the least impressive. These were years when the Kentish group needed assistance. For instance, at the death of Ethelbert in 616 a pagan reaction nearly overthrew the whole establishment.[8] It would seem that the papacy felt incapable of doing anything more for Gregory's establishment.

Occasionally, but not consistently, the papacy tried to encourage the spread of the faith beyond Kent, as the first mission had envisioned. The struggle to spread Christianity to the East Saxons and the East Angles, both of which areas were closely associated with the Kentish church, did not concern Rome.[9] On the other hand, Pope Honorius I acted vigorously to bring about the conversion of Northumbria. The opening of the Northumbrian mission was not the result of papal initiative. Edwin of Northumbria's desire to strengthen his alliance with the royal house of Kent presented an opportunity to introduce Christianity into Northumbria. Edwin was allowed to marry Ethelberga of Kent only on the condition that priests be allowed to accompany her and that her husband would consider accepting Christianity. Paulinus, one of the monks Gregory had sent into England in 601, was assigned to accompany Ethelberga. He was consecrated bishop by Justus in 625, a step obviously fitting him for a greater role that that of chaplain for the queen.[10] The Kentish church had finally found an opportunity to carry out Gregory's plans to extend the faith outside its original seat in southeastern England.

The papacy entered the scene only after the Kentish clergy had established a foothold in Northumbria. Boniface V (619-625) wrote two powerful letters to Northumbria to appeal to Edwin and Ethelberga.[11] It has usually been presumed that the pope wrote these letters to promote the cause of Paulinus. Boniface did not indicate clearly that he was aware of the full situation in Northumbria. He knew of Ethelberga's marriage, of Edwin's paganism, and of his refusal to "yield obedience or give ear to the voice of the preachers." Since he knew of the

[6] *Ibid.*, II, 4, p. 88.
[7] *Ibid.*, II, 19, pp. 122-124.
[8] *Ibid.*, II, 5-6, pp. 89-93.
[9] *Ibid.*, III, 18-20, 22-23, pp. 162-169, 171-177.
[10] *Ibid.*, II, 9, pp. 97-100, for the circumstances marking the opening of the Northumbrian mission. It is not unlikely that Edwin was contemplating accepting Christianity prior to his marriage; at least Bede suggests that he had contacted Christianity during his exile in East Anglia prior to his victory over Ethelfrith in 616 and his accession to power in Northumbria; see *ibid.*, II, 12, pp. 106-112.
[11] For the texts of these two letters see *ibid.*, II, 10-11, pp. 100-106.

marriage, he presumably knew of Paulinus' presence in Northumbria. The letters, however, make no mention of Paulinus. Neither is there a letter of commendation designed to give papal blessings to a missionary whose task it is to present the case for the new religion. Instead Boniface attempted by direct argument to persuade the royal pair to support the conversion of England. In the letter to Edwin Boniface stated that he "thought fit to extend our priestly care to make known to you the fullness of the Christian faith . . . ,"[12] suggesting that the papacy felt that it had the duty and the power to affect conversions on its own. Boniface then stated the case for Christianity. He began with a discussion of the power of the Christian God, creator of all things and ruler of all things, including earthly kingdoms. He especially tried to demonstrate that the power of the kings of Kent was a result of their conversion. The pagan deities and rituals to which Edwin was a victim were excoriated by Boniface. Finally, he presented a strong case for the eternal rewards that could come to Edwin only if he accepted Christianity. The pope sent the pagan king a shirt with a golden ornament and a garment of Ancyra as a demonstration of his friendship. This letter, so strongly flavored with religious arguments in favor of Christianity and opposed to paganism, represents an addition to papal missionary weapons. It represents the first instance of direct papal appeal to a pagan king asking him to accept a superior religion and presenting him with a reasoned argument for such a move. The letter to Ethelberga was more conventional, being primarily an appeal to her, a Christian, to assume the responsibility for converting her husband. Boniface told her to strive for this noble goal by her prayers, by insinuating divine precepts into the king's mind, and by informing him of the rewards that he might gain by becoming a Christian. The pope asked the queen to inform him of her progress so that he might return thanks to God and St. Peter.

Whether this papal action had an effect on the conversion of Edwin is unknown. Bede's account of his acceptance of Christianity and its subsequent spread in Northumbria makes no mention of papal influence in the process. Rather he stresses the skill of Paulinus and the zealous assistance of Edwin as the determining factors.[13] Not until 634 did the papacy again act with reference to Northumbria. Perhaps there was no need for papal action prior to this. Apparently Paulinus followed the missionary pattern established in Kent, preaching, baptizing, ordaining priests, building churches, and destroying pagan temples. Whatever problems arose might well have been disposed of on the basis of precedents established in Kent, with which Paulinus had been closely associated, or in consultation with the present clergy of Kent, well versed in missionary problems. The papacy acted in Northumbria only when the mission had reached the point where organization became a necessity in order to make permanent the first successes. In 634 Honorius I elevated Paulinus to the rank of archbishop and sent him a pallium. He also ordered that York be Paulinus' archiepiscopal see and that it be co-equal with that of Canterbury.[14] This was in effect an order for Paulinus to begin creating bishoprics in Northumbria and to proceed toward the completion of the plans of Gregory I. Honorius also wrote once again to Edwin to encourage him to continue his support of the true religion in his realm and to incite him to a more perfect practice of Christianity, especially by reading the works of Gregory the Great.[15]

Unfortunately, Honorius wrote these letters without knowing that Edwin had fallen at the battle of Hatfield or that Paulinus had fled to Kent and had apparently abandoned hope of returning to Northumbria, since he accepted the

---

[12] *Ibid.*, II, 10, p. 101: ad adnuntiandam uobis plenitudinem fidei Christianae sacerdotalem curauimus sollicitudinem prorogare. . . .

[13] *Ibid.*, II, 12-16, pp. 106-118.

[14] *Ibid.*, II, 18, pp. 120-122; this letter is to Honorius of Canterbury in which Pope Honorius reveals his actions in the north.

[15] *Ibid.*, II, 17, pp. 118-120.

bishopric of Rochester.[16] The one serious attempt made to convert more of England from a base in Kent had failed, certainly leaving the papacy with little glory as a missionary agency. Northumbria reverted to paganism for some years. It was then reconverted permanently by Irish clergy whose source of guidance was not Rome. Nor did the Irish confine themselves to Northumbria. With the backing of Oswald and Oswy Irish influences spread into several other kingdoms, whose conversion and organization progressed rapidly around the middle of the seventh century.[17] The papacy had no part in all of these affairs; perhaps one might conclude that it had no interest. Even Rome's great victory at Whitby was won without any direct action by the papacy. The papal cause was borne by personalities like Wilfrid, a native Northumbrian and a product of the Irish monastery at Lindesfarne, Eanfled, the wife of Oswy, Agilbert, the Frankish bishop who had served as bishop of Dorchester in West Saxony, all of whom seem to have received their original inspiration to serve Rome and its ecclesiastical ways by some connection with Kent.[18] Only in Kent did the papacy retain a relatively active influence, and even there its activity was limited.

However, the rather uninspiring record of papal participation in the progress of Christianity in seventh-century England must not hide at least one papal act of decisive importance in the conversion of the English—the sending of Theodore of Tarsus to England as archbishop in 667. All the evidence suggests that this act was decided upon by Rome on its own initiative and that the decision was made with a clear purpose in mind, namely, the solution to several grave problems bearing on the organization and discipline of the new English church. The drift of affairs[19] in England prior to 667 was disturbing in spite of the steady addition of new converts, the occasional creation of new bishoprics, the foundation of new monasteries, and the dissolution of the struggle between the Roman and Celtic forces. There was a trend toward the establishment of national churches headed by independent bishops. Most episcopal sees were too large. There was an obvious lack of coordinated action among the bishops. Discipline was not rigorously maintained. The last of the Romans who had been connected with Gregory's first mission were gone; for instance, in 653 Honorius was succeeded as archbishop of Canterbury by a West Saxon, Frithonas, who assumed the name Deusdedit.[20] To make the whole situation worse a plague decimated the clergy of England about the time of the council of Whitby.[21]

The English were certainly aware of their own difficulties. Oswy of Northumbria and Egbert of Kent apparently decided to take some decisive action to correct the situation. Their plan consisted in installing someone in the vacant see at Canterbury who would restore order in the whole of England. The man of their choice was Wighard. Feeling that he would need special authority, they sent him to Rome, an unprecedented act in the history of the English church. Wighard bore with him letters which apparently revealed the intentions of the kings.[22] However, before Pope Vitalian (657-672) could do the bidding of the kings, Wighard died. Thereupon the pope took matters in his own hands. He sent a letter to Oswy speaking as follows on the matter of the archbishop: "We have not been able now to find, considering the length of the journey, a man docile and qualified in all respects to be a bishop according to the tenor of your letter. But as soon as such a suitable person will be found, we will send him with

---

[16] *Ibid.*, II, 20, pp. 124-126.
[17] Bede supplies the essential account of this missionary effort in *ibid.*, III, *passim*, pp. 127-200.
[18] See Caspar, *Geschichte des Papsttums* II, pp. 676-689, for a description of the formation of a pro-Roman party in Northumbria and for the antecedents of the members of that party.
[19] Hunt, *The English Church* (597-1066),

pp. 128-131.
[20] Bede, *Hist. eccl.* III, 20, p. 169.
[21] *Ibid.*, III, 27, 30; IV, 1, pp. 191-192, 199-200, 201-202, for some of the drastic effects of this pestilence.
[22] Bede's account of the sending of Wighard to Rome seems to indicate clearly that the two kings had a plan in mind; see *ibid.*, III, 29; IV, 1, pp. 196-199, 201.

63

instructions to your country, so that he may by word of mouth and through divine oracles and with divine consent root out all the enemy's tares throughout your island."[23] In these words the papacy demonstrated a revival of Gregory's bold policy toward England. In the hands of a man of its own choice, instructed in his task by the pope himself, lay the solution to England's grave religious problems. Vitalian was confident that papal influence was great enough in England to assure the acceptance of an archbishop of his choice and that the pro-Roman sentiment was well enough entrenched to secure conformity to any regulations imposed from Rome. Vitalian picked his man carefully, settling finally on the learned and virtuous monk Theodore. Apparently Theodore was told what he must do, since Vitalian sent Hadrian with him to watch that he did not veer from orthodoxy and since a few years later a certain abbot named John was sent to England by order of Pope Agatho (678-681) to inquire concerning the condition of the faith in England and to report his findings to Rome.[24]

The papal action was decisive in the completion of the Christianization of England. To inject into the English scene at this crucial moment a figure who had no prior involvement in either the political struggles or the ecclesiastical structure of England and who had a clear concept of what was needed to be done was a highly important step toward completing the organization and perfecting the discipline of the newly converted nations. Theodore's often described program need not be reviewed here in detail.[25] Let it only be said that his policy of creating new bishoprics of manageable size, of subordinating them to a metropolitan, of holding regular synods, of instituting uniform regulations for clergymen and laymen, of promoting a thorough educational program in order to create an adequate native clergy, of conducting regular episcopal visitations, of spreading a uniform liturgy all savor of Roman influence and inspiration. By the time of Theodore's death in 690 missionary efforts in England were no longer necessary. Gregory's dream of bringing the pagan Anglo-Saxons to sing alleluias in praise of Christ was a fact, due in no little part to the efforts of him and his successors.

The record of papal participation in the Christianization of England during the seventh century would not be complete without some reference to an indirect, intangible, yet powerful contribution made by the papacy. It is next to impossible to fashion an adequate description of what Englishmen of all orders seemed to draw from their own contacts with Rome and the see of St. Peter by way of inspiration and zeal for the Christian way of life. Yet no one could tell the story of the progress of Christianity in England without introducing this factor. The attraction that Rome had for Englishmen shaped the destiny of many of them, causing kings to lay down their crowns to spend their last days at the see of St. Peter, compelling clergymen to take every opportunity to make a pilgrimage to the Englishmen's holy of holies, encouraging numerous men of lesser position to leave behind family and property to die in the holy city.[26] Such an attraction must surely have played a role in making the English subservient to Rome's orders and suggestions and zealous to emulate the religion sponsored by Rome's bishop. Perhaps Bede's account of the council of Whitby

[23] Ibid., III, 29, pp. 197-198: Hominem denique docibilem et in omnibus ornatum antistitem, secundum uestrorum scriptorum tenorem, minime ualuimus nunc repperire pro longinquitate itineris. Profecto enim dum huiusmodi apta reppertaque persona fuerit, cum instructam ad uestram dirigemus patriam, ut ipse et uiua uoce, et per diuina oracula omnem inimici zizaniam ex omni uestra insula cum diuino nutu eradicet.

[24] For the careful choice of Theodore with its implication of equally careful instruc-

tion, see ibid., IV, 1, pp. 202-204; for the papal concern over checking Theodore, see ibid., IV, 1, 18, pp. 202-203, 240-242.

[25] Hodgkin, A History of the Anglo-Saxons I, pp. 303-366; J. H. Maude, The Foundations of the English Church (London, 1909), pp. 139-191; Hunt, The English Church (597-1066), pp. 132-161.

[26] For a brief discussion of the numerous pilgrimages to Rome by the English and of the larger issue of the influence of St. Peter's on English thinking, see Haller, Das Papsttums I, pp. 371-383.

illustrates how decisive was the papal reputation during this century. He recounts that Wilfrid won the day for Rome by using the argument that St. Peter and his successors were keepers of the keys to heaven to counteract the Celtic argument that their customs were held on the authority of St. Columba. It was this point that won Oswy to the Roman position and forced the Celt, Colman, to concede Rome's supremacy.[27] Here was a force operating in men's minds that stemmed from Rome and played a key role throughout the period of conversion.

At times its operation had a direct influence on the actual conduct of ecclesiastical affairs in England. The case of Wilfrid illustrates this well. It was his five year stay in Gaul and in Rome after he had been educated at Lindesfarne under Irish influence that inspired him to play his important role as founder of monasteries, converter of pagans, bishop and archbishop, and constant protagonist for Roman observances and ideas in England.[28] Even a better case in point is the career of Benedict Biscop.[29] Giving up a promising worldly career in the service of Oswy, this young nobleman decided to follow the religious life. Whereupon, he left England in 653 to see Rome and to worship where the bodies of the holy apostles lay. Returning to England he took up the religious life with great zeal. In about 665 he set out again for Rome as a companion of Alchfrid, the son of Oswy. Although the young prince was recalled, Benedict went on. He spent several valuable months in Rome, whereupon he withdrew to Lerins to become a monk, perhaps at papal instigation. Leaving Lerins he again returned to Rome in time to be commissioned papal guide for Theodore and Hadrian. After a brief pause in England Benedict made his fourth trip to Rome. His main purpose this time was to obtain books. Upon his return he found his way back to Northumbria, prepared for his most important work, the foundation of Wearmouth and Jarrow. For this task Benedict was ready with monastic rules, books, and relics, the fruits of his numerous trips to Rome and the continent. A necessary grant of land was made by the Northumbrian king and the monastery was built with technical help from Gaul. Benedict still did not have and could not secure in England all he needed to complete his monastery. Therefore, he made his fifth trip to Rome, returning with more books, relics, a papal privilege for his monastery, a variety of art objects to decorate his new church, and a Roman monk named John, sent by Pope Agatho to teach the correct Roman liturgical usages. Benedict made still another trip to Rome before the end of his life, again in search of books and materials to adorn his two monasteries. Here was a man shaped largely under the influence of Rome. Benedict Biscop himself sought out this guidance, constantly being attracted to the holy see for whatever he needed to achieve the kind of ecclesiastical career he desired. The contribution made by his monasteries, shaped under Roman influences, to the intellectual history of England needs no discussion when one recalls the career of Bede, a direct product of Wearmouth and Jarrow, or of Alcuin, a product of the episcopal school at York, which was an offshoot of Biscop's establishments. Both Wilfrid and Benedict Biscop, and certainly many more whose careers are not so well known, can thus be called products of papal influence in England. Although the papacy made no special effort to influence these men, still its great reputation in England attracted them and created the opportunity for them to be influenced. They in turn put what they gained in Rome to practice in England. In this indirect way the papacy played an important part in incorporating England into the Christian world and in causing the English church to develop along certain lines.

[27] Bede, *Hist. eccl.* III, 25, pp. 181-189.
[28] Eddius Stephanus, *The Life of Bishop Wilfrid*, text, translation, and notes by Bertram Colgrave (Cambridge, 1927), for Wilfrid's connections with Rome.
[29] The following is based on Bede, *Historia Abbatum*, 1-13 in *Venerabilis Baedae Opera Historica* I, ed. Carolus Plummer (Oxford, 1896), pp. 364-377.

The record traced above demonstrates that the papacy was never completely removed from English missionary affairs in the seventh century and sometimes acted decisively to affect the progress of the conversion and organization of England. In contrast, its participation in seventh-century continental missionary affairs was almost negligible.[30] Perhaps the best explanation of Rome's small part in seventh-century continental missionary history lies in the confusion that characterized that effort, a confusion arising from the numerous agencies trying to convert pagans and from the variety of methods these agencies employed. A brief glance at the continental situation must precede an evaluation of Rome's limited activity.

The Merovingian rulers were active in missionary affairs, seeking to push the cause of Christianity into semi-pagan and pagan principalities as a means of incorporating those principalities into the Frankish sphere of influence. Their means of achieving this end were varied. Frankish conquest usually resulted in the establishment of a pro-Christian ruling dynasty in pagan territories, as might be illustrated by the history of the Thuringians and the Bavarians.[31] These dynasties were expected to Christianize their subjects and usually made an effort to do so. The Frankish bishops, usually tools of the Merovingian kings, and always desirous of enlarging their sees, pushed their influences into pagan areas. For instance, Dagobert made important grants of land around Utrecht to Cunibert of Cologne, on the condition that the bishop convert the pagans in the area.[32] The eastern bishoprics in Francia also exercised powerful influences in southern Frisia, Alemannia, and Thuringia, probably again with royal support.[33] The Merovingian rulers even tried on occasion to send missionaries into these principalities in an attempt to speed up the process of Christianization and thus enhance the prospects of Frankish overlordship. Columban's personal activity as a missionary in Alemannia was certainly encouraged, if not actually ordered, by Theudebert.[34] Amandus began his missionary career in the border area between the Frisians and the Franks under the direct auspices of the Merovingians. Clothair was instrumental in his elevation to the episcopal rank without a see, a step that immediately preceded his missionary activities around Ghent. Dagobert complied with Amandus' desire for a decree that made baptism compulsory in the same area. After a series of other activities Amandus returned to missionary work in this general area, this time as bishop of Maastricht, an office that he must surely have received with the blessing of the Merovingian ruler.[35]

Another force adding to the missionary confusion on the continent in the seventh century was the activity of the Irish *peregrini*. The seventh century witnessed a steady stream of these wanderers coming to the continent. Not all of them turned to missionary work. However, some of them journeyed to the Christian frontier, founded their cells, and in the Irish fashion began to care for the religious life of the population in the vicinity, including the task of

[30] The best account of the expansion of Christianity during this period is Albert Hauck, *Kirchengeschichte Deutschlands* I (3rd and 4th ed., Leipzig, 1904-1920), pp. 320-389. One might add an almost infinite number of studies of the penetration of Christianity into local areas; for a sample of such valuable studies see Dahlmann-Waitz, *Quellenkunde der deutschen Geschichte* (9th ed., Leipzig, 1931), #5190-5209.
[31] Hauck, *Kirchengeschichte* I, 367-371, 385-388; E. de Moreau, "Les missions médiévales" in Baron Descamps, *Histoire générale comparée des missions* (Paris, 1932), pp. 185-186; Sigmund Riezler, *Geschichte Baierns* (2nd ed.), in *Allgemeine Staatengeschichte*, hrsg. Herman Oncken, 1. Abt.: *Geschichte*

der europäischen Staaten XX (Stuttgart and Gotha, 1927), I¹, pp. 169-172.
[32] Boniface, *Ep.* #109; ed. Tangl, pp. 235-236.
[33] Hauck, *Kirchengeschichte* I, 322-328, 332, 338, 385-386; for examples of the operations of such bishops see *Vita Hugberti episcopi Traiectensis*; ed. W. Levison, MGH, SS. rer. Merov. VI, 482-496; *Vitae Landiberti episcopi Traiectensis*; ed. B. Krusch, MGH, SS. rer. Merov. VI, 353-429.
[34] Jonas, *Vitae Columbani abbatis discipulorumque eius Libri Duo* I, 27; ed. Bruno Krusch, MGH, SS. rer. Merov. IV, 101-104.
[35] *Vita Amandi episcopi* I, 13-18; ed. B. Krusch, MGH, SS. rer. Merov. V, 436-443.

converting those who were still pagan. Fridolin, for instance, seems to have followed this line of activity in Alemannia.[36] Kilian came from Ireland to settle eventually in the area around Würzburg, where he found a supporter in the local prince and carried on missionary work until he was murdered, allegedly at the instigation of the prince's wife.[37] There were numerous others like them who worked in Thuringia, Bavaria, and Alemannia in the seventh century without leaving their names behind them.[38] Usually the achievement of these Irishmen was nebulous. While each was alive his own personality, his zeal, his asceticism won many followers in the locality where he labored. But his death usually marked the end of his influence. He provided no permanent establishment to continue what had been begun. Many who accepted Christianity under the guidance of the Irish reverted to paganism after the departure of the missionary; at least Boniface, who later worked over much of the area where the Irish had been most active as missionaries, often found such to be the case. For all its zeal, the Irish missionary venture on the continent tended to add to the general religious confusion.

The Irish monks were joined in missionary work by continental monks, whose efforts were often as futile as those of the Irish. Amandus[39] and Eligius,[40] both of whom carried on missionary work among the southern Frisians, are typical examples of continental monks who were moved by missionary zeal. The Irish monasteries at Luxeuil and St. Gall produced several monks who spent part of their careers in missionary work, especially in the semi-pagan areas of Bavaria and Alemannia; among these were Gall, Ailus, Eustasius, and Agrestius.[41] Bavaria seemed especially attractive to continental monks searching for souls to win; Rupert, Emmeran, and Corbinian[42] all seem to have labored there around 700 and to have found numerous pagans to convert. Although the careers of nearly all of these monastic missionaries are clouded with legend and difficult to reconstruct, it is clear that their efforts were haphazard and disorganized. Some of them acquired the position of wandering bishops, traveling over wide areas with a brief pause at any spot that struck their fancies. Others founded cells in the midst of some island of paganism. Some found a place to work by winning the attention of a local prince. The results of their labors, however conducted, were extremely impermanent and contributed to a great deal of confusion in the religious situation along the Frankish border.

This many faceted missionary effort on the continent created a limited opportunity for papal missionary activity. The major missionary agencies mentioned above were not accustomed to seek the aid of the papacy for any purpose. The Frankish royal house pursued an ecclesiastical policy that relied on Rome for nothing; there was no reason for the Merovingian kings to ask the papacy for assistance in missionary affairs. The Irish monks were not only extremely individualistic but also were at odds with Rome on several matters that touched very close to the missionary scene—principles of church organization,

[36] Baltherus, *Vita Fridolini confessoris Seckingensis;* ed. B. Krusch, MGH, SS. rer. Merov. III, 350-369.

[37] *Passio Kiliani martyris Wirziburgensis;* ed. W. Levison, MGH, SS. rer. Merov. V, 722-728.

[38] Hauck, *Kirchengeschichte* I, 371, ff. Louis Gougaud, *Christianity in Celtic Lands* (London, 1932), pp. 129-184.

[39] *Vita Amandi episcopi I;* ed. Krusch, MGH, SS. rer. Merov. V, 428-449; see also Edouard de Moreau, *Saint Amand, apôtre de la Belgique et du Nord de la France* (Louvain, 1927).

[40] *Vita Eligii episcopi Noviomagensis II;* ed. B. Krusch, MGH, SS. rer. Merov. IV, 634-742.

[41] Jonas, *Vita Columbani* II, 8-9; ed. Krusch, MGH, SS. rer. Merov. IV, 121-124; Wettinis, *Vita Galli,* 6; ed. B. Krusch, MGH, SS. rer. Merov. IV, 260.

[42] *Vita Hrodberti episcopi Salisburgensis;* ed. W. Levison, MGH, SS. rer. Merov. VI, 140-162; Arbeo, *Vita vel passio Haimhrammi episcopi et martyris Ratisbonensis* in *Arbeonis episcopi Frisingensis vitae sanctorum Haimhrammi et Corbiniani;* ed. Bruno Krusch, SS. rer. Germ. in usum schol. (Hanover, 1920), 1-99; Arbeo, *Vita Corbiniani episcopi Baiuvariorum* in *ibid.,* 100-234. See also *De Conversione Bagoariorum et Carantanorum libellus,* 1-3; ed. W. Wattenbach, MGH, SS. XI, 4-7.

ritual, etc. They were not likely to turn to Rome for advice. Perhaps Rome was cool toward aiding them; for example, the famous Columban complained to Pope Sabinian (604-606) that he had written several letters to Gregory I without receiving an answer.[43] Even the continental monastic establishments usually had only few contacts with Rome. The Frankish episcopate of the seventh century, and especially the dioceses along the pagan frontier, were seldom in communication with Rome. Only by a bold policy of sending Roman missionaries into these areas could the papacy have become involved in view of the lack of communications with the agencies already doing the work.

Since those actively engaged in missionary ventures did not rely on Rome's assistance and since the papal policy of the seventh century found bold action impossible, Rome's participation in continental missionary work during the seventh century was incidental and of little importance. Many of the missionary personalities of the era, including Amandus, Corbinian, and Kilian, were in Rome at one time or another.[44] These excursions were probably inspired by a desire to visit the tombs of the apostles rather than by an interest in gaining missionary assistance from the contemporary occupant of the holy see. However, Amandus is reported to have received his inspiration to do missionary work while he was in Rome and to have gained papal blessing for his work.[45] The biography of Kilian says that this Irish wanderer was received in Rome by Pope Conon (686-687), consecrated a bishop at the instigation of the pope, and sent to Thuringia to preach the gospel.[46] This biography is so late and the story told of Kilian is so similar to Boniface's career that one cannot accept it as proof of any such papal action. Amandus apparently did depend upon the papacy for advice in his missionary work. A letter addressed to him by Pope Martin I (649-654) reveals that, while serving as bishop of Maastricht, he wrote to Rome complaining of the poor quality of his clergy and of his inability to wipe out paganism as a result; his situation was so difficult that he desired to abdicate his see. Martin wrote back to dissuade him from any such move. The pope sent Amandus some acts of church councils, a recent papal directive, and relics, all intended to aid in missionary activity.[47] Perhaps the papacy also influenced some of the continental missionaries indirectly. For instance, Columban asked Gregory I for a copy of his Pastoral Rule and other writings.[48] Beyond these few cases, none of decisive importance, the Christian frontier advanced northward and eastward during the seventh century without Rome's assistance.

Perhaps the papacy gave at least a thought to missionary work among the Slavs during the seventh century. John IV (640-642), a native Dalmatian, sent an abbot named Martin into Dalmatia and Istria to purchase captives from the pagans.[49] A much later Greek source suggests that his venture had a missionary purpose. The Croatian prince at the moment appealed to the Emperor Heraclius for Christian teachers. Heraclius referred him to Rome. John obliged by sending a bishop and priest into the area. They baptized many, whereupon the papacy took the new converts under its special protection and sought to impose on them more Christian modes of conduct.[50] This account is extremely suspect, especially with respect to papal authority over the Croats at such an early date.[51]

[43] Columban, Epistolae #3; ed. Wilhelmus Gundlach, MGH, Ep. III, 164-165.
[44] Vita Amandi episcopi I, 6-7; ed. Krusch, MGH, SS. rer. Merov. V, 433-434; Passio Kiliani, 4-5; ed. Levison, MGH, SS. rer. Merov. V, 723-724; Arbeo, Vita Corbiniani, 6-9; ed. Krusch, MGH, SS. rer. Germ. in usum schol., pp. 194-197.
[45] Vita Amandi episcopi I, 7; ed. Krusch, MGH, SS. rer. Merov. V, 434.
[46] Passio Kiliani, 5; ed. Levison, MGH, SS. rer. Merov. V, 724; see Levison's comments, ibid., 714-715.

[47] This letter is included in Vita Amandi episcopi II. auctore Milone; ed. W. Levison, MGH, SS. rer. Merov. V, 452-456.
[48] Columban, Ep. #1; ed. Gundlach, MGH, Ep. III, 156-160.
[49] Liber Pontificalis I, ed. L. Duchesne (Paris, 1886-1892), p. 330.
[50] Constantine Porphyrogenitus, De Administrando imperio liber, 32; PG 113, 288-292.
[51] For some of the difficulties connected with this account, see F. Dvornik, Les Slaves, Byzance et Rome au IXe siècle

However, one might well conclude that John instructed his envoy to try to win converts in an area that was rapidly losing its Christian characteristics. Certainly the venture was not successful; nearly two centuries were to pass before the Slavs of this area were converted.

III.

Before the seventh century ended, the papacy once again found the opportunity to participate in an important way in missionary activity and to end its isolation from the main areas of missionary work. Perhaps a harbinger of the new day was the pause in Frisia made by the Anglo-Saxon bishop Wilfrid on one of his trips to Rome. Detained by inclement weather and by certain political considerations, this persistent champion of Rome passed the winter of 678-679 preaching to the Frisians and converting many of them.[1] Certainly he must have recounted his experiences and revealed his enthusiasms over the prospects for a Frisian mission while in Rome. The new missionary movement was brought more forcibly to Rome's attention when in 692 another Anglo-Saxon, Willibrord, appeared in Rome "in order that he might go about his desired work of converting pagans with the licence and blessing of Sergius."[2] Both Wilfrid and Willibrord were pioneers in a new phase in the history of western European missions, the heralds of a stream of Anglo-Saxon monks and priests who came to the continent during the period from about 690 to 770 and who devoted their major efforts to missionary work on the northern and eastern fringes of the Frankish kingdom. Their arrival resulted in the confluence of several missionary forces and in a period of feverish missionary activity. One of these forces was the papacy, which acted promptly and with vigor in furthering the missionary activities of the Anglo-Saxons and, consequently, exerted an important influence on the missionary history of the period.

Conditions had changed considerably in Western Europe since the accession of Gregory the Great. As a result the papal role in this new missionary wave was bound to be different than it had been in his era. For one thing, the Anglo-Saxon monks were already inspired with a zeal for missionary work; the papacy no longer had to create such a zeal. The Anglo-Saxon zeal was perhaps derived chiefly from Irish influences. For instance, Egbert, who was responsible for arousing interest in a Frisian mission among some of his disciples, left England for Ireland in order to gain greater grace; it was while in Ireland that he conceived his desire to migrate to the continent as a "soldier of Christ."[3] Wigbert, Willibrord, and the brothers Ewald, all early missionaries in Frisia, had spent several years in Ireland prior to the beginning of their missionary work.[4] However, the English monasteries, beginning to reach their full vigor by the end of the seventh century, likewise inspired an urgent missionary zeal in the hearts of their members. Proof of the missionary urge generated by English monasticism might be found in the early career of Boniface,[5] who left England for Frisia and Rome with a "pious purpose"[6] firmly in mind, or of Willehad, the Northumbrian monk who felt the urge to do missionary work so strongly that he appealed to his king for permission to work in Frisia.[7] Whatever the source of the zeal, England produced a troop of missionaries who for three-

(Paris, 1926), pp. 71-74.

[1] Eddius Stephanus, *The Life of Bishop Wilfrid*, 26; ed. Colgrave, p. 52.

[2] Bede, *Hist, eccl.* V, 11, p. 301: ut cum eius licentia et benedictione desideratum euangelizandi gentibus opus iniret.

[3] *Ibid.*, V, 9, pp. 296-298.

[4] *Ibid.*, V, 9-10, pp. 298-301; Alcuin, *Vita Willibrordi*, 4; ed. W. Levison, MGH, SS. rer. Merov. VII, 118-119.

[5] Willibald, *Vita Bonifatii*, 1-2, in *Vitae sancti Bonifatii archiepiscopi Moguntini*; ed. Wilhelmus Levison, MGH, SS. rer. Germ. in usum schol. (Hanover and Leipzig, 1905), 4-11, for the monastic influence on Boniface.

[6] At least this was the designation given by Pope Gregory II to Boniface's plans on his first trip to Rome; Boniface, *Ep.* #12; ed. Tangl, p. 17.

[7] *Vita sancti Willehadi*, 1; ed. Albertus Poncelet, *Acta Sanctorum*, Nov. III, 842-843.

quarters of a century worked to advance the Christian frontier without any great urging of the kind that Gregory the Great had to give to his missionaries before they were more than a few hundred miles from Rome.

Neither was it any longer necessary for the papacy to select the areas suitable for missionary work. The English monks had settled this question in their own minds. Repeatedly one finds references to a sympathetic feeling which the English harbored for their kinfolk on the continent. When Egbert received the urge to become a missionary, his thoughts were directed immediately to Germany, where there lived many nations—the Frisians, the Rugii, the Danes, the Huns, the Old Saxons, and the Bructeri—from whom the English had had their origins and who had not yet heard the word of God.[8] Boniface, addressing himself to the English nation in a plea for help in converting the Saxons, saw fit to remind the English that they and the Saxons "were of one blood and one bone."[9] Willehad was prompted to become a missionary chiefly because he had heard of the deplorable condition of the pagan Saxons and Frisians.[10] The English thus came to the continent with a definite area in mind in which to work.

Finally, the situation had changed between 590 and 690 in another significant way. Missionary work after 690 gained on an ever increasing scale the support of the rising Carolingian dynasty. This support became more and more decisive in missionary affairs, chiefly because the new family represented a unity of policy and a purposiveness of action that had been lacking among the Merovingians of the late sixth and seventh centuries. The Carolingian house was inspired to aid missionaries partly out of religious motives; the members of this dynasty felt a strong sense of responsibility as champions of Christianity and conceived of missionary work as an especially notable good work in the Christian cause. However, their support of missionary activity was chiefly based upon their awareness of the intimate connection between Frankish expansion and the conversion of conquered peoples. The destruction of paganism was accepted as the surest way to destroy resistance to the Franks. The emergence of this new dynasty with its willingness to aid missionary work meant that any missionary effort in the eighth century could rely upon the patronage of the Carolingians, a lay patronage more powerful than had hitherto been lent to missionary ventures. The activity of the Carolingian patrons removed a part of the missionary burden from the papacy, thus seeming to decrease the papal role. This should not lead one to conclude that there emerged a rivalry between popes and Carolingians for control and direction of eighth-century missionary work. The papacy fully approved and encouraged Carolingian support of missionary work. The rising need that the papacy and the Carolingian house felt for one another's good offices brought these two agencies ever closer together in missionary policies as well as in other areas of ecclesiastical policy.

Against this background of events, all coinciding to create a favorable atmosphere for missionary work, one can now proceed to describe the part the papacy played in what might be called the Anglo-Saxon phase of continental missionary history. The missionary zeal of the Anglo-Saxons, coupled with the expansionist aims of the Carolingian mayors of the palace, resulted in a two-pronged missionary thrust. One was in the direction of Frisia. The other was eastward from the Frankish kingdom into Hesse, Thuringia, and Bavaria. The papacy played a role in each of these, although one of much greater magnitude in the venture east of the Rhine than in Frisia.

The Frisian mission was begun without papal participation.[11] English monks

---

[8] Bede, *Hist. eccl.* V, 9, p. 296.
[9] Boniface, *Ep.* #46; ed. Tangl, p. 75: Miseremini illorum, quia et ipsi solent dicere: 'De uno sanguine et de uno osse sumus. . . .'

[10] *Vita Willehadi*, 1; ed. Poncelet, *Acta Sanctorum*, Nov. III, 842-843.
[11] For descriptions of the Frisian missionaries see Hauck, *Kirchengeschichte* I, 431-437; II, 354-370; Josef Jung-Diefenbach,

had apparently singled out Frisia as a likely place to work. Wilfrid was perhaps responsible for this decision. His accidental delay in Frisia in 678-679 revealed that King Aldgisl was willing to tolerate missionaries.[12] Although Wilfrid had more pressing problems to deal with than the conversion of the Frisians, he perhaps carried the word back to Northumbria that an opportunity existed in Frisia. Egbert, another Northumbrian living in Ireland, also contemplated a Frisian mission. He was responsible for sending Wigbert to Frisia about a decade after Wilfrid's short stay. Wigbert encountered the hostility of the new ruler Radbod and was forced to return to Ireland after two years.[13] Still another Northumbrian, Willibrord, a pupil of both Egbert and Wilfrid, next came to Frisia in 690. He found conditions more suitable due to a defeat inflicted on Radbod by Pepin of Heristal, a defeat that resulted in Frankish annexation of territory in south Frisia. Willibrord turned to Pepin's court immediately upon his arrival in Frisia; there he found a willing patron.[14] Thus the conversion of the Frisians opened as a joint venture of English monks and Carolingian rulers and remained so over most of its history.

The papacy, however, was not excluded. Shortly after his arrival in Frisia and after his arrangement with Pepin, Willibrord made a trip to Rome.[15] He sought to gain the permission and the blessing of Pope Sergius (687-701) for the Frisian venture. He also wanted to acquire relics for use in the new churches he contemplated building as paganism was wiped out. And "he desired to learn there or receive thence many other things that so great a work required."[16] This journey to Rome, which certainly must have been made with the approval of Pepin, clearly demonstrates the conviction on the part of the Christian world that papal recognition of a mission had a bearing on its success. Willibrord himself must also have felt that Sergius could give him advice on the task of converting the pagans of Frisia.

The Frisian mission was not yet finished with Rome after Willibrord's first trip there. "After they who had come over to Frisia had taught there a few years, Pepin, with the consent of all, sent the venerable Willibrord to Rome, where Sergius was still pope, requesting that he be ordained archbishop of the Frisian people. What was requested was done in the year of the Lord 696 . . . And he was sent back to his episcopal see fourteen days after he came to Rome."[17] Bede's account makes Pepin responsible for this important step. Perhaps such was the case. Pepin may have felt that he could allay Frisian hostility to Frankish domination by encouraging a church organization dependent upon Rome rather than upon the hated Franks. However, the decision to create a province of this order was certainly a departure from previous Frankish ecclesiastical policy. The suppression of the archiepiscopal see at Utrecht by Charles Martel after Willibrord's death also makes one suspicious of Bede's

---

Die Friesenbekehrung bis zum Martertode des hl. Bonifatius (Post Mödling bei Wien, 1931); Gabriel H. Verbist, Saint Willibrord. Apôtre des Pays-Bas et fondateur d'Echternach (Louvain, 1939); Alexander Grieve, Willibrordi by Alcuin of York 691-739. Including a translation of the Vita Willibrordi by Alcuin of York (Westminster, 1932).
[12] Eddius Stephanus, The Life of Bishop Wilfrid, 26; ed. Colgrave, p. 52.
[13] For Egbert and Wicbert see Bede, Hist. eccl. V, 9, pp. 296-298.
[14] Ibid., V, 10, p. 299; Alcuin, Vita Willibrordi, 5; ed. Levison, MGH, SS. rer. Merov. VII, 120-121.
[15] Bede, Hist. eccl. V, 11, p. 301.
[16] Ibid., pp. 301-302: Sed et alia perplura, quae tanti operis negotium quaerebat, uel ibi discere uel inde accipere cupiebat.
[17] Ibid., pp. 302-303: Postquam uero per annos aliquot in Fresia, qui aduenerant, docuerunt, misit Pippin fauente omnium consensu uirum uenerabilem Uilbrordum Romam, cuius adhuc pontificatum Sergius habebat, postulans, ut eidem Fresonum genti archiepiscopus ordinaretur. Quod ita, ut petierat, impletum est, anno ab incarnatione Domini DCXCVI . . . ac mox remissus ad sedem episcopatus sui, id est post dies XIIII, ex quo in urbem uenerat. See also Alcuin, Vita Willbrordi, 6; ed. Levison, MGH, SS. rer. Merov. VII, 121. Bede's date is wrong; see Wilhelm Levison, "Willibrordiana," Neues Archiv der Gesellschaft für ältere deutsche Geschichtskunde, XXXIII (1908), 528.

statement. At least it might be suggested that Willibrord's return to Rome to be made archbishop was the result of Sergius' instructions delivered during Willibrord's visit in Rome in 692. Thus the papal role in directing the Frisian mission along a certain line might have been larger than Bede has suggested.

Beyond this point one finds little evidence that the papacy played a part in the Frisian mission as long as Willibrord was archbishop (until 739). The archbishop enjoyed the support of Pepin and Charles Martel, both of whom granted property to support the mission and used their armies to protect and broaden its field of action. The Frisian mission depended heavily upon England for many of the things it might have gained from Rome, e.g., recruits and advice.[18] In spite of the obvious dependence on England and on the Carolingians, the Frisian mission probably still remained in contact with Rome and perhaps consulted it on important matters. Numerous Anglo-Saxon pilgrims undoubtedly passed through Frisia on their way to Rome. Wilfrid spent a winter in Utrecht in 704-705.[19] Boniface was in Frisia, working in close cooperation with Willibrord, for three years after his first trip to Rome in 719.[20] A certain Marchelm, a disciple of Willibrord, was in Rome in 738 while Boniface was there on his third Roman trip.[21] Any of these instances might have offered ample opportunity for consultation with the papacy about missionary problems, although no direct evidence to prove this point can be produced.

Only once more did the papacy take a direct part in the history of the conversion of Frisia, again in connection with the problem of organization. After Willibrord's death Utrecht ceased to be an archbishopric.[22] Boniface, with the assistance of Carlomann, sought to gain control of the see as one of his suffragans with the right to appoint and consecrate a bishop. His efforts were undoubtedly inspired by a desire to insure the continuation of missionary work. However, his claims conflicted with those of the archbishop of Cologne. Boniface called upon Rome to decide the case in his favor.[23] Whether the pope acted upon this request is not clear; Boniface seems to have won his point, but probably with the aid of the Carolingians rather than of the papacy. Hardly had Boniface gained control of the situation when he was martyred trying to win converts in northern Frisia. His passing threatened the continuation of missionary work in Frisia, since the Frankish bishops, almost devoid of missionary interests, were grasping for control over Frisia. Pepin the Short and Pope Stephen II (752-757) collaborated to insure the continuation of missionary activity in Frisia, irrespective of the fate of the episcopal see. The two commissioned Gregory, a longtime disciple of Boniface, abbot of the monastery of St. Martin at Utrecht and charged him with the direction of the existing missionary establishment. For about twenty years (until 775) Gregory of Utrecht continued to direct the slow, laborious progress of Christianity into central and northern Frisia, his authority resting primarily on royal and papal approval of his efforts as missionary abbot.[24]

The expansion of Christianity on the eastern frontier of the Frankish kingdom

[18] For examples of this close contact see Bede, *Hist. eccl.* V, 11, p. 302; *Vita Willehadi*, 1; ed. Poncelet, *Acta Sanctorum*, Nov. III, 842-843; Liudger, *Vita Gregorii abbatis Traiectensis;* ed. O. Holder-Egger, MGH, SS. XV, 66-79; Altfrid, *Vita Liudgeri* I, 9-13, in *Die "Vitae sancti Liudgeri";* ed. Wilhelm Diekamp, *Geschichtsquellen des Bistums Münster* IV (Münster, 1881), pp. 13-18.

[19] Bede, *Hist. eccl.* III, 13, p. 152.

[20] Willibald, *Vita Bonifatii*, 5; ed. Levison, MGH, SS. rer. Germ. in usum schol., pp. 23-26.

[21] Altfrid, *Vita Liudgeri* I, 13; ed. Diekamp, p. 18. designates Marchelm thus: servum Dei de genere ortum Anglorum et a sancto episcopo Willibrordo a pueritia sancti instructum moribus. . . . Liudger, *Vita Gregorii*, 8; ed. Holder-Egger, MGH, SS. XV, 73, speaks of Marchelm being in Rome in 738.

[22] For the complicated question of the disposition of the bishopric of Utrecht after Willibrord's death see Jung-Diefenbach, *Die Friesenbekehrung*, pp. 107-118; Hermann Nottarp, *Die Bistumserrichtung in Deutschland im achten Jahrhundert* (Stuttgart, 1920), pp. 17-27.

[23] Boniface, *Ep.* #109; ed. Tangl, pp. 234-236.

[24] Liudger, *Vita Gregorii*, 10; ed. Holder-Egger, MGH, SS. XV, 74-75.

provided the papacy with a greater opportunity than did the Frisian mission.[25] This opportunity came to it as a result of Boniface, whose career in one way or another completely dominated the missionary effort involved in converting the remaining pagans in Hesse, Thuringia, Bavaria, and to some extent Frisia. Thus the papal participation in this phase of missionary history is primarily an account of Rome's connection with Boniface.

The papacy cannot be credited with taking the initiative in this missionary venture in the sense that Gregory the Great took the initiative in opening the English mission. Not until the Anglo-Saxon missionaries offered their services to end paganism on the eastern frontier of Francia did Rome show any interest. When Boniface made his first trip to Rome, he presented the papacy with a unique problem for which there was no precedent in papal missionary experience. He came, not as the English missionaries in Gregory's day, asking for papal advice on how to conduct affairs in a mission started by the pope. Nor did he come as Willibrord had, seeking authority to do what had already begun and was likely to continue, whatever the papacy chose to do. Boniface came to Rome inspired with an urge to do missionary work but without any specific program of action in mind. His zeal was a product of the monastic atmosphere in which he had been nurtured in England. He was a monk struck with the idea of paying greater service to God than he could by remaining in England. He had first tried to exercise that zeal in Frisia, only to find the situation there impossible.[26] So he turned to Rome for further guidance. Besides being a monk zealous for missionary work, Boniface was also an Englishman willing to accept papal authority as the highest in Christendom and to serve the pope as an obedient servant. Rome therefore was a natural place to turn for religious guidance. In a letter written on May 15, 719, commissioning Boniface to do missionary work, Gregory II (715-731) stated with great clarity Boniface's manner of presenting himself: "Your pious purpose, as it has been declared to us, demands of us that we make use of you as our co-worker in spreading the divine words. Knowing . . . that you now wish, for the love of God, to extend the talent divinely entrusted to you, by dedicating yourself ceaselessly to missionary work and the teaching of the mystery of the faith among the heathen, carrying to them the saving knowledge of divine oracle, we rejoice in your loyalty and desire to further the work of grace vouchsafed to you."[27] In all likelihood Boniface had suggested a desire to convey Christianity to those Germanic peoples with whom the English felt a special kinship, an idea that was common in England at the time.[28] Moreover, he could, on the basis of his own experience, recommend

[25] No attempt will be made in the following section to describe in detail the missionary work of Boniface. As guides for that activity the following might be recommended: Hauck, Kirchengeschichte I, pp. 448-594; Gustav Schnürer, Die Bekehrung der Deutschen zum Christentum: Bonifatius (Mainz, 1909); Godfrey Kurth, Saint Boniface, tr. from 4th French ed., Rt. Rev. Victor Day, with insertions . . . by Rev. Francis S. Betten (Milwaukee, 1935); Johann Joseph Laux, Der heilige Bonifatius. Apostel der Deutschen (Freiburg im Breisgau, 1922); Theodor Schieffer, Winfrid-Bonifatius und die christliche Grundlegung Europas (Freiburg, 1954); Heinrich Böhmer, "Zur Geschichte des Bonifatius," Zeitschrift für hessische Geschichte und Landeskunde, L (n.f., XL) (1917), 171-215; Michael Tangl, "Bonifatiusfragen," Abhandlungen der preussischen Akademie der Wissenschaften, Philosophisch-Historische Klasse, Jhrg. 1919 (Berlin, 1919); Michael Tangl, "Studien zur Neuausgabe der Bonifatius-Frage," Neues

Archiv, XL (1916), 639-790; XLI (1917), 21-101.

[26] Willibald, Vita Bonifatii, 1-4; ed. Levison, MGH, SS. rer. Germ. in usum schol., pp. 4-18, for Boniface's monastic career and its resultant missionary zeal.

[27] Boniface, Ep. #12; ed. Tangl, p. 17: Exigit manifestata nobis relegiosi propositi tui pie in Christo flagrantis intentio et adprobata sincerissima fidei tuae perlata relatio, ut ad dispensationem verbi divini, cuius per gratiam Dei curam gerimus, te conministro utamur. Experientes . . . te . . . indolem ad augmentum crediti caelitus talenti prospectu divini amoris extendere, videlicet gratiam cognitionis caelestis oraculi in laborem salutiferę praedicationis ad innotescendum gentibus incredulis mysterium fidei instanti conatu expendere: conlaetamur fidei tuae et adiutores effici cupimus gratiae praerogatę.

[28] See above, p. 69. Boniface was certainly aware of this feeling of kinship with the continental Germans; see Boniface, Ep.

the unlikelihood of missionary success in Frisia. This evidence hardly warrants a conclusion that Boniface had a definite plan in mind as to where he wanted to go or that he had come to Rome to secure approval for a specific missionary venture. He presented himself to Gregory as a missionary ready to serve the highest authority in Christendom in fulfilling a task of vital interest to all Christians, spreading the faith. Thus there was thrust upon the pope the need to make an important decision and the opportunity to once again make the papacy a significant missionary force.

According to Boniface's biographer, Gregory II took considerable time in deciding upon an answer to Boniface's request.[29] Eventually he acted by granting Boniface a papal commission entitling him to "go forth . . . to those peoples who are still in the bonds of infidelity . . . to teach the service of the kingdom of God . . ."[30] Gregory granted such a commission on the basis that missionary work was the "special care" of the papacy. He had satisfied himself that Boniface was qualified by learning and by zeal to serve as "co-worker in spreading the divine words,"[31] and that he was willing to obey the papacy "as a single member of a body submits itself to the sovereignty of the head."[32] Gregory further instructed Boniface to go as a teacher, persuading the pagans of the truth and pouring into their minds the knowledge of the Old and the New Testament in a manner suited to their understanding. Finally, Boniface was ordered to use "the sacramental discipline prescribed by the official ritual formulary of the Holy Apostolic See."[33] The letter which contained these ideas and instructions was placed in Boniface's hands, obviously as the authority for any action that he might take.

The concepts presented in this letter demonstrate a new stage in the papal role in missionary work. Any reading of Gregory the Great's connection with missionary work suggests that he acted in missionary affairs in order to give aid to those doing a work he would personally have preferred to do were he not pope. He conceived his role as that of a monk aiding other monks but not that of a pope exercising his papal function. His successors usually confined their support of missionaries to exercising powers already defined by canons, e.g., elevating bishops to the archiepiscopal rank, or to serving as spiritual fathers to Christians needing aid or encouragement, e.g., writing letters of encouragement or advice on specific problems. Gregory II advanced beyond these ideas. His letter defined the position of the papal office relative to all missionary activity. By virtue of his succession to St. Peter the pope had the duty to spread the faith. To fulfill that function he must discover workers, judge of their fitness, and commission them to go to their labors. He must instruct them whenever necessary in the techniques of missionary work. He must assume responsibility for guarding the results of their labors lest deviation from the true faith be instituted among the ignorant pagans. In short, Gregory's letter to Boniface stated the principle that proper missionary activity could only be conducted under papal direction, since the spreading of the faith was a definite function of the papal office. Those historians who interpret this letter as the first step in a preconceived plan to reform the Frankish church or as the opening wedge in a papal scheme to arrange an alliance with the Frankish state or as an attempt of the papacy to construct an ecclesiastical domain independent of the existing *Landeskirchen* are perhaps reading too much into its content. True, all of these developments emerged as a result of the events of 719. At the time Gregory

---

#46; ed. Tangl, pp. 74-75.
[29] Willibald, *Vita Bonifatii*, 5; ed. Levison, MGH, SS. rer. Germ. in usum schol., p. 21.
[30] Boniface, *Ep.* #12; ed. Tangl, pp. 17-18: ideo . . . ad gentes quascumque infidelitatis error detentas properare . . . ministerium

regni Dei . . . designes. . . .
[31] See above, note 27, for these passages.
[32] *Ibid.*, p. 17: . . . ut membrum ex membro proprii corporis caput requirens. . . .
[33] *Ibid.*, p. 18: Disciplinam denique sacramenti . . . ex formula officiorum sanctae nostrae apostolicae sedis. . . .

II revealed absolutely nothing to show that such schemes were his intention. His commission to Boniface was only a definition of the papal role in missionary work, a definition that the pope was compelled to make because an English monk who wanted to serve God as a missionary and who was convinced that Rome was the highest authority in Christendom presented himself to the pope and asked to be put to work.

The papal assumption of the obligation of missionary work plus the willingness of Boniface to live within its implications resulted in a flurry of papal activity in the ensuing years. The connection of Gregory II, Gregory III (731-741), Zacharias (741-752), and Stephen II to the missionary events of the times allows them to be recorded as great missionary popes, making a notable contribution to the expansion of Christendom along the eastern borders of the Frankish kingdom.

Gregory II was especially important in the successful outcome of Boniface's work. Boniface left Rome in 719 with no definite program of action, his papal commission making no specific references as to where he was to work. His first task as co-worker of the pope was to discover an area where actual missionary work might have a chance of success. During the next three years he traveled through Bavaria, Thuringia, Frisia, and Hesse, seeking such a spot. He finally found the proper scene in Hesse and there began to win a considerable number of converts.[34] Of equal importance was the fact that he as a missionary began to draw others into his orbit to help in his work. His correspondence reveals that the news of the work he had undertaken had reached England and that the English were already offering their assistance,[35] a development that was of vital importance to his success. Boniface began to establish connections in Francia that also were significant, since he was laboring in territory that was under Frankish lordship.[36] He was also beginning to recruit a body of missionaries for his work.[37] These developments, coupled with the actual success of Boniface in winning converts in Hesse, spelled a fulfillment of the missionary venture conceived in Rome in 719. True to his position as decided upon in Rome, Boniface once again turned to the papacy, sending a letter to Gregory II reporting his success and requesting advice on the problems connected with his daily work as a missionary. Gregory II replied by summoning Boniface to Rome in 722,[38] obviously exercising his recently claimed authority as the director of missionary effort.

The transactions in Rome in 722 represented a further clarification of the papal part in missionary work as well as a major contribution of the papacy to Boniface's success. Gregory II again took care to ascertain Boniface's fitness to conduct missionary work, fitness being defined in terms of knowledge and acceptance of the apostolic tradition and of a willingness to obey Rome. This careful scrutiny of missionary personnel demonstrates the seriousness with which the papacy took its position in missionary affairs and contrasts rather vividly with Gregory the Great's lack of concern with questions of orthodoxy. Willibald reports that after Gregory had ascertained Boniface's orthodoxy, he gave his missionary elaborate instructions. Perhaps the two discussed the whole procedure to be followed in the future with respect to missionary work. Being satisfied that Boniface was qualified for greater responsibility, Gregory II vested him with episcopal authority in order that he could perform his missionary work

---

[34] The essential source for Boniface's activity after leaving Rome in 719 is Willibald, *Vita Bonifatii*, 5-6; ed. Levison, MGH, SS. rer. Germ. in usum schol., pp. 22-27.
[35] Boniface, *Ep.* #13-15; ed. Tangl, pp. 18-28.
[36] Willibald, *Vita Bonifatii*, 5; ed. Levison, MGH, SS. rer. Germ. in usum schol., p. 23; Luidger, *Vita Gregorii*, 2-3; ed. Holder-Egger, MGH, SS. XV, 67-70.
[37] Liudger, *Vita Gregorii*, 2; ed. Holder-Egger, MGH, SS. XV, 67-69.
[38] Willibald, *Vita Bonifatii*, 6; ed. Levison, MGH, SS. rer. Germ. in usum schol., p. 27.

more adequately.[39] Boniface's elevation was sealed by an oath which the missionary himself wrote, placing himself under papal authority and binding himself to work and teach only as Rome prescribed.[40] Boniface was the first missionary who had received his consecration as a missionary bishop from the pope himself; previously it had been thought sufficient if a missionary clergyman received this rank from anyone canonically qualified to consecrate bishops. This unusual procedure in 722, for which Gregory had obviously called Boniface to Rome, again demonstrates the new vigor of papal overlordship of missionary work and the new feeling that the papacy was now exercising an official function comparable to filling an episcopal office in the Roman province, that is, a function which belonged to the papacy by right. Whereas previously the elevation of a missionary to the episcopate had been a matter of expediency, it now had become a step in the papal method of exercising its rightful power.

Once having made Boniface a missionary bishop, Gregory took further steps to aid his labors. He presented Boniface with a series of constitutions and canonical collections that were to serve as guides in future missionary work.[41] He also provided Boniface with a series of letters designed to permit the new bishop to exercise his new power more readily. These letters show that the papacy had helped Boniface to decide the area that was to be proselytized next, that is, Thuringia, and was ready to lend its authority to help Boniface receive a hearing in Thuringia. The first[42] was addressed to the Christians living in Thuringia. They were informed that Boniface was being sent to convert pagans and to correct fallen-away Christians. They were exhorted to lend every possible aid to the bishop, including guides for his journeys and food. Their reward for any help they gave would be "fellowship with the saints and martyrs of Jesus Christ . . ." Any hindrance would result in eternal damnation. The second letter[43] especially commended Boniface to five Thuringian nobles who had resisted falling into paganism and thus were especially likely to aid the missionary bishop. These nobles were asked to obey and aid Boniface. Apparently Boniface knew from his own experience in Hesse prior to his coming to Rome how important the aid of local nobles could be;[44] thus the papacy took special steps to encourage such assistance. A third letter[45] was a conventional notification of Boniface's elevation to the episcopate addressed to all laymen and clergy in Thuringia. Apparently this document was designed to insure Boniface's acceptance as a bishop. The fourth letter[46] was addressed to Charles Martel. The letter informed him of Boniface's consecration and of his papal commission to convert the pagans "on the eastern side of the Rhine." Gregory II wrote as follows: "For their sakes we warmly commend him to your high favor and pray you to help him in every need, to defend him against every enemy over whom you may prevail in the Lord's name, bearing in mind that whatever support you solicitously give to him will be given to God, who said that those who received his holy apostles, sent forth as a light to the Gentiles, would be receiving Himself."[47] Lay assistance and recognition was thought to be vital to missionary success; Gregory II as the spiritual head of the mission was asking Charles to

[39] Ibid., 6, pp. 28-30 for these transactions.
[40] Boniface, Ep. #16; ed. Tangl, pp. 28-29.
[41] Willibald, Vita Bonifatii, 6; ed. Levison, MGH, SS. rer. Germ. in usum schol., pp. 29-30.
[42] Boniface, Ep. #17; ed. Tangl, pp. 29-31.
[43] Ibid., #19, p. 33.
[44] For instance, two Hessian nobles had provided him with the land upon which his missionary monastery at Amöneberg was built; see Willibald, Vita Bonifatti, 6; ed. Levison, MGH, SS. rer. Germ. in usum schol., p. 26.

[45] Boniface, Ep. #18; ed. Tangl, pp. 31-33.
[46] Ibid., #20, pp. 33-34.
[47] Ibid., p .34: Pro quibus eum gloriosae benivolentiae tuae omnimodo commendamus, ut eum in omnibus necessitatibus adiuvetis et contra quosibet adversarios, quibus in Domino prevaletis, instantissime defendatis certissime retinentes Deo vos exhibere, quaecunque huic promptissimo impenderitis favore, qui sanctis apostolis suis ad lucem gentium destinatis suscipientibus eos se suscipiendum predixit.

fulfill his religious duty by lending his aid. Moreover, there is implicit in the letter the request for the mayor of the palace to recognize the authority of the papacy to undertake missionary work and to take the steps necessary for its completion.

The whole course of papal action in 722 indicates that Gregory II and Boniface together had conceived a comprehensive missionary plan. Boniface, properly tested, instructed, and fortified with the necessary offices, was entrusted fully to win converts and instruct them in the new faith. To succeed he would need the assistance of the whole Christian society. The pope threw his prestige and authority behind mustering that assistance, supplying his missionary with letters instructing all people in their obligations and promising anyone who aided a share in eternal salvation, the keys to which Rome possessed.

Armed with his new authority and fortified with the moral prestige of Rome, Boniface returned to Germany. He labored in Hesse and Thuringia during the rest of Gregory's pontificate, aided by agencies other than the papacy, including especially Charles Martel, the laity in the region in which he was working, and the English. Gregory II entered the scene again only as Boniface asked for his aid. On December 4, 724, the pope replied[48] to a letter from Boniface in which the latter had reported his success and had requested papal aid in certain matters. Boniface reported that the bishop of Mainz was intruding into his area of operation and interfering with his work. Gregory wrote to Charles Martel, asking him to curb the bishop. Boniface also requested another papal letter to the Thuringians and other Germans. Gregory assured him that he would write such a letter. This he did in December, 724,[49] again reminding the Thuringians that in fulfillment of his apostolic function he had sent Boniface to preach to them, to baptize them, and to show them the way to salvation. He explicitly laid before them their duty: "But be obedient to him in all things; honor him as your father; incline your hearts to his teachings. For we have sent him to you not for acquiring any temporal gain, but for the profit of your souls. Therefore, love God and receive baptism in His name because the Lord our God has prepared for those who love Him things which the eye of no man has seen and which has never entered the heart of man. Leave off evil deeds and do good. Do not worship idols or sacrifice flesh because God does not accept these things. Instead do what our brother Boniface directs and you and your sons will be saved. Make a house where your father and our bishop may live, and churches where you might pray, so that God will forgive your sins and give you eternal life."[50] The tenor of these remarks makes it clear that Boniface wanted this letter to be addressed to the real pagans in his missionary field and not to the Christians, as had been the case with previous papal letters. Papal admonitions were apparently useful in overcoming pagan opposition.

Sometime before November 22, 726, Boniface sent another letter to Rome requesting advice on a series of problems arising from his work with pagans. Gregory II answered on that date,[51] supplying specific information on the way to handle the troublesome situations and stating that Boniface had acted wisely in consulting Rome, since "the blessed apostle Peter stands as the fountainhead of the apostolate and the episcopate." The pope laid down regulations on such

---

[48] *Ibid.*, #24, pp. 41-43.
[49] *Ibid.*, #25, pp. 43-44.
[50] *Ibid.*, pp. 43-44: Sed vos ei in omnibus oboedite et sicut patrem vestrum illum honorate et ad eius doctrinam corda vestra inclinate, quia illum non pro lucro aliquo temporali conquirendo direximus, sed pro lucro animarum vestrarum ad vos eum misimus. Diligite ergo Deum et in nomine eius baptismum suscipite, quia dominus Deus noster, quod oculus hominis numquam vidit nec in cor hominis ascendit, praepara-vit diligentibus se. Iam recedite a malis operibus et agite bene. Non adoretis idola nec immoletis carnes, quia Deus non recipit ista, sed in omnibus, secundum quod vos frater noster Bonifatius docuerit, observate et agite; et salvi eritis et vos et filii vestri in sempiternum. Facite ergo et domum, ubi debeat ipse pater vester episcopus habitare, et ecclesias, ubi orare debeatis, ut Deus indulgeat peccata vestra et donet vobis vitam perpetuam.
[51] *Ibid.*, #26, pp. 44-47.

matters as marriage practices, the ritual, the problem of baptism in a situation where many had been irregularly baptized previously, clerical discipline, and the persistence of pagan practices. The pope's advice was generally in line with a rather strict conformance with regular canonical rules, although he advocated leniency in some cases. The whole letter indicates that Boniface found papal authority helpful in completing his work in Hesse and Thuringia, especially in matters pertaining to the institution of Christian practices among those recently converted.

The contribution which Gregory II had made to Boniface's work explains the missionary's concern when the pope died in 731. Boniface immediately sent a delegation to Rome bearing a letter[52] which requested that the new pope continue the existing arrangement. Boniface also reaffirmed his obedience to Rome and requested a renewal of the pact between pope and missionary. In the same letter Boniface reported his progress, spoke of his difficulty in controlling his far-flung theater of operations, and presented the new pope with a series of problems upon which advice was needed. Gregory III answered in 732 in a fashion that not only reassured Boniface that the papacy still supported him but also indicated that Rome was retaining its position as the director of missionary activity. He raised Boniface to the rank of archbishop and sent him the pallium. This step was not merely a reward to a faithful missionary; it was a part of missionary strategy. Recognizing that Boniface had been successful, the pope judged the time ripe for the completion of an ecclesiastical organization through the consecration of new bishops for Germany. Having given Boniface the authority for this next step, Gregory III left the matter of choosing the bishops and establishing the sees to the new archbishop. He thereby established a goal toward which Boniface could work. While issuing these important orders, Gregory III did not neglect to answer Boniface's immediate problems. After the fashion of Gregory II he ruled on a series of problems presented by Boniface. The most difficult problem with which Boniface had to deal was the persistence of certain pagan practices, such as eating horse meat, making sacrificial offerings for dead pagans, irregular baptisms performed by pagans, and selling slaves to other pagans for sacrifices. All of these practices were condemned. Boniface must have known that they would be, asking the papacy to rule on such matters only so that he could use papal authority as an argument against his new converts. Boniface also needed further advice on marriage regulations, the treatment of certain criminals, and the discipline of the clergy. On all of these matters Gregory supplied canonical regulations.[53]

For some years after his elevation in 732 Boniface went on with his work in Hesse and Thuringia, doing nothing to abide by the papal order to complete the organization of the church. In 735 he made an excursion to Bavaria, perhaps simply as a preacher desirous of correcting the abuses that existed there. He perhaps also contemplated opening a Saxon mission about this time. These projects, however, still left undone the task imposed on him in 732. Thus in 737 Boniface again departed for Rome, apparently to consult with the papacy on the matter.[54] Out of the consultations came an order from the papacy to undertake the complete organization of Bavaria, Alemannia, Hesse, and Thuringia. These decisions were announced in three letters written by Gregory III when Boniface left Rome. One of the letters was addrssed to the bishops, priests, and abbots of all lands, calling upon them to give Boniface their support as he returned to his work.[55] The pope especially requested that clergymen aid Boniface

[52] Willibald, *Vita Bonifatii*, 6; ed. Levison, MGH, SS. rer. Germ. in usum schol., pp. 34-35.
[53] Boniface, *Ep.* #28; ed. Tangl, pp. 49-52.
[54] There is no agreement on why Boniface took the third trip to Rome; see the authorities cited in note 25, above, for various opinions. Most of them agree that Boniface came to Rome for permission to do *something*, thus proving his reliance on Rome for all things.
[55] Boniface, *Ep.* #42; ed. Tangl, pp. 67-68.

in gaining clerical recruits for his work. A second was sent to the nobles and people of Hesse and Thuringia, asking that they accept the priests and bishops Boniface annointed for them by virtue of apostolic authority.[56] A third was addressed to five bishops in Bavaria and Alemannia.[57] Boniface was announced as the papal representative and vicar, charged primarily with reforming the Bavarian and Alemannian churches according to Roman usage and with establishing a system of synods that would insure the continuance of sound discipline. A letter from Gregory III to Boniface about a year later[58] makes it clear that Boniface was ordered to constitute three new bishoprics in Bavaria, as well as recognizing one that already existed, to ferret out unfit clergy, and to hold a synod to institute a reform program. This program was apparently a revival of the abortive plan of Gregory II, instituted in 716 with the collaboration of the Bavarian princes.[59] Finally, Gregory III put into Boniface's hands a letter addressed to the Saxons, asking them to abandon their pagan religion and supplying them with reasons why they should become Christians.[60] These letters taken together again demonstrate the papal assumption of the authority to direct a missionary program to its conclusion and its willingness to buttress its missionaries with the proper authority to complete the work.

Boniface carried out these instructions during the next few years.[61] He instituted four bishoprics in Bavaria, three in Hesse-Thuringia, and one in Nordgau. Sometime before October 29, 739, he reported to Rome on his work in Bavaria; Gregory III confirmed it in a letter written on that date.[62] Early in 742 Boniface wrote to the new pope, Zacharias, to reaffirm his obedience to Rome and to report the creation of bishoprics at Würzburg, Buraburg, and Erfurt. He requested that the pope confirm them with his charters.[63] Zacharias, after a considerable delay (until April 1, 743), wrote to Boniface approving the new bishoprics.[64] He indicated that his approval was not merely a formality by questioning the wisdom of building bishoprics in places so small. He also wrote letters to two of the new bishops, confirming each new see and forbidding any interference with them in the future. Likewise, he ruled that these new sees could only be filled with the approval of the representative of Rome.[65] A little later still another see was created at Eichstätt. An Englishman, Willibald, who had been sent into Germany with Boniface by Gregory III, was made bishop. Again the papacy confirmed the new see.[66]

The papacy had one more step in mind to conclude the development of the church in Germany—the creation of a metropolitan see for Boniface. For a long time this had not been desirable in the missionary district. As late as 739 Gregory III ordered Boniface to refrain from lingering in one place.[67] However, by 745 Boniface's work had progressed far enough to permit an end to his wanderings. A Frankish synod and the Frankish rulers chose Cologne as a metropolitan see for the missionary archbishop. Zacharias approved this act and sent a charter instituting Cologne as a metropolitan church.[68] However, this plan did not come to pass. In 748 Boniface reported to Rome that the Franks had not kept their word and that he was now residing at Mainz. He requested that the pope permit him to find a suitable successor, since he was growing old. Zacharias refused this

[56] Ibid., #43, pp. 68-69.
[57] Ibid., #44, pp. 70-71.
[58] Ibid., #45, pp. 71-74.
[59] For Gregory II's instructions see Lex Baiuwariorum: Additio II; ed. Johannes Merkel, MGH. Leges III, 451-454.
[60] Boniface, Ep. #21; ed. Tangl, pp. 35-36.
[61] For a description of the erection of the bishoprics in Bavaria, Hesse, and Thuringia, see Nottarp, Die Bistumserrichtung in Deutschland im achten Jahrhundert, passim.
[62] Boniface, Ep. #45; ed. Tangl, pp. 71-74.

[63] Ibid., #50, p. 81.
[64] Ibid., #51, pp. 86-87.
[65] Ibid., #52-53, pp. 92-95.
[66] Vita Willibaldi episcopi Eichstetensis auctore sanctimoniali Heidenheimensi, 5; ed. O. Holder-Egger, MGH. SS. XV, 104-105.
[67] Boniface, Ep. #45; ed. Tangl, p. 73, where Gregory III wrote to Boniface: Nec enim habebis licentiam frater, percepti laboris in uno morari loco.
[68] Ibid., #60, pp. 121-122, 124.

request, insisting that Boniface remain in his office, still that of archbishop without a fixed see.[69] Boniface remained at Mainz until he departed for Frisia for his last missionary effort in 753. Mainz was not raised to the rank of a metropolitan see.

With the completion of the episcopal structure there perhaps remained no more real missionary work to be done in the areas where Boniface had labored so long. Boniface himself became involved in the reform of the Frankish church, thus eliminating any new missionary plans for a decade. However, in reading his correspondence one is aware that he never felt that his missionary work was finished in Hesse, Thuringia, and Bavaria. In 741 he requested the protection of Grifo for his establishment in Thuringia.[70] On other occasions he wrote to England telling of the great burdens facing him.[71] As late as 752 he asked Fulrad, abbot of St. Denis, to petition Pepin to make provisions for supporting his disciples working in Germany.[72] Sometime between 750 and 754 he wrote to Optatus, abbot of Monte Cassino, asking him to pray that the heathen be shown the light.[73] The source of Boniface's concern emerges clearly; in spite of having baptized most of the pagans, of creating a definite organization, and of establishing priests and monks over the land, there still remained the tremendous task of teaching the newly won Christians the real meaning of their religion and of compelling them to put it into practice. Thus he and his disciples labored on, trying to impose a more Christian life on his charges. In that task the papacy remained a faithful and valuable supporter of Boniface, supplying him with whatever advice he needed. And Boniface continued to follow his well-established custom of deferring to Rome. When Zacharias and Stephen II succeeded to the papal see, he wrote letters to each reaffirming his obedience and asking that friendly relations be maintained.[74]

For the most part Boniface's dependence on the papacy after about 741 consisted in securing papal authority to enforce canonical regulations and asking the papal opinion on how to handle situations arising out of the ancient customs of people who had not been Christian long enough to forget their pagan ideas and practices. For instance, the problem of rebaptism of those improperly baptized was presented to Rome on several occasions.[75] Questions concerning proper liturgical usage were also referred to Rome.[76] Boniface asked the papacy for a ruling on certain dietary practices which were holdovers from pagan times and received authority to prohibit them.[77] Marriage regulations caused trouble and demanded papal rulings.[78] Boniface was constantly faced with a shortage of adequate priests to labor in newly converted districts. In an attempt to solve this problem Boniface asked Pope Zacharias for permission to ordain priests before the accustomed age of thirty; the pope gave him permission to ordain men of twenty-five in view of the urgent need. He also sanctioned Boniface's custom of ordaining at irregular times, again because of missionary necessity.[79] Even more disturbing to Boniface was the ignorant, vice-ridden, corrupt clergy that he was forced to deal with and that often impeded his work. He repeatedly asked papal assistance against this element.[80] Many of these requests sprang from his reforming work in the whole Germanic world. Occasionally, however, these clergymen interrupted his work in recently converted or organized territories.[81] For instance, Zacharias gave Boniface authority in 744 and again in 748 to depose a false priest in Bavaria who claimed he had papal authority to hold one of the

[69] Ibid., #80, pp. 179-180.
[70] Ibid., #48, pp. 77-78.
[71] Ibid., #63, 65, 66, 67, 73, 74, 76, 78, 91, pp. 129-132, 137-138, 138-139, 139-140, 146-155, 155-156, 158-159, 161-170, 206-208.
[72] Ibid., #93, pp. 212-214.
[73] Ibid., #106, pp. 231-232.
[74] Ibid., #50, 108, pp. 80-81, 233-234.

[75] Ibid., #68, 80, pp. 141, 173-177.
[76] Ibid., #87, pp. 192-201.
[77] Ibid., #80, 87, pp. 172-180, 192-201.
[78] Ibid., #50-51, pp. 80-92.
[79] Ibid., #87, p. 198.
[80] Ibid., #50, 60, 80, 87, pp. 80-86, 122-123, 172-180, 194-201.
[81] Ibid., #63, pp. 132-136.

bishoprics established by Boniface in 739 and who was trying to cause friction between Boniface and Duke Odilo. In 748 Zacharias wrote to Theodo of Bavaria on the matter and also summoned the culprit to Rome.[82] Boniface knew he could depend upon the papal curia for canonical collections and any other documents he might need to strengthen his work.[83] Upon Boniface's request Zacharias granted a privilege to Boniface's new monastery at Fulda, so located that it could serve as a center for strengthening the faith among those whom Boniface had converted.[84] The papacy continued to encourage Boniface to keep at the heavy labor among the new Christians, assuring him that the reward would be in proportion to the labor spent.[85] This praise and honor may have been a great consolation and aid to the aging and sorely beset missionary. All these cases are eloquent proof that the papacy never ceased to lend its aid to Boniface's work and that Boniface always felt a need for papal guidance.

Boniface's death in 754 saw the main missionary work east of the Rhine completed. As subsequent events were to show, his passing proved a blow to papal missionary activity. The harmonious union of Rome and the Anglo-Saxon monk had worked out to make each a vital contributor in the expansion of Christendom. Again, as in the case of the conversion of England after Gregory I's death, the basis of papal missionary policy began to dissolve after Boniface's death. Between 690 and 754 each successive pope had counted on the presence of a pliant, obedient, inspired troop of Anglo-Saxon missionaries, willing to defer their problems to Rome and to accept Rome's overall guidance of their missionary work. The papacy constructed its missionary policy almost entirely on these missionaries. To such a group Rome could and did serve a vital function and thus earned due glory as a missionary agency. Her success, however, depended upon the continuation of these pliant Anglo-Saxon soldiers for Christ. Boniface's death heralded the passing of such a group, thus leaving Rome without the necessary support to continue her existing policy. Neither did Rome have the resources to adapt her policy to the rapidly shifting missionary picture. Again a definite age in papal missionary history had ended.

IV.

By the middle of the eighth century a profound change began to emerge in missionary affairs, negating the entire papal missionary policy of the moment. The rapidly rising Carolingian house was in the process of seizing the initiative in the expansion of Christendom and of subordinating all other missionary agencies to its leadership. The signs of this revolution in missionary affairs were clearly evident throughout the first half of the eighth century. However, it was only with the accession of Charlemagne in 768 that the Carolingians completed the process of assuming the responsibility for missionary work. For nearly a century thereafter Christian expansion was almost invariably organized and directed by the Frankish crown.

This new development resulted in a vigorous burst of missionary activity and several notable additions to Christendom. Charlemagne's efforts resulted in the conversion of the Saxons, the Frisians, and a large number of Slavs and Avars in the area of Pannonia and Carinthia. Louis the Pious, capitalizing on the desire of a faction of the embattled Danish royal house for a Frankish alliance, was responsible for sending Anskar to seek converts among the Danes. As a result of this foothold in the Scandinavian world, Anskar was also able to extend his activities to Sweden. Under the auspices of Louis the German Christian mis-

[82] Ibid., #58, 80, pp. 107-108, 178-179.

[83] Ibid., #54, 62, 75, pp. 96-97, 127-128, 156-158.

[84] Ibid., #86, 87, 89, pp. 193-194, 196, 203-205.

[85] Ibid., #57, 60, 80, 85, pp. 102-103, 120-121, 172-173, 179, 190-191.

sionaries were able to advance into the Slavic world of central Europe, especially among the Czechs and Moravians. These successes establish the century after 768 as one of the most notable in the history of the expansion of Christianity.[1]

The numerous accounts which record the achievement of the Carolingian kings and emperors as missionary leaders leave no doubt of their domination of every phase of missionary activity. Royal armies were employed in Frisia, Saxony, and the Avar empire to convince pagans of the advisability of accepting Christianity; so completely was missionary effort tied up with the Frankish military policy in Charlemagne's day that one can fully agree with the ninth-century author who said that Charlemagne "preached with an iron tongue."[2] Royal diplomacy consistently created missionary opportunities by holding out the prospect of a Frankish alliance to any pagan prince who would commit himself to the conversion of his people. The full authority of royal legislation was thrown into the battle against paganism. The Frankish crown assumed the responsibility for the recruitment of missionaries. The material support for missionary efforts was supplied by the rulers, especially through grants of land to the missionaries and through the imposition of tithes in territories recently incorporated into the Frankish state. The rulers took the initiative in organizing newly converted areas into an episcopal structure. Even the problem of missionary method was completely pre-empted by the Frankish crown. Almost nothing in missionary affairs escaped the attention of the Frankish rulers; they had indeed become the fountainhead of the missionary effort of the era.[3]

This ascendance of the Carolingian rulers obviously limited the role of the papacy in missionary affairs. The sources reveal conclusively that the papacy participated in the conversion of pagans only insignificantly from the pontificate of Paul I (757-767) through that of Benedict III (855-858), quite in contrast to the papal activity of the half century preceding Paul I. Even more striking is the revelation that on those occasions when the papacy did take part in missionary activity, it operated as an agency completely subservient to the Carolingian rulers, merely lending its support to policies established by them.

At the accession of Charlemagne there were only two active centers of missionary work. One was in Frisia, where monks operating from Utrecht continued to try to win converts in northern Frisia. Pope Stephen II had sanctioned the decision made in 755 to place one of Boniface's disciples, Gregory, in charge of the continued efforts to convert the pagans who had murdered Boniface. Until Gregory's death in 775 missionary work continued without any spectacular successes. The papacy played no role in this work. It remained primarily an effort carried on by Anglo-Saxons and by native Frisians, educated at Utrecht, supported by the material resources of the monastic establishment at Utrecht, and directed by the steady hand of Gregory.[4] The second missionary venture of the period centered on the southeastern border of Bavaria, where the episcopal see at Salzburg supplied missionaries and material support and the Bavarian princes lent political support in the effort to persuade Slavic groups

---

[1] For general accounts of missionary activity during this period, see Hauck, *Kirchengeschichte* II, *passim*; Latourette, *The Thousand Years of Uncertainty: A.D. 500-A.D. 1500*, pp. 98-119, 155-159; Amann, *L'époque carolingienne*, pp. 188-200, 247-255, 447-450; Hans von Schubert, *Geschichte der christlichen Kirche im Frühmittelalter. Ein Handbuch* (Tübingen, 1921), pp. 333-346, 502-514.

[2] *Translatio sancti Liborii*, 5; ed. G. Pertz, MGH, SS. IV, 151: . . . ferrea quodammodo lingua praedicavit.

[3] Any attempt to document these many cases of royal control of missionary activity for the century following the beginning of Charlemagne's rule would involve citing nearly the whole body of missionary literature from this period and will not be undertaken here. The general accounts cited in note 1, above, will supply examples.

[4] The chief sources for this activity are Liudger, *Vita Gregorii*, 10-15; ed. Holder-Egger, MGH, SS. XV, 74-79; Altfrid, *Vita Liudgeri* I, 1-20; ed. Diekamp, pp. 7-24; *Vita Lebuini antiqua*; ed. A. Hofmeister, MGH, SS. XXX², 789-795; Hucbald, *Vita Sancti Lebwini*; PL 132, 875-894; *Vita Willehadi*, 1-4; ed. Poncelet, *Acta Sanctorum*, Nov. III, 842-843.

to accept the new religion.[5] Pope Paul seems to have lent his authority to this venture by assigning the area being Christianized to the jurisdiction of Salzburg; however, in doing this he was only confirming a policy of his more vigorous predecessors, Zacharias and Stephen II.[6] Other than this the papacy had no interest in the conversion of the Slavs.

In 772 Charlemagne led his first campaign against the Saxons and thereby began a new phase of missionary effort. For the rest of his career Charlemagne was almost constantly engaged in the conquest, conversion, and ecclesiastical organization of the Saxons and of their allies, the Frisians. The papacy played an extremely minor role in these stirring events, in spite of the fact that the final conversion of the Saxons and the Frisians involved several basic changes in missionary policy and caused considerable concern among some of Charlemagne's advisers.[7] Only once was the papacy consulted by Charlemagne on matters pertaining to the Saxon mission. Early in 786 Hadrian I (772-795) replied to a request made by Charlemagne about how to deal with Saxons who had once been Christians but had reverted to paganism. Hadrian, citing the examples of his predecessors, laid down the general principle that the circumstances under which apostasy occurred ought to govern the penance required for readmission to the ranks of the faithful. Otherwise, he shifted the burden to the clergy "in those parts."[8] One wonders why Charlemagne requested advice on this rather insignificant matter when he considers that by 786 Charlemagne had, without recourse to the papacy, laid down the major lines of his missionary policy in Saxony and Frisia. By that time he had employed forced baptisms, diplomacy, and bribery to win converts, had used his armies to destroy Saxon shrines, had charged already established bishoprics and monasteries in Francia with the responsibilities of converting the Saxons, had personally commissioned individual missionaries to work in Saxony, and had issued his *Capitulatio de partibus Saxoniae*. There is no evidence that Rome had any part in such decisions or any interest in their implications as missionary techniques. There was at least a tradition in later centuries that Hadrian I had lent his authority to the establishment of the bishoprics of Verden, Bremen, and Osnabruck.[9] However, that tradition was based on grounds so shaky that it does not permit one to attribute to Hadrian a part in the arduous task of organizing a Saxon church, a task which the Frankish rulers assumed to themselves.

Otherwise, Hadrian's role in the Saxon mission was confined to offering congratulations to Charlemagne. In 774 he wrote to the king expressing his joy at the latter's "immense victory" over the Saxons and informing Charlemagne that he had ordered the Roman clergy and monks to pray for further victories and for the king's prosperity.[10] Early in 786 Hadrian again wrote to Charlemagne to congratulate him on having converted the Saxons. Hadrian again reported to the king that he had ordered all those under papal jurisdiction to offer prayers for this great victory. However, this action was taken only at the specific request of Charlemagne. Repeatedly throughout the letter Hadrian gave the king full credit for converting the Saxons; nowhere did he suggest that the papacy was concerned with intervening in the procedure or had any suggestions to offer to the king.[11] On several other occasions Hadrian expressed a hope that Charlemagne

[5] *De conversione Bagoariorum et Carantanorum libellus*, 2-5; ed. Wattenbach, MGH, SS. XI, 6-9.

[6] *MGH, Diplomatum karolinorum* I; ed. Engilbert Mühlbacher, 282-283.

[7] Aside from the works cited in note 1 above, the best study of the conversion of the Saxons is H. Wiedemann, *Die Sachsenbekehrung*, in *Veröffentlichungen des internationalen Instituts für missionswissenschaftliche Forschungen: Missionswissen-*schaftliche Studien, ed. J. Schmidlin, neue Reihe, V (Münster i. W., 1932).

[8] *Codex Carolinus* #77; ed. Wilhelmus Gundlach, MGH, Ep. III, 609.

[9] See the falsified charters for Verden, Bremen, and Osnabruch in *MGH, Diplomatur karolinorum* I; ed. Mühlbacher, 333-338, 344-346, 399-402, 403-405.

[10] *Codex Carolinus* #50; ed. Gundlach, MGH, Ep. III, 569-570.

[11] *Ibid.*, #76, pp. 607-608.

would emerge victorious over "all barbarian peoples" and over "all adversaries of the church of God."[12] These messages, so often repeated that they seem to have become formulae, cannot be said to apply to any one of Charlemagne's numerous military ventures, and thus have no special missionary significance. Perhaps Hadrian served the Saxon mission indirectly by giving encouragement to the missionaries themselves. When Willehad was driven out of Saxony in 782 by a revolt, he traveled to Rome, where he voiced a fear that everything accomplished until then would be undone. But he soon returned to Francia, "not a little strengthened by the consolation of the venerable Pope Hadrian."[13] Hadrian is also credited with receiving Liudger with high honor when he was forced to flee from his missionary work and with giving him relics to be used in a monastery the missionary proposed to build.[14] It must be noted, however, that neither missionary returned to missionary work until ordered to do so by Charlemagne.[15]

Pope Leo III (795-816) added little to Hadrian's restrained policy. During his sojourn in Francia in 799 Leo participated in the creation of an episcopal see at Paderborn, dedicating the episcopal church and placing in it the relics of the martyr Stephen he had brought from Rome.[16] However, the papal contribution to the ecclesiastical organization of Saxony must not be overestimated from this one case. Leo's participation in the creation of the see at Paderborn was prompted merely by his presence in Saxony; certainly he had not made the trip from Rome for this purpose.[17] Charlemagne had already demonstrated that he had assumed the responsibility for the organization of Saxony by instituting a bishopric at Bremen in 785.[18] Perhaps there were also bishoprics at Minden and Verden by 799. In none of these cases was papal authority required by the Frankish rulers.[19] Even the account describing the proceedings at Paderborn in 799 make it perfectly clear that the new see was created by royal orders and that its institution did not depend upon papal authority. In the years after 799 Charlemagne proceeded toward the completion of the organization of Saxony without papal help, as could be illustrated by the creation of the see at Münster with Liudger as bishop.[20] Leo is also credited with aiding in the organization of the new Saxon church by dedicating certain chapels and churches during his trip in 799.[21] Again this was only prompted by his presence in Saxony and was not a matter of papal policy.

While Charlemagne was completing the conversion and the organization of the Saxons and the Frisians, his armies opened a new area for missionary work by destroying the political power of the Avars. Again the royal management of the missionary effort was complete. A synod held in 796, just prior to the opening of the decisive military campaign of that year, defined the procedures to be used in converting the Slavs and Avars about to be conquered.[22] The actual missionary

[12] For example, ibid., #52, 53, 55, 61, 62, 66, 68, 72, 73, 75, 88, 89, pp. 573-574, 575-576, 578-580, 588-589, 589-590, 594, 597-598, 602-603, 604, 606-607, 624-625, 626.

[13] Vita Willehadi, 7; ed. Poncelet, Acta Sanctorum, Nov. III, 844.

[14] Vita secunda s. Liudgeri I, 13; ed. Diekamp, p. 60.

[15] Vita Willehadi, 8; ed. Poncelet, Acta Sanctorum, Nov. III, 845; Altfrid, Vita Liudgeri I, 22; ed. Diekamp, pp. 26-27.

[16] Translatio sancti Liborii, 4; ed. G. Pertz, MGH, SS. IV, 150.

[17] Liber pontificalis II, ed. Duchesne, 4-6; Annales regni Francorum, a. 799; ed. Fridericus Kurze, MGH, SS. rer. Germ. in usum schol. (Hanover, 1895), pp. 106-107, for the occasion of Leo's journey to Charlemagne's court.

[18] Vita Willehadi, 8; ed. Poncelet, Acta Sanctorum, Nov. III, 845.

[19] This is assuming that the tradition reflected in the charters, cited in note 9 above, is false.

[20] Altfrid, Vita Liudgeri I, 23-24; ed. Diekamp, pp. 27-29. For the complicated question of the foundation of the Saxon bishoprics see Wiedemann, Die Sachsenbekehrung, pp. 67-95.

[21] Widukind, Rerum gestarum Saxonicarum Libri Tres II, 11; ed. Karolus Andreas Kehr, MGH, SS. rer. Germ. in usum schol. (Hanover and Leipzig, 1904), p. 65. See also a spurious letter of Leo III in PL 102, 1028-1029.

[22] Concilia aevi karolini I, #20; ed. Albertus Werminghoff, MGH, Leges, Sectio III, Tomus II¹, 172-176.

work was assigned to the bishopric of Salzburg, then occupied by one of Charlemagne's chief lieutenants, Arn, and perhaps later to the sees at Aquileia and Passau.[23] Another royal adviser, Alcuin, offered Charlemagne and his court extensive advice on how to win converts among the Slavs and Avars without engendering the violent resistance that had accompanied the conversion of the Saxons.[24] In the struggle against the Avars Charlemagne did not even leave it to Rome to order prayers to celebrate the Christian victory; he took that responsibility himself.[25] Rome's only noteworthy contribution to the institution of Christianity in this new area was the elevation of Arn to the rank of archbishop and the granting to him of the pallium, thus permitting him to create bishoprics in the newly converted territories. Leo III's letters concerning this matter indicate that the initiative lay with Charlemagne and that the pope was merely enacting the will of the king.[26] Leo expressed the situation perfectly when, in a letter to Charlemagne announcing that he had made Arn an archbishop as the king ordered, he began as follows: "Since the holy catholic and apostolic Roman church, enriched in all good things, has been exalted through your laborious royal efforts, it is fitting that we fullfil in every way your legislative wishes."[27] Since the victory for the true faith was completely the work of the king, the least the pope could do was to accede to royal plans and lend his authority to their completion.

If Charlemagne's missionary policy almost excluded the papacy, that of his successors made only slightly more room for Roman participation. The Scandinavian mission, initiated by Louis the Pious and continued by Louis the German, was no less a royal missionary venture than were the efforts that resulted in Charlemagne's conversion of the Saxons, Frisian, and Avars.[28] The only thing that was absent from ninth-century missionary activity in Denmark and Sweden was the Frankish army. Although every phase of the attempt to convert the Danes and the Swedes was instigated and controlled by the emperors, the ultimate progress of the mission required papal assistance. Both Louis the Pious and Louis the German called on Rome's services to implement their policies more frequently than did Charlemagne. Their actions identified the papacy more closely with missionary affairs than was the case in the last half of the eighth century, but left no more room for papal initiative.

Louis the Pious' first move to introduce Christianity into Denmark came in 822, when it was decided, probably at a diet at Frankfort,[29] to permit Ebo, archbishop of Rheims, to undertake a mission to Denmark. Before Ebo left for

[23] For the question of responsibility for converting the newly conquered Avars see *De conversione Bagoariorum et Carantanorum libellus*, 6; ed. Wattenbach, MGH, SS. XI, 9; Alcuin, Ep. #99, 107, 113; ed. Dümmler, MGH, Ep. IV, 143-144, 153-154, 163-166; MGH. *Diplomatum karolinorum* I, #211; ed. Mühlbacher, pp. 282-283.

[24] Besides his letters cited in the preceding note, see also Alcuin, *Ep.* #110, 111, 112; ed. Dümmler, MGH, Ep. IV, 157-163.

[25] *Epistolae variorum Carolo Magno regnante scriptae* #20; ed. Ernestus Dümmler, MGH, Ep. IV, 528-529.

[26] *Epistolae selectae pontificum Romanorum Carolo Magno et Ludowico Pio regnantibus scriptae* #3, 4, 5; ed. Karolus Hampe, MGH, Ep. V, 58-63; *De conversione Bagoariorum et Carantanorum libellus*, 8; ed. Wattenbach, MGH, SS. XI, 9-10.

[27] *Ep. sel. pont. Romanorum Carolo Magno et Ludowico Pio regnantibus scriptae* #4; ed. Hampe, MGH, Ep. V, 59: Dum per vestra laboriosa regalia certamina sancta catholica et apostolica Romana ecclesia de omnibus bonis ditata exultat, convenit nos in omnibus adimplere vestris legalibus votis.

[28] The essential sources revealing royal domination in the Scandinavian mission are *Ann. regni Franc.*, a. 823, 826; ed. Kurze, pp. 162-163, 169-170; Rimbert, *Vita Anskarii*; ed. G. Waitz, MGH, SS. rer. Germ. in usum schol. (Hanover, 1884), pp. 5-79; Ermoldus Nigellus, *In honorem Hludowici . . . carmen* IV, vv. 1882-1993, 2164-2529; ed. and tr. Edmond Faral in *Les Classiques de l'histoire de France au moyen âge* (Paris, 1932), pp. 144-152, 166-192.

[29] *Ann. regni Franc.*, a. 822; ed. Kurze, p. 159, mentions that Danish legates were present at the diet of Frankfort in October, 822. A letter of Anskar (PL 128, 1031-1032) says: . . . Ebo Rhemensis archiepiscopus . . . temporibus domini Ludovici imperatoris, cum consensu ipsius ac pene totius regni ejus synodi congregatae, Romam adiit. . . . This would suggest that Ebo's trip to Rome resulted from the diet at Frankfort and that the decision to send him to Denmark was made at that time.

Denmark in 823, he was sent to Rome by Louis to secure papal authorization for his missionary work.[30] Pope Pascal I (817-824) acceded to the imperial request, giving to Ebo a letter,[31] addressed to all clergymen, princes, and the Christian faithful, in which the archbishop was granted full authority to preach to the pagans in "northern lands."[32] Pascal based his grant upon his responsibility as pope to care for the flock and spread the heavenly word, repeating to a large extent the ideas of Gregory II in his commission to Boniface in 719.[33] Ebo was constituted a papal legate armed with full authority to do whatever was necessary by way of preaching and teaching the pagans he encountered. Pascal commissioned Halitgarius, bishop of Cambrai, as a colleague of Ebo, in order that communications could be maintained between Ebo and Rome. He especially enjoined Ebo to refer any difficulties he encountered in fulfilling his office to Rome for advice and decision. As a further means of assisting the conversion of the north, Pascal ordered all Christians to aid the missionaries in every way possible and especially by supplying the needs of the journey. He promised eternal rewards to those who were helpful to the missionaries and excommunication for those who acted in such a way as to impede the work. Implicit throughout the letter is the assumption that the constitution of missionary ventures was a papal prerogative. Christian society must have placed some value on this aspect of papal authority; otherwise Louis would not have taken the trouble to send Ebo on a special journey to Rome. Perhaps Pascal had gone beyond Louis' request when he sought to make Ebo accountable to Rome for the conduct of the mission, since there is no evidence to suggest that the connection of Halitgarius to the mission was inspired by Louis. At least by implication Pascal was reasserting the policy of Gregory II toward missions and was again pressing the papacy into missionary affairs.

Ebo's mission was not a success[34] and he soon returned to Francia, apparently having no further relations with the papacy on the matter. Further political developments were necessary to encourage the Frankish crown to send another mission to Denmark. In 826 Harald, his family, and some of his followers were baptized under the sponsorship of Louis.[35] When Harald returned to Denmark, it was decided to send with him a priest who could serve as his chaplain and try to promote the spread of Christianity in Denmark. Louis and his advisers chose Anskar.[36] Again the papacy was called upon to lend its authority to this venture. Eugenius II (824-827), at the request of Ebo, commended Anskar and his associates to all the faithful.[37] Beyond this the new venture proceeded without papal aid. Anskar's efforts in Denmark were not encouraging, especially in view of the fact that Harald was forced to flee in 827.[38] Anskar next turned his efforts to Sweden, encouraged by the appearance of Swedish legates at the Frankish court in 829 bearing a report that their king would permit Christian missionaries in his land.[39] A two year stay in Sweden convinced Anskar that prospects were good for a major Christian victory. In 831 he returned to his

[30] Ann. regni Franc., a. 823; ed. Kurze, p. 163, says that Ebo went to Denmark "consilio imperatoris et auctoritate Romani pontificis praedicandi gratia. . . ."

[31] Ep. sel. pont. Romanorum Carolo Magno et Ludowico Pio regnantibus scriptae #11; ed. Hampe, MGH, Ep. V, 69-71.

[32] Ibid., p. 69: partibus quilonis.

[33] See above, pp. 73-74.

[34] Ann. regni Franc., a. 823; ed. Kurze, p. 163, and Ermolus Nigellus, In honorem Hludowici . . . carmen IV, vv. 2028-2061; ed. Faral, pp. 154-156, give Ebo credit for many converts. However, absolutely no other evidence can be found to suggest that Christianity had made any permanent foot-

holds when Anskar went to Denmark in 826.

[35] For accounts of this event, see Ann. regni Franc., a. 826; ed. Kurze, pp. 169-170; Ermoldus Nigellus, In honorem Hludowici . . . carmen IV, vv. 2164-2529; ed. Faral, pp. 166-192.

[36] Rimbert, Vita Anskarii, 7; ed. Waitz, pp. 26-29.

[37] See addition to a letter of Pascal in MGH, Ep. V, 70, note 4.

[38] For Anskar's first mission to Denmark, see Rimbert, Vita Anskarii, 8; ed. Waitz, p. 30.

[39] Ibid., p. 30.

chief benefactor, Louis the Pious, to urge the broadening of the northern mission.[40] Louis immediately took steps to promote the conversion of the north. His new plan again required the services of the papacy. The emperor "burning with the ardor of the faith began to seek how he might be able to constitute an episcopal see in the northern parts, that is, on the frontiers of his empire; for thence it would be suitable for the bishop seated there to go more frequently into those parts in order to preach and thence all of the barbarian nations would be able to take the sacrament of divine mystery more easily and more fully."[41] The result was the creation of a new archbishopric at Hamburg and the elevation of Anskar to the new see. Although this whole action was taken by the imperial court, Rome's approval was sought, "so that all of this would retain the perpetual vigor of stability."[42] Anskar was sent to Rome along with imperial emissaries to request papal confirmation for the new see. Gregory IV (827-844) confirmed the new see. He granted Anskar the pallium, further strengthening the new archbishop's position. Gregory also made Anskar papal legate to the Danes, Swedes, Slavs, and all other people in the north, with full authority to evangelize, a position that Anskar was to share with Ebo, who already had such a commission from Pascal. Gregory threatened to punish those who interfered with Anskar. Especially important from a missionary viewpoint was a grant of authority to ordain new bishops.[43]

The remainder of Anskar's missionary career evolved around the attempt to Christianize the Danes and Swedes from an archiepiscopal center located within Frankish boundaries. Anskar and his associates enjoyed only minor successes until his death in 865. What little help Anskar did receive came from the Frankish crown, and especially Louis the German, who sought to reconstruct a base for missionary activity by joining the sees of Hamburg and Bremen after Hamburg had been destroyed by a Danish raid. The royal hand was not strong enough to command permanent respect in the north and thus Anskar usually had to rely on his own personal appeal in his attempt to win converts. The division of the empire in 840 deprived him of his property outside the kingdom of Louis the German and forced him to close his school in Hamburg.[44] Certainly the papacy did little to promote the work of its legate. Sergius II (844-847) apparently renewed in a bull of 846 the concessions of Gregory IV, reaffirming Anskar as archbishop of Hamburg, extending his authority over all converts won in the north, and granting him the use of the pallium. Along with that new concession went words of encouragement and especially the advice to construct new churches, ordain priests, and consecrate new bishops.[45] Perhaps this renewal was of significance at the moment, since Anskar had only recently been forced to flee from Hamburg before a Danish raid which had wiped out the fruits of his labor in that city. Leo IV (847-855) may also have confirmed Anskar's authority, although the only evidence for such action rests on a falsified bull of 849.[46] It was only with the pontificate of Nicholas I (858-867) that the papacy took a renewed and more positive interest in the Scandinavian mission. However, Nicholas' missionary

[40] For Anskar's work in Sweden between 829 and 831, see ibid., 9-11, pp. 30-33.

[41] Ibid., 12, p. 33: . . . ardore fidei succensus, quaerere coepit, quomodo in partibus aquilonis, in fine videlicet imperii sui, sedem constituere posset episcopalem, unde congruum esset episcopo ibi consistenti causa praedicationis illas frequentius adire partes, et unde etiam omnes illae barbarae nationes facilius uberiusque capere valerent divini mysterii sacramenta. For Louis' part in the creation of the new see, ibid., 12, pp. 33-34, and Ludowici Pii Praeceptum de missione S. Anskarii ejusque ordinatione; PL 118, 1033-1036.

[42] Rimbert, Vita Anskarii, 13; ed. Waitz, p. 34: . . . ut haec omnia perpetuum suae stabilitatis retinerent vigorem. . . .

[43] For Gregory IV's grant, see ibid., 13, p. 35; Gregory's letter of confirmation in PL 118, 1035-1036. The text of this letter is heavily interpolated.

[44] For Anskar's missionary work after he became archbishop of Hamburg, see Rimbert, Vita Anskarii, 15, ff.; ed. Waitz pp. 36 ff.

[45] PL 129, 997-1000.

[46] PL 129, 999.

policy in the north was a part of a new papal missionary program and must be left for a later treatment.

While Anskar was attempting to extend Christianity into the Scandinavian world, missionaries were also pressing into the Slavic world on the eastern frontier of the Frankish empire. The effort was especially successful in Carinthia and Pannonia, where Charlemagne's armies had crushed Avar power in 796. The main missionary burden was borne by the bishops of Salzburg, Aquileia, and Passau. The Frankish rulers, and especially Louis the German, gave vital support to this effort by maintaining constant military pressure, encouraging colonization, furnishing liberal endowments to the missionary bishops, and supporting Christianized Slavic princes in the area.[47] Farther to the north Christianity gained some ground among the Czechs, Bohemians, and Moravians. Again it was a combination of Bavarian bishops and Frankish rulers that accounted for success. Progress was not rapid among these peoples and the Christian establishment always lacked stability because of the pronounced resistance offered by some Slavic rulers, apparently fearful that the new religion spelled German domination. However, by the middle of the ninth century some evidence suggests that many Slavs in this area had accepted Christianity. The Slavs along the lower course of the Elbe were hardly touched by missionary activity, even though this area was part of the missionary territory of Anskar.[48]

In all of the missionary activity among the Slavs the papacy took no part. There is not a trace of papal interest in the diplomacy and warfare involved in extending the Christian frontier, in the activities of the Bavarian bishoprics, or in the efforts of Christianized Slavic princes to convert their subjects. Probably the papal lack of concern offers further proof of the absence of a papal missionary policy throughout the last half of the eighth and first half of the ninth centuries. Unless the Frankish rulers needed assistance and requested or ordered papal compliance, the popes left missionary matters to other agencies. In the case of the missionary work among the Slavs nothing was needed from Rome. The conversion of these territories had not progressed far enough to require a special organization. The ambitious Bavarian bishops were eager to supply the personnel for missionary work and to retain any converts under their authority. Frankish diplomacy and military might, plus the interest of Slavic princes in currying Frankish favor, created sufficient opportunity for Christian expansion. Disciplinary questions and missionary procedural problems arising out of the Slavic missionary effort were settled at the Frankish court. Rome had nothing to add to this armory of missionary weapons and thus was excluded.

The failure of the papacy to continue after 750 the aggressive missionary policy it enacted before 750 perhaps needs no comment beyond the paucity of evidence of papal participation in the stirring missionary successes outlined above. However, the whole atmosphere surrounding the ferocious assault of the Carolingian princes on paganism suggests that the papacy contributed more to the course of missionary affairs than is revealed in the record of actual missionary events. Charlemagne himself gave the major clue to his missionary zeal in a letter to Leo III in 796. Writing to define his concept of the relationship between

[47] The chief source describing the expansion of Christianity in this area from Charlemagne's death until the pontificate of Nicholas I is De Conversione Bagaoriorum et Carantanorum libellus, 9-14; ed. Wattenbach, MGH, SS. XI, 10-14, dealing with the activities of the archbishop of Salzburg. See also Hauck Kirchengeschichte II, pp. 711-715; Ernst Dümmler, Geschichte des ostfränkischen Reiches I (2 ed., Leipzig, 1887-1888), pp. 29-38; II, pp. 174-178.

[48] The information revealing the progress of Christianity among the Czechs, Bohemians, and Moravians is extremely limited and scattered through a variety of sources. For reviews, see Hauck, Kirchengeschichte II, pp. 716-718; Dümmler, Geschichte des ostfränkischen Reiches I, pp. 32-33, 285-286, 298-299, 345-346, 356, 388-390, 416-417, 426-427; II, pp. 21-25, 51, 178-179.

king and pope, he argued as follows: "This is our power: to defend by arms with the aid of divine piety the Holy Church of Christ everywhere from the incursions of pagans and from the devastations of infidels from without and to fortify the knowledge of the Catholic faith within."[49] Wars against the pagans and their subjugation were an important part of Charlemagne's theocratic concept of the role of the secular prince in Christian society.[50] He had a God-given duty "to defend the Church of Christ from the incursions of pagans and to propagate the faith."[51] Throughout the whole missionary picture of this era there existed an underlying assumption that the expansion of the Christian realm was a duty impinging on kingship, that every victory over the pagans was a testimonial of divine favor shining upon the Frankish rulers.[52] Royal missionary effort was a concomitant of Carolingian theocracy.

Leo III must have been pleased to read Charlemagne's letter. All the popes of the period must have, in the words of Hadrian I, "extended their palms to heaven, giving the highest praises to the King of Kings and the Lord of Lords, beseeching His divine and ineffable clemency that . . . He grant [the Frankish rulers] many victories over [their] enemies and bring all pagan nations under [their] heels,"[53] when they heard of the missionary successes of the Frankish kings. Throughout almost the whole eighth century the papacy had been beseeching the Frankish monarchs to assume the very attitude Charlemagne expressed above and to do what Hadrian was expressing thanks for, namely, to crush those who stood in the way of the Church. Even a sampling of papal thinking will illustrate how strongly the popes urged the Carolingians to assume a more positive role in caring for the Church. Repeatedly the papacy begged Pepin the Short, Carlomann, and Charlemagne to become defenders of the Church.[54] Pope after pope avowed that "God Almighty having predestined" the Frankish rulers "from their mothers' wombs, and blessed and annointed them as kings, constituted them defenders and liberators of His Holy Church."[55] The Franks were often referred to as God's chosen people, especially selected for the defence of Christendom.[56] God was on their side in their wars.[57] Their kings were the only refuge after God, left to the papacy and the Church as a whole,[58] standing as an "unconquerable wall"[59] against the evils of the day. Again and again the papacy called on the Frankish king to arise as a new Moses or David or Constantine to deliver the Church from its perils.[60] The papacy never ceased

[49] Alcuin, *Ep.* #93; ed. Dümmler, MGH, Ep. IV, 137: Nostrum est: secundum auxilium divinae pietatis sanctam undique Christi ecclesiam ab incursu paganorum et ab infidelium devastatione armis defendere foris, et intus catholicae fidei agnitione munire. For other expressions of the same idea by Charlemagne, see *Capitularia regum Francorum;* ed. Alfredus Boretius, MGH, Leges, Sectio II, Tomus I, #12, 1, p. 44; #33, 5, p. 93; #45, 15, p. 129.
[50] The best discussion of the general idea involved here is H. X. Arquillière, *L'Augustinisme politique* (Paris, 1934).
[51] Alcuin, *Ep.* #171; ed. Dummler, MGH, Ep. IV, 282.
[52] *Epistolae variorum Carolo Magno regnante scriptae* #20; ed. Dümmler, MGH, Ep. IV, 528-529, for a letter written by Charlemagne to Queen Fastrada expressing the idea that the victory over the Avars in 796 was a God-given one.
[53] *Codex Carolinus* #50; ed. Gundlach, MGH, Ep. III, 570: extensis palmis ad aethera, regi regum et domino dominantium opimas laudes retulimus, enixius deprecantes ineffabilem eius divinam clementiam . . . multipliciter de hostibus victorias tribuat

omnesque barbaras nationes vestris substernat vestigiis.
[54] Nearly every letter in the *Codex Carolinus* centres around this idea.
[55] *Ibid.,* #16, p. 513: . . . Deus omnipotens ex utero matris tuae te predistinatum habens, ideo te benedicens et in regem ungens, defensorem te et liberatorem sanctae suae ecclesias constituit. . . For the same idea, see *ibid.,* #6, 20, 22, 26, 33, 35, 36, 98, 99, pp. 488-489, 522, 526, 530, 539-540, 543, 544, 649-650, 652; Leo III, *Epistolae X,* #2; ed. Karolus Hampe, MGH, Ep. V, 89.
[56] For examples, see *Codex Carolinus,* #39, 45; ed. Gundlach, MGH, Ep. III, 551-552, 561.
[57] *Ibid.,* #61, pp. 588-589.
[58] *Ibid.,* #22, 34, pp. 526, 541-542; Leo III, *Epistolae X,* #2, 9; ed. Hampe, MGH, Ep. V, 89, 101.
[59] For the use of this expression see *Codex Carolinus* #17, 20; ed. Gundlach, MGH, Ep. III, 516, 522.
[60] *Ibid.,* #3, 11, 33, 39, 42, 43, 68, 98, 99, pp. 479-480, 505, 539-540, 551-552, 554-555, 557, 597, 649, 652.

praying that the Franks would win tremendous victories over all pagan nations and that their boundaries would expand without hindrance.[61] Rome repeatedly gave guarantees that, since the pope held the keys to the eternal kingdom, the Frankish rulers were assured of salvation as long as they cared for the Church.

These expressions demonstrate that the reasoning used by the popes to justify their pleas for Frankish help in the eighth and early ninth centuries reflected most of the ideas upon which Carolingian theocratic concepts were based. The popes who argued so insistently in the context cited above ought to be given credit for their contribution in schooling the Carolingian princes in the ideas that produced the brilliant missionary successes. The feat of inspiring the heirs of a Merovingian mayor of the palace to become rulers with a deep sense of responsibility for the welfare of Christendom was perhaps the most fundamental development of the eighth century. Those who partook of the effort were shapers of almost every success enjoyed by the Carolingian rulers. In this sense, then, one might conclude that the papacy played a larger missionary role than the missionary record spanning the years 750 to 850 alone shows. Several popes helped to mold the thinking of the dynasty of kings who dedicated themselves to serving the Church and defending it against its enemies. Out of this sense of duty came, at least in part, the Carolingian urge to spread the faith and as a result the successful wars against paganism. The papacy felt no misgivings about the course of events; their "adopted sons"[62] performed well in doing what the popes had so long begged them to do, namely, to assume the responsibility for the safety and welfare of Christendom. They were in no sense aware of being deprived of participation in the missionary ventures of the period; instead they stood in their rightful position as shepherd of the flock, having shaped a mighty instrument for defeating God's enemies in the shape of the "strong right arm"[63] of the Franks, "the propagators and defenders of the Christian religion."[64]

V.

By the middle of the ninth century the royal missionary effort of the Carolingians began to falter. Internal difficulties continually detracted the rulers from missionary affairs and interfered with missionary work already in progress.[1] Barbarian assaults against the weakened Carolingian state became bolder, resulting in devastating effects on newly established Christian outposts.[2] Slavic states on the eastern frontier defied the Carolingians more openly than ever and caused a growing concern, especially in the realm of Louis the German.[3] By 860 the troubled empire was considerably less able to uphold the cross than it had been earlier in the century. Certainly the hopes for expansion had dimmed considerably, as Anskar's travail in Denmark and Sweden demonstrated so clearly.

The paralysis among the Franks set the stage for a new outburst of papal missionary activity. Nicholas I, exhibiting the same forcefulness that characterized his whole policy, was chiefly responsible for thrusting the papacy into a

[61] *Ibid.*, #8, 13, 17, 24, 26, 35, 37, 50, 52, 53, 55, 62, 66, 68, 72, 73, 75, 88, 89, 92, 99, pp. 498, 510, 516, 528, 531, 543, 550, 570, 574, 575, 579, 589-590, 594, 597, 603, 604, 606, 625, 626, 630, 652.

[62] *Ibid.*, #10, p. 501.

[63] For examples of the papal use of this expression, see ibid., #13, 59, 98, 99, pp. 510, 585, 649, 651.

[64] As Charlemagne was addressed by Theodomar, abbot of Montecassino; *Epistolae variorum Carolo Magno regnante scriptae* #13; ed. Dümmler, MGH, Ep. IV, 510.

[1] Rimbert, *Vita Anskarii*, 21; ed. Waitz, pp. 46-47, relates how the death of Louis the Pious and the division of his empire deprived Anskar of a monastery located in western Francia which had been one of his chief sources of material support in his northern mission.

[2] *Ibid.*, 16-18, pp. 37-39, for the drastic effects of a Danish raid on the missionary center at Hamburg and the repercussions on missionary work in general.

[3] See especially, Dümmler, *Geschichte des ostfränkischen Reiches* I, 426, 427; II, 21-25, for an estimate of the Slavic threat, especially from the Moravians.

position of leadership in missionary affairs after a long period of inactivity. Indeed, his far-reaching schemes for adding to the Christian realm, all of them powerfully motivated by his strong sense of papal overlordship over Christian affairs, was one of the most notable features of his pontificate. His policies virtually determined papal missionary interests for the rest of the ninth century.

One of Nicholas' first missionary concerns was to lend his assistance to the tenuous Scandinavian mission. Anskar had for many years been struggling to win new advantages in Denmark, chiefly by exerting his personal influence over the Danish rulers. He enjoyed some success in his relationship with Horic II, in spite of the latter's initial hostility to Christianity.[4] In 864 an emissary of Louis the German was able to report to Nicholas that Horic would soon accept baptism, news which prompted Nicholas to rejoice and to pray that the conversion would soon occur. Horic himself added to these high hopes by sending gifts to Rome.[5] Nicholas, in an action that had not been paralleled since the pontificate of Gregory II, immediately addressed a letter to Horic urging his conversion. The pope's argument centered around two fundamental points: the power of the Christian God and the blessings of eternal life. He took pains to contrast the impotence of the "deaf, mute, and blind idols" that Horic now worshipped with the "Almighty, all-embracing, indescribable, immense, infinite, simple, unchangeable, uncircumscribed, immortal, all good, all merciful, all holy" Christian God. Only the Christian God could provide the king with a relief from the miseries, dangers, strife, insecurity, and fleeting glory of the present life, where all the kingdoms that man could create disappear as a result of the ambitions of other men or of death. Only the true God could give that life "where there is joy without sorrow, fullness without nausea, continued health, indefinite life, peace without end, constant security, and eternal glory." Moreover, the Christian God was alone capable of aiding his servants in the affairs of this life.[6] Throughout the appeal Nicholas sought to place Christianity in a context that might be understood by a Danish prince who ruled over a state long torn by internal strife and constantly engaged in warfare and who perhaps had demonstrated his envy for his prosperous Christian neighbors, the Franks, by his raids on their territories.

Nicholas also acted to strengthen the Scandinavian mission by lending his authority to the settlement of the long standing dispute over the combined see of Hamburg-Bremen, which Louis the German had created as a missionary outpost. The archbishop of Cologne insisted that Bremen pertained to his province and demanded that it be returned to him. In 864 Louis referred the case to Rome in order to confirm a decision made by a royal synod in opposition to the claims of Cologne. Anskar sent a representative to present his case.[7] Nicholas ordered that the existing arrangement be respected. Bremen was to remain separate from Cologne and was to continue to serve as archiepiscopal see for the Danes and the Swedes. Nicholas' defence of his action was based primarily on the necessity of this arrangement as a missionary step. He called attention to the poverty of Hamburg, especially since it had lost the monastery of Turholt, located in the kingdom of Charles the Bald. Following the action of Gregory IV he also granted Anskar the pallium and renewed the commission of Anskar to preach to the Danes, Swedes, Slavs, and all others located in those parts. Nicholas threatened to anathematize any who interfered with this settlement in the future.[8] In no sense did Nicholas' action represent a radical departure from

---

[4] Rimbert, *Vita Anskarii*, 31-32; ed. Waitz, pp. 63-64.

[5] Nicholas, *Ep.* #26, 27; ed. Ernestus Perels, MGH, Ep. VI, 292-294, reports these events.

[6] *Ibid.*, #27, pp. 293-294.

[7] The main events of this dispute are outlined in Rimbert, *Vita Anskarii*, 23; ed. Waitz, pp. 48-51.

[8] Nicholas reported his decision to Louis the German in *Ep.* #26; ed. Perels, MGH, Ep. VI, 291-292. His bull confirming the see of Hamburg-Bremen (see PL 119, 876-879; Rimbert, *Vita Anskarii*, 23; ed. Waitz, pp. 49-51) supplies his justification for his action and grants to Anskar once again the necessary missionary powers.

established policy. He repeatedly indicated that his action was nothing more than a confirmation of a previous papal action and the dictates of the German rulers. Nonetheless, his firm support of the attempt to maintain an archiepiscopal see as a spearhead for missionary work in Scandinavia probably proved valuable to Anskar. Just prior to his death in 865 Anskar sent to the German king and to German bishops a letter containing his papal privileges. He begged everyone to respect their provisions as an assurance of the future well-being of the mission in the north.[9] Certainly he was able to end his life with his archiepiscopal see intact and to leave as his successor a tried disciple, Rimbert, who soon received the pallium from Nicholas and thus was able to carry on the missions.[10]

Nicholas may also have tried to lend papal assistance in still another area in the process of being converted. Sometime during his pontificate he wrote to a certain Osbald in Carinthia, giving him instructions on how to deal with disciplinary problems among the clergy there, including that of handling priests who had killed pagans.[11] Osbald was serving as chorepiscopus in Carinthia, having been assigned to that position by the archbishop of Salzburg, to whose province Carinthia pertained. Heretofore, this missionary venture had been tightly controlled by Salzburg.[12] Osbald's request for guidance from Rome and Nicholas' reply without reference to the archbishop of Salzburg indicate a more independent papal policy. Perhaps Nicholas was aware that the Slavic princes in that area were restive under German rule and was encouraging a more independent attitude.

Meanwhile, a new victory for Christianity was in the making, offering to the papacy an opportunity for action in an area that had not previously been a concern of the western Church. In 865 the Bulgar king, Boris, accepted baptism from a Byzantine ecclesiastic and undertook to convert his kingdom.[13] His decision was probably influenced by the steady penetration of his kingdom by Greek influences, including Christianity, for many years prior to 865. Diplomatic considerations, however, provided the immediate impetus. Boris had allied himself with the Franks in 863 for the purpose of destroying the powerful Moravian state that had disquieted both Boris and Louis the German. Boris indicated a willingness to accept Christianity as a part of the Frankish agreement, although no immediate steps were taken to affect his conversion.[14] The Moravians countered this alliance by seeking aid in Constantinople. When a famine struck Boris' kingdom in 864, the Byzantine armies invaded his territory and forced Boris to surrender. Included in the price he paid for peace was the acceptance of Christianity. Once having made his decision and in spite of a revolt by some of his subjects against the new religion,[15] Boris went about the task of converting

---

[9] *Epistolae variorum inde a saeculo nono medio usque ad morten Karoli II (Calvi) imperatoris collectae* #16; ed. Ernestus Dümmler, MGH, Ep. VI, 163; Rimbert, *Vita Anskarii*, 41; ed. Waitz, p. 75; *Vita Rimberti*, 11; ed. G. Waitz, MGH, SS. rer. Germ. in usum schol. (Hanover, 1894), pp. 89-90.

[10] PL 119, 962.

[11] Nicholas, *Ep.* #142; ed. Perels, MGH, Ep. VI, 660-661.

[12] For missionary developments in this area about this time, see *De Conversione Bagoariorum et Carantanorum libellus*, 9-14; ed. Wattenbach, MGH, SS. XI, 10-14.

[13] The chief sources for the actual conversion of the Bulgar king are Greek and present conflicting accounts. For an examination of these sources and for the background of Boris' conversion see Dvornik, *Les Slaves, Byzance, et Rome au IXe siècle*, pp. 99-104, 184-190; J. B. Bury, *A History of the Eastern Empire from the Fall of Irene*

to the Accession of Basil I (A.D. 802-867) (London, 1912), pp. 381-386; Matthew Spinka, *A History of Christianity in the Balkans*, in *Studies in Church History* I, ed. Matthew Spinka and Robert Hastings Nichols (Chicago, 1933), pp. 25-33.

[14] Louis so reported to Rome; Nicholas, *Ep.* #26; ed. Perels, MGH, Ep. VI, 293. See also *Annales Bertiniani*, a. 864; ed. G. Waitz, MGH, SS. rer. Germ. in usum schol. (Hanover, 1883), p. 72.

[15] *Ann. Bertiniani*, a. 866; ed. Waitz, pp. 85-86, describes this revolt; there are also references to it in Nicholas, *Ep.* #99; ed. Perels, MGH, Ep. VI, 577; Ioannes Zonoras, *Epitomae Historiarum* XVI, 2; ed. Theodoro Büttner-Wobst, *Corpus Scriptores Historiae Byzantinae* III (Bonn, 1897), 387-389; Theophanes Continuatus, *Chronographia* IV, 14-15; ed. I. Bekker, *Corpus Scriptores Historiae Byzantinae* (Bonn, 1838), pp. 163-165.

his people with vigor. At first he was guided by the Byzantine church. Not only were Greek clergymen sent into his territory; no less a person than the patriarch Photius sent a long letter of guidance to Boris, laying upon his royal shoulders most of the responsibility for the Christianization of the Bulgars and pointing out the steps which the Bulgars needed to take before being acceptable as civilized Christians.[16] For some reason, perhaps the refusal of Photius to concede ecclesiastical independence to the Bulgar church, Boris grew tired of his bargain with the Greeks. In 866 he sent representatives to the West seeking aid for his new Christian establishment.

One Bulgar delegation appeared at Regensburg to solicit the aid of Louis the German. In 867 the bishop of Passau went to Bulgaria with a party of priests equipped for missionary work. Upon his arrival the bishop found the field already occupied by a mission sent from Rome and thereupon withdrew.[17] The presence of Roman missionaries in Bulgaria was the result of Nicholas' prompt response to Boris' other delegation, which had been sent to Rome, where it arrived in August, 866. The Bulgars arrived in Rome bearing gifts and requesting from Nicholas priests for missionary service and advice on a series of pressing problems connected with the institution of the new religion in Bulgaria.[18] This perhaps was a development Nicholas had not expected. Two years before in 864 he seemed content to entrust the spread of Christianity in Bulgaria to the Germans; at that time he had received the news of a treaty between the Franks and the Bulgars with joy and indicated his anticipation of the news of the Bulgar conversion, which Louis the German reported was imminent, offering only to pray for the success of the venture.[19] In 866 he showed no such deference to other potential missionary agencies. Instead he promptly assumed the leadership of the new Christian establishment in Bulgaria and undertook to shape it according to his wishes.

His first action was to direct a party of missionary priests to Bulgaria, ordering them to preach to the Bulgars, many of whom were not yet baptized. Nicholas was not content to let the Bulgar situation rest at this point. At the head of the mission he placed two important bishops, Formosus of Porta and Paul of Populonia. These men were carefully prepared for their task. Nicholas gave them instructions prior to their departure.[20] He empowered them to settle a wide variety of problems posed by Boris in his request for information from the pope. The bishops were fully equipped with a collection of canons, a missal, and a penitential to serve as guides in their assault on paganism and their attempts to create a religious establishment in Bulgaria.[21] Most important of all, the legates were authorized to take steps toward organizing the Bulgarian church. Nicholas empowered them to consecrate new bishops when necessary. They were ordered to report back to Rome on the number of Christians in Bulgaria, whereupon the papacy would decide whether an archiepiscopal see was warranted and would create one if necessary. He would permit the Bulgars to choose a candidate for that see from among the bishops operating in their land. Nicholas made it perfectly clear, however, that Boris' dream of a patriarchate was out of the question.[22] In setting forth so clear a program for his legates, the

---

[16] PG 102, 628-698. Nicholas' long letter to Boris in 866 (*Ep.* #99; ed. Perels, MGH, *Ep.* VI, 568-600) shows the heavy influence of the Greek clergy in Bulgaria and makes several references to the presence of the Greeks.

[17] *Ann. Bertiniani*, a. 866; ed. Waitz, p. 86; *Ann. Fuldenses*, a. 866, 867; ed Fridericus Kurze, MGH, SS. rer. Germ. in usum schol. (Hanover, 1891), pp. 65-66.

[18] *Liber pontificalis* II, ed. Duchesne, p. 164.

[19] Nicholas, *Ep.* #26; ed. Perels, MGH, *Ep.* VI, 293.

[20] *Liber pontificalis* II, ed. Duchesne, p. 164; Anastasius Bibliothecarius, *Epistolae sive Praefationes* #5; ed. E. Perels and G. Laehr, MGH, *Ep.* VII, 412.

[21] The nature of Nicholas' orders to his bishops is revealed in his letter to Boris containing the one hundred and six responses to questions raised by the latter; *Ep.* #99; ed. Perels, MGH, *Ep.* VI, 568-600; see especially 106, pp. 599-600.

[22] *Ibid.*, 72-73, pp. 592-593.

pope created a definite procedure within which the conversion and final organization of Bulgaria could be completed.

Nicholas, realizing the role that the Bulgar king must play in the Christianization of the Bulgars, did not neglect to encourage and enlighten him. The papal legates departed for Bulgaria bearing books that Boris requested, including a collection of laws, penitentials, and a missal. They also bore a remarkable document containing answers to questions raised by Boris through his ambassadors to Rome.[23] The content reveals that the papacy realized clearly the difficulties besetting Boris in his new venture. "You [Boris] beseeched us as a suppliant that we bestow upon you just as on other peoples a true and perfect Christianity, having no blemishes or flaws. You say that there came into your land many from diverse places, i.e., Greeks, Armenians, and those from elsewhere, who according to their own will, spoke in many and various ways. On account of this you ask to be told which of all of these in their various interpretations to obey and what you ought to do." Confusion, lack of order, absence of a final authority thus offset all the good intentions of Boris in his attempts to convert his people. The papacy could fill this need. "In truth we are not sufficient in these things, but our sufficiency is in God. Blessed Peter, who lives and presides in his see, gives to those who seek the truth. For the Holy Roman Church was always without blemish or flaw . . ."[24] Nicholas placed himself as the final authority on any problem concerning the faith and its practice. In this capacity he had an answer for any problem presented by Boris and proceeded to set forth his answers in full.

Nicholas' responses ranged over a variety of subects. The question of proper religious observances was obviously foremost in Boris' mind. Nicholas laid down concise rules on such things as the performance of baptism (c. 14, 15, 71, 104), the administration of communion (c. 9, 65, 71), burial customs (c. 98, 99, 100), conduct of the laity at church services (c. 54, 58, 66, 68), the necessary religious preparations prior to battle (c. 33, 35, 36), prayer (c. 53, 56, 61), religious processions (c. 7, 8), dietary observances (c. 4, 5, 53, 57, 60, 90, 91), and the observance of feast days (c. 10, 11, 12, 33, 36). He sent a missal and a penitential for enlightening the Bulgars on the proper reading of the mass and on the treatment of sinners (c. 75, 76), entrusting to his legates to explain the use of each. He was especially explicit in explaining the major observances for the Lenten season (c. 44, 45, 46, 47, 48, 50). Marriage regulations and sexual practices also received major attention (c. 2, 3, 4, 29, 39, 48, 49, 50, 51, 63, 64, 68, 96). From this list it becomes obvious that Nicholas intended to be considered the final authority on all matters concerning ritual and discipline. What topics had not been dealt with in his letter were left to his legates, "who would instruct [Boris] and inform [him] abundantly of what [he] ought to do."[25] Rome, then, assumed the responsibility for instituting the proper religious observances in a newly converted land.

Nicholas did not confine his advice on religious matters to problems of ritual and discipline only. He provided Boris with a set of principles to be used in completing the conversion of his subjects. He ordered that the king refrain

[23] This letter, cited above in note 21, will be referred to in the following paragraphs simply by inserting the proper chapter number into the text, unless there is some necessity of including additional material, in which case a footnote will be used.

[24] *Ibid.*, 106, pp. 599-600: Postremo deprecamini nos suppliciter, ut vobis, quemadmodum ceteris gentibus, veram et perfectam Christianitatem non habentem maculam aut rugam largiamur, asserentes, quod in patriam vestram multi ex diversis locis Christiani advenerint, qui, prout voluntas eorum existit, multa et varia loquuntur, id est Graeci, Armeni et ex caeteris locis. Quapropter juberi poscitis, utrum omnibus his secundum varios sensus eorum oboedire an quid facere debeatis. Verum nos in his non sumus sufficientes, 'sed sufficientis nostra ex Deo est;' et beatus Petrus, qui in sede sua vivit et praesidet, dat quaerentibus fidei veritatem. Nam et sancta Romana ecclesia semper sine macula fuit et sine ruga. . . .

[25] *Ibid.*, 106, p. 600: qui vos instruant et, quid agere debeatis, abundanter erudiant.

from forceful conversions. Admonitions and pleas were the only valid means of softening the hardened hearts of pagans. Nicholas suggested that it might be effective to cease dining or associating with pagans as a means of impressing upon them the gravity of their adherence to paganism. In the final analysis God would act in His own time to convert them (c. 41, 102). The case of apostates was somewhat different. The pope advised stern measures for those who would not return to Christianity after proper warning (c. 18). As a step towards the completion of the conversion of Bulgaria Nicholas explained the basic principles of the organization of the universal church and informed Boris of the position of the Bulgar church in that scheme (c. 72, 73, 92, 93, 106). Wherever church organization was considered, Nicholas made Rome's primacy explicit. He warned Boris that the problem of discipline of the clergy was not within royal power, laying down the principle that temporal authorities were to be judged and not to judge wherever the interests of the clergy were at stake (c. 83). Nicholas again demonstrated a broad concept of papal missionary responsibility. Everything from proselytizing to the organization of a new church must proceed under papal supervision and through papal guidance.

On still another score Nicholas placed himself in a position of guide and mentor to the recently converted king. He undertook to furnish advice concerning a wide range of civil affairs connected with Boris' governance of his people. Nicholas made the assumption throughout his letter that temporal affairs had a relevance to the spiritual order and fell within the papal domain. As a guide to the conduct of civil affairs Nicholas sent a law code with his legates, advising Boris to use it only with the advice of those capable of interpreting it (c. 13). Besides this general guide in civil affairs, Nicholas offered the king his opinion on such problems as treatment of rebels (c. 17, 19), judicial procedures (c. 12, 45, 84, 86), handling of fugitives (c. 20, 21, 25), the conduct of war (c. 23, 33, 36, 40, 46), the punishment of certain criminals (c. 24, 26, 27, 28, 30, 31), diplomatic relations (c. 80, 81, 82), and the treatment of slaves (c. 97). Boris was led to believe that the Church through its head possessed the wisdoms to guide a king in his rule over a Christian kingdom.

As impressive as the range of subjects on which Nicholas offered guidance was the spirit in which the advice was offered. The pope approached all the Bulgar problems with an attitude of leniency arising from his realization that he was dealing with new converts who could not be expected to practice Christianity perfectly. Strict observance of the laws of abstinence were not required because the pope, realizing that the Bulgars "were up to now pagan and still ought to be nourished on milk, could not put a heavy yoke on [them] until [they] were ready for solid food."[20] He took special pains to refute those teachers of the Bulgars who were insisting on a strict observance of Old Testament rules, especially in matters of diet (c. 43), seeking to avoid making the new faith too heavy a burden. Nicholas was satisfied that for the moment the Bulgars believed in God and were baptized. He was firm in counseling a repudiation of pagan customs, especially those that reflected idolatry (c. 33, 35, 40, 55, 63, 67, 79). However, he did not heap scorn on Bulgar customs and conceded that some of them, like the custom of wearing pantaloons (c. 59) or of the king taking his meals apart from all company (c. 42), need not be rejected. Whenever he called upon Boris to end an obnoxious practice, Nicholas was careful to supply a substitute. For instance, he advised that the Bulgars carry a cross into battle as an insignia in place of the traditional horse's tail (c. 33; see also c. 35, 40, 55). Even where he was aware that the Bulgars were being misled by the Greeks, Nicholas engaged in no vituperation, which might have been expected in view of his quarrel with the Greek church. He simply disposed of Greek error by

[20] Ibid., 4, p. 571: Nos tamen vobis, qui, ut praetulimus, adhuc rudes estis, et lacte tamquam parvuli nutriendi, non grave possumus iugum, donec ad solidum cibum veniatis, imponere.

citing Roman practices or teachings (c. 6, 54, 57, 77). He almost always justified his comments on any problem by giving a reason for his decision, thus avoiding an authoritarian attitude. For instance, when condemning the Bulgar practice of killing anyone who tried to flee his native land, Nicholas argued that there might be a just reason for flight and cited cases from sacred history to prove his point (c. 20, 25). Everywhere in the letter Nicholas tried to insinuate a teaching which would uplift his new pupil to a higher level of morality and fuller understanding of Christian doctrine. Boris, for instance, was concerned over his own brutal treatment of those who had rebelled against him when he had first undertaken to convert his subjects. Nicholas pointed out his failure but offered mercy and forgiveness (c. 17; see also c. 1, 2). Boris upon receipt of this letter must have been convinced that he had found a fitting guide for his task. He must have been assured that his work was progressing properly. The pope was thereby furthering the expansion of religion by his gentle, persuasive, encouraging attitude toward a king with great troubles and a people only slightly aware of the implications of the new religion.

The Bulgar mission, so thoroughly prepared by the papacy, started its work auspiciously. According to Roman sources,[27] Nicholas' missionary party began teaching, baptizing, building churches, instituting the Christian ritual, and imposing the Christian way of life on the Bulgars. Even Greek sources vouch for the effectiveness of the papal move. Photius complained to the eastern patriarchs that heretical teachings and practices were being instituted among the Bulgars by the Romans and asked for support in offsetting this development.[28] Boris was reported to have been so well pleased that he drove out all alien clergymen and declared that he would never adhere to any authority except Rome. Papal leadership had seemingly shaped a splendid and rapid victory for Christ.

However, the Bulgar mission was not entirely free from difficulties. Two situations, neither of them having too much to do with the actual missionary problem, disturbed the scene. First, Boris was not happy with the provisions Nicholas made for the ecclesiastical organization of Bulgaria. In 867 he sent a new emissary to Rome asking that Formosus be made archbishop for Bulgaria. Nicholas refused the request, but sought to avoid alienating Boris by preparing a new mission, headed by two more Italian bishops, Dominic and Grimoald, and including carefully selected priests. He prepared letters advising Boris that he might select an archbishop from this group.[29] A second situation arose from the fact that the Greeks were bending every effort to reestablish the authority of the patriarch of Constantinople over the Bulgars. Nicholas revealed their efforts in a series of letters written to various lay and ecclesiastical personages in Francia in 867. He related that the Greek emperor was using diplomatic pressure to discredit the papal legates and that the Greeks were spreading rumors of Roman heresy among the Bulgars.[30] Other sources suggest that the Greeks used bribes and "sophisticated arguments" to detach the Bulgars from Rome.[31] A jurisdictional struggle was emerging to confuse the situation among the Bulgars and divert the papacy from missionary work in the strict sense.[32] However, Nicholas' death in November, 867, relieved him both of the burden of dealing

[27] The chief ones reporting on the progress of the first mission of Nicholas are *Liber pontificalis* II, ed. Duchesne, pp. 165, 185; Anastasius Bibliothecarius, *Epistolae sive Praefationes* #5; ed. Perels and Laehr, MGH, Ep. VII, 412.

[28] PG 102, 722-738.

[29] *Liber pontificalis* II, ed. Duchesne, p. 165.

[30] Nicholas, *Ep.* #100-102; ed. Perels, MGH, Ep. VI, 600-610; *Ann. Fuldenses*, a. 868; ed.

Kurze, pp. 66-67.

[31] *Liber pontificalis* II, ed. Duchesne, p. 185; Anastasius Bibliothecarius, *Epistolae sive Praefationes* #5; ed. Perels and Laehr, MGH, Ep. VII, 413.

[32] For the background and larger issues of that jurisdictional dispute, see F. Dvornik, *Les Légendes de Constantin et de Méthode vues de Byzance* (Prague, 1933), pp. 248-283.

with the Greek offensive and of answering Boris' demands for greater ecclesiastical independence.

Before his death Nicholas had still another opportunity for exerting an influence on missionary affairs. In 863 the Moravian prince, Rastislav, appealed to Constantinople for aid in completing the conversion of his people. Christianity had already made some progress in Moravia, chiefly as a result of German activity. Rastislav was not completely happy either with the religious state of his subjects or with the German political power which accompanied German missionaries. The Greeks answered his request by sending two Slavic speaking missionaries, Cyril and Methodius, to Moravia. They enjoyed immense success, due chiefly to their use of a Slavic ritual. By 867 there was a need for an organization for Moravia. Since neither of the missionaries was a bishop, the pair left Moravia to find authorities qualified to assist them in organizing the Moravian church. Their exact destination has remained a mystery. Nicholas, having heard of their fame and perhaps suspicious of their orthodoxy, invited them to Rome. Probably he was chiefly interested in assuming leadership over this new missionary venture. However, he did not live to greet the missionaries or direct their future work.[53]

Nicholas died leaving a great deal of missionary work unfinished. A new Bulgar mission was almost ready to leave Rome to continue a major project there. Two successful Greek missionaries with powerful though disputed influence in Moravia were on their way to Rome to consult with the papacy. These ventures, coupled with his efforts in Scandinavia, mark him as a major influence in missionary affairs. True, he had not taken the initiative in planting Christianity in pagan lands. His policy was opportunistic. However, he acted with vigor wherever there was a chance of advancing the Christian cause. He used his personal influence to persuade princes to promote Christianity. He was especially effective in organizing missionary resources. He was quick to proffer practical advice on any kind of problem relative to the Christianization of a new territory. In all of this he was bolder than any pope had been for a long time, seldom deferring to another missionary agency that had a stake in a missionary venture. He came close to making the papal see a missionary headquarters from which emanated missionary personnel, regulations, advice, and final decisions extending to far-flung missionary frontiers. Once again the papacy was a major force in missionary affairs after lingering so long in the shadows of the Carolingian rulers.

Hadrian II (867-872) acted promptly to carry on Nicholas' policy. The Bulgar mission demanded his first attention. He immediately dispatched Nicholas' mission, led by the bishops Dominic and Grimoald, to Bulgaria, sending with them the letters which Nicholas had prepared but to which Hadrian now added his name. Boris had requested this mission in order to secure a satisfactory archbishop. Throughout the next two years that problem dominated the relationship between Rome and Bulgaria. Late in 867, after the departure of the above mentioned mission, Boris sent another representative to Rome in the company of bishops Paul and Formosus, whom Nicholas had first sent to Bulgaria. This time Boris requested that Hadrian send a certain deacon, Marinus, or some cardinal to be made archbishop. Hadrian refused this request on the grounds that Marinus had been assigned as a legate to a forthcoming council in Constantinople. The pope

[53] The chief sources for the beginning of the Moravian mission are chapters 14-17 of the Slavic biography of Cyril and chapters 5-6 of the Slavic biography of Methodius. For the text of these chapters in a French translation see Dvornik, *Les Légendes de Constantin et de Méthode vues de Byzance*, pp. 372-379, 385-386. These biographies will be cited hereafter as *Vie de Constantin*, tr. Dvornik, and *Vie de Méthode*, tr. Dvornik, with appropriate chapter and page numbers. See also *Vita* [sancti Cyrilli] *cum translatione s. Clementis*, 7-8, *Acta Sanctorum*, March II, 21. Dvornik's comments on these accounts are especially valuable in settling some of the difficulties connected with them.

sent a subdeacon, Sylvester, who was accompanied by bishops Leopard of Ancona and Dominic of Trevi. Sylvester was also unsatisfactory, since Boris soon made a new request that Formosus or some other suitable candidate be sent. Once again Hadrian wrote asking that Boris select another.[34] Obviously the organization of the Bulgar church under Roman auspices had reached an impasse resulting from Boris' desire for independence. Hadrian had little power to compel the king to accept papal dictates.

While negotiations between Hadrian and Boris continued, Boris apparently decided to seek his ends in Constantinople. As has previously been mentioned, the Greeks had continued to exert pressure on Boris since he first turned to Rome in 866. It is entirely possible that he was promised his archbishop if he would again accept allegiance to Constantinople. Internal troubles in his kingdom increased the frightful possibility of Greek intervention in Bulgar affairs, a threat that Rome could not utilize in pressuring Boris to accept its program. For whatever reason, Boris sent an emissary to Constantinople in 869 at the time that an important council was being held to restore peace between Rome and Constantinople.[35] At the conclusion of that council in February, 870, the Bulgars were given an audience before the Roman legates, the representatives of the eastern patriarchs, and the patriarch of Constantinople, Ignatius, and asked for a decision as to which authority, Rome or Constantinople, Bulgaria pertained. In spite of the attempts of the papal legates to defend Rome's rights on grounds of Rome's possession of the Bulgar territory prior to the barbarian invasions and Rome's leading role in the conversion of Bulgaria, the decision went in favor of Constantinople. Boris' return to Constantinople had probably been arranged prior to this meeting. Beyond threatening Ignatius with papal retaliation for permitting this development, the papal legates were powerless. Hadrian, who did not know of the procedure until long after it had happened, had been completely outmaneuvered by Greek diplomacy.[36]

The return of the Bulgars to Constantinople was fatal to the papal missionary establishment in Bulgaria. Ignatius immediately appointed an archbishop[37] for the Bulgars and sent Greek clergymen into the territory. The Romans, including Grimoald, who was serving as papal legate at the time, were expelled. The Bulgar king presented Rome with a series of complaints as an excuse for his move.[38] Hadrian took the only course open to him, namely, to pressure the Greeks to repudiate the affair, threatening the emperor and especially Ignatius with dire consequences if they did not acquiesce.[39] His efforts were fruitless; the Christian establishment in Bulgaria had escaped Rome and with it Nicholas' dream of a major addition to Rome's sphere of influence.

Hadrian's failure in Bulgaria was offset, however, by his successful exploitation of the Moravian missionaries, Cyril and Methodius. Nicholas' death made it necessary for Hadrian to greet them when they arrived at Rome. This he did in a most fitting fashion, creating the impression that Rome accepted their work without question. Especially significant was the fact that Hadrian in a public ceremony blessed the books containing the Slavic liturgy used by the Greek missionaries and permitted the performance of that liturgy in several important churches in Rome. He also ordained certain of the disciples of the missionaries as priests; perhaps Methodius was in that group. While the missionaries were thus honored by the papacy, Cyril died. Methodius desired to

[34] Liber pontificalis II, ed. Duchesne, p. 185.

[35] For the background of this important council, see Amann, L'époque carolingienne, pp. 465-489.

[36] Liber pontificalis II, ed. Duchesne, pp. 182-185; Anastasius Bibliothecarius, Epistolae sive Praefationes #5; ed. Perels and Laehr, MGH, Ep. VII, 413-415.

[37] A letter of John VIII identifies Ignatius' appointee as an archbishop; John VIII, Fragmenta Registri #9; ed. Ericus Caspar, MGH, Ep. VII, 278.

[38] Liber pontificalis II, ed. Duchesne, p. 185.

[39] Hadrian II, Ep. #41-42; ed. E. Perels, MGH, Ep. VI, 759-762.

return his body to his home, but was persuaded either by Hadrian or by Cyril before his death to abandon that project. This was an important matter, since a new missionary venture in which Methodius would play an important part was being constructed by Hadrian.[40]

Cyril and Methodius had obviously pleased Rastislav in Moravia. On their journey to Rome they had passed through the lands of Kocel, a prince of Moravian origin ruling in Carinthia under the tutelage of Louis the German. Kocel had also been impressed by the Greeks and especially by their Slavic ritual and desired their services in his land. He requested that the papacy send the Greeks to Carinthia to serve as teachers. Here was a situation comparable to that presented to Nicholas when Boris of Bulgaria sent his legates to Rome in 866. Here were princes of partially Christianized lands asking Rome for assistance, bypassing those parties who already had an interest in their territories. Hadrian acted with as much vigor as did Nicholas. He sent Methodius and his disciples back to the Slavic princes. He also sent a letter addressed to Kocel, Rastislav, and Svatopluk, another Moravian prince, informing them that Methodius, a man of perfect orthodoxy and intelligence, was being sent as their teacher. Methodius had been commissioned to teach from the Slavic scripture, celebrate the mass in Slavic, and baptize in Slavic, the only reservation being that the epistle and gospel had to be read in Latin prior to the reading of the Slavic version. Hadrian threatened to punish anyone who interfered with the work of the papal missionary. He exhorted the princes to follow the guidance of Methodius.[41] Once again a missionary territory under the direct authority of Rome was staked out. Once again the papacy assumed the right to commission missionaries and guide their activities. Especially bold was Hadrian's permission to use the Slavic ritual, a practice that had already aroused suspicion in the West. Undoubtedly this precedent-breaking step was a concession to the Slavs in an attempt to attach them to Rome. Nonetheless, in view of the popularity of the native ritual, it proved a noteworthy addition to the western missionary method.

Methodius, upon leaving Rome on the papal mission, was greeted well by Kocel. Within a short time he was back in Rome in the company of a considerable number of nobles from Kocel's court, who asked that he be made bishop for Pannonia. Hadrian gladly elevated Methodius to the rank of archbishop, with a see at Sirmium, the site of the ancient see of Illyricum. Methodius was apparently given authority over Moravia as well as Pannonia. The pope now intended that the ecclesiastical organization of this vast new province proceed as rapidly as possible, this step to mark the conclusion of the missionary process which had begun independently of the papacy.[42]

Hadrian's death in 772 resulted in no major shift in papal policy. John VIII tried valiantly to sustain the papal program of lending assistance to the newly Christianized peoples, although he was sorely beset by serious problems nearer to Rome. He was especially concerned with developments in Bulgaria. His many letters on the Bulgar question show little interest in actual missionary problems, in spite of the fact that there were still many pagans in Bulgaria.[43] Occasionally he fretted lest certain Greek teachings and practices, considered heretical by Rome, become any more deeply implanted in the yet untutored minds

[40] Vie de Constantin, 17-18, tr. Dvornik, pp. 378-380; Vie de Méthode, 6-7, tr. Dvornik, p. 386; Vita [sancti Cyrilli] cum translatione s. Clementis, 8-12, Acta Sanctorum, March II, 21-22.
[41] Vie de Méthode, 8, tr. Dvornik, pp. 387-388.
[42] Ibid., 8, p. 388. For a discussion of the territory assigned to Methodius, see Ernst Dümmler, "Die pannonische Legende vom

heilige Methodius." Archiv für österreichische Geschichts-Quellen, XIII (1854), 185-189; Dvornik, Les Légendes de Constantin et de Méthode vues de Byzance, pp. 267-275.
[43] A biography of one of Methodius' disciples, driven out of Moravian territory in 885, gives evidence of the existence of paganism as a major problem in Bulgaria after that date; see Vita s. Clementis, 17-18; PG 126, 1224-1225.

of the Bulgars. John's real preoccupation centered around persuading Boris to return to Roman overlordship and compelling the imperial court to repudiate its claim to ecclesiastical authority over Bulgaria. To gain the first aim John kept a steady stream of letters flowing to Boris.[44] These letters were essentially the same in content. John tried to convince Boris that the Greeks taught a heretical brand of Christianity and that whoever followed it ran the danger of eternal damnation. In connection with this argument, John sought to build a case for the long-standing orthodoxy of Rome, a situation resulting from Rome's primacy dating from the time of St. Peter. John also tried to persuade Boris that Bulgaria had historically pertained to Rome and that Constantinople's assumption of authority in 870 was illegal. He insinuated into his letters the idea that the Greek motive for intervention in Bulgaria was chiefly the hope of gaining political control, whereas Rome's motive was not tainted by worldly ambitions but was concerned only with the care of souls and the proper organization of the infant church of Bulgaria. This line of argument was intended to prod the Bulgar spirit of independence against the ever-present danger of Greek political domination. Finally, John reminded Boris that the king had once made a promise to obey Rome and was now violating his oath. In addition to his letters to Boris, John sought to use his influence on the relatives, confidants, and advisers of Boris, asking them to plead the papal case before the king.[45] In spite of his efforts, Boris made no move toward repudiating Constantinople. His attitude excluded Roman influences completely from Bulgaria. Nothing but empty claims of authority remained of the papal attempt to take the responsibility for the Christianization of the Bulgars.

John also battled to force the Greeks to concede Bulgaria to Rome. His policy centered around exploiting the religious difficulties within the Empire and the imperial desire for peace with Rome. He pleaded with Basil I to correct the injustice committed by the patriarch of Constantinople in assuming authority over Bulgaria.[46] Against Ignatius and his clergy John was more severe. In a letter written in April, 878, he demanded that Ignatius withdraw all Greek clergy from Bulgaria within thirty days and threatened to depose the patriarch if he did not comply. John indicated that this action was the culmination of previous warnings.[47] The same order was directed to the Greek bishops and other clergy in Bulgaria.[48] This policy of threatening to use ecclesiastical weapons to cause trouble within the Byzantine church seemed to bear fruit in 879 and 880, when the emperor was seeking papal recognition for Photius, chosen to succeed Ignatius but extremely suspect in Rome as a result of his previous career as patriarch. As one of the conditions for recognizing Photius John was able to secure a repudiation of Greek authority over Bulgaria.[49] Seemingly the papacy had gained its end. John was again free to send his ministers into Bulgaria to complete the conversion of that land, as he indicated was his intention in his letter to the Greek clergy in Bulgaria in 878.

However, his victory was a hollow one, as two letters written to Boris in 881 and 882 so clearly reveal. In the midst of fulsome expressions of joy over the turn of events that had put Boris under Roman authority, John wondered why the king had failed to send messengers to Rome for instructions. He reminded

---

[44] John VIII, *Ep.* #66, 182, 192, 198; ed. Caspar, MGH, Ep. VII, 58-60, 146, 153-154, 158-159; John VIII, *Fragmenta Registri* #7, 37; ed. Caspar, MGH, Ep. VII, 277, 294-295.

[45] John VIII, *Ep.* #67, 70, 183; ed. Caspar, MGH, Ep. VII, 60-62, 65-66, 147.

[46] *Ibid.*, #69, pp. 63-65; John VIII, *Fragmenta Registri* #40; ed. Caspar, MGH, Ep. VII, 296.

[47] John VIII, *Ep.* #68; ed. Caspar, MGH, Ep. VII, 62-63.

[48] *Ibid.*, #71, pp. 66-67.

[49] John's conditions are revealed in three letters written in August, 879, to Basil and his sons, to the bishops of the eastern patriarchates, and to Photius; see *ibid.*, #207-209, pp. 173-174, 179, 185-186. For the decisions of the council of Constantinople in 879-880, see Joannes Dominicus Mansi, *Sacrorum conciliorum Nova et amplissima collectio*, new ed., XVII (Venice, 1762), cols. 373-526.

Boris that Bulgaria now adhered to Rome and that it behooved the king to act.[50] The stony silence that greeted these letters must have demonstrated to John the true situation. Boris had no intention of reestablishing contacts with Rome. The Greeks had been safe in conceding to Rome authority over the Bulgars, since Rome would never be able to capitalize on it. Cultural and political ties oriented the Bulgars toward Constantinople, assuring that Rome would exert small influence. Moreover, subsequent years were to show that the Bulgars were intent on an autocephelous church, built on a Slavic liturgy. Thus the hope of Roman control faded even more completely, leaving the papacy with only the consolation that it had lent an important hand while the Bulgars were being converted.

John inherited another missionary venture from his predecessors. Methodius was carrying on his work in Pannonia and Moravia under papal auspices. John acted as his champion in the face of the difficulties which he encountered in these areas. The gravest problem in connection with Methodius' mission did not result from opposition by pagans. By the time of John's pontificate the Christianization of Pannonia and Moravia had made extensive progress. The chief problem arose out of conflicting claims concerning the organization of new converts, a process that Hadrian II had tried to control by making Methodius an archbishop for a huge area in Pannonia and Moravia. The major obstacle to papal policy in this case was the Bavarian clergy supported by the German crown.

Methodius' initial activities in his new province immediately aroused the opposition of the Bavarian clergy which had interests in Pannonia. The Bavarians claimed the Greek was intruding into their territory and perhaps added the charge that he was a teacher of false doctrines.[51] A Germany military offensive against Moravia, which resulted in the captivity of Rastislav and his replacement by Svatopluk, who was pro-German at the moment, emboldened the Bavarian bishops to act against Methodius.[52] He was captured, put on trial, and sentenced to prison with scant attention paid to serving justice. After he had remained in prison for over two years and had suffered vile treatment, the whole affair came to the attention of John. In May, 873, he acted with decision to free his legate and protect the new Slavic organization. He first wrote letters to Louis the German and his son, Carlomann, to remind them that Pannonia pertained to Roman jurisdiction and that Rome's provisions for its organization must be respected. Strict orders were given to Carlomann to allow Methodius to act freely in Pannonia in order to carry out papal orders.[53] John's action against the Bavarian bishops was more severe. Adalwin, archbishop of Salzburg, was accused of being the author of the plot against Methodius and was ordered to restore him to his see immediately.[54] For their part in the attack on Methodius Emeric of Passau and Anno of Friesing were both deposed of their authority until they made their peace with Rome by making a journey to the papal court.[55] To assure that all complied with his orders John sent a legate, Paul, bishop of Ancona, to Germany with specific instructions as to how to deal with the case. Paul was to remind Louis the German that Pannonia had formerly pertained to Rome and could not be claimed by right of conquest. To Rome

[50] John VIII, *Ep.* #298, 308; ed. Caspar, MGH, Ep. VII, 260, 266-267.
[51] *Vie de Méthode*, 9, tr. Dvornik, pp. 388-389, says the quarrel was over jurisdiction. *De conversione Bagoariorum et Caran-tanorum libellus*, 14; ed. Wattenbach, MGH, SS. XI, 14, suggests that the German bishops felt that Methodius was guilty of new teachings. John VIII, *Ep.* #201; ed. E. Caspar, MGH, Ep. VII, 160-161, written several years after the clash between Methodius and the Bavarian bishops, implies that the question of the Slavic ritual agitated the bishops.
[52] For the relations between the Germans and the Moravians in this period, see Dümmler, *Geschichte des ostfränkischen Reiches* II, 294, ff.
[53] John VIII, *Fragmenta Registri*, #15-16; ed Caspar, MGH, Ep. VII, 280-281.
[54] *Ibid.*, #20, p. 283.
[55] *Ibid.*, #22, 23, pp. 285-286.

alone belonged the right of ordination and deposition of clergy. Paul was also instructed to reprimand the bishops involved and see to it that Methodius was freed. The papal legate was instructed to send Methodius safely on his way to Moravia.[56] Apparently the pope also tried to appease the Germans somewhat after this assault on their claims. He ordered Methodius to abandon the use of the Slavic ritual, a reversal of papal policy that perhaps threatened Methodius' work among the Slavs.[57]

The papal action bore immediate results. Methodius was freed and returned to his work. His actions were largely confined to Moravia after 873. John's order for him to go there after being freed from prison in Germany was perhaps prompted by the fact that Svatopluk had turned against the Germans and regained his independence. Svatopluk's anti-Germanism perhaps inclined him favorably toward Rome's project of an independent Slavic church. Methodius was greeted well in Moravia. He carried on his campaign against paganism and continued his efforts to perfect the Slavic liturgy. Eventually he encountered new trouble, again from the Germanic clergy. New charges of unorthodoxy were brought against him.[58] Svatopluk reported the situation to Rome, expressing concern over the religious welfare of his people and apparently placing considerable trust in Rome's ability to decide such matters. John wrote to the prince in June or July, 879, assuring him that Rome was the proper source of the true religion and ordering the prince to see to it that the Roman faith was observed. He reported his surprise that Methodius was guilty of deviation but added that he was summoning the archbishop to Rome to test his teaching. At the same time John wrote to Methodius and ordered him to Rome, not only to test his orthodoxy but also to inquire into the charge that Methodius had violated papal orders by using the Slavic liturgy.[59]

A year later in June, 880, John reported to Svatopluk again. Methodius had in the interim been in Rome and had been cleared of all charges. He was now being sent back as archbishop of the Moravian church. John also reported that he had consecrated a certain Wiching as bishop of Nitra and suffragan of Methodius. Wiching had apparently been the ringleader in the charges brought against Methodius and a representative of the pro-German faction in Moravia. John was trying to remove the conflicts that were disturbing Moravia. He ordered that Svatopluk send another priest to Rome for consecration as soon as such a step was necessary. The creation of a third bishop in Moravia would make possible the consecration of still other bishops without recourse to outside assistance. John was still promoting and directing the organization of Moravia. All clergy, whatever their rank or nationality, were to be subject to Methodius. Finally, John gave his consent to the use of the Slavic liturgy, assuring Svatopluk that it would be beneficial to his people and that its use was not illegal.[60]

Methodius' troubles were not yet ended. His foes, led by Wiching, again raised doubts of his orthodoxy. They fell back on papal authority by spreading a rumor that they possessed letters from Rome ordering them to drive Methodius out of Moravia as a heretic. Methodius appealed to Rome for vindication. John sent another letter on March 23, 881, assuring Methodius that the archbishop had full papal support. John expressed his certainty of Methodius' orthodoxy and vehemently denied sending letters to Wiching giving him authority to do anything. The archbishop was ordered to put aside his doubts and continue his missionary work. John would summon the case to Rome if further trouble occurred.[61] This

[56] Ibid., #21, pp. 283-285.
[57] John VIII, Ep. #201; ed. Caspar, MGH, Ep. VII, 160-161.
[58] Vie de Méthode, 10, tr. Dvornik, p. 389.
[59] John VIII, Ep. #200-201; ed. Caspar,
MGH, Ep. VII, 160-161.
[60] Ibid., #255, pp. 222-224.
[61] Ibid., #276, pp. 243-244; Vie de Méthode, 12, tr. Dvornik, p. 390.

papal order apparently settled the case for the remainder of Methodius' life. He is reported to have continued his work in peace.

John's pontificate ended in December, 882, without further contact with the work of Methodius. There can be little doubt, however, that papal support had been a valuable asset in the face of the opposition aroused by Methodius' revolutionary method and by papal boldness in staking out a territory for his efforts. Papal power sufficed to curb factious clergymen and papal influence aided in swaying lay assistance to support Methodius. John's success in connection with the Slavic mission offset his inability to persuade the Bulgars to complete their Christianization under papal overlordship.

The passing of John and Methodius led almost immediately to a reversal of the course of Christian growth in Moravia. Methodius had selected one of his disciples, Gorazd, as his successor and had left behind a loyal party to carry on his work. Almost immediately Moravia was divided by a struggle between the party of Methodius and the German clergy. The Germans succeeded in winning the support of Svatopluk, a success perhaps partly explained by a restoration of peace between Svatopluk and Arnulf of Germany.[62] The German faction, having gained the confidence of Svatopluk, turned to Rome to seal the victory. Wiching appeared in Rome as the spokesman of the party. Stephen V (885-891) was completely won over. When Wiching left Rome, he bore a papal letter to Svatopluk in which Stephen denounced the party of Methodius. Apparently he was convinced that their teachings were heretical, since he gave Svatopluk instructions concerning the doctrine of the Trinity and fasting regulations. Most significantly, he condemned the use of the Slavic ritual, accusing Methodius of having broken an oath in which he swore to refrain from the use of that liturgy. Stephen probably gave his blessing to Wiching as the new leader of the Moravian church.[63] The pope also sent a legate to Moravia to arrange the affair, giving him authority to instruct the populace in orthodox teachings, to stop the use of the Slavic rite, and to prohibit Gorazd from exercising his office until he appeared in Rome for judgment.[64] Stephen's action spelled the end of Methodius' work. Svotopluk ordered that the adherents of the Greek be driven from their offices, imprisoned, and finally expelled from Moravia. Some of them fled to Bulgaria, where Boris greeted them warmly and enlisted their talents in his program of creating an independent Bulgarian church.[65] Rome thus lost control over these valuable missionaries. There is no evidence that the ecclesiastical party in control of Moravia had further contact with Rome. Perhaps it is safe to assume that Moravia was oriented toward the German church after the disciples of Methodius had been ousted. This is suggested by the fact that the Moravians made an attempt about 900 to regain their ecclesiastical independence and appealed to Rome for aid. John IX (898-900) was party in an attempt to create an archbishop and three bishops for Moravia. This effort resulted in a violent protest from the Bavarian hierarchy which probably prevented its success.[66]

Throughout the closing years of the ninth century the papacy also sought to sustain the Scandinavian mission. Actually, there was little to be accomplished in this area. The deepening hostility between Norsemen and the Christian world virtually eliminated any hope of the conversion of the Scandinavians, as the limited activities of Rimbert and Adalgar, the first two successors of Anskar as archbishop of Hamburg, revealed. Still every effort was made to maintain

[62] The main outlines of the struggle for ecclesiastical control in Moravia are given in the biography of one of Methodius' disciples; see *Vita s. Clementis*, 7-10; PG 126, 1208-1213. This account is, in part at least, substantiated by the letters of Pope Stephen V, cited below.

[63] Stephen V, *Epistolae passim collectae*

#1; ed. G. Laehr, MGH, Ep. VII, 354-358.

[64] Stephen V, *Fragmenta Registri* #33; ed. E. Caspar, MGH, Ep. VII, 352-353.

[65] *Vita s. Clementis*, 11-29; PG 126, 1213-1232.

[66] *Regesta pontificum romanorum: Germania pontificia* I, ed. Albertus Brachman (Berlin, 1910, ff.), p. 163.

Hamburg as a missionary outpost. Rome tried to aid that effort. Successive archbishops were confirmed in their privileges and granted the pallium. Encouragement was extended to the archbishops to create suffragans and to carry on missionary work. Especially vigorous was the action of Stephen V and Formosus (891-896) to prevent the archbishop of Cologne from recovering the bishopric of Bremen, which had been joined with Hamburg as a means of providing material support for Hamburg's missionary activities. Both of these popes refused to divide the two sees, at least until Hamburg possessed suffragans in the still pagan world to the North. They justified their actions on the grounds that Hamburg was a missionary outpost and needed the support of Bremen. However, the papal action was of little consequence, since there was small opportunity for missionary work from Hamburg, irrespective of its material condition. Moreover, the German bishops were inclined to flout papal orders with impunity; for instance, in 895 a synod at Tribur ordered that Bremen be returned to the jurisdiction of Cologne, in spite of the papal orders cited above, issued between 890 and 892.[67]

The debacle that marked papal missionary efforts in Bulgaria, Moravia, and Scandinavia in the last years of the ninth century were symptomatic of a general decline of western missionary effort at that time. The papacy was fast becoming embroiled in Roman politics and the victim of the feudal chaos engulfing Italy. The Carolingians were no longer masters of the territory which made up Charlemagne's empire and were thus incapable of action against pagans. The new barbarian invasions by the Magyars and the Norsemen not only made missionary work difficult but drove back the Christian frontier, as was the case when the Magyars overran Moravia. The universal debilitation of western Europe at the end of the ninth century makes the year 900 a dividing point in missionary history. A new alignment of forces was necessary to supply the drive for another era of expansion. In the general paralysis that halted the spread of Christianity around 900, perhaps no missionary agency suffered a greater loss of independence of action than did the papacy. Not for a long time would it be able to exert a significant force on missionary affairs in the West. Thus the year 900 marked a definite conclusion of that phase of papal missionary effort that had been inaugurated when Gregory I dispatched his monks to England in 596.

VI.

The evidence presented in the preceding pages suggests certain general statements characterizing the role of the papacy in the expansion of Christianity in the early Middle Ages.

Gregory the Great's policy certainly overshadowed all papal activity for the three following centuries. He struck out boldly along a line that involved papal responsibility for almost every aspect of missionary effort. His program included selecting a missionary field, choosing missionary personnel, defining the objectives of missionaries, rallying Christian society to their support, proposing methods to be used in attacking paganism, supplying guidance to missionaries whenever extraordinary problems arose, organizing the new converts into a church, and glorifying missionary effort as a proper activity for dedicated Christians. No other agency in western society had as yet devised such a comprehensive program for dealing with paganism. Gregory's concept and practice of missionary work thus promised to establish the papacy as the leading agent in expanding the earthly realm of Christ.

[67] For the missionary activity among the Scandinavians from the death of Anskar to the end of the ninth century, see *Vita Rimberti*, ed. Waitz, pp. 80-100; Adam of Bremen, *Gesta Hammburgensis Ecclesiae Pontificum* I, 37-52; PL 146, 485-495. For the papal part in trying to protect Hamburg, see Stephen V, *Ep.* #2, 5; ed. Laehr, MGH, Ep. VII, 358-359, 364-365; Formosus, *Ep.* #1-3; ed. G. Laehr, MGH, Ep. VII, 366-370. For the synod at Tribur, see Adam of Bremen I, 51; PL 146, 492-493.

The history of the next three centuries demonstrated that his plan was abortive. Christendom expanded, but the papacy must be eliminated as an important contributor in many phases of missionary activity. The papacy never again took the initiative in the struggle against paganism. No matter how seriously paganism might threaten Christendom or how ripe a pagan people might be for conversion, Rome took no action until some other missionary agency made the initial move and then presented Rome with an opportunity for intervention. The papacy did not make a serious attempt to recruit personnel for missionary work. Occasionally it commanded an Italian cleric to assume at least a temporary responsibility in a missionary field or suggested to a monk that missionary work might befit his urge to serve Christ. Rome had no troop of servants to assign to missionary work during these centuries and thus missionaries had to emerge from other levels of society. The papacy supplied none of the material resources needed to begin and maintain missionary projects. The popes might plead with those who did possess wealth to contribute to the support of missionaries, but its pleas lacked compulsion. The papacy was almost silent on the crucial and troublesome question of the methods to be used in convincing pagans to accept Christianity. Even when the papacy was so deeply immersed in missionary affairs as it was in the case of Boniface, it did little more to define a missionary method than utter a generality about the need for preaching and teaching. The missionary was left to devise his own method or to seek guidance elsewhere than from the papacy. Only occasionally did the papacy condone a particular method being employed by a missionary, and then with some reluctance, as might be illustrated by the papal vacillation on the use of the Slavic liturgy in the later part of the ninth century. The silence of the papacy on missionary method was quite clearly the result of papal ignorance of conditions and problems in most missionary areas.

With papal policy lacking in so many ways, one is compelled to conclude that papal missionary activity over the three centuries under consideration was largely opportunistic. As a rule, the papacy waited to be asked to help in the struggle for converts. In some exceptional cases, a pope might try to exploit a situation presented to him and thus broaden the scope of papal activity beyond the intention of the missionary seeking Rome's help. However, these cases do not contradict the fundamental opportunism of papal policy. The viability of a new Christian establishment depended upon the strength of a Christian ruler backing missionary work or of a newly converted native king or of a dedicated, persistent, and persuasive band of missionary monks, but never on the papacy. Rome could only assist those agencies and usually admitted its limitations by awaiting their request for assistance.

Having severely delimited the extent of papal contribution to early medieval missionary effort, it still needs to be said that Rome cannot be eliminated as a missionary force. As one assault after another was made on paganism, Rome provided a limited but significant share in the victory.

First, the papacy, more consistently and more effectively than any other agency, provided legitimacy to missionary undertaking. A papal letter of commendation for a missionary, a papal bull confirming the activities of a missionary, a papal plea to a pagan king, a papal directive to Christian laymen were almost invariably necessary parts of a successful missionary venture, eagerly sought by anyone engaged in missionary work. In numerous situations Rome alone could speak with authority enough to clear away difficulties. This contribution was especially vital in offsetting conflicts that arose among the several Christian agencies engaged in missionary activity, although it occasionally served to open doors in the pagan world. However a missionary chose to use the papal name, he could almost depend upon it to strengthen his position and to aid him win converts.

Second, the papacy played a major role in impressing on the missionary effort of the early Middle Ages the principle that organization was the most important step in the conversion process. From Gregory I's time onward Rome injected into every missionary venture the idea that the institution of an independent episcopacy must accompany the establishment of the Christian religion in any pagan territory. The popes accomplished this end in many ways. Sometimes they thrust upon missionaries seeking papal aid the episcopal or archiepiscopal rank. They ordered these emissaries to give priority to the creation of new bishoprics. They enthusiastically confirmed the efforts of kings who established episcopal sees in newly converted areas. They encouraged newly converted rulers to think in terms of a speedy division of their realms into bishoprics. They did everything in their power to prevent newly established bishoprics from being phantom organizations, manipulated by power-seeking kings or empire-building ecclesiastics. The importance of this steadfast policy must be judged in the context of an era when other possible modes of treating converts were bidding for supremacy. In her insistence on the institution of an independent episcopacy Rome was competing with the Irish idea of permitting the appealing, dedicated "saint" to form the center of cohesion among new converts, the Benedictine tendency to let the monastery serve as a Christian center, the royal or princely urge to devise an ecclesiastical structure that would serve purely political ends, and the Byzantine custom of creating "national" churches as components of an imperial order. The supremacy of any of these would certainly have changed the ecclesiastical face of Europe and perhaps all other aspects of the emerging western European civilization. At Rome's urging, however, the ancient Roman concept of the organization of newly conquered territories was impressed upon western society in the form of new bishoprics established in even barely Christianized regions. Without papal guidance the conversion process might have resulted in a multiplicity of organizational forms left behind to add to the other particularistic institutions that resulted from the fall of the Roman Empire and the ascendancy of the Germanic barbarians.

Third, Rome performed a vital missionary function by serving as a fountainhead of direction in the transmission of ritual, dogma, and discipline to converts. By its very nature missionary effort confronted western society with unusual complications. Missionary agents of every description turned repeatedly to Rome for instructions on how to handle these problems. Rome always replied with specific guidance, thus arming every missionary agency with authorized and practicable solutions to its immediate problem. Not only did this aid the missionary in his immediate situation, it also tended to unify the religious system transmitted to the pagan world and ease the entrance of pagan people into the main stream of western culture. Again no other agency—with the possible exception of the Carolingian state under Charlemagne—possessed the grasp of the total Christian tradition or the authority to act as a source of guidance to overcome the mountainous problems posed by the meeting of Christianity and paganism.

Finally, as a concomitant to its role as adviser and legislator in the areas of ritual, liturgy, and discipline, the papacy helped immeasurably in keeping Christianity supple and adaptable as it was transmitted to barbarian converts. It is not difficult to find evidence that some missionary agencies tried to pursue a counsel of perfection in imposing the new religion on converts, while others concerned themselves so little with the religious side of the conversion process that there was a danger of complete superficiality. Rome always sought to avoid both extremes. In every possible fashion the papacy sought to restrain the perfectionists by advising a modification of Christianity fitted to the traditions, culture, and mentality of prospective or recent converts. Just as frequently the popes sought to inculcate the idea that conversion must result in a real change of heart and an obvious change of habits for the convert. Perhaps in this intermingling of Christianity and barbarism lay the secret of the vitality of Christianity in this critical era; only its adaptability permitted it to escape the fate of other aspects of Graeco-Roman civilization. The papacy with unceasing consistency advocated a compromise with barbarism and paganism. Thereby it made a major contribution to the shaping of the new civilization and of its most recent additions, the recently converted Germanic and Slavic groups brought into the Christian fold between 590 and 900.

KHAN BORIS AND THE CONVERSION OF BULGARIA:
A CASE STUDY OF THE IMPACT OF CHRISTIANITY ON A BARBARIAN SOCIETY

In 601 Pope Gregory the Great sent the following exhortation to King Ethelbert of Kent:

> Therefore, glorious son, take care with a solicitous mind of the grace you have divinely received. Hasten to extend the Christian faith among the people subjected to you. Multiply the zeal of your righteousness for their conversion. Suppress the worship of idols. Overthrow the temples. Edify the manners of your subjects by great cleanness of life, by exhorting, terrifying, soothing, correcting, and illustrating with the example of good works, so that you will find in heaven your rewarder whose name and reputation you have spread on earth.[1]

This passage tempts the historian of Christian expansion in the early middle ages to think that he has within his grasp important clues relating to a vital issue in missionary history, namely, the nature of the impact of Christianity on a pagan society. Pope Gregory unmistakably implies that the introduction of the new faith into a pagan land would work profound changes on the entire culture of that land. He indicates that traditional institutions, manners, ethical standards, ideas, and values would be transformed under the weight of a completely new order. He broadly hints that this transformation would eventuate in so striking an improvement in the condition of the converts that God Almighty would be pleased and the fame of the reborn people would rise in the view of the entire world. Gregory further suggests that the ruler of a people in the process of conversion holds the key to this great transformation. Upon the ruler's assiduousness, devotion, and skill in the execution of his heavy responsibilities would hinge not only the success of the conversion of a whole nation but also the nature of the impact of the new religion on an entire cultural pattern.

However, sober reflection on this passage—seemingly so rich in terms of assessing the impact of conversion—suggests caution. Gregory was not

1. *Gregorii I papae Registrum Epistolarum*, XI, 9, eds. Paulus Ewald and Ludowicus M. Hartmann, *MGH, Epistolae*, II, 308–9.

Reprinted from *Studies in Medieval and Renaissance History*, volume III, by permission of the University of Nebraska Press. Copyright © 1966 by the University of Nebrasksa Press.

reporting what had actually happened in Kent as a consequence of the acceptance of Christianity by the people living there, nor was he recording what Ethelbert had done to assure the successful conversion of his people and to effect a change in their customary pattern of culture; the pope was expressing only a pious expectation which suggests the possibilities of the revolutionary impact of Christianity without revealing what actually happened.

Most of the sources that deal with Christian expansion in the early middle ages suffer from this basic limitation. Although they broadly hint that Christianity exerted a powerful transformational influence on pagan cultures and that the role of princes was decisive in the conversion process, they provide exceedingly scant information about the exact way the new religion worked to change pagan societies and about the issues posed for newly converted rulers as they undertook to introduce Christianity into their realms. Ranging over the whole era, from the conversion of Clovis at the end of the fifth century to the conversion of Scandinavia in the twelfth century, one finds little evidence upon which to construct an adequate picture of what conversion implied for newly converted kings and the societies under their command. This lacuna in the sources, attributable chiefly to the fact that most material dealing with missionary history was written to glorify the deeds of missionaries and to laud the support given them by their lay and ecclesiastical sponsors dwelling behind the religious frontier, has long made any attempt to discuss early medieval Christian expansion somewhat one-sided and incomplete. More significantly, it has made any firm grasp of the impact of the conversion process on primitive societies virtually impossible. Although the conversion experience was decisive in the history of these societies, the modern historian has been unable to adequately discuss this critical aspect in the making of medieval civilization.

However, at least one case appears to offer a good opportunity for penetrating the darkness that surrounds the impact of conversion on the policies and actions of a newly converted ruler and on the culture of the society over which he ruled. This case is the conversion of the Bulgars during the reign of Khan Boris (c. 852–889). Because this event became involved in the larger issues of the so-called Photian schism, a relatively greater amount of information pertaining to Boris' activities has survived than is usual for the early middle ages, and this study will analyze this information primarily with the view of reconstructing the situation in Bulgaria during the conversion period. A correlative attempt has been to extract from this information as precise a description as possible of the manner in which the coming of the new religion affected Bulgar institutions and ideas. Moreover, the scrutiny of this material, primarily from the Bulgar point of view, seems to suggest valuable new insights into the tasks facing a newly converted ruler bent on completing the conversion of his people, and it also seems to throw considerable light on the impact of the new religion on a primitive, undeveloped culture.

The impact of Christianity on Bulgaria is much more easily discernible than in most other cases involving the conversion of entire nations during the early middle ages because of the unique nature of the sources pertaining to the conversion process in Bulgaria. These sources, in turn, derive their special quality primarily from the historical situations that produced them. Therefore a brief description of the major documents and an explanation of the circumstances surrounding their creation is a necessary preliminary step for a study of the impact of Christianity on Bulgar society.

The conversion process commenced in Bulgaria long before the reign of Boris. As early as the seventh century, when the Bulgars made their first assaults on Byzantine territory south of the Danube, these invaders began to feel the impact of Byzantine civilization, including its religion. In the incessant wars between these two states, Christian prisoners who were captured by the Bulgars continued to practice their religion among the pagans. On the other hand, Bulgar captives were carried off to Constantinople, converted to Christianity, and later returned to their native land, where they remained Christian. Byzantine merchants and ambassadors circulated in Bulgaria and Bulgars traveled in the Byzantine Empire. Bulgar rulers also established diplomatic relationships with the Frankish kings and consequently learned something of the religion and culture of the western European world. However, despite these important penetrations of the Bulgar state by Christian influences during the seventh, eighth, and early ninth centuries, the Bulgars remained, officially, a pagan people until 864.

In that year, however, a dramatic turn of events occurred. Byzantine forces, provoked by Boris' efforts to form an alliance with the kingdom of the East Franks against Moravia, suddenly attacked and defeated the Bulgars. As a part of the peace settlement that followed the Greek victory, Boris agreed to accept baptism and to convert his people under Greek auspices. This decision, as we shall see, caused a considerable stir not only in Bulgaria but throughout the Christian world. The interest of outsiders in Bulgar affairs was intensified in 866 when Boris turned his back on Constantinople to seek help from Rome. And it reached a crisis when, in 870, the Bulgars returned to Byzantium for religious guidance. Thus, as the Christianization of Bulgaria proceeded under the leadership of Boris, a vigorous competition arose between Rome and Constantinople for jurisdiction over the Bulgars. That dispute raged throughout the reign of Boris. Out of the combination of circumstances connected with the original conversion, the transfer of allegiance, and the jurisdictional battle, several documents emerged which permit us to see with unusual clarity how Boris and his kingdom were affected by the ruler's acceptance of Christianity and by his decision to impose the new religion on his subjects.[2]

By far the most important piece of evidence relating to this problem is a long pastoral letter written to Boris by Pope Nicholas I in 866.[3] Nicholas' letter was prompted by the appearance in Rome, in 866, of a delegation sent by the khan, who had become displeased with the Greek clergymen who entered his realm in 864 to help in the task of converting his people. Through his legates, Boris made known his willingness to

---

2. For a treatment of the early history of the Bulgars, their relationships with the Byzantine Empire and the Franks, and the penetration of Byzantine-Christian influences into Bulgaria, see Francis Dvornik, *Les Slaves, Byzance, et Rome au IX*[e] *siècle* (Paris, 1926), pp. 99–103, 184–86; Matthew Spinka, *A History of Christianity in the Balkans: A Study in the Spread of Byzantine Culture among the Slavs*, Studies in Church History, Vol. I (Chicago, 1933), pp. 25–36; Steven Runciman, *A History of the First Bulgarian Empire* (London, 1930), pp. 22–98; W. N. Slatarski, *Geschichte der Bulgaren*, Pt. I: *Von der Gründung des Bulgarischen Reiches bis zur Türkenzeit (679–1396)* (*Bulgarische Bibliothek*, ed. Gustav Weigand, No. 5) (Leipzig, 1918), pp. 1–41; Christian Gérard, *Les Bulgares de la Volga et les Slaves du Danube. Le problème des races et les barbares* (Paris, 1939), pp. 6–182. These accounts deal adequately with the major Greek literary sources concerning Byzantine-Bulgar relations prior to the conversion; however, some interesting new insights may be gained from a study of inscriptions from the pre-conversion period; see V. Beševliev and H. Grégoire, "Les inscriptions protobulgares," *Byzantion*, XXV–XXVI–XXVII (1955–56–57), 853–80; XXVIII (1958), 253–323; XXIX–XXX (1959–60), 477–500, for the texts of some of these inscriptions, a translation into French, and extensive commentary (this work has not yet been completed). An extensive bibliography concerning Bulgaria is provided by Gyula Moravcsik, *Byzantinoturcica*, Vol. I: *Die byzantinischen Quellen der Geschichte der Türkvolker* (2d ed.; Berlin, 1958), pp. 112–19.

3. *Nicolai I. Papae Epistolae*, No. 99, ed. Ernestus Perels, *MGH, Ep.*, VI, 568–600. Hereafter this letter will be cited as Nicholas, *Ep.*, No. 99, with appropriate chapter and page number. This letter has also been published with a Bulgarian translation in *Fontes Latini Historicae Bulgaricae*, eds. Ivan Dujčev, Mihail Vojnov, Strašimir Lišev, and Borislav Primov (Academia Litterarum Bulgarica. Institutum Historicum. *Fontes Historiae Bulgaricae*, VII) (2 vols.; Sofia, n.d.), II, 65–125.

accept Roman spiritual overlordship and to place the missionary undertaking in Roman hands. The Bulgar legates brought with them a series of topics upon which the khan desired information. Nicholas framed his responses with care and dispatched them to Bulgaria, along with books and a law code, in the hands of two bishops, Paul of Populonia and Formosus of Porto.[4]

An analysis of Nicholas' responses provides several clues which demonstrate the crucial importance of his document in reconstructing the situation in Bulgaria at this critical moment in the conversion process. Nicholas indicates that Boris had directed a list of specific questions to the papal curia. At the very beginning of his letter the pope speaks of *vestra consulta* and apologizes for not being able to answer at length *per singula*.[5] In another place he refers to Boris' *questiones*.[6] Nicholas repeatedly reveals the manner in which the khan had addressed him in search of guidance. In many places he indicates that Boris had made a positive statement to him on some matter about which a papal opinion was desired, and in these cases the pope began his response with expressions like *dicitis, asseritis, enarratis,* and *indicatis*.[7] In other places the pope indicates that the khan had asked a question, and in these cases he employed such expressions as *consulitis, nosse cupitis, scire cupitis, inquiritis, interrogatis, exquiritis, investigatis, scire velle significatis, sciscitamini, requisites, requiritis, postulatis,* and *desideratis nosse*.[8] These terms, followed in each case by a dependent clause introduced by "that. . . ," leave little doubt that Nicholas repeatedly paraphrased Boris' statements or questions in framing the opening sentence of each response, and it is sometimes obvious that he simply restated Boris' words exactly as they had been received.[9] Furthermore, there is evidence that in composing his letter Nicholas

---

4. The chief sources discussing the appearance of the Bulgar delegation in Rome are the following: the biography of Nicholas I in *Le Liber Pontificalis*, text, introduction, and commentary by Abbé L. Duchesne (*Bibliothèque des écoles françaises d'Athènes et de Rome*) (2d ed., 3 vols.; Paris, 1955–57), II, 164; the biography of Pope Hadrian II, *ibid.*, p. 185; *Annales Bertiniani, annus* 866, ed. G. Waitz, *MGH, Scriptores rerum Germanicarum in usum scholarum* (Hanover, 1883), pp. 85–86; *Iohannis VIII. papae Epistolae*, No. 192, ed. Ericus Caspar, *MGH, Ep.,* VII, 154; and *Anastasii Bibliothecarii Epistolae sive Praefationes*, No. 5, eds. E. Perels and G. Laehr, *MGH*, VII, 412.

5. Nicholas, *Ep.*, No. 99, p. 568.

6. *Ibid.*, Chs. 1, 13, pp. 568, 575, also in the concluding statement, p. 600.

7. *Ibid.*, Chs. 3, 6, 14, 25, 33, 35, 38, 40, 42, 54, 55, 57, 62, 66, 67, 77, 78, 79, 86, 94, 103, 104, pp. 569, 572, 575, 579–83, 587–91, 593–95, 597, 599.

8. *Ibid.*, Chs. 7–13, 15–18, 34, 37, 39, 45, 47–49, 51–53, 56, 59–61, 63, 68–75, 80, 81, 83–85, 87, 88, 90, 92, 93, 95, 98, 99, 101, 103–5, pp. 572–75, 576, 577, 581, 582, 585–99.

9. *Ibid.*, Chs. 4, 20, pp. 570–71, 579.

followed an order dictated by the listing he had received from Boris. He began his first response by writing *in prima questionum vestrorum*, and he occasionally used such words as *praeterea* and *porro* for introducing a new topic. He opened his last response with *postremo*.[10]

This internal evidence convincingly demonstrates that Nicholas' letter provides a direct link with Bulgar affairs. Boris had, through his legates, placed a list of specific questions before Nicholas, and had, it seems evident, compiled these questions on the basis of problems that had arisen in Bulgaria between his conversion in 864 and the dispatch of his legation to Rome in 866. Nicholas I, ignorant except for the most general knowledge of affairs in Bulgaria prior to the appearance of the legates bringing these questions, was content to organize his pastoral responses around Boris' questions, and in almost every answer he restated, in some form, the statement or question with which the Bulgar khan had confronted him. The papal letter is therefore filled with reflections on genuine Bulgar problems that had been formulated by the Bulgar ruler. It is not, in other words, a document which the pope composed by bringing together a variety of ideas and admonitions which he thought ought properly be called to the attention of any newly converted prince. The letter—when looked at in terms of what Boris asked—supplies precious details about the problems and situations which confronted a ruler and a society during the early stages of the conversion process; but it has not received adequate attention from this point of view. In the pages that follow, this document will constitute not only the fundamental source of information about the impact of Christianity on Bulgaria but also the major control for the evaluation of several other sources.

Less revealing, but still important, is another pastoral letter dispatched to Boris, this one written by Photius, patriarch of Constantinople.[11] This lengthy document was composed after the baptism of Boris, which probably occurred in the summer of 865, and before the replacement of

10. *Ibid.*, Ch. 1, p. 568, Chs. 6, 7, 14, 15, 34, 49, 63, pp. 572–73, 575–76, 581, 586, 590, Ch. 106, p. 599.

11. Φωτίου . . . Πατριάρχου Κωνσταντινουπόλεως ᾿Επιστολαί (No. 6) ὑπο Ιωαννου N. Βαλεττα (London, 1864), pp. 200–248. This work will be cited hereafter as Photius, *Ep.*, ed. Valetta, with appropriate letter and page numbers. The letter is also printed in Migne, *PG*, CII, cols. 628–96. Basil Laourdas, "A New Letter of Photius to Boris," ᾿Ελληνικα, XIII (1954), 263–65, provides a pertinent letter missing from the Valetta edition. In this letter Photius announced to Boris the death of the Emperor Michael; but it does not throw any specific light on the situation in Bulgaria.

Greek missionaries in Bulgaria by those sent from Rome in 867.[12] Photius' letter was not, like Nicholas', prompted by any specific request for information. The patriarch gratuitously conceived it to be his duty to instruct his spiritual son, Boris, at a vital moment in the prince's career.

> I place these few out of many tokens of friendship and filiation from God, these original notes of virtue before you, O my true and genuine spiritual son, so that when you turn your eyes to them and conform and compare yourself to them, you will not have difficulty in observing and understanding what sort are the actions which will make beauty flourish in your mind.[13]

To this end, Photius drew together a series of remarks touching on two major issues. First he set forth the orthodox tenets of the faith, basing his discussion on the decisions of the seven ecumenical councils and highlighting the heretical ideas disposed of by these councils; then he turned to a discourse on the moral qualities befitting a Christian and especially a Christian prince. His concerns ranged over a great variety of matters, indicating that he intended his letter to serve as a handbook for the moral education of an audience unfamiliar with Christian ethical concepts. All of these matters are treated with considerable grandiloquence, which gives the tract a sophisticated tone.

At first glance Photius' letter seems to have little bearing on the situation in Bulgaria. Its tone and manner appear too stilted to answer to the needs of a newly converted prince wrestling with the problems of Christianizing his primitive subjects, and the theological issues are treated on a level that seems beyond the grasp of the neophyte Bulgars—including the khan. These features of the letter have led some authorities to suggest that Photius was simply displaying his vast learning to impress an untutored barbarian recently brought under the sway of Byzantium,[14] but such a judgment is unwarranted and unjustified. An analysis of this letter in the light of other sources—especially Pope Nicholas' responses—

12. V. Grumel, *Les regestes des actes du patriarchat de Constantinople* (Istanbul, 1932), I, Pt. 2, No. 478, 87, thinks that the letter dates from May, 866. Moravcsik, *Byzantinoturcica*, I, 475, says the letter was sent "um das Jahr 866."

13. Photius, *Ep.*, No. 6, Ch. 114, ed. Valetta, pp. 247–48. For an interesting discussion of the intent of Photius' letter, see I. Dujčev, "Au lendemain de la conversion du peuple bulgare. L'Épitre de Photius," *Mélanges de science religieuse*, VIII (1951), 211–16. Dujčev concludes, somewhat surprisingly, that the tone of Photius' letter played a significant role in forcing Boris to turn to Rome.

14. J. Hergenröther, *Photius, Patriarch von Constantinopel. Sein Leben, seine Schriften und das griechische Schisma* (3 vols.; Regensburg, 1867–69), I, 604.

reveals that Photius' discussion was pointed toward the very issues that Boris found difficult to handle in his efforts to convert his subjects: the problem of orthodoxy; the question of moral reform (especially as the prince should exemplify Christian conduct for his people); the problem of adding Christian principles to the administration of justice, to the choice of the royal advisers, and to other political processes; and the means of offsetting resistance to these new policies.

Photius was in an excellent position to possess considerable knowledge of Bulgar problems by virtue of his relationship with Greek clergymen who worked there as missionaries and with Greek and Bulgar diplomatic agents who passed back and forth between Byzantium and Bulgaria during the period of the letter's composition. The crucial importance of Bulgaria to imperial policy must certainly have prompted high Greek officials to seek information on Bulgar affairs, information which Photius shared by virtue of his high office. On other occasions Photius had demonstrated a keen interest in Byzantine missionary expansion, the prime case being the dispatch of Cyril and Methodius to Moravia just prior to the opening of the Bulgar mission. This experience also armed the patriarch with some knowledge of what was significant to a newly converted prince.

In analyzing his letter in detail it would appear that it takes its tone of sophistication not so much from the issues dealt with as from the exalted role its author assigns to a prince in a Christian society. One would hardly expect less from an ardent admirer of the Byzantine imperial court and of the refinements of the Byzantine court circle. The patriarch's exaltation of the Christian prince in a Christian society need not preclude the possibility that he can also direct his spiritual son's attention to those practical issues which the patriarch knew were vital to the advance of Christianity in Bulgaria. Nor did Photius' grandiose style necessarily preclude Boris' understanding the letter's ideas upon the essential features of the conversion process.

What the patriarch seemed determined to achieve by sending his letter to Boris was to place in the hands of his spiritual son a set of principles and a list of practical suggestions which would be useful in facing the problems likely to confront the newly converted ruler. As a promoter of Byzantine missionary expansion, and as an astute political figure well informed in imperial relationships with foreign powers, Photius was in all likelihood fully aware of some of the actual problems in Bulgaria and fully capable of anticipating problems that might arise to face a newly converted prince struggling to Christianize his subjects.

Thus there appear to be many justifications for using Photius' letter as a source that indirectly reflects conditions and problems existing in Bulgaria shortly after the official introduction of Christianity. On the basis of our knowledge of Photius' interests and inclinations, it also appears that his letter mirrors with some accuracy those problems relating to the role of the prince in the conversion process, to the political impact of the new religion on a primitive regime, to dogmatic and disciplinary issues, and to the intellectual life in a newly converted realm. Although not as directly derived from a specific Bulgar source as was Nicholas' letter, the patriarch's letter to Boris warrants respect as an indirect reflection of the Bulgar situation as seen by a sagacious ecclesiastical statesman; it is worthy of respect because of Photius' knowledge of a wide range of issues.

These two pastoral letters are supplemented by other letters that throw light on the situation in Bulgaria during the years between Boris' conversion and his retirement to a monastery. All of these documents originated either in the papal curia or at the Byzantine court, and all in some way bore on the bitterly debated issue of ecclesiastical jurisdiction over Bulgaria.[15] Some were addressed by Popes Hadrian II and John VIII to the Byzantine court and the patriarch, threatening the use of strong measures if the Greeks did not leave Bulgaria to Roman jurisdiction.[16] Others went from Rome to Bulgaria, pleading with Boris and his advisers to return to Roman jurisdiction after the Bulgar defection from Rome in 870.[17] Internal evidence offers excellent grounds for believing that the popes based these letters, in part, on a knowledge of

15. The quarrel over Bulgaria is traced in detail by Hergenröther, *ibid., passim*; by Dvornik, *The Photian Schism, History and Legend* (Cambridge, 1948); by Émile Amann, *L'époque carolingiennne* (*Histoire de l'église depuis les origines jusqu'à nos jours*, publiée sous la direction de Augustin Fliche et Victor Martin, T. VI) (Paris, 1947), pp. 465–501; and by A. Lapôtre, *L'Europe et le Saint-Siège à l'époque carolingienne*, Pt. 1: *Le pape Jean VIII* (Paris, 1895), *passim*.

16. *Hadriani II. Papae Epistolae*, Nos. 41, 42, ed. Ernestus Perels, *MGH, Ep.*, VI, 759–62; *Iohannis VIII. Papae Epistolae*, Nos., 68, 69, 207–9, 259, ed. Caspar, *MGH, Ep.*, VII, 62–65, 173–74, 179–80, 185–86, 229; *Fragmenta Registri Iohannis VIII. Papae*, No. 40, ed. Ericus Caspar, *MGH, Ep.*, VII, 296. See also Jaffé-Wattenbach, *Regesta Pontificum Romanorum*, No. 2915 (Leipzig, 1885), I, 371.

17. *Iohannis VIII. Papae Epistolae*, Nos. 66, 67, 70, 71, 182, 183, 192, 198, 298, 308, ed. Caspar, *MGH, Ep.*, VII, 58–62, 65–67, 146–47, 153–54, 158–59, 260, 266–67; *Fragmenta Registri Iohannis VIII. Papae*, Nos. 7, 37, ed. Caspar, *MGH, Ep.*, VII, 277, 294–95. The parts of these papal letters pertaining to Bulgar affairs, as well as those cited in the preceding note, are printed with a Bulgarian translation in *FLHB*, eds. Dujčev *et al.*, II, 129–31 (Hadrian's letters), 137–81 (John VIII's letters).

64

affairs in Bulgaria derived from their agents who had journeyed there or from Bulgar legations to Rome.

One letter of Photius to the patriarchs of the eastern churches sought to enlist their aid in attaching Bulgaria to Constantinople.[18] This letter reflects the patriarch's extensive knowledge of the activities of Roman missionaries in Bulgaria; it also suggests not only that Photius was interested in Bulgar affairs but that he had means of keeping informed of developments there even when the Romans were in command of the missionary operation. Pope Nicholas I wrote Archbishops Hincmar of Rheims and Luitbertus of Mainz, informing them at some length on Bulgar affairs, and attempting in this fashion to involve them, their kings, and their suffragans in the struggle over Bulgaria.[19]

The Bulgar issue was dealt with by the papal secretary, Anastasius Bibliothecarius, in a prefatory letter to his Latin version of the decrees of the general council held in Constantinople in 869–870.[20] Anastasius was in Constantinople at the time of this council, before which a Bulgar legation appeared to request a decision on the question of whether Bulgaria was subject to Roman or Greek jurisdiction. Thus he was in a position to garner some first-hand information about Bulgar affairs. (However, he was not present at the sessions of the council when the Bulgar issue was debated; his account of that event is derived from other papal legates who were in attendance.)

As might be expected, all these documents are strongly partisan and given to distortion in the hope of gaining advantage in the struggle for Bulgaria. Most of the authors felt the need to explain what had happened in Bulgaria, but most of the recipients were also aware of the course of events in Bulgaria, which made it pointless to misrepresent the truth too badly. As a result, these letters rather accurately reflect the progress made in the Christianization of Bulgaria. From them emerges additional and definite information on the problems encountered by Boris in converting his people.

Finally, there are some miscellaneous sources that touch upon the situation in Bulgaria. The biographies of Popes Nicholas I and Hadrian II

---

18. Photius, *Ep.*, No. 4, ed. Valetta, pp. 165–81.

19. See *Nicolai I. Papae Epistolae*, No. 100, ed. Perels, *MGH, Ep.*, VI, 600–609, for the letter to Hincmar of Rheims. *Annales Fuldenses, a.* 868, ed. Fridericus Kurze, *MGH, SS. rer. Germ.* (Hanover, 1891), pp. 66–67, signifies that the same letter was sent to the bishops of the East Frankish kingdom.

20. *Anastasii Bibliothecarii Ep. sive Praef.*, No. 5, eds. Perels and Laehr, *MGH, Ep.*, VII, 411–15. That portion of this document appropriate to Bulgar affairs is printed with a Bulgarian translation in *FLHB*, II, 196–203.

made careful record of the conversion of Bulgaria, especially in view of Boris' submission to Rome in 866 and his ultimate return to Constantinople.[21] Both Byzantine and Latin chroniclers were impressed enough by the baptism of Boris and the events connected with it to supply some information, although, unfortunately, they did not remain sufficiently interested in Bulgar affairs to complete the story of the Christianization of the land.[22] There is also a biography of St. Clement of Ochrida, a disciple of the famous Moravian missionary, Methodius. Clement entered Bulgaria about 885, after being driven from Moravia, and he spent the rest of his life working as a missionary in various part of Bulgaria.[23] A fragmentary life of St. Nahum, another refugee from Moravia who labored in Bulgaria, also survives.[24] From these sources one catches an occasional glimpse of Boris' actions and problems, although this information hardly permits a full reconstruction of the progress of Christianity in Bulgaria.

21. *Liber pontificalis*, ed. Duchesne, II, 164–65, 182–85. The portions of these papal lives relevant to Bulgar affairs are printed with a Bulgarian translation in *FLHB*, II, 184–95; however, the Latin version supplied here has been taken from the inferior edition in Migne, *PL*, CXXVIII, cols. 1379–96.

22. *Annales Bertiniani*, a. 864, 866, ed. Waitz, *MGH, SS. rer. Germ.*, pp. 72, 85–86; *Annales Fuldenses*, a. 863, 866, 867, ed. Kurze, *MGH, SS. rer. Germ.*, pp. 56, 65–66; Regino of Prum, *Chronicon*, a. 868, ed. F. Kurze, *MGH, SS. rer. Germ.* (Hanover, 1890), pp. 95–96; Georgius Monachus (Continuatus), *Vitae imperatorum recentiorum: De Michaele et Theodora*, Ch. 16, ed. I. Bekker, *Corpus Scriptorum Historiae Byzantinae* (Bonn, 1838), p. 824; Georgius Cedrenus, *Compendium Historiarum*, ed. I. Bekker, *CSHB* (2 vols.; Bonn, 1838–39), II, 151–53; Josephus Genesius, *Regum Liber IV de Michaele Theophili Filio*, ed. C. Lachmann, *CSHB* (Bonn, 1834), p. 97; Theophanes Continuatus, *Chronographia*, IV, Chs. 13–15, ed. I. Bekker, *CSHB* (Bonn, 1838), pp. 162–65; Symeon Magister ac Logotheta, *Annales: De Michaele et Theodora*, Chs. 21–22, 25, ed. I. Bekker, *CSHB* (Bonn, 1838), pp. 664–66; Ioannas Zonaras, *Epitomae Historiarum libri XIII–XVIII*, XVI, Ch. 2, ed. T. Büttner-Wobst, *CSHB* (Bonn, 1897), pp. 387–89; Theophylactus Bulgariae Archiepiscopus, *Historia Martyrii XV Martyrum*, Chs. 28–55, Migne, *PG*, CXXVI, cols. 189–221. The portions of the Latin chronicles relevant to Bulgarian history are printed with a Bulgarian translation in *FLHB*, II, 43–45 (*Annales Fuldenses*), 287–88 (*Annales Bertiniani*), 306–7 (Regino).

23. Theophylactus Bulgariae Archiepiscopus, *Vita s. Clementis*, Migne, *PG*, CXXVI, cols. 1193–239. A better edition of this work, A. Milev, *Teofilakt Ohridski, Žitie na Kliment Ohridski. Prevod ot grŭckija original, uvod i beležki* (Sofia, 1955), was not available for this study. For the authorship of this life, see Methodie Kusseff, "St. Clement of Ochrida," *Slavonic (and East European) Review*, XXVII(1948–49), 193–215, and especially I. Snegarov, "Les sources sur la vie et l'activité de Clément d'Ochrida," *Byzantinobulgarica*, I (1962), 79–119.

24. The old Slavonic text and an English translation of this life are provided by Methodie Kusseff, "St. Nahum," *Slavonic and East European Review*, XXIX (1950–51), 142–44.

66

Viewed collectively, these several sources leave much to be desired when one contemplates the task of assessing the impact of Christianity on Bulgar society and the role of the prince in promoting the conversion of Bulgaria. None of them emanated directly from Bulgaria, a fact which obviously precludes certainty in their treatment of affairs in Bulgaria. The historian is forced to proceed by inference in using these sources, never an ideal—or even adequate—mode of argument. Many of the documents are surcharged with partisan issues, which very likely caused their authors to disregard more significant factors existing in Bulgaria simply because these matters had no direct relevance to the issue under dispute. Moreover, all were written by men who, at best, had limited contact with the Bulgars and who had never been in Bulgaria as eye-witnesses to the events they treated. Such reporters were bound to suffer serious limitations in their grasp of realities in Bulgaria and conclusions derived from such evidence must be tentative. Nevertheless, these documents abound in quick glimpses and veiled allusions to conditions in Bulgaria. This is so primarily because their authors had a vital interest in conditions in Bulgaria. The winning or losing of jurisdiction over that important realm depended, to some degree, upon a grasp of the situation there. Unlike so many other cases in missionary history, these documents were not composed to recount the heroic deeds of missionaries and to record the victories won for the faith. A careful, systematic exploitation of these documents, governed by a firm effort to see the conversion process from the Bulgar position, yields a considerable body of information bearing on the problems raised for a prince by his decision to convert his people and on the influences exerted on the culture of a nation by the new religion. At least the harvest is richer than in most other cases involving the conversion of entire nations in the early middle ages.

The sources dealing with the Christianization of Bulgaria dramatically highlight the first problem facing Boris when he decided to become a Christian. His decision plunged his kingdom into a grim crisis during which the khan was in grave danger of losing control over his subjects. This crisis was compounded of several factors which can be clarified only by an examination of the precise circumstances surrounding Boris' decision to become a Christian.

As has already been noted, Christianity began to penetrate the area controlled by the Bulgars as early as the seventh century. The new religion was introduced by war prisoners, merchants, and by Bulgars who had lived for a time in the Byzantine Empire and then returned to the Bulgar state. While this process of slow penetration continued, the Bulgar state remained officially pagan. As nearly as can be ascertained, the Bulgar khans for a long time paid no attention to the growing number of Christians in their realm. However, by the ninth century they could no longer overlook the fact that Christianity was becoming an important factor among their people. One account has it that during the reign of Khan Ormatog (814–831) there were even Christians in the khan's household, seeking, with some success, to influence major decisions.[25] The khans of the early ninth century attempted to solve this problem by persecuting the Christians, although apparently with no success.[26]

By the middle of the ninth century, then, when Boris became khan, Christianity was a force in Bulgaria of sufficient importance to concern the prince, and some decision about this new religion would soon have to be made. Factors other than the presence of Christians were also emerging to drive the khan toward a decision in favor of the official conversion of Bulgaria to Christianity. Boris' kingdom was made up of Bulgars and Slavs, the former actually being a minority group long accustomed to dominating the latter. Like his predecessors, Boris searched for forces which would unite these disparate and often hostile elements into a single nation.

A common religion was certainly a possible solution, and the promise of its efficiency as a unifying force must have led Boris to think in terms of imposing Christianity on his subjects. Perhaps he sensed that the only way to persuade the Slavic element in his kingdom to accept the authority of a Bulgar lord was to make that lord a Christian ruler, and he was probably convinced that Christianity would also enhance his power as head of the state. Knowing from the experience of his predecessors that the Bulgar nobles, the *boyars*, were jealous of the khan's authority, he perhaps hoped that the institution of a new religion and the creation of a new church in his realm would give him prestige enough to curb the *boyars* and power enough to rule over his subjects after the fashion of the Byzantine *basileus* or the Frankish *augustus*.

25. Theophylactus, *Historia Martyrii XV Martyrum*, Chs. 29–30, Migne, *PG*, CXXVI, cols. 192–93.

26. For evidence of persecution under Ormatog, see *ibid.*, Ch. 30, col. 193; Theophanes Continuatus, *Chronographia*, V, Ch. 4, ed. I. Bekker, *CSHB*, pp. 216–17; Ioannes Zonaras, *Epitomae historiarum*, XVI, Ch. 6, ed. T. Büttner-Wobst, *CSHB*, p. 408; Theodore of Studite, *Sermones Catechatici*, No. LXIII, Migne, *PG*, XCIX, col. 591. See also Gérard, *Les Bulgares*, pp. 162–78; Spinka, *A History of Christianity in the Balkans*, pp. 27–29; Dvornik, *Les Slaves, Byzance et Rome au IXᵉ siècle*, pp. 99–101.

68

The religion of the Bulgars was surely a significant factor in the international policy pursued by the Bulgar khans. Beginning with the reign of Krum (802–814), the khans followed an aggressive, expansionist policy against the Byzantine Empire, the Serbs, the Croats, the Moravians, and the Franks. To succeed against so wide a variety of foes required alliances, and Boris certainly realized that his chances of winning favor from most of these potential allies were poor so long as he was a pagan. The acceptance of Christianity might contribute substantially toward engendering respect among foreign powers for a people long thought of as destructive, cruel barbarians, who were capable of such an act of savagery as using the skull of a dead Byzantine emperor for a drinking cup.[27] The success of the Moravians in winning Byzantine support (in 863) by agreeing to become Christians under the aegis of Cyril and Methodius could hardly have been lost on Boris or ignored in his diplomatic calculations.[28]

There were, perhaps, even personal forces at work pushing Boris toward conversion. One account tells that his sister had long been in Constantinople as a hostage, had been converted, and had returned to Boris' courts, where she exerted an influence on him.[29] Other sources speak of the presence at the Bulgar court of Greek monks who were seeking to persuade the khan to accept the true faith.[30] In view of the strong religious bent Boris demonstrated after his conversion, one might well conclude that he was personally attracted to Christianity quite aside from political and diplomatic considerations. It appears beyond question, then, that throughout the early years of Boris' reign there were numerous pressures recommending that the khan accept Christianity for himself and his people.

27. *Theophanis Chronographia*, ed. Carolus de Boor (2 vols.; Leipzig, 1883–85), I, 491.

28. See Dvornik, *Les légendes de Constantin et de Méthode vues de Byzance* (Prague, 1933); idem, *Les Slaves, Byzance et Rome au IXe siècle*, pp. 147–83, 259–96; J. Bujnoch, *Zwischen Rom und Byzance. Leben und Wirken des Slavenapostel Kyrillos und Methodios* (*Slavische Geschichtsschreiber*, I) (Gratz, 1958); Franz Grivec, *Konstantin und Method, Lehrer des Slaven* (Weisbaden, 1960); and Zdenek R. Dittrich, *Christianity in Greater Moravia* (Gronigen, 1962), for a full discussion of the problem of the conversion of the Moravians and the activities of Cyril and Methodius.

29. Theophanes Continuatus, *Chronographia*, IV, Ch. 14, ed. I. Bekker, *CSHB*, pp. 162–63; Ioannes Zonaras, *Epitomae historiarum*, XVI, Ch. 2, ed. T. Büttner-Wobst, *CSHB*, pp. 387–88.

30. Theophanes Continuatus, *Chronographia*, IV, Chs. 14–15, ed. I. Bekker, *CSHB*, pp. 163–64; Georgius Cedrenus, *Compendium Historiarum*, ed. I. Bekker, *CSHB*, II, 152–53; Symeon Magister, *Annales: De Michaele et Theodora*, Ch. 22, ed. I. Bekker, *CSHB*, p. 664; Ioannes Zonaras, *Epitomae historiarum*, XVI, Ch. 2, ed. T. Büttner-Wobst, *CSHB*, p. 388.

With these rather powerful forces operating to drive Boris toward conversion, it seems that the khan would have been free to decide the time and the circumstance for the introduction of the new religion into his realm. The first years of his reign were marked by a series of triumphs, especially in the diplomatic field. No one, inside or outside his realm, seemed to be in any position to dictate to him, and the evidence suggests that Boris, of his own volition, had decided by the early 860's to accept Christianity at a time and under circumstances that would permit him to reap a diplomatic reward.

The tantalizing prize was the prospect of an alliance with Louis the German against Rastislav of Moravia. A German alliance, aimed at victimizing Rastislav, promised to give Boris greater freedom to extend his control over the Slavic world and to provide him with a strong ally against Bulgaria's greatest foe, the Byzantine Empire, which at the moment was deeply engaged in a crucial struggle with the Moslems. Boris apparently chose to accept Christianity as part of the price to be paid for a firm alliance with Louis the German. The treaty between Boris and Louis was agreed upon in a meeting at Tuln in 862, and shortly thereafter reports reached Rome that Boris was willing to accept Christianity, apparently under the guidance of German clergymen.[31]

However, Boris' clever attempts to capitalize on his conversion by extracting a diplomatic advantage for Bulgaria were unavailing. The Byzantine government discerned his game, and, acting to offset the Bulgar advantage, made an alliance with the sorely tried Rastislav. Soon thereafter, they sent Cyril and Methodius to Moravia as missionaries, thereby counteracting the influence of the German clergy operating there. The government of Emperor Michael III, fortunately freed from the Arab threat as a result of an important victory in 863, sent a military expedition into Bulgaria in 864. Surprised by these speedy moves and crippled because of a famine in his land, Boris surrendered to the Byzantine forces without a struggle. The skillful diplomacy of the Greeks apparently made his choice easier by allowing him to retain all his territory, insisting only that he give up his alliance with the Franks. Indeed, the chief condition imposed on Boris was that he accept Christianity under Greek auspices. With almost unseemly haste the final settlement was negotiated in Constantinople, and a group of Greek clergymen, led by a bishop, was sent to baptize Boris and to assume the burden of converting his subjects.

31. *Nicolai I. Papae Epistolae*, No. 26, ed. Perels, *MGH, Ep.*, VI, 293; *Annales Fuldenses*, a. 863, ed. Kurze, *MGH, SS. rer. Germ.*, p. 56; *Annales Bertiniani*, a. 864, ed. Waitz, *MGH, SS. rer. Germ.*, p. 72.

The whole process was completed by the summer of 865. Boris was a Christian and the conversion of his subjects was under way.[32]

This chain of events obviously negated whatever plans Boris had made in 862, 863 and 864 for the conversion of Bulgaria with the help of German missionaries. More significantly, the sudden shift of affairs permitted a foreign power to become involved within Bulgaria in a fashion which appeared to compromise Bulgar sovereign power and to subordinate the khan to an external authority. By 865, foreign priests, sponsored by a government that had just won a military victory over the Bulgars, were streaming into Boris' realm and telling his subjects to do strange things.[33] Officials in Constantinople were assuming that they had certain powers over Boris and his subjects.[34] In accordance with Christian usage, the khan had been persuaded to assume a foreign name, Michael, as a result of his acceptance of Emperor Michael III as his godfather.[35] This arrangement, however innocent in spiritual terms, had definite implications of Bulgar political subordination to a superior authority. For the moment there was no telling how far the influence of the Greeks over the Bulgars' internal affairs might extend.

To many Bulgars, and perhaps even to the khan, their defeat at the hands of the Byzantine forces in 864 was greater than any defeat the Bulgars had previously suffered. Earlier defeats had involved loss of territory, the payment of tribute, and the sending of hostages to the

32. The chief sources informing us (not very adequately) on the events leading to the conversion of Boris are Theophanes Continuatus, *Chronographia*, IV, Ch. 15, ed. I. Bekker, *CSHB*, pp. 163–65; Georgius Monachus (Continuatus), *Vitae recentiorum imperatorum: De Michaele et Theodora*, Ch. 16, ed. I. Bekker, *CSHB*, p. 824; Ioannes Zonaras, *Epitomae historiarum*, XVI, Ch. 2, ed. T. Büttner-Wobst, *CSHB*, pp. 387–89. For a careful analysis of these sources and their meaning, see Dvornik, *Les Slaves, Byzance et Rome au IX⁰ siècle*, pp. 184–89; Spinka, *A History of Christianity in the Balkans*, pp. 25–33; Gérard, *Les Bulgares*, pp. 183–205; and Runciman, *The First Bulgarian Empire*, pp. 102–5. See A. Vaillart and M. Lascaris, "La date de la conversion des Bulgares," *Revue des études slaves*, XIII (1933), 5–15, for a discussion of the problems connected with the date of the conversion.

33. At least Boris complained of this condition to Pope Nicholas I; see Nicholas, *Ep.*, No. 99, Chs. 6, 14–16, 54–55, 57, 66, 77, 94, 103–6, pp. 572, 575–76, 587, 588, 590–91, 593, 597, 599–600.

34. Photius, *Ep.*, No. 6, Ch. 20, ed. Valetta, p. 220, where Boris is referred to as the "spiritual son" of Photius (. . . πνευματικὲ ἡμῶν υἱέ).

35. Theophylactus, *Hist. Martyrii XV Martyrum*, Ch. 34, Migne, *PG*, CXXVI, col. 200; Georgius Monachus (Continuatus), *Vitae recentiorum imperatorum: De Michaele et Theodora*, Ch. 16, ed. I. Bekker, *CSHB*, p. 824; Theophanes Continuatus, *Chronographia*, IV, Ch. 14, ed. I. Bekker, *CSHB*, p. 163; Josephus Genesius, *Regum Liber IV de Michaele Theophilii Filio*, ed. C. Lachmann, *CSHB*, p. 97; Symeon Magister, *Annales: De Michaele et Theodora*, Ch. 25, ed. I. Bekker, *CSHB*, p. 665.

victor; this defeat had loosed upon the Bulgars the agents of a foreign power who engaged themselves—as we shall see in detail—in changing Bulgar society in profound ways. All of this had come about because Boris had already decided to Christianize his subjects and was now willing to accept foreign assistance in this task as a condition for a peace settlement.

The presence of these missionaries, a by-product of a military defeat, appeared to assure Greek predominance in Bulgaria and to preclude complete freedom of action for the Bulgars in the realm of diplomacy. Boris had suffered a serious setback by being forced to do—at a moment and under circumstances not of his choosing—something he had already decided to do: to become a Christian and to assume responsibility for converting his subjects. Put another way, his position would have been much more secure had he been free to "invite" German missionaries to his land under terms that would have permitted the world to think that Bulgaria was accepting Christianity out of free choice and with the assistance of missionaries who had entered Bulgaria by the grace of the khan. Because of his skill as a leader, Boris escaped the potential consequences of his subordination to a foreign power, but, for a brief time between 864 and 866, his position was indeed tenuous.

The seriousness of the crisis surrounding the conversion of the Bulgars in 864 probably resulted from a serious miscalculation by Boris. In spite of the fact that he felt many internal pressures forcing his nation toward conversion, he deliberately sought to exploit his willingness to accept Christianity as a diplomatic ploy, first to gain an ally and then to soften the exactions of a victorious foe. He seemingly failed to realize the significance the Christian world attached to the conversion of an entire people of some prominence in the contemporary world scene, and he therefore underestimated the extent to which outsiders would insist on being involved in Bulgar affairs in the name of Christianizing his land.

Perhaps Boris should not be blamed for his limited grasp of the situation. So far as we can determine, no Christian prince or prelate had taken any interest in the spiritual state of the Bulgars during the nearly two centuries prior to the reign of Boris, when Christianity was slowly penetrating the pagan land. However, the moment it became obvious that Boris was inclined to accept Christianity and convert his people, it became a matter of universal concern. Kings and emperors had maneuvered furiously to force Boris' hand, and then had vied to be on hand when Boris was ready for baptism. They hoped that by having assisted in the conversion process and the institution of the new religion they would be in a position to exercise a degree of control over the newly converted prince and his land, or that they could entrench their ecclesiastical representatives in his realm as agents capable of controlling the policy of Bulgaria in their favor. Everyone seemed to assume that the movement of the Bulgars toward conversion would result in a profound transformation of Bulgar society which would make that people more desirable as allies and more formidable as foes. No one could stand aside and permit the pagan Boris to proceed toward the conversion of his people at his own speed.

In spite of the fact that Boris enjoyed a reputation as a powerful ruler, he was not strong enough or skillful enough to control the actions of those outside his realm once they were convinced that his land was open to Christianity. Nor could he prevent foreigners from using his willingness to accept their aid in carrying forward the conversion process as evidence of Bulgar subordination to their overlordship. This sudden aggressive thrust by outsiders, justified in the name of assisting with conversion, introduced elements into the Bulgarian scene that seriously compromised the power of the prince, threatening—at least momentarily—to reduce him to a dependent position.

The crisis accompanying the decision to accept Christianity had another dimension which likewise threatened the ruler's power, and this was its effect on the people within the Bulgar state. Considerable confusion developed at all levels of the populace, centering around a conviction that the acceptance of a new deity and the repudiation of the old gods involved tampering with the foundations of the cosmic order, and that drastic consequences might result. This state of mind bred resentment, fear, and doubt among those being converted, and it contributed to the general atmosphere of crisis accompanying Boris' decision to accept Christianity.

Several sources relating to the conversion of the Bulgars suggest the existence of religious tension and uneasiness. Certain scraps of evidence also indicate that Boris himself had wrestled seriously with the religious implications of the acceptance of Christianity. A Greek chronicler insists that a vivid painting of the Last Judgment (by a Christian artist named Methodius, living at the khan's court) aroused in Boris a fear of eternal damnation and hellfire strong enough to help persuade him to become a Christian.[36] It was also said that Boris was convinced that the famine which afflicted his land in 864 (the year of his conversion) was caused by

36. Theophanes Continuatus, *Chronographia*, IV, Ch. 15, ed. I. Bekker, *CSHB*, pp. 163–64; see also Georgius Cedrenus, *Compendium Historiarum*, ed. I. Bekker, *CSHB*, II, 152–53.

the wrath of the Christian God and could be alleviated only by surrender to that God.[37] These instances are hardly sufficient for a valid generalization but they imply that the coming of the new religion posed disturbing questions for the Bulgars about the powers of their old gods and the possible dire consequences of a failure to take account of the Christian God.

The *boyar* revolt that occurred in Bulgaria as an immediate reaction to Boris' decision to impose Christianity on his subjects offers further confirmation of a state of uneasiness in the land. The following account of that revolt, provided by a western European source, contains some interesting reflections of the state of mind prevailing in Bulgaria during the initial stages of the conversion process:

> The king of the Bulgars . . . received holy baptism. Because his nobles thought themselves injured, they incited the people against him in order to kill him. [Everybody] in the ten provinces gathered themselves around his palace. He, having invoked the name of Christ and being accompanied by forty-eight men all fervent Christians who remained with him, emerged against all that multitude. And then as he passed out of the gates of the city, there appeared to him and to those with him seven priests; each of them held a burning candle in his hand. And thus they led the way for the king and those who were with him. To those who had rebelled against him it seemed that a great palace burning over their heads was about to fall on them; and in front the horses of those who were with the king stood erect and struck the rebels with their front legs. So great a fear seized them that they neither tried to flee nor to defend themselves, but prostrated themselves unable to move.[38]

This account highlights the extremes to which opinion ran at the decisive hour of conversion: from belligerent opposition to abject surrender in the face of an outward display of the symbols of the new religion.

One might dismiss these scraps of information simply as fanciful attempts by later historians to explain the miraculous working of God so

37. Theophanes Continuatus, *Chronographia*, IV, Ch. 14, ed. I. Bekker, *CSHB*, p. 163; Theophylactus, *Hist. Martyrii XV Martyrum*, Ch. 34, Migne, *PG*, CXXVI, cols. 197–200; Georgius Cedrenus, *Compendium Historiarum*, ed. I. Bekker, *CSHB*, II, 151–52; Ioannes Zonaras, *Epitomae Historiarum*, XVI, Ch. 2, ed. T. Büttner-Wobst, *CSHB*, p. 388; Symeon Magister, *Annales: De Michaele et Theodora*, Ch. 22, ed. I. Bekker, *CSHB*, pp. 664–65.

38. *Annales Bertiniani, a.* 866, ed. Waitz, *MGH, SS. rer. Germ.*, p. 85. The revolt is also noted by Theophanes Continuatus, *Chronographia*, IV, Ch. 15, ed. I. Bekker, *CSHB*, p. 164; Ioannes Zonaras, *Epitomae Historiarum*, XVI, Ch. 2, ed. T. Büttner-Wobst, *CSHB*, pp. 388–89; and Symeon Magister, *Annales: De Michaele et Theodora*, Ch. 25, ed. I. Bekker, *CSHB*, pp. 665–66; these sources do not, however, supply such full details.

as to assure the spread of his true religion. They are corroborated, however, by the questions Boris sent to Pope Nicholas, many of which reflect concern and tension in the minds of the Bulgars as they began to face the implications of their conversion. Repeatedly, the khan asked the pope's opinion about the necessity for abandoning ancient practices, and the tone of these requests suggests that the new converts were torn by indecision and doubts as they proceeded to divest themselves of their time-sanctioned customs.[39] Boris and his subjects needed papal reassurance of the wisdom of their acceptance of Christianity; probably the khan also needed papal authority to help persuade his subjects that the abandonment of pagan religious practices was both necessary and safe.

In several other instances Boris sought papal direction for the exact way Christians should go about certain activities with which pagan religious practices were associated: preparation for battle, the supplication of the spirit world for relief from drought, praying at mealtime, and the disposal of animals killed in unusual ways.[40] In these cases the khan seemed to be fearful lest he and his subjects innocently anger their new God by some ritualistic indiscretion and thus bring disaster on themselves in matters absolutely essential to their daily lives. Perhaps the most poignant request made by Boris—one symbolical of all the uncertainty surrounding the acceptance of a new religion and the abandonment of the old—was his query about the propriety of praying for his dead pagan ancestors.[41] The khan seemed to have realized that the pope would answer that a Christian was not allowed to pray for dead pagans, yet the new convert felt compelled to raise this question on a vital matter so as once more to set his mind at rest that no catastrophe would descend on those who had abandoned their ancient gods for a new one. Throughout Nicholas' response there are indications that the new convert was uneasy, doubtful, and ready to grasp at anything for assurance that his recent religious choice was one that would benefit rather than harm him.

It appears, then, that there are grounds for concluding that the decision to become a Christian brought personal anxiety and uneasiness to the khan. Moreover, some of the *boyars* were seriously enough moved by the khan's decision to attempt regicide, which earned them the reward they must have known would result from failure: execution by the khan. It is perhaps not unwarranted to assume that the general populace shared

39. Nicholas, *Ep.*, No. 99, Chs. 33, 62, 79, 89, pp. 580–81, 589–90, 594, 596.
40. *Ibid.*, Chs. 34, 53, 56, 90–91, pp. 581, 587–88, 596.
41. *Ibid.*, Ch. 88, p. 596.

the misgivings and doubts of their superiors. Indeed, the tenor of some of Boris' questions to Pope Nicholas I strongly suggests concern among the mass of people over fundamental issues: whether the old gods would be displeased by being abandoned, whether the cessation of ancient usages would deprive men of accustomed benefits, and whether their clumsy, amateurish approach to the new deity would provoke wrathful responses ruinous to their fortunes.

This state of mind hardly made it easier for the ruler to sustain his authority. Coupled with the onslaught of foreign influences, this internal uneasiness undermined, at least temporarily, the sovereign's control over his realm, as is evident in the *boyar* revolt. Nor did the unsettled condition vanish quickly. When Boris abdicated his office (in 889) in favor of his son, Vladimir, a new effort was made by the *boyars*, with the new khan's cooperation, to return to paganism.[42] Apparently, resentment of the new religion had existed covertly for a quarter of a century, having posed a permanent problem for the khan that had demanded his constant vigilance.

Boris was able to survive the disturbances that gripped his realm at the moment of his decision to Christianize his people, but serious problems still awaited him. Shortly after his baptism, he was reminded by Photius that after he had been liberated from error and freed from darkness, it was his duty to turn his faculties to the beauty of divine worship.[43] To the khan, only recently relieved of the crisis that accompanied his conversion, this command pointed to what all sources indicate was the most onerous burden facing a newly converted prince: the institution among his subjects of the outward forms of the new religion and the instruction of his people in the basic tenets of the new faith. Of course, a newly converted king could expect aid in this task, but he was made to feel that the responsibility was primarily his. The whole burden of Photius' letter to Boris was to remind the newly converted prince of the extent of his obligation in guiding his subjects to a full understanding and proper practice of Christianity.[44] Pope Nicholas was no less positive in assigning the burden of the institution of Christian practice in Bulgaria to Boris.[45]

42. Regino of Prum, *Chronicon*, a. 868, ed. Kurze, *MGH, SS. rer. Germ.*, pp. 95–96; Theophylactus, *Hist. Martyrii XV Martyrum*, Ch. 47, Migne, *PG*, CXXVI, col. 213.

43. Photius, *Ep.*, No. 6, Ch. 2, ed. Valetta, p. 203.

44. *Ibid.*, Chs. 25–28, pp. 224–26.

45. Nicholas, *Ep.*, No. 99, Chs. 17, 35, 40, 41, 82, 84, 106, pp. 577, 581, 582–83, 595, 599–600.

Boris did not shrink from this obligation. From the time of his baptism until the end of his reign, a major portion of his energies was absorbed in instituting Christian practices and spreading Christian doctrine among his subjects. His efforts, quite clearly, were marked with success, for by the end of his reign the outward Christianization of Bulgaria was far advanced. Moreover, the sources definitely indicate his dedication to this task. Never is there a hint—for instance, in the many papal letters sent to Boris to try to win him back under Roman control after he had given his allegiance to Constantinople in 870—that the khan had been negligent in fulfilling his obligations to Christianize his subjects; and in some cases the popes openly admit his devotion to that cause.[46] Furthermore, in the course of his lifetime Boris earned a great reputation for personal piety, dedication to duty, and steadfastness in pursuit of the goal of converting his people.[47] It is especially noteworthy that the Bulgar khan enjoyed a very high repute in western Europe, where he might have been regarded with suspicion because of his defection to Constantinople after his temporary acceptance of Rome's spiritual guidance.

Perhaps the most dramatic proof of his personal contribution to the Christianization of Bulgaria came after his abdication in 889. That event was the signal for a pagan reaction, led by his son and successor, Vladimir, and supported by a faction of the *boyars*. The fate of the new religion was in the balance until Boris left his monastic retreat to save the day.[48] However, the same sources which testify to Boris' successes in implanting the Christian faith and practices also demonstrate the magnitude of his task. They conclusively indicate that the progress of the new religion depended on the ruler's ability to cope with several different problems simultaneously.

Boris' first problem was providing for the baptism of his people. He himself set the pattern by accepting baptism from a Byzantine bishop who had been sent into Bulgaria; and some members of his court circle were baptized at the same time.[49] This initial step still left the bulk of

46. *Iohannis VIII. Papae Ep.*, Nos. 66, 67, 182, 192, ed. Caspar, *MGH, Ep.*, VII, 59, 61, 146, 153–54.
47. *Liber pontificalis*, ed. Duchesne, II, 164; Regino of Prum, *Chronicon*, a. 868, ed. Kurze, *MGH, SS. rer. Germ.*, pp. 95–96; Theophylactus, *Hist. Martyrii XV Martyrum*, Chs. 34–36, Migne, *PG*, CXXVI, cols. 200–201; Theophylactus, *Vita s. Clementis*, Chs. 16–19, Migne, *PG*, CXXVI, cols. 1221–28.
48. Regino of Prum, *Chronicon*, a. 868, ed. Kurze, *MGH, SS. rer. Germ.*, pp. 95–96.
49. Theophanes Continuatus, *Chronographia*, IV, Chs. 14–15, ed. I. Bekker, *CSHB*, pp. 163–64; Symeon Magister, *Annales: De Michaele et Theodora*, Ch. 25, ed. I. Bekker, *CSHB*, p. 665; Ioannes Zonaras, *Epitomae Historiarum*, XVI, Ch. 2, ed. T. Büttner-Wobst,

the population to be brought to the baptismal font. Holding that it was his personal duty to assure this fundamental step in the Christianization of Bulgaria,[50] Boris was concerned with this problem for the remainder of his reign. Between the time of his conversion in 864 and his appeal to Rome in 866, the chief burden of baptizing Bulgars was borne by priests from the Byzantine world. Boris obviously tried to keep them under surveillance, for he complained to Nicholas of abuses perpetrated by these priests and asked for guidance in correcting the consequences.[51] After the Greek priests were replaced, priests from western Europe took up the burden. Again, Boris was concerned with the progress being made, since he sought to recruit additional clergymen for that purpose in the kingdom of Louis the German, as well as at Rome.[52] Twenty years later, Boris had not yet completely solved this problem. In 885 he greeted with open arms the disciples of Methodius, who had been forced to flee Moravia, and put them to work baptizing Bulgars in remote regions of the kingdom.[53] One can only conclude that from the moment of his conversion Boris felt he had to be alert for unbaptized subjects and to devise ways of bringing them to the baptismal font.

However, the baptism of the Bulgars presented complexities that extended beyond the mere task of finding priests in sufficient numbers to baptize every Bulgar. There were some who refused to become Christians.[54] Others apostasized after baptism and rose in rebellion against the ruler they held responsible for having caused them to be baptized.[55] Some, apparently, tried to flee the land to escape baptism.[56] This recalcitrant element in the population must have caused Boris no end of uneasiness, especially in the initial stages of the effort to baptize all Bulgars. With so many to lead to the baptismal font, Bulgaria was apparently attractive to clergymen with dubious credentials, for Boris complained that a

CSHB, p. 388; Theophylactus, Hist. Martyrii XV Martyrum, Ch. 34, Migne, PG, CXXVI, col. 200.

50. Nicholas, Ep., No. 99, Ch. 17, p. 577.

51. Ibid., Chs. 14, 104, pp. 575, 599.

52. Liber pontificalis, ed. Duchesne, II, 165; Anastasii Bibliothecarii Ep. sive Praef., No. 5, eds. Perels and Laehr, MGH, Ep., VII, 412; Annales Fuldenses, a. 866, 867, ed. Kurze, MGH, SS. rer. Germ., pp. 65–66.

53. Theophylactus, Vita s. Clementis, Chs. 17, ff. Migne, PG, CXXVI, cols. 1224 et seqq.

54. Nicholas, Ep., No. 99, Ch. 41, pp. 582–83.

55. Ibid., Chs. 17–19, pp. 577–78; Annales Bertiniani, a. 866, ed. Waitz, MGH, SS. rer. Germ., p. 85.

56. Nicholas, Ep., No. 99, Ch. 20, p. 579.

Greek, who falsely claimed to be a priest,[57] and a Jew[58] were busily engaged in baptizing Bulgars. Not only was it necessary for the khan to discover such charlatans, he also had to worry whether the sacrament they had administered was valid.

Certain technical questions about the administration of baptism arose: the nature of baptismal sponsorship, the proper season for baptism, the number of times a year the sacrament could be administered, and fasting regulations on days of baptism.[59] Although nowhere explicitly stated, it appears likely that many of the questions posed by Boris in his letter to Nicholas were issues raised by people about to be baptized. For example, it seems logical to infer that Boris asked Nicholas about the legitimacy of the Bulgar custom of hanging a wooden pendant about the neck as a healing device because many about to be baptized had asked whether part of the bargain included giving up such sacred objects.[60] An abundance of such questions must have been a burden to the khan and his priests. Clearly, the baptism of large numbers was no simple task; rather, the process raised numerous questions and caused uneasiness everywhere.

Although the baptizing of the Bulgars continued slowly, the khan was faced with the problem of inculcating into the minds of his subjects the basic concepts of Christian dogma. It was no doubt the complexity of this task which prompted Boris to end his letter to Nicholas with a humble appeal that the pope instruct him as he would anyone not having true and perfect Christianity.[61] This sense of inadequacy could well have been induced in Boris by the stress his mentors placed on *knowledge* of the faith as a key to merit.

Photius was especially insistent in his pastoral letter that every prince must be responsible for guarding his subjects against heterodoxy. The proper discharge of this responsibility demanded that the prince know the tenets of the faith and that he see to it that his subjects learned about Christian doctrine. Lest out of ignorance Boris take this task too lightly, Photius deemed it best to instruct him in the fundamentals of the faith. Nearly a third of his tract to Boris consists of a summary of decisions by all of the ecumenical councils on matters of dogma. Nor did Photius neglect to insinuate the idea that heresy breeds contention and tumult

57. *Ibid.*, Chs. 14–15, pp. 575–76.
58. *Ibid.*, Ch. 104, p. 599.
59. *Ibid.*, Chs. 2, 69, pp. 569, 591–92.
60. *Ibid.*, Ch. 79, p. 594.
61. *Ibid.*, Ch. 106, pp. 599–600.

in a nation, providing Boris with a special reason for concerning himself with the responsibility of teaching the true faith.[62] As one reads the patriarch's presentation of the central tenets of Christian dogma, it seems possible that Boris may have felt smothered by doctrinal points beyond his comprehension. Photius, in fact, plunged him straight into the intricate questions which dominated the ecumenical councils—in addition to quoting him the Nicene Creed as the starting point for dogmatic knowledge. Nicholas I, although not so expansive on dogmatic matters, did not fail to remind Boris that there were many things for him to learn about the faith and to transmit to his people.[63]

The sources are extremely vague on the procedures employed to assure the instruction of the new converts in the rudiments of the faith, and their vagueness may indicate that this was a process that did not occupy the center of attention from the Bulgar point of view. Usually, the sources state only that priests went through the land preaching;[64] and the missionaries may well have taken it upon themselves to decide what dogmatic matters were suitable to their audiences. Both Photius and Nicholas made it perfectly clear that they did not place any great confidence in the khan's grasp of Christian doctrine. This, then, might suggest that when missionaries came to Bulgaria they were not inclined to look to the royal court for guidance, or even cooperation, in the task of teaching the Bulgars the essentials of the faith.

Boris' major concerns in his requests to Nicholas strongly imply that he did not see the Christianization process basically in terms of the instruction of his people in dogma. He seldom asked the pope anything that was concerned directly with dogma; his interest was almost exclusively with the external practices and with the disciplinary aspects of the new religion. This is not to imply that Boris was completely ignorant of Christian doctrine, for his questions indicate an acquaintance with the sacramental system, the nature of sin, the doctrine of immortality, and prayer.[65] However, the occasional references that demonstrate some doctrinal awareness must be matched with evidence of the khan's doctrinal naïveté. Boris' confusion on the nature of baptism and penance, on the

62. Photius, *Ep.*, No. 6, Chs. 2–22, ed. Valetta, pp. 203–23, esp. Chs. 2, 20, 21, pp. 203, 220–22.

63. Nicholas, *Ep.*, No. 99, Chs. 1, 106, pp. 566–67, 599–600.

64. *Anastasii Bibliothecarii Ep. sive Praef.*, No. 5, eds. Perels and Laehr, *MGH, Ep.*, VII, 412; *Liber pontificalis*, ed. Duchesne, II, 165, 185.

65. Nicholas, *Ep.*, No. 99, Chs. 9, 14–16, 65, 75, 78, pp. 573, 575–76, 590, 593–94, on the sacraments; Chs. 16, 24, 26, 28, 29, 31, 32, 83, 85, 98, pp. 576, 579, 580, 595, 598, on sin; Chs. 38, 56, 61, pp. 582, 587–89, on prayer; Ch. 88, p. 596, on immortality.

efficacy of prayer and the sign of the cross, and on the role of the priest in administering the sacraments[66] may well have prompted Nicholas' rather uncomplimentary remark that the Bulgars, like little children, must be fed on milk until they were old enough to handle solid food.[67] It undoubtedly convinced the pope of the advisability of urging Boris to check with bishops and priests in Bulgaria to clear up difficult points.[68]

These scraps of evidence lead one to conclude that although the Bulgar ruler may have honored in the abstract the admonitions addressed to him to instruct his people in the faith, he had no particular program for achieving this end. The lack of a program stemmed from the khan's inadequate grasp of the doctrinal side of the new faith and from his inclination to see Christianity as a ritual and an external discipline. Perhaps toward the end of his reign, after the conversion of Bulgaria had made considerable progress, Boris began to realize the need for a systematic effort to assume royal direction over the doctrinal instruction of his people. This realization may have been part of his reason for sending Bulgars to Constantinople for instruction[69] and for encouraging the founding of monastic schools for the education of native Bulgars.[70] Until these efforts bore fruit, doctrinal instruction was in the hands of foreign missionaries, who operated as they saw fit.

Although it seems true that Boris did not develop a program for doctrinal instruction, and that he was not inclined to see the Christianization of his land primarily in terms of dogmatic issues, doctrinal matters nevertheless constituted a major problem for the khan and forced him to engage in an arena where he was confused and uncertain. Boris became involved simply because the missionaries upon whom he had to depend insisted upon making Bulgaria a theological battleground and upon establishing adherence to a certain doctrinal line as a criterion for true conversion.

As early as 866, Boris revealed that he was confused by various versions of Christian truth. He wrote to Nicholas that "many Christians from diverse lands had come into [his] land, . . . speaking in various tongues, that is, Greek, Armenian, and so forth," and he asked the pope

66. *Ibid.*, Chs. 2, 7, 14–16, 33, 38, 53, 56, 61, 71, 74, 78, 104, pp. 569, 572–73, 575–76, 580–82, 587–89, 592–94, 599.

67. *Ibid.*, Ch. 4, p. 571.

68. *Ibid.*, Chs. 9, 56, pp. 573, 587–88.

69. Photius, *Ep.*, No. 255, ed. Valetta, p. 556.

70. Theophylactus, *Vita s. Clementis*, Ch. 18, Migne, *PG*, CXXVI, col. 1225; "Life of St. Nahum" in M. Kusseff, "St. Nahum," *Slavonic and East European Review*, XXIX (1950–51), 142–44.

to tell him "whether he should obey all of these according to the various meanings or what he ought to do."[71] Nicholas told him what to do: follow the guidance of the church of Rome. Boris accepted this advice for the moment, and his appeal to Nicholas resulted in a new crop of missionaries from Rome, who, with the help of Boris, expelled the Greeks.[72]

Nicholas definitely instructed his representatives to root out the error established by the Greeks.[73] That they followed papal instructions is dramatically revealed in an angry letter addressed by Photius to the eastern patriarchs, accusing the Latins of spreading heresy in Bulgaria.[74] Prior to writing this letter Photius had apparently had these teachings condemned by a local synod, and he tried to use this decision to influence Boris. A letter from Emperors Michael and Basil was sent to Boris, informing him that a synod had condemned the teachings of the Roman missionaries. This was obviously an attempt to undermine the confidence of the Bulgars in their new spiritual masters, as was the spreading of pamphlets among the Bulgars condemning the Latins.[75]

Having, however, failed to persuade Boris that his adherence to Rome involved him in heresy, Photius enlarged the conflict. He summoned the patriarchs of the east to a general council in 867 to condemn the Latin doctrines being spread in Bulgaria. As F. Dvornik has shown, this meeting was held primarily to undermine the Roman position in Bulgaria.[76] Latin sources indicate that the Greeks used the decisions of this council to weaken Boris' attachment to Rome.[77] And it seems likely that confusion about the source and the content of the true Christian doctrine had a bearing on Boris' ultimate decision to abandon his second set of missionary teachers. In 870 his legates appeared at a council in Constantinople and asked the assembled prelates to decide to which jurisdiction the Bulgars pertained. The council ruled in favor of Constantinople. Thereupon a new set of clergymen passed into Bulgaria to drive out the

71. Nicholas, *Ep.*, No. 99, Ch. 106, p. 599.

72. *Liber pontificalis*, ed. Duchesne, II, 164.

73. Nicholas, *Ep.*, No. 100, ed. Perels, *MGH, Ep.*, VI, 601; *Liber pontificalis*, ed. Duchesne, II, 165.

74. Photius, *Ep.*, No. 4, ed. Valetta, pp. 165–81; see especially Chs. 3 and 4, p. 168, for Photius' version of what happened in Bulgaria after the Roman missionaries arrived and expelled the Greeks.

75. Nicholas, *Ep.*, No. 100, p. 603. Nicholas knew of these matters because Boris turned the imperial letter and other inflammatory writings over to the papal legates in Bulgaria.

76. Dvornik, *The Photian Schism*, pp. 119–31.

77. *Liber pontificalis*, ed. Duchesne, II, 185; *Anastasii Bibliothecarii Ep. sive Praef.*, No. 5, eds. Perels and Laehr, *MGH, Ep.*, VII, 413.

Latins and to correct the errors that had so agitated the Greeks since 867.[78]

Still the Bulgars found no relief. For many years the papacy tried to win back the Bulgars, primarily by arguing that the new converts were being led into grave doctrinal errors which endangered the newly established faith. The papal argument was embodied in a series of letters sent by Pope John VIII to Boris[79] and to his chief confidants.[80] John's argument in all these letters was fairly standard. The Bulgars had begun on the right path toward orthodoxy under Rome's direction, but now that the Greeks had infested Bulgaria, the pope feared that the Bulgars would be led into diverse heresies, schisms, and errors. John denied any interest in governing the Bulgars but he intimated that the Greeks' motives may not be apolitical. He also cited cases of other peoples who had been doctrinally misled by consorting with the Greeks. To avert the menace of heresy—with all its implications for the salvation of souls— the Bulgars must return to Rome, the fountain of the true faith. One motive governs all these letters: to kindle among the Bulgars a distrust for the Greeks which might lead the khan and his nobles to repudiate them and take the initiative in returning to Roman jurisdiction. John must have been convinced that the Bulgars were sensitive to doctrinal issues and the problem of orthodoxy for he pinned his hopes of victory almost entirely on the doctrinal level.

Boris and his advisers were not, to our knowledge, moved by the papal letters, nor by the personal appeals of a papal agent who was sent to Bulgaria presumably to argue the same cause.[81] Perhaps more worrisome to the khan was a letter addressed by John to the Greek clergy in Bulgaria that threatened to excommunicate them if they did not depart immediately.[82] The news of such a drastic step may well have raised serious alarm among new converts, clinging to the word of their priests that the faith was the answer to their spiritual problems.

We can therefore say with some certainty that the implantation of Christian doctrine generated troublesome clashes between missionary groups in Bulgaria which required vigilance by the ruler. Although

78. *Liber pontificalis*, ed. Duchesne, II, 181–85, for the events of this council and the appearance of the new missionary force in Bulgaria.

79. *Iohannis VIII. Papae Epistolae*, Nos. 66, 70, 182, 192, 198, 298, 308, ed. Caspar, *MGH, Ep.*, VII, 58–60, 65–66, 146, 153–54, 158–59, 260, 266–67; *Fragmenta Registri Iohannis VIII. Papae*, Nos. 7, 37, pp. 277, 294–95.

80. *Iohannis VIII. Papae Epistolae*, Nos. 67, 183, pp. 61–62, 147.

81. *Ibid.*, Nos. 184, 190, pp. 147, 152.

82. *Ibid.*, No. 71, pp. 66–67.

evidence is far from conclusive, the problem may well have been more serious. Divergent dogmatic positions presented to the populace in rapid succession may have bred confusion through the land. That such confusion existed is implicit in the tenor of John VIII's letters. Given the penchant of the Bulgars to fret over propriety—dramatically manifested in Boris' requests to Nicholas—one might surmise that the problem of coping with divergent dogmas left the entire population worried and uncertain during the early years after Christianity became the official religion.

Although the teaching of Christian doctrine was a significant and difficult aspect of the Christianization of Bulgaria, the institution of the outward practices of Christian worship was of greater concern to Boris. His requests to Nicholas I are so completely concerned with this issue that one is tempted to conclude that Boris saw the conversion process primarily as an exercise in changing the modes of worship of his people. This would be too strong a position, however, for we have already seen—or will see—that Boris realized other matters were also involved in the conversion process. What his queries indicate is that the introduction of the Christian cult raised major problems and that the khan was constantly involved in the issues that emerged from the institution of Christian worship.

A summary listing of the several aspects of Christian religious worship and observance that had to be introduced into Bulgaria will give some indication of the magnitude of the task facing Boris and his missionaries. Churches had to be built.[83] Public services, new to the Bulgars, had to be introduced into these churches: the mass, baptism, communion, confession, public prayer, marriages, confirmation, preaching, singing, funeral services, processions, veneration of relics, the use of Christian symbols.[84]

83. The literary sources say little about this matter except to note that churches were built; e.g., *Anastasii Bibliothecarii Ep. sive Praef.*, No. 5, eds. Perels and Laehr, *MGH, Ep.*, VII, 412; Theophylactus, *Vita s. Clementis*, Ch. 23, Migne, *PG*, CXXVI, cols. 1229–31. A proper treatment of this subject would involve a more thorough investigation of recent archaeological findings than has been made for this paper; for helpful suggestions see Bogdan D. Filov, *L'Art antique en Bulgarie* (Sofia, 1925); André Grabar, *La peinture religieuse en Bulgarie* (Paris, 1928); and Dimiter Dimitrov, *Bulgaria: Land of Ancient Civilizations* (Sofia, 1961), and the bibliography indicated there.

84. Nicholas, *Ep.*, No. 99, Ch. 76, p. 593, for mass; Chs. 14–16, 69, pp. 575–76, 591–92, for baptism; Chs. 9, 55, 65, 71, pp. 573, 587, 590, 592, for communion; Chs. 11, 38, 56, 61, 74, 88, 100, pp. 574, 582, 587–89, 593, 596, 598, for prayer; Chs. 2, 3, 39, 48, pp. 569–70, 582, 586, on marriage; Chs. 35, 75, 78, pp. 581, 593–94, on confession and penance; Ch. 94, p. 597, on confirmation; Chs. 11, 14, 105, pp. 574, 575, 599, on preaching; Ch. 11, p. 574, for singing; Chs. 98–100, p. 598, on burial; Chs. 7, 8, pp. 572–73, for

84

New converts had to be taught how to comport themselves in the churches at these various ceremonies: how to dress, how to prepare for baptism and communion, how to take communion, how to pray.[85] They had to be acclimated to the obligation to attend church on Sundays and feast days, and to refrain from work, public activities, and private pleasures on these days.[86] Dietary laws had to be introduced.[87] A special set of regulations for the Lenten season had to be defined, a matter which apparently perplexed and irritated the Bulgars no end, if we can judge from Boris' repeated queries to Nicholas on the subject.[88] The Bulgars had to be taught the Christian manner of praying at meals, of invoking rain, of preparing for battle, of taking an oath, of arranging a betrothal, and of praying for the ill—matters that were often conducted outside the churches and individually.[89] Obviously, the Bulgars were striving to institute the whole range of Christian observances, a task that could have been completed for all Bulgaria only after a long time and only with monumental effort. A concomitant problem was the suppression of pagan practices of worship.

Formidable as all of this was, the sheer labor of acquainting the Bulgars with the basic forms of Christian worship was only part of the problem. In turning to Nicholas for advice, Boris provided abundant evidence that his labors to teach his people how to worship were complicated by a vast ignorance of Christian usage. His requests to Nicholas reflect the desperation of one who knows in a general way the Christian practices that should be inaugurated in order that the new deity may be honored properly, but who is often at a loss about the specific nature of Christian usage. He began his message to Nicholas by asking that "the Christian law" be sent to him, evidently expecting that Nicholas would be able to supply a simple guide that would inform the Bulgars of proper Christian usage. Nicholas could only reply that this would require "innumerable volumes."[90] Lacking a concise compendium to explain how the Christians

---

veneration of relics and the use of the cross. See also Theophylactus, *Vita s. Clementis*, Chs. 18, 22, 29, Migne, *PG*, CXXVI, cols. 1224–25, 1228–29, 1237–38, for the labors of St. Clement of Ochrida along these lines.

85. Nicholas, *Ep.*, No. 99, Chs. 7–9, 54, 55, 58, 65, 66, pp. 572–73, 587, 590–91.

86. *Ibid.*, Chs. 10–12, 34, 63, pp. 574–75, 581, 590.

87. *Ibid.*, Chs. 4–5, 42, 43, 56, 57, 60, 69, 90, 91, pp. 570–72, 583–84, 587–89, 591–92, 596; Photius, *Ep.*, No. 4, Ch. 5, ed. Valetta, pp. 168–70.

88. Nicholas, *Ep.*, No. 99, Chs. 44–48, 50, pp. 585–86; Photius, *Ep.*, No. 4, Ch. 5, ed. Valetta, pp. 168–70; Nicholas, *Ep.*, No. 100, ed. Perels, *MGH*, *Ep.*, VI, 603.

89. Nicholas, *Ep.*, No. 99, Chs. 33, 35, 40, 53, 56, 62, 67, 79, pp. 580–82, 587–91, 594.

90. *Ibid.*, Ch. 1, pp. 566–67.

worshipped, Boris could only search for advice on particular matters where his knowledge was inadequate; he could only ask Nicholas to tell him exactly how to do what he realized should be done. No doubt he frequently turned to missionary clergymen to resolve the problems that arose from his ignorance of Christian usage.

To analyze the full extent of the ignorance plaguing the Bulgar ruler as he struggled to institute the proper forms of Christian worship would require a discussion too lengthy for this paper, but a few examples drawn from his requests to Nicholas will suffice to reveal the nature of his quandary. Boris knew that Christians must observe fast days, but he had to ask Nicholas what days these were. He had trouble deciding who could carry the cross in processions. He wanted to know whether communion could be received daily during Lent. He was confused about what to do in cases where an unworthy priest had administered baptism. He fretted over the proper manner of praying while in military camp, presumably away from a church. He asked for a specific list of animals and birds that the Bulgars might eat. He did not know how to pray at mealtime when a priest or deacon was absent. The exact requirements for fasting were not clear in his mind. He asked Nicholas to tell him how to swear an oath. He was at a loss about how long a woman who had just borne a child should be kept from attending church. He requested specific advice on how many times a year baptism may be administered and what fasting conditions should be imposed on those being baptized. He asked Nicholas for a penitential.[91] All of this strongly suggests that there were nettlesome problems pertaining to Christian worship ever awaiting the king's decision. It also indicates that once the question of Christian propriety was resolved an effort would have to be made to correct the erroneous practices that had grown up as a result of Bulgar ignorance.

In some of these cases Boris' concern certainly extended beyond a need for information. He, and very likely his subjects, appear to have been beset by a fear that as neophyte practitioners of the Christian cult they might commit some minor or unintentional fault which would displease the Christian God and result in grave consequences. When Boris asked if it is lawful to receive communion daily during Lent, one suspects that he was concerned not so much with securing papal sanction for partaking of divine grace more frequently as with the possibility that an unusual departure from a ritualistic practice would affect him adversely.

91. *Ibid.*, Chs. 4, 7, 8, 14, 15, 38, 43, 53, 60, 67–69, 88, pp. 570–73, 575–76, 582–84, 587–89, 591–92, 596.

His keen concern about those days in which it was forbidden to do battle and about the precise preparations for battle reflects a fear that violation of Christian usages would end in defeat. When he sought to discover whether a risk might be involved if he uttered an improper prayer when he was in military camp and without the services of a priest, or if he prayed the wrong number of times a day outside the church, or if he simply made the sign of the cross over his meals when no priest was present, Boris suggested that his every supplication of the new deity involved grave concern lest erroneous usage might negate the efficacy of prayer or even anger Almighty God. One can almost visualize the perturbed state of mind that afflicted the Bulgars as they struggled to abide by the admonitions of Greek missionaries that they would be guilty of sin if they did not stand in church with their hands clasped to their breasts, if they took communion without wearing a belt, and if they entered a church wearing a linen headbinding.[92] The list could be lengthened; there was apparently no end of the instances in which a sincere convert felt timorous as he went about worshipping in a new way, hoping that he would not commit some mechanical fault which would provoke divine wrath.

There are veiled hints in Boris' questions which imply not only that ignorance and temerity impeded the institution of the Christian cult but also that a subtle form of resistance by the new converts complicated the entire process. The clue to this difficulty lies in certain cases where Boris asked the pope to render a judgment on a Christian usage about which the khan almost certainly knew the correct position. For instance, Boris asked Nicholas whether it is lawful to work and to judge cases in the courts on Sundays and feast days. In spite of evidence that his knowledge of Christian practice was not perfect, it is impossible to believe that the khan did not know the Christian usage on this point. Nor is it possible to think that the missionaries were spreading confusion on this matter. One must suppose that Boris needed an authoritative statement from Rome—perhaps accompanied by a rationale—concerning the sanctity of Sundays and feast days in order to convince some elements among his subjects who were reluctant to accept this particular usage. The same issue seems to have been involved when Boris asked Nicholas what insignia should replace the horse's tail, traditionally carried into battle by the Bulgars. Boris must surely have encountered enough Christian armies and heard enough from missionaries to have known what a Christian army should display as a battle insignia. Again, the khan's

92. *Ibid.*, Chs. 9, 34, 35, 38, 43, 53–55, 57, 61, 66, 90, 91, pp. 573, 581–84, 587–91, 596.

concern must have been to obtain a definite papal opinion that could be used for persuading his subjects to abandon a convention that did not conform to Christian usage.[93]

Boris' persistent questioning on matters of this order implies that one of his most difficult tasks in introducing Christian cult observances lay not in breaking down the resistance of adamant supporters of ancient religious usages but in justifying to sincere converts the religious significance of certain Christian practices. The issue appears to have been especially troublesome in cases where the new system of worship involved the abandonment of ancient habits of life that previously had had no special ritualistic significance. The khan apparently sought to resolve this issue by citing the word of a recognized authority, a word that he himself had invoked by asking Rome's position on specific situations that had been encountered in Bulgaria.

When his subjects wondered why they must become involved in a complex ritualistic procedure involving church-going, confession, penance, prayer, the freeing of prisoners and slaves, and almsgiving in preparation for battle, Boris and his priests could answer best by citing Rome's position on the matter. Those women who protested covering their heads in church could be confronted with a papal opinion buttressed by scriptural citations. The pope's commands may have helped to supply a persuasive reply to those men who felt no meaningful compulsion to refrain from the conjugal bed on Saturday night and Sunday as an aspect of honoring God. (In this particular case, the papal argument that such conduct constituted work on the Lord's day may have been harder to respect than papal authority.)

Boris seems to have encountered his greatest trouble with respect to Lenten observances. Apparently the Bulgars could see little reason why they must stop hunting, holding court, waging war, celebrating parties, and marrying during Lent in favor of fasting, penance, prayer, and church-going. The khan's careful and extensive questioning of Nicholas on Lenten observances indicates that the difficulty arose not from the new converts' opposition to the Christian usages suitable to Lent but from their inability to see the religious implications of eliminating customary pursuits as a mode of worshipping God. The presence of this spirit among the Bulgars strongly suggests that there was a constant demand upon those responsible for introducing Christian practices to explain the meaning of what converts were being asked to do. The Bulgars were not dumb, silent victims, ready to do what they were told;

93. *Ibid.*, Chs. 10–12, 33, pp. 574–75, 580–81.

at least in some cases, especially where they were asked to give up parts of their traditional modes of living, they demanded that the innovations make religious sense to them.[94]

In reviewing the whole range of activities involved in instituting the Christian religion in Bulgaria, one is inevitably struck by how often the critical issue seems to have rested with relatively minor matters of a highly formal nature. Boris' constant concern with these issues and Nicholas' meticulous care in providing explanations for what seem to be petty technicalities may well provide the secret to the Christianization process. There is no solid evidence to indicate that the great mysteries of the Christian faith or the subtle issues of dogma emerging from these mysteries vitally influenced the reception of the new faith in Bulgaria. There is abundant evidence that the Bulgars readily accepted and entered into the major forms of Christian public worship—the mass, baptism, communion, confession, prayer, burial rites, and the like; the only troublesome issue on this score was learning the correct manner of performing these rites. What disturbed them, provoked questions, and even engendered resistance was a whole range of minor practices which in the name of religion required them to put aside customs which previously had had little or no religious meaning, or which demanded the abandonment of traditional usages without an obvious substitute. The surviving sources leave no hint that the triune God or the *filioque* question or any other fundamental point embodied in the creed quoted to Boris by Photius acted as an obstacle to the conversion of the Bulgars. But Lenten regulations created no end of formidable problems. Everything suggests that the Bulgars viewed the mass as no loathsome innovation but rather accepted it quickly as a suitable substitute for pagan sacrificial and propitiatory rites. What agitated the new converts was the insistence of the missionaries that the new mode of worship be conducted without those activities that customarily had formed an integral part of their great religious ceremonies: judging cases, battle preparations, gaming, singing, etc. Probably the Bulgars felt no great hardship in substituting the Christian procedure of betrothal for their customary practice; the equivalence was fairly obvious. What left them frustrated was the insistence of the missionaries that they abandon their dead pagan kinsmen; and it was here the new religion left an empty spot in their lives.

One is thus drawn to the conclusion that the decisive element in the process of instituting Christian practices was the ability of the missionary forces to provide two things: substitute religious practices for the every-

94. *Ibid.*, Chs. 35, 44–48, 50, 58, 63, pp. 581, 585–86, 588, 590.

day, simple pagan usages not acceptable to Christians, and meaningful explanations which would persuade the Bulgars to abandon practices which had no religious significance but which ran counter to Christian usages. Conversion apparently did not involve the glorious rebirth which Photius and Nicholas spoke of so eloquently; it entailed a tortuous process of substituting Christian practices as recognizable equivalents ✤ for time-sanctioned pagan usages. The burden upon the ruler and his missionary forces was to make evident the equivalence between the old and the new. The process constantly ran the risk of asking the converts to abandon too wide a range of conventional usages that did not seem intimately linked to religious life as they understood religion. When the demand to suppress conventional modes of life extended beyond the religious comprehension of the converts, the missionary forces had to try to supply a rationale capable of persuading the Bulgars to conform to Christian standards. This necessity often arose when the Bulgars were asked to accept practices that had become attached to Christianity by virtue of its evolution in a Judaic-Roman environment for which there were no corresponding experiences or precedents in the Bulgar tradition.

This examination of the problems involved in the institution of Christian worship and the propagation of Christian doctrine among the Bulgars prompts one final remark. The task was obviously one that required a monumental expenditure of labor. It seems safe to assume that the entire process involved nothing less than the full concentration of the nation's energies for an entire generation. It is difficult not to admire those who were willing to persist in the face of so great a task. Obviously, the ruler was the vital force, alone capable of concentrating the needed energy on the work to be accomplished.

While contending with the numerous burdens associated with the institution of Christian beliefs, rites, and practices, Boris plunged into another problem that he obviously felt was critical to his undertaking. He sought to assure the development of a formal organization of the emerging Bulgar Christian community after a pattern that reflected current usage in the Christian world. This problem was complicated not only by the newness of Christianity in his realm but also by the necessary involvement of external elements which had to be respected in establishing an ecclesiastical organization.

There is no evidence to clarify the organizational pattern involved in Bulgaria when the first Greek missionary parties appeared in 864 and

865 to baptize Boris and to proceed with the work of conversion. The imperial government sent a bishop to Bulgaria to baptize Boris, but there is no suggestion that this move had any organizational significance.[95] Perhaps the Byzantine authorities only imitated for Bulgaria the procedure that had been employed in 863 in Moravia. In the latter case the imperial regime, backed by Photius, had commissioned two men to lead a missionary expedition into a land ready to accept the cross. These men were qualified for the task by their piety, learning, linguistic skill, and experience with people of Slavic origin and non-Christian faiths. Neither leader had high ecclesiastical standing or dignity at the time of the mission to Moravia; Cyril was a man of learning and a teacher, while Methodius was a monk. Nor did a prestigious rank seem necessary during the early stages of their work in Moravia.[96] If the same procedure held in Bulgaria, we can suppose that the original Greek mission was composed of a body of men led by one or two figures whose authority rested primarily on their reputation as pious, learned men of exemplary Christian life and on their designation as missionary chiefs by the imperial government and the patriarch. Photius made it clear to Boris from the outset that the spiritual head of the emergent Bulgar church was in Constantinople.[97] Nowhere in his pastoral letter did he indicate the need for the formal establishment of an ecclesiastical organization in Bulgaria.

Boris apparently was not satisfied with this arrangement, for in 866 he asked Nicholas I if it was lawful for his nation to have a patriarch, how such a patriarch ought to be ordained, and whether the king could constitute a patriarch. Obviously, he had begun to envisage a hierarchical arrangement of the most ambitious kind; and perhaps he was also a little overawed by the audacity of his request, for, further on in his letter, he requested information on how many true patriarchs there were and which was second after Rome. Nicholas quickly dismissed the possibility of a Bulgar patriarch, but in his responses to these questions he laid out a plan for the organizational evolution of the Bulgar church, at least as Rome saw it. He explained the true patriarchates in some detail and the reasons or rights upon which this dignity was based.

---

95. Theophanes Continuatus, *Chronographia*, IV, Ch. 14, ed. I. Bekker, *CSHB*, p. 163: "παρὰ τοῦ πρὸς ἐκεῖνον ἀποσταλέντος ἀρχιερέως ἀπὸ τῆς βασίλιδος τῶν πόλεων"; Ioannes Zonaras, *Epitomae Historiarum*, XVI, Ch. 2, ed. T. Büttner-Wobst, *CSHB*, p. 388: "καὶ ἀποστάλη μὲν ἀρχιερεὺς πρὸς αὐτόν. ὁ δὲ καὶ ἐμυήθη καὶ ἐβαπτίσθη."

96. For a discussion of the work of Cyril and Methodius, see the works cited in n. 28, above.

97. Photius, *Ep.*, No. 6, Chs. 20, 114, ed. Valetta, pp. 220–21, 247–48.

His remarks could hardly have encouraged Boris to believe that the Bulgars would soon, if ever, have their own patriarch. The pope stated clearly that under no circumstances could a king establish a patriarchate, nor even an archbishopric or bishopric. Nicholas would first appoint a bishop for Bulgaria, and this bishop would be granted the archiepiscopal honor by the pope as soon as the Christian population had increased to Rome's satisfaction. This archbishop could then consecrate other bishops for Bulgaria, and they, in turn, would be permitted to elect the first archbishop's successor. The first archbishop would not have to come to Rome for his *pallium*, but all his successors would be required to discharge this obligation before assuming their new position.[98] This plan left no question that Bulgaria was destined to remain a province fully subordinated to Rome.

Nicholas launched this program by commissioning two bishops to go to Bulgaria, Paul of Populonia and Formosus of Porto, bearing his famous responses to Boris' questions.[99] The pope obviously intended that these bishops would exercise the episcopal function for he commanded Boris to seek guidance from them on several matters.[100] However, it was not the pope's intention that either of these men would be elevated to a permanent position as head of the Bulgar hierarchy. He made this clear when he refused to honor Boris' request to make Formosus archbishop of Bulgaria, justifying his refusal on the grounds that it was uncanonical to transfer an already established bishop from one see to another.[101] The task of Paul and Formosus was to travel, preach, baptize, confirm, build churches—in short, to direct a missionary establishment.[102] Not long after their arrival another missionary bishop, Hermanrich of Passau, arrived from the East Frankish kingdom with a retinue of clergy and a supply of religious materials, but he left when he found that the Romans were in control.[103]

The sources are unanimous in reporting that Boris was pleased with the work of Paul and Formosus. However, the situation may not have

98. Nicholas, *Ep.*, No. 99, Chs. 72–73, 92–93, pp. 592–93, 596–97.

99. *Liber pontificalis*, ed. Duchesne, II, 164, 185; Nicholas, *Ep.*, No. 100, ed. Perels, *MGH, Ep.*, VI, 603; *Anastasii Bibliothecarii Ep. sive Praef.*, No. 5, eds. Perels and Laehr, *MGH, Ep.*, VII, 412.

100. Nicholas, *Ep.*, No. 99, Chs. 24, 26, 28–30, 50, 51, 81, 95, pp. 579, 580, 586, 594, 597.

101. *Liber pontificalis*, ed. Duchesne, II, 165.

102. *Ibid.*, p. 164; *Anastasii Bibliothecarii Ep. sive Praef.*, No. 5, eds. Perels and Laehr, *MGH, Ep.*, VII, 412.

103. *Annales Fuldenses*, a. 867, ed. Kurze, *MGH, SS. rer. Germ.*, p. 65.

been completely satisfactory from an organizational viewpoint. We have already noted[104] that the Greeks, having been driven out of Bulgaria upon the arrival of the Roman party, launched a counter-attack which sought to impugn the orthodoxy of the Latins. Boris, perhaps feeling the need for a stronger organization to combat this threat, sent a legate to Rome asking Nicholas that Formosus be elevated to the archiepiscopal rank and that more priests be sent to Bulgaria. Nicholas dispatched carefully selected priests, but he refused to accede to the request for the promotion of Formosus. Arguing that it was illegal to transfer the bishop of Porto to another see, he sent two more bishops to Bulgaria, Dominic of Treviso and Grimoald of Polimarti. He ordered Dominic and Formosus to proceed to Constantinople to conduct papal business; and Paul and Grimoald were charged with the conduct of the Bulgar mission.[105]

Hadrian II pursued Nicholas' organizational program—still without notable success in terms of Boris' interests. In 869 another Bulgar legate, Peter, came to Rome to request that a certain deacon Marinus be made archbishop of the Bulgars. If this was not possible, Boris asked that "someone from among the cardinals" be sent to the Bulgars to be examined as a candidate for archbishop, and the Bulgars would send him back to Rome for ordination if he met their approval. Since the "cardinals" at this time comprised clergymen of all ranks who were associated with certain churches in the city of Rome and who often served as functionaries in the papal curia, Boris' request seems to indicate an interest in obtaining for the leadership of the Bulgar hierarchy the services of a man closely associated with papal affairs and trusted by the pope. Because Marinus had already been assigned to Constantinople as a papal legate, Hadrian sent the subdeacon Silvester to the Bulgars as an archiepiscopal candidate. Boris promptly sent Silvester back to Rome, along with a second request that Formosus of Porto be made archbishop. The pope was still not willing to consent to Boris' wish to entrust the leadership of the Bulgar church to Formosus, who apparently had made a powerful impression on Boris. In response to the khan's request, Hadrian wrote that anyone else whom the Bulgars wished to be their archbishop would receive papal approval. While these negotiations were in progress, the leadership of the Bulgar mission remained in the hands of the missionary bishops previously sent from Rome. The chief figure was Grimoald, who had been commissioned to work in Bulgaria by Nicholas I; his working companion, Paul of

104. See above, p. 81.
105. *Liber pontificalis*, ed. Duchesne, II, 165; Nicholas, *Ep.*, No. 100, ed. Perels, *MGH, Ep.*, VI, 603.

Populonia, had returned to Rome in 869 in the company of the khan's legate, Peter.[106]

It may well have been that Rome's failure to constitute a hierarchy suitable to the Bulgars severely disappointed Boris, for by 870 he was beginning to waver in his allegiance to the see of St. Peter and to think of a return to the ecclesiastical jurisdiction of Constantinople. However, other pressures were also driving Boris toward Constantinople. The Greeks had made a powerful effort to convince him that the Latins were spreading heresy among his people. He was, moreover, faced with internal resistance, which the Greeks may have been exploiting, and so successfully that the khan felt the need to establish friendlier relations with the imperial court. Western writers insist that the Greeks used "gifts and promises" to weaken the Bulgar attachment to Rome, and "promises" may in some way have involved discussions of the organizational future of the Bulgars.[107] Whatever the reason, Boris sent a legation to Constantinople in 870 to ask the important general council, then in session, to decide whether Bulgaria's jurisdiction pertained to Rome or to Constantinople.[108] Despite a stout defense of Rome's claims in Bulgaria by papal legates, the council decided that Bulgaria pertained to the authority of Constantinople.[109]

This decision, obviously approved by Boris, once again reoriented the entire organizational evolution of the Bulgar church. The Latin clergy were expelled, and among those required to leave was Bishop Grimoald, apparently none the worse for his experiences, since it was reported that he had become rich while in Bulgaria.[110] A letter of Hadrian II, written in 871, indicates that Patriarch Ignatius had by that date appointed a bishop for Bulgaria;[111] and this seems to be confirmed by an inscription which speaks of a Greek bishop named Nicholas working in Bulgaria.[112] Greek priests again entered Bulgaria to carry on missionary

106. *Liber pontificalis*, ed. Duchesne, II, 185.

107. *Ibid.*, p. 185; Nicholas, *Ep.*, No. 100, ed. Perels, *MGH, Ep.*, VI, 603; *Anastasii Bibliothecarii Ep. sive Praef.*, No. 5, eds. Perels and Laehr, *MGH, Ep.*, VII, 413.

108. For the larger implications of this council, see Dvornik, *The Photian Schism*, pp. 145–58; Amann, *L'époque carolingienne*, pp. 483–89.

109. For a full account of the treatment of the Bulgar requests at the council of Constantinople, see *Liber pontificalis*, ed. Duchesne, II, 182–85; *Anastasii Bibliothecarii Ep. sive Praef.*, No. 5, eds. Perels and Laehr, *MGH, Ep.*, VII, 411–15.

110. *Liber pontificalis*, ed. Duchesne, II, 185.

111. *Hadriani II. Papae Epistolae*, No. 41, ed. Perels, *MGH, Ep.*, VI, 760.

112. H. Grégoire, "Une inscription datée au nom du Roi Boris-Michel de Bulgarie," *Byzantion*, XIV (1939), 227–34.

work. All this aroused the wrath of the papacy and prompted Popes Hadrian II and John VIII to engage in a long battle of words in an attempt to regain jurisdiction over Bulgaria.

We need not follow this struggle, since papal efforts had no significant impact on church organization in Bulgaria,[113] but the papal letters supply some evidence on the development of the ecclesiastical organization under Greek aegis. We have already noted that in 871 Hadrian II spoke of a Greek bishop residing in Bulgaria. In a letter written in late 872 or early 873, John VIII indicated that Ignatius had "sent there [to Bulgaria] some schismatic with the title of archbishop,"[114] who may well have been the "antistites" referred to by Hadrian II in his letter of 871. In another letter, written to Boris at about the same time, John spoke of the presence of Greek "bishops and priests" in Bulgaria.[115] Such evidence indicates that the Bulgars had finally got an archbishop, which may have been a concession made by Constantinople to gain the victory of 870. Moreover, bishops had been consecrated under the archbishop and were actively engaged in episcopal functions. This is confirmed by a letter from John VIII to Boris, in 878, ordering the deposition of "a certain eunuch, Sergius, a Slav by birth," who had been made bishop of Belgrade by George, "who had falsely assumed to himself the title of bishop."[116] A native episcopacy appears to be emerging and the division of Bulgaria into dioceses has begun. Nor is it impossible that Sergius had been one of those Slavs who had been educated in Constantinople about this time.[117]

There is further proof of the existence of several bishops in Bulgaria by 878 in a letter of John VIII addressed to "all Greek bishops and other clergy who are invaders of the *dioceses* of Bulgaria," threatening them with excommunication if they did not leave their offices within thirty days. Some of these churchmen had come from outside Bulgaria already holding the episcopal office, for John assured those who obeyed his command that they would be restored to their former sees.[118] It may have occurred to John that if he could not oust the Greek hierarchy then emerging in Bulgaria, he could at least influence it, for in June, 879, he wrote to Boris

113. See Dvornik, *The Photian Schism*, pp. 151 ff.; Runciman, *The First Bulgarian Empire*, pp. 114–23.
114. *Fragmenta Registri Iohannis VIII. Papae*, No. 9, ed. Caspar, *MGH, Ep.*, VII, 278.
115. *Ibid.*, No. 7, p. 277.
116. *Iohannis VIII. Papae Epistolae*, No. 66, ed. Caspar, *op. cit.*, p. 60.
117. Photius, *Ep.*, No. 255, ed. Valetta, p. 556.
118. *Iohannis VIII. Papae Epistolae*, No. 71, ed. Caspar, *MGH, Ep.*, VII, 66–67. A second letter dealing with the same matter was sent at the same time to Patriarch Ignatius; see *ibid.*, No. 68, pp. 62–63.

asking whether the khan wished to receive a papal legation and an apostolic visitation.[119] Apparently Boris felt no such need, for he did not request Rome's guidance. The ecclesiastical organization of Bulgaria was apparently taking a shape that was satisfactory to him.

One of the concessions John VIII extracted from the imperial government at the synod held at Constantinople in 879–880 in return for his recognition of the reinstallation of Photius as patriarch was the restoration of Bulgaria to Rome's jurisdiction. This decision was clearly an arrangement between Rome and Constantinople; Boris was not involved in any of the negotiations,[120] and he apparently refused to adhere to the decision taken in Constantinople. The imperial regime undoubtedly was aware of his devotion to Byzantium and therefore quite willing to concede to Rome nominal jurisdiction over Bulgaria.

Because Boris paid no heed to the decisions of 879–880, there was no exodus of the Greek hierarchy in favor of a new crowd of Romans. John may initially have intended that this would happen for he ordered Photius to see that "the bishops consecrated there and all lower clergy leave the country."[121] However, as Dvornik has shown, John eventually was willing to compromise the issue of allowing the Greeks to remain in Bulgaria provided they would admit his jurisdiction, come to Rome for installation in higher offices, and refrain from depending in any way on Constantinople. Photius and the imperial government were not averse to this arrangement,[122] but Boris provided the roadblock, refusing to accept Rome's jurisdiction. Papal appeals in 881 and 882 produced not so much as an answer.[123]

All of this would suggest Boris' satisfaction with the organization that had developed since 870. Probably by 880 the hierarchy in Bulgaria was sufficiently pliable to his will and so oriented to Bulgar problems that it felt no burning interest in the disputes and negotiations involved in establishing the jurisdiction to which Bulgaria belonged. Thus Boris could see no advantage in inviting a complete upheaval of the existing organization by permitting the pope to oust the Greeks and introduce a new and inexperienced leadership in Bulgar problems, especially since

119. *Ibid.*, No. 192, pp. 153–54.
120. For an analysis of this council see Dvornik, *The Photian Schism*, pp. 159–219; Amann, *L'époque carolingienne*, pp. 492–98.
121. *Iohannis VIII. Papae Epistolae*, No. 209, ed. Caspar, *MGH, Ep.*, VII, pp. 185–86.
122. Dvornik, *The Photian Schism*, pp. 210–13.
123. *Iohannis VIII. Papae Epistolae*, Nos. 298, 308, ed. Caspar, *MGH, Ep.*, VII, pp. 260, 266–67.

Rome had previously been reluctant to permit an independent hierarchy in Bulgaria.

Toward the end of his reign Boris took steps to increase the number of native clergy in Bulgaria. This move may at first have been intended only to complement the Greek hierarchy, but it is very likely that Boris already planned to create a Bulgar hierarchy that could ultimately replace the Greeks. We have noted that Boris had begun to send Bulgars to Constantinople for a monastic education, and presumably some of these Bulgars returned to serve as clergymen in their homeland (although we have no precise confirmation of this). At any rate, Bulgars trained in Byzantium would probably have been thoroughly Hellenized and thus little different in their outlook from the Greeks who had entered the Bulgar kingdom to serve in a missionary capacity. The Greek missionary forces also elevated some natives to the clerical rank, although this does not appear to have been a regular procedure.[124] Perhaps, then, it was especially significant that, about 878, Boris sent his second son, Symeon, to Constantinople to be educated and then to become a monk.[125] It appears not unlikely that already the khan planned that Symeon would ultimately return to Bulgaria to assume the role of patriarch, thoroughly prepared for that exalted task by the intellectual and spiritual experiences he had gained while associating with the circle surrounding the great Photius.[126]

About 885 a new and unexpected opportunity presented itself to Boris that permitted him to move toward the creation of a native clergy.[127] After the death of St. Methodius, a German-inspired reaction occurred

124. *Ibid.*, No. 66, p. 60; Theophylactus, *Vita s. Clementis*, Ch. 22, Migne, *PG*, CXXVI, col. 1229, which says that many priests in Bulgaria used Greek so poorly that they could not understand Scripture. This would suggest a more numerous native clergy by the end of the reign of Boris.

125. Luidprandus of Cremona, *Antapodosis*, III, Ch. 29, in *The Works of Luidprand of Cremona*, trans. F. A. Wright (New York, 1930), p. 123.

126. For a somewhat imaginative review of Symeon's career in Constantinople and suggestions on the purpose for which he was sent there, see G. Sergheraert (Christian Gérard), *Syméon le Grand (893–927)* (Paris, 1960), pp. 15–47.

127. The following section is based on Theophylactus, *Vita s. Clementis*, Chs. 14–29, Migne, *PG*, CXXVI, cols. 1217–40, and on the old Slavonic *life* of St. Nahum, the text of which is given, along with an English translation, by Kusseff in *Slavonic and East European Review*, XXIX (1950–51), 142–44. Kusseff's "St. Nahum," *ibid.*, 139–52, and "St. Clement of Ochrida," *ibid.*, XXVII (1948–49), 193–215, and I. Snegarov's "Les sources sur la vie et l'activité de Clément d'Ochrida," *Byzantinobulgarica* (Sofia, 1962), I, 79–119, provide careful analyses of these sources; they are especially useful because of their use of Slavic studies unavailable to the present author.

in Moravia. The Slavic-speaking disciples of this Apostle of Moravia were forced to flee, abandoning their effort to develop a Slavonic liturgy and a Slavonic literary tradition in Moravia. Some went directly from Moravia to Bulgaria, and many of these clergymen found a warm welcome in Bulgaria. Others were sent to the slave markets of Venice, where an emissary of Emperor Basil rescued them and returned them to Constantinople, and from there they were eventually transferred to Bulgaria. The biographies of two of these missionaries, Clement of Ochrida and Nahum, provide insight into Boris' use of the talents of these skilled missionary workers and illuminate his plans for a Bulgar hierarchy.

Upon their arrival in Bulgaria, Clement and Nahum were taken to Boris by the governor of Belgrade, who, according to Clement's biography, "knew that Boris was friendly to such men." The khan greeted them joyfully, placed them in the houses of Bulgar nobles, and asked them many questions. After a short time, Boris moved to make better use of Clement's talents. In the Macedonian area of his realm, where the population was predominantly Slavic, he divided a larger province so as to create a smaller territory, and commissioned Clement to be "teacher" (διδάσκαλος) over this area. The title suggests that Clement's role was that of a missionary leader; however, the description of his position indicates that he enjoyed a considerably larger authority, which permitted him to order affairs so as to expedite missionary work. A secular official, named Dobeta, was installed in the territory to share responsibility with Clement and to assist his missionary work, perhaps submitting to his authority in some matters. Boris provided Clement with houses in Devol, Ochrida and Glavinitze, commended Clement to the Slavic population of the area, and ordered them to support his work with material gifts. The entire arrangement suggests that Clement, representing the tradition of a Slavonic church established earlier in Moravia by Cyril and Methodius, was being given a jurisdiction independent of the Greek archbishop in Bulgaria and separate from the court. He was being used to rally Slavs to the new religion and to represent the Bulgar khan among these Slavs, where Bulgar overlordship may not have been popular.

For seven years Clement occupied himself spreading the Word in his area, laboring with a population given to superstition and ignorance. As a part of this effort, Clement established schools which taught reading and writing, and the number of students in these centers was reported to be 3,500. From those taught to read, Clement apparently singled out certain ones who became his constant companions, and their training was apparently more thorough. From these, selected pupils were eventually ordained lectors, subdeacons, and priests, perhaps in large enough numbers that they could be sent to serve elsewhere in Bulgaria. Clement and his disciples at the same time labored to create a body of theological and liturgical literature suited to the needs of the Slavs, who could not comprehend Greek. These efforts were a continuation of the work begun in Moravia by Cyril and Methodius; indeed, from the work of Clement and his disciples there soon evolved the first flowering of a Slavonic literary culture, which reached its full fruition during the reign of Symeon (893–927).[128] This cultural activity, prompted by the needs of a newly established religion, proved to be a powerful force in bridging the gap between the ruling Bulgars and the subject Slavs. As the fame of Clement spread—along with the religious works produced by his disciples—the importance of the Greek hierarchy in Bulgaria undoubtedly receded.

The outcome of the role in which Clement had been cast was inevitable. Shortly after Symeon became khan (893), the widely known and greatly respected Clement was elevated to the episcopacy, the first Bulgar-speaking man to be so honored. With this event, the native element in Bulgaria had moved to the forefront. The perpetuation of the tradition of Cyril and Methodius had produced a circle of ecclesiastical figures deeply schooled in Byzantine learning but possessed of the linguistic skills and the experience to put their talents to work in Bulgaria. Their presence made unnecessary any further dependence on Greeks as ecclesiastical leaders among the Bulgars. Boris' reception and utilization of the fugitives from Moravia in 885 was the initial step toward the establishment of a Bulgar patriarchate in 925.

But Clement was not the only man to serve the khan's effort to produce a native clergy. Nahum had spent the years 885 to 893 as a leader of scholarly activity at the newly established monastery of St. Panteliemon, near Preslav. The monks there were chiefly engaged in translations and copying, producing numerous works in the Slavonic tongue to serve the rapidly emerging native church. After Clement had been made a bishop, Nahum went to Clement's territory in Macedonia to serve as missionary leader and teacher. He built another important monastery on Lake Ochrida and made it an important educational center.

128. For a review of Bulgarian cultural activity in the reign of Symeon, see Sergheraert, *Syméon le Grand (893–927)*, pp. 88–115; also see pp. 180–89 for an excellent bibliography on the subject. Likewise suggestive are the remarks of Dvornik, *The Slavs: Their Early History and Civilization (Survey of Slavic Civilization, Vol. II)* (Boston, 1956), pp. 147–88.

Meanwhile Boris had taken his last step to shape the organization of the Bulgar church. After returning from his monastic retreat to thwart the efforts of his son and successor, Vladimir, to overturn the Christian establishment and restore paganism, Boris sought to give formal sanction to the ecclesiastical organization. In 893 he summoned an assembly of important men to approve a series of crucial decisions. The Slavonic rite was made official. Symeon, who had been living as a monk at St. Pantelie-mon, was made khan. Seven metropolitan sees were formally proclaimed: Drista, Philippopolis, Sardica, Provadia, Margum, Bregolnitsa and Ochrida, all to be under the archbishop of Bulgaria, whose see was now moved to Preslav, the new capital. Most of these cities or towns had been the centers of ancient provinces and had served as ecclesiastical centers between the years 864 and 893. Bishoprics already existed in several provinces.[129]

When Boris died, in 907, the organization of the Bulgar church had progressed far from its state of forty years earlier, when the khan had pleaded with Rome to designate a foreign archbishop to serve Bulgaria. It is obvious, however, that progress in this direction had created many problems that had been added to the burden imposed on the khan by the conversion process as a whole. The creation of an ecclesiastical organiza-tion had depended on foreigners; there had been the initial problem of securing adequate help from abroad. The missionary bishops, priests, and monks who could be recruited were then confronted by a population whose language and culture were strange, a condition that must have led to misunderstandings. Furthermore, the clergy that came to Bulgaria initially owed prime allegiance to superiors outside the Bulgar kingdom; and these superiors, in Rome and/or Constantinople, had preconceived notions of how an ecclesiastical organization should evolve in a missionary territory.

These ideas had often prevented the khan from promoting the organizational growth which he judged suitable to his realm, especially since the two major sources of missionary aid for Bulgaria were engaged in bitter competition for jurisdiction over Bulgaria. As a consequence, both had insisted on the exclusive right to proselytize among the Bulgars, a condition which had forced Boris to choose one or the other as the source of assistance. Each choice had resulted in the exodus of one group of missionaries and the appearance of a new group. Roman and Greek missionaries, whichever were in command, had to combat pressures from

129. Runciman, *The First Bulgarian Empire*, pp. 135–36; Sergheraert, *Syméon le Grand (893–927)*, pp. 51, 55–58.

the out-group, insisting that their work was tainted in some way. This contentious situation must certainly have compromised the authority of ecclesiastical leadership and thereby endangered the progress of the missionary effort. As far as can be determined from the evidence, neither the Roman nor the Greek missionary forces strove to develop a native clergy from which a native hierarchy could emerge. This crucial step had to await a happy accident, which put at the service of Boris a capable missionary group which was also willing to prepare native Bulgars for responsible ecclesiastical posts. Boris' skill in utilizing this new talent was a decisive turning point in the Christianization process in Bulgaria and a mark of his effective leadership of that process.

As one studies the problems connected with the establishment of an ecclesiastical organization in Bulgaria he becomes more sympathetically understanding of Boris' constant concern with this problem. Most authorities have accepted without question the position that Boris' pre-occupation with securing an autonomous ecclesiastical authority for Bulgaria was dictated by ambition and premature dreams of Bulgar glory.[130] Indeed, it is not difficult to arrive at such a conclusion when one finds Boris asking the pope, within two years after his conversion, how one goes about establishing a patriarchate. Yet in view of what has been established in the preceding pages as the practical problems that faced the Bulgar khan in establishing Christian doctrine and practice, it is also easy to realize how desperately Boris must have felt the need for an ecclesiastical superior of sufficient authority—and with intimate knowledge of the Bulgar situation—to resolve the many issues that arose from day to day as the new religion spread. It is inconceivable that a ruler so intimately involved in the conversion of his people would not have immediately sensed that the task would become easier if it were supported by an ecclesiastical hierarchy self-contained in Bulgaria and answerable to no external power whose interests in the Bulgars involved more than the conversion process. Although it is conceded that excessive ambition, grandiose dreams, and national pride played a large part in Boris' attempt to establish an independent Bulgar hierarchy, it seems likely that he also saw the practical necessity of a strong hierarchy as a vital aspect of an effective and successful missionary effort.

130. For example, Spinka, *A History of Christianity in the Balkans*, pp. 37–40; Slatarski, *Geschichte der Bulgaren*, I, 43–46; Dvornik, *Les Slaves, Byzance et Rome au IXe siècle*, p. 190; Amann, *L'époque carolingienne*, pp. 477–78. Although agreeing with this view in general, Gérard (*Les Bulgares*, pp. 208–9) hints that Bulgar problems had some relationship to Boris' anxiety to secure an independent organization and to develop a hierarchy responsive to his will.

In this respect he appears to have achieved an insight common to other successful missionary leaders of his era, e.g., Boniface, Ansgar, and Gregory the Great: that ecclesiastical authority was needed in the missionary arena almost as soon as the first pagan was baptized. To gain this end, Boris had to contend with an unusual situation: he was dependent on the aid of outsiders who were reluctant to permit the growth of a Bulgar hierarchy unless they were perfectly certain of that hierarchy's first allegiance. Had Boris been free to deal exclusively with either Rome or Constantinople, he might have secured an effective hierarchy without so much difficulty. And that hierarchy might have been allowed a greater degree of independence in responding to the unique problems in Bulgaria.

As the new religion took hold among the Bulgars, a fresh range of problems arose to complicate a situation already quite complex. The introduction of Christianity called into question the art of government as traditionally practiced among the Bulgars, and, by implication, it required a wide-ranging adjustment of existing usages to new concepts of government and to new situations produced by the mere presence of Christianity. To Boris fell the responsibility of making the changes demanded in establishing a Christian government for the Bulgars. Unfortunately, we can see only the dimensions of his problem; the meager evidence does not permit us to follow the political changes actually effected as efforts were made to adjust to the new religion. Still, what emerged as new political issues, regardless of their ultimate resolution, leaves no doubt that the conversion process called into question the basic concepts and processes of government that had prevailed in Bulgaria before the conversion.

The most striking political development suggested by a synthesis of all the sources is that the Christianization of Bulgaria demanded a vast expansion of the power of the khan. Certainly the internal evolution of the Bulgar state before 864 had witnessed the slow transformation of the khan's position from that of a war chieftain, commanding a loosely knit band of warriors in incessant pursuit of the prizes of war, into that of a genuine chief of state, with authority over a set territory, with power to judge, pronounce laws, punish, tax, and conduct a foreign policy—and with at least a primitive administrative system at his command. This gradual strengthening of monarchical government was apparently nourished by at least two powerful forces: the exigencies involved in wresting from formidable foes a territory that would serve as a homeland for the Bulgars, and the example of the more-advanced political systems of these foes, especially the Byzantine Empire.[131] But with the baptism of Boris in 864, what had been a drift in Bulgar political life suddenly was presented to the khan as a necessity. Popes and patriarchs insisted that the new convert was responsible for converting his subjects, for protecting the purity of the faith among a population whose crudity endangered it, and for ordering all things in Bulgaria so as to expedite and assure the spread of Christianity. Implicit in their injunctions was a broad range of new powers for the khan, which promised to exalt his position beyond that enjoyed by his pagan predecessors.

The most eloquent testimony for the range of authority that a Christian prince could rightfully claim was the pastoral letter sent to Boris by Photius shortly after the former's baptism. For the enlightenment of his spiritual son the patriarch produced an elegant treatise on the duties of a Christian prince, replete with concepts drawn from the classical tradition. It has often been said that Photius' delineation of the prince's role could have meant little to the unsophisticated Bulgar khan. Indeed, the tract might have been more appropriate if addressed to an educated Byzantine prince (for whom it may well have been produced originally); yet one suspects that what Photius insisted Boris should do served but to suggest to the new convert what he might do to increase his royal power. Photius' epistle is therefore worth a brief description as an indication of the concept of authority a newly converted ruler earned by his journey to the baptismal font.

In his letter, Photius assumed the role of spiritual father to Boris, an office which demanded that he lead the newly initiated Christian to a fuller comprehension of the truth to which Boris had surrendered. The patriarch's task had a dual character: to acquaint Boris with the basic tenets of the faith and to provide him with a guide to those good works which are proper to a follower of Christ.[132] Photius insisted that "the excellent ornament of [his] labors"[133] understand that faith and good works are linked: "right faith produces noble habits, and purity of deeds proves that faith is fully divine."[134] Photius appears to have treated Boris

131. Slatarski, *Geschichte der Bulgaren*, I, 1–41; Gérard, *Les Bulgares*, pp. 136–82. Also see the interesting attempt of V. Beševliev, "Souveränitätsansprüche eines bulgarischen Herrschers im 9. Jahrhunderts," *Byzantinische Zeitschrift*, LV (1962), 11–20, to demonstrate that a ninth-century inscription from Bulgaria indicates that an effort was being made by the khan to imitate the powers of the Byzantine emperor.

132. Photius, *Ep.*, No. 6, Chs. 1–2, ed. Valetta, pp. 202–3.

133. *Ibid.*, Ch. 5, p. 204: "... ὦ καλὸν ἄγαλμα τῶν ἐμῶν πόνων."

134. *Ibid.*, Ch. 3, p. 203: "Καὶ γὰρ δογμάτων μὲν εὐθύτης πολιτείας προβάλλεται κοσμιότητα, πράξεων δὲ καθαρότης τῆς Πίστεως ἀπαγγέλλει Θειότητα."

as merely another catechumen; his explanation of the purpose of his letter made no mention of its being a guide for the exercise of royal power. Yet Photius inevitably had to consider that Boris was a prince, and therefore he developed arguments that Boris could interpret only as justifications for more and greater princely powers.

Having stated his general purpose, Photius devoted a long section of his letter to expanding the basic doctrines of Christianity.[135] He first set down the Nicene Creed; then he outlined the decisions of all the ecumenical councils, explaining the heretical ideas that had necessitated these councils. But the patriarch did not stop with a simple exposition of the content of the faith, he tried to convince Boris that this body of doctrine must be guarded against contrary opinions while it was being spread among the newly converted Bulgars. He therefore developed an argument suggesting how great would be the displeasure of God over any deviation from these truths, and how drastic would be the tumults, wars, contentions, and battles afflicting Bulgaria if heresy were to develop. His discourse led inevitably to one conclusion: upon the ruler falls the burden of guarding orthodoxy and preventing the disorders that emerge from heresy.[136]

As Boris pondered the strictures of his spiritual father, he must have envisaged, from his position as prince, a new area of authority that had not been his as a pagan. There had been handed over to him a body of truth whose sanctity must be guarded. By the very nature of the universe, diabolic forces would be laboring constantly to subvert that truth. If such subversion occurred, God would be displeased and the society over which the khan ruled would be rent with tumult and struggle. To prevent such catastrophes he was entitled, and duty-bound, to use whatever powers he could muster; indeed, the exercise of extraordinary powers was divinely sanctioned. As his subjects came to understand the pure faith, having grasped the evil consequences of heterodoxy, they would certainly acquiesce to whatever authority the prince needed to protect them from error and strife. In brief, the institution of the Christian faith in Bulgaria involved a special kind of responsibility for the prince, and a new range

135. *Ibid.*, Chs. 4–18, pp. 203–19.
136. *Ibid.*, Chs. 19–20, pp. 219–21. Photius speaks in such terms as these: "Ταύτην προσήκει καὶ τὴν ὑμετέραν θεοφρούρητον σύνεσιν, ἤδη πρὸς τὸν ἡμέτερον κλῆρον τῆς εὐσεβείας ἀφορῶσαν, εἰλικρινεῖ διαθέσει, καὶ γνώμης εὐθύτητι, καὶ ἀδιστάκτῳ πίστει ἀποδέχεσθαι καὶ στέργειν, καὶ μήτε δεξιᾷ μήτε ἀριστερᾷ, μηδὲ ἐπὶ βραχὺ ταύτης ἀποκλίνειν. . . . Ἄρχοντος γὰρ ὡς ἀληθῶς μὴ τῆς ἰδίας μόνον σωτηρίας ποιεῖσθαι φροντίδα, ἀλλὰ καὶ τὸν ἐμπιστευθέντα λαὸν τῆς ἴσης ἀξιοῦν προνοίας, καὶ εἰς τὴν αὐτὴν τῆς θεογνωσίας χειραγωγεῖν τε καὶ προσκαλεῖσθαι τελειότητα."

of powers followed that could not be shirked by a Christian prince worthy of that rank. As protector of the faith, Boris had become something he had not been as a pagan ruler, and he was therefore constrained to act in ways that had not been proper to his office before he was baptized.

Having charged his pupil with new and grave responsibilities as the guardian of orthodoxy, Photius turned to a discourse on good works.[137] His argument turned on a simple proposition: having accepted the new faith, Boris was obligated to remold his life, to bear witness to his faith by the nature and quality of his deeds. Once again Photius wrote in terms that were applicable to all Christians,[138] outlining a moral code for Boris that was the same as for any other Christian. However, the patriarch could not escape the fact that he was instructing a prince, revealing his awareness of this fact when, at the very outset of his exposition, he admonished Boris to emulate Constantine the Great.[139] Thus his moral precepts repeatedly emerge as suggestions that pointed to ways in which careful observance of the new religion might enhance royal power—or as commands indicating new powers which the newly converted king should assume.

A few examples will suffice to illustrate the political overtones of Photius' moral advice. The patriarch was especially skillful in tempting Boris to think that a modification of his moral conduct would exalt him in the eyes of his subjects. "The habits of princes are as the law among subjects."[140] This means that if the prince by his example can induce his people to love one another, they will refrain from bloodshed, theft, adultery, false witness, fighting, and the desire for the goods of others.[141] If the prince can cause his subjects to pray and worship together, they will then be bound in a new kind of unity.[142] In the administration of justice, the spirit of Christian mercy, benevolence, and moderation will gain greater praise and respect than rigid adherence to the letter of the law.[143] Subjects will respect him who orders his desires and dominates his pleasures.[144] Kindness and pious feelings toward compatriots will win a prince

137. *Ibid.*, Chs., 21–114, pp. 221–48.
138. *Ibid.*, Ch. 24, p. 224: " 'Αλλὰ ταῦτα μὲν ἀνθρώπῳ παντὶ πάσῃ δυνάμει παραφυλακτέον, ἄρχοντι καὶ ἀρχομένῳ νέῳ καὶ πρεσβύτῃ, πλουσίῳ καὶ πένητι. Κοινὴ γὰρ ἡ φύσις, καὶ κοινὰ τὰ προστάγματα, καὶ κοινῆς τῆς παραφυλακῆς καὶ ἐπιμελείας δεόμενα."
139. *Ibid.*, Ch. 22, p. 222.
140. *Ibid.*, Ch. 47, p. 233: " 'Ο τῶν ἀρχόντων τρόπος νόμος γίνεται τοῖς ὑπὸ χεῖρα."
141. *Ibid.*, Ch. 23, pp. 223–24.
142. *Ibid.*, Chs. 25–27, pp. 224–25.
143. *Ibid.*, Chs. 42–43, 54, pp. 232–35.
144. *Ibid.*, Ch. 53, p. 234.

greater favor than successful conduct of war.[145] Anger, passion, distrustfulness, voluptuousness and drunkenness debase the power of a prince, but virtues will enhance his position.[146] As he followed Photius' discourse point by point, Boris could easily have convinced himself that a close observance of Christian morality would exalt his prestige and enhance his respect among his subjects. If his people came to admire his moral qualities, they would unquestioningly permit him to do what he pleased.

At times, Photius' letter probably suggested new political activities to which the khan must commit himself. Certainly it was clear that he must do whatever was necessary to spread the faith and to protect orthodoxy. If Christianity demanded good works as a complement to correct belief, then Boris was obliged to do whatever was necessary to "reform" the morals of his subjects; this would not only please God but would also make his subjects more appreciative of his virtues and more respectful of his power. The khan was unequivocally commanded to build churches for his subjects, a new activity that required new powers.[147] He was exhorted to examine the qualifications of those who advised him,[148] a command that implicitly broadened the princely power over administrative personnel and procedures. The administration of justice needed rethinking in the light of Christian principles,[149] and obviously such a review would broaden the khan's authority in this area. In fact, virtually all that Photius mentioned by way of moral instruction for his spiritual son contained an invitation for Boris to assume new authority in the interests of improving his own and his subjects' conduct.

There seems little question, then, that Photius—and no doubt the popes involved in the conversion of Bulgaria—thought in terms of an increase of royal power as a necessary concomitant of the Christianization of a pagan land. Did Boris react to this stimulus by seeking a more exalted role among his subjects? And was he able to increase his authority?

A response to these questions is difficult in the light of the sources. Some evidence can be cited to suggest that Boris assumed certain new powers as a consequence of the existence of Christianity in his realm. We have already noted the khan's role in summoning and dismissing missionary parties and in seeking to establish an ecclesiastical organization.

145. *Ibid.*, Ch. 56, p. 235.
146. *Ibid.*, Chs. 85–87, 91, 92, 94, pp. 241–43.
147. *Ibid.*, Ch. 27, p. 225.
148. *Ibid.*, Ch. 57, p. 235.
149. *Ibid.*, Chs. 39–41, pp. 231–32.

Boris sought from Pope Nicholas "worldly laws," evidently for the purpose of clarifying his regal position.[150] He wielded his power arbitrarily to punish false clergymen who sought to prey upon the Bulgars during the conversion period,[151] and to crush those who revolted in protest against the introduction of Christianity.[152] These measures suggest autocratic action in the cause of the new religion. He was at least tempted to take severe steps against those who resisted conversion or rejected the faith once they had received it.[153] When it came time to provide a missionary setting for Clement, Boris moved boldly to dismantle an existing administrative district and place part of it under the authority of a missionary leader.[154] To say the least, such a procedure appears unusual, and it is indicative of the khan's power to act as he chose.

These scraps of evidence hardly prove that the Bulgar khan became *basileus* or *autocrator* immediately after Christianity was introduced into his realm, but they indicate that the presence of the new religion and the issues raised by it gave the khan an opportunity to extend his authority into fresh areas. These opportunities, coupled with the vision of authority suggested by Boris' mentors, especially Photius, may indeed have been significant in shaping a stronger central government in Bulgaria than had existed prior to the Christianization of that land. The glorious reign of Boris' son, Symeon, would also seem to bear out this conclusion.

While hinting that Boris may have been inspired to autocratic political conduct by Christian ideals and religious problems, the evidence more strongly suggests another and perhaps more troublesome political consequence of the conversion process. The document that draws us closest to Boris himself, the letter of Pope Nicholas, repeatedly implies that the introduction of Christianity raised great confusion in the khan's mind about the conduct of ordinary, routine political processes. He appears to have believed that a Christian prince is bound to act differently than he did when he was a pagan, and that time-sanctioned political practices had to be recast to fit a Christian style of statecraft. These beliefs or inclinations appear to have bred uncertainty in the khan's mind that drove him to seek guidance on what should be done to refurbish his government to meet Christian standards.

The major political concerns reflected in Boris' requests to Nicholas

150. Nicholas, *Ep.*, No. 99, Ch. 13, p. 575.
151. *Ibid.*, Chs. 14–16, pp. 575–76.
152. *Ibid.*, Chs. 17–19, pp. 577–78.
153. *Ibid.*, Chs. 18, 41, 102, pp. 578, 582–83, 599.
154. Theophylactus, *Vita s. Clementis*, Ch. 17, Migne, *PG*, CXXVI, col. 1224.

can be grouped under a few broad headings. By far the most prominent issue centers around the administration of justice. In this connection, Boris was troubled on three points: he repeatedly asked the pope to define the position he, as judge, should take toward certain criminal groups in society; he was concerned about punishments proper for various kinds of crime; and he was worried lest conventional judicial procedures violate the Christian religion.

In seeking information about how various lawbreakers should be judged, Boris was often concerned with types of criminals that had been present in Bulgar society long before Christianity had entered the land. He asked Nicholas to tell him what should be done with fugitives from battle, those who refuse to fight, parricides, those trying to flee the country, murderers of relatives, adulterers, those guilty of incest, rapists, animal thiefs, kidnappers, those who castrate others, false accusers, poisoners, and slaves who accuse their masters.[155] We must assume that Bulgar custom and law had long ago established that those who were guilty of these acts were criminals, and Boris knew—under the old order—what to do with them; but for some reason he felt that conventional usages had been outmoded by the coming of Christianity. The fact that he asked what should be done with such common types of criminal action forces one to conclude that he was ready to change ancient usage to fit new standards. Nicholas must have interpreted his requests in this fashion, for he sent Boris a code of laws[156] and constantly directed the khan to this document for specific instructions on revamping the Bulgar judicial system.

The coming of Christianity introduced a new range of crimes and confronted the khan with the problem of the judicial treatment of his subjects who were found guilty of these new offenses. Boris now needed to know what should be done about apostates, those who flee the country to escape the new religion, those who refuse to become Christian, those who copulate with their wives during Lent, bigamists, married priests, adulterous priests, those who try to force widows to become nuns against their will, criminals who seek asylum in churches, those who divorce their spouses, suicides, false missionaries, and troublesome preachers.[157] From

155. Nicholas, *Ep.*, No. 99, Chs. 22–26, 28–32, 52, 84, 85, 97, pp. 579–80, 586, 595, 597–98.

156. *Ibid.*, Ch. 13, p. 575. M. Conrat, "Römisches Recht bei Papst Nikolaus I," *Neues Archiv*, XXXVI (1911), 724, argues that this code was a Lombard law code enlarged by certain Carolingian capitularies; he denies that it was the Code of Justinian, as some have suggested.

157. Nicholas, *Ep.*, No. 99, Chs. 18–20, 41, 50, 51, 70, 71, 87, 95, 96, 98, 104, 105, pp. 578, 579, 582–83, 586, 592, 595–99.

108

a modern point of view, Boris encroached upon private ground, for he compounded criminals and sinners, and at one point asked Nicholas how he should treat sinners in general.[158] However, what is more significant than these niceties is the fact that the introduction of the new religion thrust upon the ruler the responsibility for rendering justice on matters previously unknown in Bulgar society. Again, the conversion process had introduced complications into the ordinary processes of government and had left the ruler uncertain of his responsibility.

Not only did Boris want to know his position vis-à-vis the perpetrators of a wide range of criminal acts, he also worried about the punishment he should mete out to criminals. Apparently convinced that a mark of Bulgar barbarity was its savagery in punishing lawbreakers, Photius had cautioned the khan against imposing weighty punishments according to the exact letter of the law.[159] It seems almost certain that the new convert was moved by this admonition and that he was gravely concerned lest customary Bulgar severity in punishing criminals violate Christian teaching. At one place in his letter to Nicholas, Boris submitted a sample of Bulgar justice for papal evaluation: if a thief or a robber is apprehended and denies what is charged against him, the judge strikes his head with a rod and pierces his sides with iron picks until he tells the truth.[160] He asked the pope to tell him if this is a just treatment of a criminal.

In two other cases he asked for a judgment on Bulgar treatment of criminals by making a personal confession to the pope. Boris had apprehended a "lying Greek who claimed to be a priest" performing baptism; he judged him, and then punished him by cutting off his ears and nose, lashing him, and expelling him from the country. He begged the pope to tell him whether he should do penance for such conduct.[161] Boris then recounted that when some of his subjects had rebelled against him for having introduced Christianity into the land, and had sought to kill him, he had killed the nobles involved and their progeny. His chief concern was whether his conduct as judge had been sinful.[162]

In each of these three instances the Bulgar penal code is held up for scrutiny, and Boris would hardly have raised these issues had he not felt that the new religion demanded less severe punishments. We must presume that in all his requests for guidance in dealing with criminals he was

158. *Ibid.*, Ch. 83, p. 595.
159. Photius, *Ep.*, No. 6, Chs. 42–44, ed. Valetta, pp. 232–33.
160. Nicholas, *Ep.*, No. 99, Ch. 86, p. 595.
161. *Ibid.*, Chs. 14, 16, pp. 575, 576.
162. *Ibid.*, Ch. 17, pp. 577–78.

also seeking to discover the approved Christian punishments as replacements for the savage habits of the Bulgars. Nicholas apparently sensed Boris' sentiment, for he repeatedly counseled his protégé to temper the law with mercy and moderation. The law code he sent to Boris provided specific information for establishing a new penal code.

In the matter of justice, finally, Boris was concerned with the propriety of certain judicial procedures as he was forced to cope with new factors introduced by Christianity. The new religion required that he cease holding courts and imposing death sentences on Sundays, feast days and during Lent.[163] The customary ways of extracting confessions from accused criminals were no longer permissible;[164] and the khan was now expected to entrust to the clergy the final authority in deciding certain kinds of cases, especially those involving marriage problems,[165] sexual abuses,[166] and rights of asylum for criminals.[167] This latter requirement inevitably involved the clergy in the routine procedures of the courts. However, Boris was given to understand that the ruler had no right to judge clerics in any matters,[168] so clerical discipline necessitated the creation of another judicial system in Bulgaria. The conventional form of oath-taking had to be changed to fit Christian usage, thereby introducing a foreign element into judicial administration.[169] These cases were not sufficiently numerous to warrant the conclusion that the whole procedure for the administration of justice had to be scrapped, but they suggest that enough modifications had to be made that they disturbed accustomed patterns and caused confusion.

Another area of political concern for Boris lay in the area of foreign relations. He worried over several matters relating to the waging of war, reflecting a fear that improper procedures would provoke divine wrath and lead to defeat. He asked Nicholas to tell him if there were certain days or seasons when it was not proper to engage in war.[170] He requested guidance on what battle insignia was proper for a Christian army and what kinds of preparation were suitable prior to a military engagement.[171] He wondered if he could still send his agents through the land to check

---

163. *Ibid.*, Chs. 12, 45, pp. 574–75, 585.
164. *Ibid.*, Ch. 86, p. 595.
165. *Ibid.*, Chs. 28, 50, 51, 70, pp. 580, 586, 592.
166. *Ibid.*, Chs. 29, 50, 51, pp. 580, 586.
167. *Ibid.*, Chs. 24, 26, 28, 95, pp. 579, 580, 597.
168. *Ibid.*, Chs. 70, 83, pp. 592, 595.
169. *Ibid.*, Ch. 67, p. 591.
170. *Ibid.*, Chs. 34, 36, 46, pp. 581, 585.
171. *Ibid.*, Chs., 33, 35, pp. 580–81.

that all his subjects had the horses, arms, and other necessities required for battle.[172] The khan was greatly concerned over battle preparations; and he even asked Nicholas to tell him what ought to be done when, in the midst of prayer, a messenger brings news of an enemy's approach.[173] Obviously, the khan and his warriors had been accustomed to trust that the gods would assure their victory, and they wanted to be sure that their new God was properly and adequately placated so that their military fortunes would continue to flourish. One suspects that, at least for a time, the changes in military procedures necessitated by Christianity caused the Bulgars to enter battle somewhat less confidently than in former days, when there had been no new-fangled usages to respect.

Boris also felt a need to clarify the procedures involved in making peace.[174] He asked Nicholas to instruct him in how to make and keep peace with foreigners who came seeking it. Nicholas interpreted this request to mean that Boris was concerned about pacts with pagan nations, and he responded by telling Boris to make sure that a treaty in no way compromised the faith. Indeed, Boris was concerned about Bulgar relations with pagans for he specifically asked about diplomatic dealings with them. And he was troubled about his rights and responsibilities in cases where a pact with a Christian people was broken by the other party.

Again it would appear that the introduction of the new religion had cast doubts on existing political usages and had raised serious questions about the validity of Bulgar commitments to neighboring peoples. Our limited knowledge of Bulgar foreign relations suggests that Boris' questions touched on vital matters: the treaty with the Greeks in 864, Bulgaria's hostile policy toward the Moravians prior to Boris' conversion, the treaty of 862 with the East Franks, and Bulgar relations with several Slavic tribes adjacent to the Bulgar frontiers. If Christianity demanded a new code of diplomacy, Boris may have felt that the Bulgar position must be changed as it pertained to some of her neighbors. One suspects that the khan was hopeful that his adhesion to the new religion and his willingness to observe Christian principles in his foreign policy would elevate his status in the eyes of the great powers of his generation: the Christian states of Byzantium and the East Franks.

Still another political issue posed by the conversion of Bulgaria was the problem of the relationship between the Church and the state. Our discussion of Boris' efforts to establish a church organization has already made

172. *Ibid.*, Ch. 40, p. 582.
173. *Ibid.*, Ch. 34, p. 581.
174. *Ibid.*, Chs. 80–82, pp. 594–95.

it clear that the khan was convinced it was a matter of urgency to institute the Church as a corporate entity in his realm. Boris obviously felt free to use his secular authority to manipulate this new organization emerging in his realm. He punished religious leaders whom he felt were acting in error;[175] he expelled missionary bishops and priests who no longer suited his needs;[176] he commanded his noble supporters to provide hospitality for Clement in the newly formed missionary district and ordered those living in that district to support his efforts.[177] The Roman missionary Grimoald could hardly have grown rich in Bulgaria except through the generous support given him by Boris.[178] The khan was at least inclined to exert his power to correct the religious shortcomings of his subjects and to compel them to observe his version of the Christian law.[179] All these cases indicate that Boris was willing and even eager to assume considerable authority over the religious establishment and to shape it according to his own lights.

It is equally obvious, however, that he could not act with complete freedom, that he was confronted with irresistible pressures to create a privileged place for the clergy in his realm and to accept considerable clerical involvement in political life. An examination of his efforts to create a church organization clearly indicates that he was heavily dependent on the will of ecclesiastical officials outside Bulgaria to secure bishops and priests as missionaries. From Nicholas' pastoral letter come clear indications that the missionary leaders came to Bulgaria primed to act positively in political affairs. The pope was good enough to respect Boris' plea for a secular law code, but he ordered that the book be returned to Rome with his legates, Bishops Paul and Formosus, so that the law would not be misinterpreted by Bulgars ignorant of its meaning. Obviously the bishops were charged with guiding Boris' use of the law in the conduct of his affairs,[180] and Nicholas repeatedly ordered Boris to refer judicial cases to the bishops.[181]

If Boris respected these orders, the clerical influence on the administration of justice was destined to be great. The Bulgar ruler was cautioned

175. *Ibid.*, Chs. 14–16, 104, 105, pp. 575–76, 599.
176. See above, pp. 81–82, 93–94.
177. Theophylactus, *Vita s. Clementis*, Ch. 17, Migne, *PG*, CXXVI, col. 1224.
178. *Liber pontificalis*, ed. Duchesne, II, 185.
179. Nicholas, *Ep.*, No. 99, *passim*; nearly every passage in this letter implies that the khan intends to use papal advice as a guide for the correction of the living habits of the people over whom he ruled.
180. *Ibid.*, Ch. 13, p. 575.
181. *Ibid.*, Chs. 24, 26, 28–30, 50, 51, 95, pp. 579, 580, 586, 597.

against assuming the right to judge the clergy, even when priests were involved in such flagrant sins as adultery, or obviously guilty of such infractions of canon law as marriage;[182] and the bishops were to be consulted in any case where there was a question of the suitability of a peace treaty.[183] Boris respected this command to involve the clergy in foreign affairs in at least one case, for he turned over to the papal legates certain letters unfavorable to Rome's cause which he had received from the Byzantine court.[184] Nor is there any reason to believe that the Greek clergy involved in Bulgar affairs during Boris' reign were any less timid than the Roman clergy in claiming an important role in guiding the khan's political actions. In short, the acceptance of Christianity brought powerful men to Bulgaria with strong convictions about the importance of the clergy in a Christian state and about the ideal configuration of a Christian political order.

Unfortunately, we cannot accurately weigh the influence of the Christian clergy in shaping Bulgar political life during the conversion period. Admittedly, Boris could have disregarded the repeated advice of Nicholas to rely on the bishops in formulating political actions, yet the very nature of the khan's situation makes this appear unlikely. Boris was trying to impose a new religion in the face of hostility from some of the *boyars*, which would seem to dictate close cooperation with the clergy and a respect for their claims to be involved in politics. He was also courting the allegiance of the Slavic elements in his realm and trying to overcome their hostility to the overlordship of the Bulgar ruling caste. The clergy, especially after the adoption of the Slavonic liturgy, was the khan's prime link with the Slavs. Boris was personally concerned that his conduct reflect the Christian ethos and that his people become Christians. To him this meant a change in old usages in favor of a Christian way of acting; almost every request he put to Nicholas bespeaks his seriousness in pursuit of this end.

Given the urge to act as a Christian, Boris had no recourse but to ask the missionary leaders for practical guidance in ways that were genuinely Christian; he was dependent on them for the enlightenment he felt he and his people required. The conversion process raised many problems of a political nature; Boris was ignorant of the Christian way of resolving these issues and had to depend on the missionary leaders for a suitable response. Thus the khan's intense search for the Christian way, coupled with the

182. *Ibid.*, Chs. 70–71, 83, pp. 592–93, 595.
183. *Ibid.*, Ch. 81, p. 594.
184. Nicholas, *Ep.*, No. 100, ed. Perels, *MGH*, *Ep.*, VI, p. 603.

admitted limitations on himself and his Bulgars, created an atmosphere that was conducive to a rapid advance of the clergy in political affairs. As the bishops moved to the center of the political stage, they must certainly have established a privileged place for themselves in society. Perhaps a fitting symbol of what happened in Bulgaria is contained in a western chronicler's account of how Boris suppressed a revolt by surrounding himself with clergymen and staging a religious procession.[185] This incident suggests strong reliance by the khan on clerical support in politics and it implies considerable involvement of the clergy in the processes of government. If the church made important advances in shaping political life, we might assume that considerable tension arose among the *boyars* who had been crowded aside. And perhaps even the great khan on occasion felt compromised by the involvement of ecclesiastical figures in the details of political life.

These reflections on the political consequences of the Christianization of Bulgaria lead one to give considerable weight to a remark that Boris made to Nicholas I. In recounting how some of his subjects had rebelled when he had introduced the new religion, Boris told the pope that the conspirators said their khan did not give them good laws, and therefore they wished to kill him.[186] One suspects that the rebels were right, if he interprets "good laws" to mean the kind of law that had been customary in Bulgaria. Inspired by the new religion, the khan set out to modify the political structure of his land in several significant ways. He caught a new vision of his own authority; he found new causes for charging his subjects with breaking the law; and he introduced new punishments for old crimes. Either by choice or by necessity, he listened to new advisers, some of whom probably knew little about Bulgar political usages but who could answer the ruler's incessant demands for knowledge of the true Christian way. He took a new view of those who were friends and enemies of the Bulgars.

All of these innovations were probably sufficient to unsettle political life in Bulgaria and to cause apprehension among those not yet convinced that the Christian style of politics represented a great advance. In short, conversion was not just a religious matter; it led to a profound unsettling of the political order in Bulgaria.

The intrusion of the new religion into Bulgaria likewise called into question conventional patterns of moral behavior. As a result, Boris and

185. *Annales Bertiniani, a.* 866, ed. Waitz, *MGH, SS. rer. Germ.*, p. 85.
186. Nicholas, *Ep.*, No. 99, Ch. 17, p. 577.

114

those associated with him in the conversion of the Bulgars were forced to question the many moral practices that prevailed among the Bulgars and to ponder ways of effecting changes in behavior. Implicit in this matter, then, was the need for a profound transformation of the mores of the society.

The sources leave little doubt that the missionary forces entering Bulgaria constantly reminded the new converts of the inadequacies of the traditional code of conduct. At several places in his letter, Nicholas I stressed that the Bulgars would have difficulty living up to Christian standards because of the crudity of their present mode of life.[187] And Photius began his letter to Boris with an austere reminder that the acceptance of the new faith called for a moral regeneration, by implication condemning the existing morality of the Bulgars.[188]

Somewhat surprisingly, the Bulgars appear to have taken the criticisms to heart. Throughout Nicholas' letter there are constant allusions to the fact that Boris approached Rome in a spirit of humility, bred of his realization of the moral shortcomings of his people. In a sense, he put his sentiments into words at the very end of his requests to Nicholas when he begged the guidance of the pope for a people "not having a true and perfect Christianity."[189] When Clement and Nahum came to Bulgaria, after having fled Moravia, there was a clamor among the Bulgar nobles to be allowed to speak to these teachers and to learn from them a more perfect manner of life; apparently the presence of saintly missionaries awakened in men an urge to learn a new way of life.[190] The introduction of Christianity thus brought into Bulgaria critics of the existing morality, and at the same time bred among Bulgars a sense of inadequacy and an urge for change.

But the missionaries came not only to show the Bulgars the inadequacies of the traditional morality, they apparently insisted that their converts accept a new morality. Indeed, this may have been the major theme in their formal presentation of Christianity. Nicholas I and Photius spoke in almost identical terms on the issue of moral regeneration in the opening sentences of their pastoral letters to Boris. Nicholas wrote: "Let it be known that the law of the Christians consists of faith and good works. For faith is the first of all virtues in the habits of believers. . . . However, good works are no less demanded of the Christian."[191] After pointing out

187. *Ibid.*, Chs. 4, 16–17, 47, pp. 570–71, 576–77, 585–86.
188. Photius, *Ep.*, No. 6, Chs. 2–3, ed. Valetta, pp. 202–3.
189. Nicholas, *Ep.*, No. 99, Ch. 106, p. 599.
190. Theophylactus, *Vita s. Clementis*, Ch. 16, Migne, *PG*, CXXVI, cols. 1221–24.
191. Nicholas, *Ep.*, No. 99, Ch. 1, p. 569.

to Boris the need to understand the Christian faith, Photius argued: "However, it must be said that virtues and good works must not be separated from faith; instead the good man ought to perfect and unite the one and the other. For right faith produces noble habits, and purity of deeds proves that faith is fully divine."[192]

These pronouncements were not idle comments, for Nicholas made it clear that the missionary leaders he was sending to Bulgaria would inform Boris in detail on everything that pertained to the fundamental Christian law.[193] It was reported of these papal missionaries that "they began to teach the people with saving warnings" and "with the grace of God caused the customs of the Bulgars to be changed over to the ways of the Christian faith, as they had been instructed by the most holy pope."[194] Another source says that Nicholas answered Boris' plea for help (in 866) "not only by giving the true faith but also [giving] a manner of living."[195]

It thus appears beyond dispute that missionary forces arrived in Bulgaria prepared and even determined to guide the crude Bulgars into new patterns of behavior. It is much more difficult to ascertain the specific content of their preachments on morality. Virtually the only source that treats this matter in detail is the pastoral letter of Photius, two-thirds of which is given over to moral strictures. This elegant, sophisticated discourse, exhorting Boris to "illustrate his faith through actions,"[196] often strikes a note that seems far removed from the Bulgar scene and asks of Boris a mode of behavior beyond his simple talents. Yet, despite its exalted tone, it touches on a range of moral problems that may well have been at issue in Bulgaria. It thus seems permissible to cite its content as a guide to the major themes stressed by missionaries in their effort to alter Bulgar conduct in the name of the new law to which the Bulgars had become subject through baptism.

Photius presented Christian morality to Boris, in part, as a series of prohibitions. Implying that the barbarian prince—and, by inference, all new converts—were apt to be accustomed to various acts that were considered sins by Christian standards, he sought to convince Boris to abandon these ways; and his admonitions were grounded in the Ten

192. Photius, *Ep.*, No. 6, Ch. 3, ed. Valetta, p. 203.

193. Nicholas, *Ep.*, No. 99, p. 568.

194. *Liber pontificalis*, ed. Duchesne, II, 165.

195. *Anastasii Bibliothecarii Ep. sive Praef.*, No. 5, eds. Perels and Laehr, *MGH, Ep.*, VII, 412.

196. Photius, *Ep.*, No. 6, Ch. 22, ed. Valetta, pp. 222–23: "ἀρεταῖς κοσμεῖν τὴν πίστιν, καὶ τῇ πίστει τάς ἀρετάς λαμπροτέρας απεργάζεσθαι." The following section is based on *ibid.*, Chs. 21–114, pp. 221–48.

⋋ Commandments, with which he presumed the khan was familiar. From these prohibitions sprang a wide range of acts that a Christian, and especially a Christian prince, must shun. He must guard against excesses and improprieties in dress, bodily adornment, and motions. Silly laughter and obscenity ought to be shunned, and accusers and sycophants. Those who ⋋ have power must avoid all abuse by that power of the powerless, and must guard against the employment of power to induce fear. Envy, pride, arrogance, deceit, vengefulness, anger, blind passion, voluptuousness, lust, bestiality, and drunkenness are dreadful offenses, bound to displease God and to destroy the authority of a prince. Whoever is in a special position in society must take great care in establishing friendships, since men will constantly press for the honor of enjoying his friendship. Once friends are made, however, every Christian has a grave moral responsibility to respect them, to treat them fairly, and to be mindful of what they have done for him. A prince is constantly in danger of using his great power to command others to a sinful action, but such conduct must be avoided at all costs. If Boris understood Photius, he must have been led to believe that leading the Christian life involved the abandonment of many actions, and a purgation of one's life that eliminated specific faults.

The patriarch was equally forceful in casting Christian morality in positive terms. If Boris hoped to do good works, he must learn to love God and his fellowmen. From this would flow numerous positive virtues: respect for parents, avoidance of shedding blood, respect for the good of others, refusal to bear false witness, avoidance of adultery. The good Christian should learn to pray, to devote himself to divine worship, and to follow the guidance of his priest. He must be merciful to those who offend him. If he is in a position of power, the good man must judge with mercy and punish with moderation, and for such a man it is especially crucial that he learn the nature of true justice and act accordingly. He should learn to control his desires and moderate his pleasures. Kindness, fairness, prudence, willingness to bear adversity, charity, generosity with one's material goods, readiness to assume labors, faithfulness to promises, beneficence, and honor toward friends mark the man who does good works in the Christian sense. Photius repeatedly made it clear that the attainment of these virtues and the consequent winning of the favor of God depended upon one's efforts. Every new Christian must understand that Christian virtue demanded an heroic struggle with the dark forces that inhabited the world, that lurked in the human soul, that distracted man from his task of earning, by his good works, the merits necessary for salvation. Again, if Boris grasped Photius' line of argument, he must have envisaged his moral responsibility not only in terms of refraining from certain acts but also in undertaking new kinds of actions that would demonstrate his willingness to do good.

If one accepts Photius' letter as the prototype of the manner in which the missionary forces confronted the Bulgars on the level of personal morality, he may wonder what the Bulgar reaction was to the double demand to purge old customs and accept new standards and patterns of behavior. The evidence does not supply any convincing proof that the Bulgars became deeply immersed in the positive side of Christian morality. No doubt the institution of the Christian cult, as previously described, altered outward modes of conduct in various ways, but mere conformance to its demands would not necessarily have involved deep moral issues. As has already been suggested, the Bulgars may have accepted Christian liturgical practices as substitutes for pagan rites; and the sources provide little indication that Christian worship evoked a new level of spiritual awareness which manifested itself in a new morality. Perhaps it was only a quest for moral regeneration that later persuaded Boris and a few of his subjects to retreat to the cloister. On the whole, it seems that the positive content of Christian morality did not deeply stir the moral sensibilities of the new converts.

What concerned the Bulgars on the moral level was whether, and to what degree, traditional moral usages differed from or violated Christian norms. This issue dominated Boris' requests to Nicholas. The khan almost never demonstrated any concern for discovering ways to put into effect Christian modes of behavior that would have been new to his people; almost never did he ask Nicholas to inform him of ways to attain the kind of moral excellence of which Photius had discoursed so eloquently. Incessantly he sought from the pope opinions about the propriety of particular Bulgar customs in terms of Christian standards. His inquiries range over a wide variety of matters, from marriage usages and sexual mores to bathing practices and the style of pants befitting true Christian life.[197] The mixture of serious moral issues and banalities in Boris' requests points toward a proscriptive concept of morality.

The moral problem before the new converts was, essentially, discovering and expurgating from habitual conduct certain kinds of behavior that

197. Nicholas, *Ep.*, No. 99, Ch. 6 (bathing), 21 (fugitive slaves), 33 (battle insignia), 35 (battle preparations), 39 (degree of kinship in marriage), 42 (royal eating customs), 43 (dietary regulations), 44, 47 (hunting), 49 (dowry), 51 (bigamy), 56 (prayers for rain), 59 (pantaloons), 63–64 (sexual mores), 79 (pendants for healing), 96 (divorce), 97 (slavery), 100 (disposal of the bodies of dead soldiers), pp. 572, 579, 580–88, 590, 594, 597–98.

violated the law observed by Christians. When that purification of prohibited usages was achieved, the converts would consider themselves morally fit as Christians. As he grasps the intent of Boris' concern over the moral life of his people, one suspects that the missionary preachers were leaning heavily on Old Testament concepts of strict adherence to a formal moral code in their efforts to Christianize Bulgar behavior. Put another way, it appears that the Bulgars took Photius' prohibitory admonitions much more seriously than his positive approach to the moral life that flowed from Christian spiritual values.

As he sought to provide intelligible and practicable answers to this barrage of questions for a judgment on Bulgar moral practices, Nicholas seems to have sensed that Boris' concern with these matters was too great. The pope was not only liberal in approving ancient Bulgar modes of conduct, he took special pains to assure Boris that whatever the Bulgars had done without sin before baptism could be done without sin after baptism.[198] Surely he emphasized this consoling principle to assure Boris that the introduction of Christianity did not require the abandonment of every manner of conduct to which the Bulgars were accustomed, and that the new converts did not have to strain over every item of their traditional code of morals to discern the propriety of each. But it appears that the Bulgar reaction was exactly this. When the missionaries descended on their land, calling for the newly baptized to abandon their old ways of life in favor of the new law, some of the most fervent Bulgars, including the khan, questioned the propriety of many aspects of the conventional morality. No doubt these same pious souls were not slow to call into question the behavior of their compatriots who were not moved by the appeals of the missionaries to take upon themselves the observance of the new law.

It would appear, then, that the conversion process disturbed the moral order in Bulgaria, which leaves the momentous question of the practical consequences of this disturbance. Did the Bulgar effort to abide by Christian moral law by purging their lives of specifically prohibited usages have any significant effect? The sources are mute; the historian cannot demonstrate the degree to which moral practices were altered in the newly converted society. All that Boris' requests to Nicholas indicate is that in their daily lives most Bulgars still followed their old customs even though they were being admonished to change. But one can at least suggest the possibility of serious tension in Bulgar society over moral conduct.

The evidence affirms that serious doubts had been cast on the validity

198. *Ibid.*, Ch. 49, p. 586.

of ancient moral standards. These doubts must surely have weakened, or perhaps even destroyed, the one element that gives any moral code its ultimate force: the unquestioning assumption of those bound by it that its provisions are valid. This condition points toward the dissolution of the old morality. The sources further attest the inability of the new converts to comprehend the positive content of Christian morality. Inevitably one is forced to envisage a situation where many Bulgars (probably the most enthusiastic converts) found themselves deprived of confidence in the old morality and fairly ignorant of the new. Such a situation could have bred moral anarchy, and perhaps Photius sensed this possibility when he so strongly stressed the need for moral excellence in a prince as a model for the rest of society. Or such a condition may have led to constant and painful soul-searching of moral issues by serious men, just as Boris had reflected uneasiness about his personal conduct in his requests to Pope Nicholas. However, this is all conjecture; the sources tell virtually nothing of changes in morality during the conversion era.

While grappling with the manifold problems accompanying the institution of the Christian religion and the adjustment of Bulgarian institutions and customs to its demands, Boris had one more major challenge to face. The sources repeatedly indicate that Christianity was presented to the Bulgars in such a way as to imply that its survival in that backward land depended upon the ability of the khan and his subjects to achieve a higher level of culture. Put another way, the acceptance of Christianity brought the Bulgars more intimately into contact with a new range of culture and made it imperative that they strive to possess this new culture not so much for its own sake but in order to comprehend the essential features of the Christian message.

In attempting to assess the cultural impact of Christianity on Bulgaria, one is first struck by the degree to which the Bulgars were belittled by those involved in introducing the new faith into the land. It has already been noted that those who offered Boris advice on the content of the faith, on its proper practice, on the arts of government suitable to a Christian society, and on the moral life proper to the sons of the Christian God were quick to assume that the Bulgars knew little of these matters, that the new converts were children who needed milk before they could feed on solid food.[199] This assumption was even more prevalent in matters that touched upon cultural life.

199. See above, pp. 78, 84–88, 106–10, 114.

The letters of Photius, Nicholas I, and John VIII are permeated with statements indicating their low opinion of the intellectual capabilities of the Bulgars; the two popes agreed with Photius' characterization of the Bulgars as a "barbarous people." [200] Repeatedly and consciously, they cast their admonitions and instructions to the Bulgars in terms which implied they were simplifying matters so as not to overstrain the limited mental abilities of the new converts. [201] Each of these potentates was quick to blame the repeated switch of ecclesiastical allegiance by the Bulgars on Bulgar simple-mindedness, which made the new converts easy prey for more subtle and sophisticated men. [202] Nicholas often advised Boris to seek the advice of the Roman bishops in his land, for "they hold the keys of knowledge"; [203] the pope clearly implied that Boris and his Bulgars suffered from a lack of knowledge. The pope would not even run the risk of allowing the Bulgars to keep the law code he sent them, for he was fearful that after his bishops left there would be no one capable of using it correctly. [204]

Although they may have done so unconsciously, the Bulgars reacted to the appearance of the culturally advanced missionaries as if to confirm their barbarous condition. Boris admitted to Nicholas that he was confused by the conflicting versions of Christianity presented in his land and that he was puzzled about what to do with "the profane books" brought to him by Moslems; he must have felt that his knowledge was too limited to cope with such complexities. [205] His eager reception of the learned Clement and Nahum, and his effort to employ their talents in developing a system of education and a literary culture in Bulgaria, suggest a strongly felt need to overcome Bulgar cultural crudity. [206] So also does Boris' decision to send his son and some of his subjects to Constantinople for a monastic education. [207]

200. Photius, *Ep.*, No. 4, Ch. 3, ed. Valetta, p. 168: "βουλγάρων ἔθνος βαρβαρικὸν."
201. For example: Nicholas, *Ep.*, No. 99, Chs. 4, 16, 17, 47, pp. 570–71, 576–77, 585–86.
202. Photius, *Ep.*, No. 4, ed. Valetta, pp. 165–81; Nicholas, *Ep.*, No. 100, ed. Perels, *MGH, Ep.*, VI, 601, 603; *Iohannis VIII. Papae Epistolae*, Nos. 66, 67, 182, ed. Caspar, *MGH, Ep.*, VII, 58–62, 146. The western version of the appearance of the Bulgars before the Council of Constantinople in 870 is based upon the assumption that the simple Bulgars had been beguiled into defecting from Rome by the Greeks; see *Liber pontificalis*, ed. Duchesne, II, 182–85; *Anastasii Bibliothecarii Ep. sive Praef.*, No. 5, eds. Perels and Laehr, *MGH, Ep.*, VII, 411–15.
203. Nicholas, *Ep.*, No. 99, Chs. 9, 106, pp. 573, 599–600.
204. *Ibid.*, Ch. 13, p. 573.
205. *Ibid.*, Chs. 103, 106, pp. 599–600.
206. Theophylactus, *Vita s. Clementis*, Chs. 16–17, Migne, *PG*, CXXVI, cols. 1221–24.

The Bulgars appear to have seized any opportunity to submit themselves to the cultural influences of their spiritual mentors, an attitude that
could only have reinforced what the outsiders already felt—the Bulgars
were "ignorant and brutish."[208] The Bulgars even capitalized on their
reputation for naïveté and crudity. When, in 870, Boris decided to turn
away from Roman supervision over his newly converted land and accept
Greek tutelage, he sent his legates to Constantinople to present the matter
to the council then in session. Upon gaining a hearing before the papal
legates and the eastern patriarchs, the Bulgar spokesman stated his case
completely in terms of Bulgar ignorance of the laws and precedents of the
Church. He asked only that his august and sacred audience decide
the proper jurisdictional disposition of his native land, then he let his more
learned judges argue the case and ultimately decide it the way they
wished.[209]

In their totality, these cases strongly suggest that the conversion process suddenly deflated the Bulgars in the opinion of both the contemporary
world and the Bulgars themselves. Whereas before 864 the Bulgars had
been treated as formidable warriors, desirable allies, and skilled diplomats,
after 864 and the coming of Christianity they were universally treated as
ignorant, crude suppliants who needed guidance in extracting themselves
from their helpless state. In their own eyes they had committed themselves, by their choice to become Christians, to a course which forced them
to admit their inadequacies and their former sins of omission and commission. Indeed, the Bulgars actually possessed about the same order of
strength and power after 864 as before, but neither the world around them
nor they themselves viewed the situation in this perspective after 864. The
introduction of Christianity revealed their cultural backwardness, and it
set the Bulgars the monumental task of making themselves culturally
worthy of the new religion.

The full proportions of this task are not entirely clear from the sources;
nor does this paper encompass a period long enough to trace in full the
cultural uplifting of the Bulgars as a result of the introduction of Christianity. However, the sources for the first stage of the conversion process
during the reign of Boris indicate that the outside world confronted the

207. Luidprandus of Cremona, *Antapodosis*, III, Ch. 29, in *The Works of Luidprand of
Cremona*, trans. Wright, p. 123; Photius, *Ep.*, No. 255, ed. Valetta, p. 556.

208. Theophylactus, *Vita s. Clementis*, Ch. 21, Migne, *PG*, CXXVI, col. 1228:
"ἀμαθέστατοι καὶ . . . κτηνωδέστατοι."

209. *Liber pontificalis*, ed. Duchesne, II, 182–85; *Anastasii Bibliothecarii Ep. sive Praef.*,
No. 5, eds. Perels and Laehr, *MGH, Ep.*, VII, 411–15.

Bulgars with the broad outlines of a new culture which that barbaric people had to master in order to comprehend Christianity in the fullest sense, and to draw from it the richest spiritual benefits. The cultural task facing the Bulgars was never stated in the form of a specific program; rather, those who addressed themselves to the problems facing the new converts repeatedly presented their arguments and appeals in terms which suggested only the broad cultural areas in which the Bulgars must acquire skill and knowledge. Even to understand their mentors fully, the Bulgars would have had to develop greater competence in a variety of cultural pursuits.

The first and most pressing task that faced the Bulgars was a mastery of Scripture. There is hardly a chapter in Nicholas' long letter to Boris which does not utilize a scriptural passage as a device for clarifying the course of action demanded of the new converts or for illustrating the exact content of Christian teaching. The letters of Pope John VIII to Boris are no less generous in the use of Scripture, and no doubt the missionary workers in Bulgaria turned with equal frequency to scriptural passages to instruct the Bulgars. Occasionally the scriptural references are only partially quoted or are paraphrased, which placed upon the reader of the papal letters the burden of seeking out the full text—assuming he had an interest in reading the original version. There is no direct evidence that the Bulgars possessed the linguistic ability to read a Latin or Greek version of the Bible; however, because of the great number of Latin and Greek letters sent to Bulgaria and Boris' specific request for law codes, penitentials, and missals in Latin,[210] we must assume there were men of learning at the Bulgar court who were capable of utilizing the Bible in Latin and Greek.

The Bulgars were faced not only with the task of mastering the literal words of Scripture in order to grasp the full meaning of Christianity, they were also confronted with the whole problem of its allegorical interpretations. Nicholas I imposed this burden on Boris in specific terms. In response to a query of whether the Greeks were right in prohibiting anyone from receiving communion unless he wore a belt, Nicholas said he was ignorant of any such command in Scripture, unless the Greeks were referring to the Lord's order: "Let your limbs be bound up" (Luke 12:35). The pope continued: "In truth this testimony of the holy gospel

210. Nicholas, *Ep.*, No. 99, Chs. 1, 13, 75, 76, pp. 568, 575, 593. For some interesting comments on the linguistic situation in Bulgaria in the pre-conversion period, see Beševliev and Grégoire, "Les inscriptions protobulgares," *Byzantion*, XXV–XXVI–XXVII (1955–56–57), 853, ff.

must be fulfilled not according to the letter, but according to the spirit," and he thereupon proceeded to enlarge on the allegorical meaning of the passage, quoting at length from a letter of Pope Celestine.[211]

On numerous occasions elsewhere in his responses to Boris, the pope himself used Scripture allegorically to illustrate the precepts he wished to convey to the Bulgars.[212] It is worth comment that Nicholas often reverted to this technique when Boris called upon him to pass judgment on a pagan practice. One suspects that he hoped to offer the khan a solution to one of his most pressing concerns; namely, the establishment of a standard against which to judge the propriety of pagan usages. The Bulgars had only to read the spiritual meaning of the Bible, as the pope so often did, and their doubts would be cleared away. However, to the unlettered Bulgars the art of interpreting "the spiritual sense" of Holy Writ may indeed have been difficult, requiring far greater learning than they possessed during the first generation of their membership in the Christian community.

If the first burden placed upon the untutored Bulgars by their spiritual guides was the learning of Scripture, certainly the second was the mastery of a new law. More accurately, one should say new laws, for the various documents addressed to the Bulgars from Rome and Constantinople refer to a variety of laws so complex that the Bulgars could well have been utterly confused, as Boris often admitted. Keeping in mind what has already been demonstrated in the attitude evinced by Christian spokesmen toward the inferiority of many Bulgar legal and moral usages, there seems to be little doubt that the Bulgars were expected to put into practice new rules that would govern all aspects of their society. Moreover, part of their obligation as Christians was the discovery of these new laws. Although Pope Nicholas was at times inclined to condone Bulgar customs, at least temporarily,[213] he did not hesitate to inform the new converts of their ultimate responsibility: "Now, however, in the same fashion that you have changed from the old men to the new, so likewise you should change from the former customs to our custom in all things."[214]

But what was *morem nostrum*? In terms of Nicholas' letter, as it is supported by other documents sent to Bulgaria, the new law was a combination of many laws with which the Bulgars must acquaint themselves.

211. Nicholas, *Ep.*, No. 99, Ch. 55, p. 587.

212. For example: *ibid.*, Chs. 1, 2, 7, 17–20, 33, 40, 41, 50, 95, pp. 568–69, 572–73, 577–83, 586, 597; and *Iohannis VIII. Papae Epistolae*, No. 66, ed. Caspar, *MGH, Ep.*, VII, 59.

213. Nicholas, *Ep.*, No. 99, Ch. 49, p. 586.

214. *Ibid.*, Ch. 59, p. 588.

Scripture itself was a prime source of the Christian law, and Nicholas and Photius repeatedly drew on scriptural commands as sanctions for their instructions to the neophyte Bulgars. It is probably this source which Photius had in mind in admonishing Boris to observe the "divine law," and what Nicholas meant when he spoke of "the sublime mandate of God."[215] Nicholas also repeatedly referred Boris to a code of secular law as his guide in shaping a Christian polity for his realm, in most cases directing the khan to the collection of *leges mundanas* which he had sent to Bulgaria.[216] It has been shown that this collection was a Lombard law code with certain Carolingian capitularies added;[217] however, the code had been influenced by Roman law, so that the Bulgars were led toward familiarity with that great body of law. Nicholas on two occasions made specific references to Roman law, clearly indicating that he presumed a Christian kingdom would utilize the code of Justinian.[218] One must suppose that Photius' numerous references to the law and its proper application were based on the presumption that the Bulgars would adopt the Roman law, probably in the form then employed in the Byzantine Empire.[219]

Equally numerous in the sources are references to the canon law, and to become adept in this body of law the Bulgar khan had to turn to several sources. Nicholas referred to "sacred canons" or "sacred rules" (*regulae*) on many occasions, which almost always meant the enactments of church councils.[220] John VIII also directed Boris to these sacred canons as a source of information on Rome's position in the ecclesiastical world.[221] And, of course, Photius' whole discussion of the disposition of past heresies rested on the decrees of the seven ecumenical councils, which the patriarch presented to Boris in capsule form.[222] However, Boris could not learn canon law simply by mastering conciliar statutes.

215. Photius, *Ep.*, No. 6, Ch. 75, ed. Valetta, p. 238: "... θεῖος ... νόμος"; Nicholas, *Ep.*, No. 99, Ch. 49, p. 586.

216. *Ibid.*, Ch. 13, p. 575, for the reference to the law code Nicholas sent to Bulgaria; Chs. 12, 19–29, 31, 32, 49, 52, 84, 85, 95, pp. 574–75, 578–80, 586, 595, 597, for allusions to the use of that law.

217. See above, n. 156.

218. Nicholas, *Ep.*, No. 99, Chs. 2, 39, pp. 569, 582.

219. Photius, *Ep.*, No. 6, Chs. 38, 42, 43, 50, 54, 59, ed. Valetta, pp. 231–36.

220. Nicholas, *Ep.*, No. 99, Chs. 4, 9, 28–30, 39, 48, 69, 93, 95, pp. 571, 573, 580, 582, 586, 591, 597. In two cases the reference is to *apostolicis regulis* (Ch. 72, p. 592) and *apostolica decreta* (ch. 79, p. 594).

221. *Iohannis VIII. Papae Epistolae*, Nos. 66, 192, 198, ed. Caspar, *MGH, Ep.*, VII, 60, 154, 159; *Fragmenti Registri Iohannis VIII. Papae*, No. 7, ed. Caspar, *MGH, Ep.*, VII, 277.

222. Photius, *Ep.*, No. 6, Chs. 5–18, ed. Valetta, pp. 204–19.

Nicholas frequently indicated to him that various popes had laid down important decretals and that the Bulgars would have to familiarize themselves with this body of law.[223] The pope sent Boris a penitential which introduced the Bulgars to another facet of the customs of the Christians.[224] He also implied that Boris would have to familiarize himself with monastic rules,[225] which became a greater necessity when monastic communities were established in Bulgaria.[226] Finally, Nicholas occasionally made vague illusions to *mos ecclesiae* and *lex Christianorum*, implying a body of Christian customs which was not written down.[227]

As the Bulgars became aware of the many sources of the law which would guide them to Christian life in the fullest sense, they perhaps began to appreciate what Nicholas meant at the opening of his letter: "If one attempted to explain [the Christian law] fully, innumerable books ought to be written."[228] It is obvious that the introduction of the new religion placed before them the need to master an immense body of legal enactments. This would be no easy task, as Nicholas warned when he ordered that the secular code he sent to Bulgaria be returned to him lest it fall into inexperienced hands and be abused.[229] Compilations of law would have to be acquired, and for this the Bulgars would have to depend on the generosity of outsiders or upon the labors of copyists who sought out the necessary texts in Rome or Constantinople. This material would then have to be studied and interpreted, and its numerous provisions would have to be applied to particular problems in Bulgaria somewhat after the fashion of Nicholas' responses to Boris' questions. At least in the beginning, the foreign priests in Bulgaria seem to have been called upon to perform this task, as Nicholas so often advised. Nonetheless, the mastery of the new law was a supreme cultural challenge to the new converts who hoped to become Christians in the real sense.

No less formidable were the theological issues. Quite aside from the rudiments of the faith which the new converts were expected to learn as catechumens,[230] those who sought to guide the neophytes to Christian

223. Nicholas, *Ep.*, No. 99, Chs. 10, 14, 15, 39, 55, 68, pp. 574–76, 582, 587, 591.
224. *Ibid.*, Ch. 75, p. 593.
225. *Ibid.*, Ch. 87, pp. 595–96.
226. Theophylactus, *Vita s. Clementis*, Ch. 29, Migne, *PG*, CXXVI, col. 1237; "Life of St. Nahum," trans. Kusseff, in *Slavonic and East European Review*, XXIX (1950–51), 142–44.
227. Nicholas, *Ep.*, No. 99, Chs. 1, 9, 51, pp. 569, 573, 586.
228. *Ibid.*, Ch. 1, p. 568.
229. *Ibid.*, Ch. 13, p. 575.
230. See above, pp. 78–80.

truth made it clear that the Bulgars would have to master a formal body of theology of no mean proportions. Nicholas quoted frequently from the fathers, always indicating that they were unerring guides to Christian truth. Among those he cited were John Chrysostom, Gregory the Great, Augustine, Jerome, and Ambrose.[231] Photius directed Boris' attention to such figures as Gregory of Nyssa, Origen, Didymus, Evagrius, and Athanasius.[232] Photius' résumé of the seven ecumenical councils drew attention to the theological issues involved in Arianism, Nestorianism, Monophysitism, Monotheletism, and Iconoclasm, and, more vehemently, to the orthodox doctrines posited to combat these heretical movements.

The learned patriarch repeatedly made it clear that a body of literature had developed in connection with each of these heresies and that only a mastery of this literature would assure an understanding of the errors of figures like Arius, Nestorius, Eutyches, and Theodore of Mopsuestia, and of the teachings of the heroic doctors who refuted them.[233] Nicholas called attention to the Novatian and Manichean heresies, without expanding on the particulars.[234] John VIII addressed Boris on the heretical group known as "pneumatomachii Macedonii," and on Arianism.[235] And when he warned Boris to beware of Greek heresy in general, he probably had in mind the *filioque* dispute, which raged around the Bulgars throughout the period of their conversion.[236] It was thus made evident that the Bulgars must immerse themselves as quickly as possible in patristic learning and in the polemical literature surrounding theological disputes if they were to get to the essence of Christian doctrine. The simple creed quoted to them by Photius was only the beginning of their theological education.

The demands of the liturgy probably posed another cultural challenge. We have already discussed the introduction of the rudiments of Christian worship in Bulgaria as a part of the conversion process, but suggestions in the sources indicate that the Bulgars were expected to go beyond the basic practices of the cult. Photius urged Boris to give attention to public services so that God would be rightly honored and the public good would

231. Nicholas, *Ep.*, No. 99, Chs. 3, 5–7, 10, 15, 43, 61, 64, 68, 71, 90, 99, 100, 104, pp. 570–74, 576, 587, 589, 590–92, 596, 598, 599.

232. Photius, *Ep.*, No. 6, Chs. 8, 14, ed. Valetta, pp. 207, 212–13.

233. *Ibid.*, Chs. 5–18, pp. 204–19.

234. Nicholas, *Ep.*, No. 99, Chs. 78, 90, pp. 594, 596.

235. *Iohannis VIII. Papae Epistolae*, No. 66, ed. Caspar, *MGH, Ep.*, VII, 56–60.

236. *Ibid.*, p. 59. For the Bulgar involvement in the *filioque* dispute, see Nicholas, *Ep.*, No. 100, ed. Perels, *MGH, Ep.*, VI, 603; and Photius, *Ep.*, No. 4, Chs. 10–22, ed. Valetta, pp. 172–75.

be served. Moreover, he commanded the khan "to build temples to God and the saints according to ecclesiastical law."[237] The force of this command may have contributed to the building of the impressive churches whose remains have been unearthed on the site of the fortress-city of Pliska (the capital of Bulgaria in Boris' time) and at Preslav.[238] What survives of the ecclesiastical structures in these cities indisputably indicates that the coming of the new religion and its liturgical demands resulted in important architectural and artistic innovations. Nicholas I likewise made clear the need for the Bulgars to elaborate their ritualistic practices, giving them instructions for observing the numerous feast days of the Church.[239]

When Boris asked how the Bulgars should prepare for battle, the pope advised them "to go to the churches, say prayers, forgive sinners, attend solemn masses, offer oblations, make confession of sins to priests, effect reconciliations and communion, open the prisons, dissolve the chains of slaves, and especially [those of] the broken and the crippled, give freedom to captives, and give alms to the poor."[240] All these acts of piety demanded some liturgical form with which the Bulgars were probably not familiar. By implication, many other aspects of life also had to be given a ritualistic dimension if the Bulgars were to act as Christians in the fullest sense. From some source, the Bulgars had to learn the proper manner in which to perform the rites which would give a Christian flavor to all of their activities. Perhaps it was this need that prompted Boris to ask Nicholas for a Roman missal.[241]

The various letters addressed to Boris abound in historical references, usually employed as examples to clarify the meaning of Christianity to the new converts. The Bulgars could hardly avoid the conclusion that they must inform themselves of a past heretofore foreign to them if they were to comprehend their new faith properly. Nicholas turned the attention of the Bulgars directly to scriptural history when, in response to Boris' inquiry about the propriety of hunting in Lent, he instructed the khan to look to "sacred history."[242] Repeatedly, throughout his responses, he utilized historical incidents from the Old and the New Testaments to

237. Photius, *Ep.*, No. 6, Chs. 26–27, ed. Valetta, p. 225.
238. See Dimitrov, *Bulgaria: Land of Ancient Civilizations*, pp. 33–38; Sergheraert, *Syméon le Grand (893–927)*, pp. 89–94.
239. Nicholas, *Ep.*, No. 99, Chs. 4, 10–12, 69, pp. 570, 574–75, 591–92.
240. *Ibid.*, Ch. 35, p. 581.
241. *Ibid.*, Ch. 76, p. 593.
242. *Ibid.*, Ch. 44, p. 585.

explicate and illustrate the conduct proper for a Christian.[243] Pope John VIII chose to demonstrate the primacy of Rome by recounting the New Testament version of the establishment of the Roman see.[244] There could have been little doubt among the Bulgars that they had the task of mastering sacred history as a part of their new cultural burden.

Almost as frequent in the literature addressed to the Bulgars were allusions to church history. Nicholas I called Boris' attention to the history of martyrs and confessors, referring not only to their feast days but also to such intriguing bits of information as the great numbers who had fled their native lands in the face of persecutions.[245] In his lengthy account of the seven ecumenical councils, Photius repeatedly introduced Boris to the great bishops, priests, and monks who had defended orthodoxy and to the wicked heretics who had threatened it. It would appear that he expected the Bulgars to desire and seek more information about these giants whose efforts had shaped the destiny of the Church. His whole account of the calling of the councils and the circumstances which required that they be held was cast in a chronological framework which invited his reader to think in terms of church history.[246] And Nicholas answered Boris' query about the origin of the patriarchates with a brief historical discourse which also invited further investigation.[247]

When the Bulgars went to the council of 869–870 in Constantinople to discover whether their land pertained to the jurisdiction of Rome or of Constantinople, they were subjected to a disputation that hinged on the history of the land they now possessed; and it must have appeared that they had to acquaint themselves with that history if they were to sustain their rights in the future. Pope John VIII likewise reminded the Bulgars of their land's distant past.[248] Occasionally the letters of Nicholas and John referred to episodes in papal history which emphasized the importance of knowing that history as well: the conversion of England by Gregory I, the dispute between Pope Felix and the Patriarch Acacius, the career of Pope Damasus. In all these cases, history was employed as an educative

---

243. For example, *ibid.*, Chs. 18, 20, 33, 38, 42, 43, 46, 47, 50, 51, 82, 89, pp. 577–86, 594–96.

244. *Iohannis VIII. Papae. Epistolae*, No. 67, ed. Caspar, *MGH, Ep.*, VII, 61.

245. Nicholas, *Ep.*, No. 99, Chs. 5, 11, 20, pp. 571, 572, 579.

246. Photius, *Ep.*, No. 6, Chs. 6, 8, 10, 12, 14, 15, 16, 17, ed. Valetta, pp. 204–7, 209–18.

247. Nicholas, *Ep.*, No. 99, Ch. 92, pp. 596–97.

248. *Liber pontificalis*, ed. Duchesne, II, 182–85; *Iohannis VIII. Papae Epistolae*, No. 71, ed. Caspar, *MGH, Ep.*, VII, 66–67.

device to which the neophytes must turn if they expected to understand the new truth to which they had subscribed.[249]

Even secular history was brought into the picture. Photius introduced Boris to the various emperors who ruled at the time of the ecumenical councils and implied a significant role for each.[250] The patriarch suggested that Boris model his life after Constantine the Great, and that he could learn something about the danger a king's concourse with women holds by studying the fate of Alexander the Great with the Persians.[251] Nicholas referred Boris to Constantine's struggle with Maxentius and to Hadrian's dealings over Jerusalem. He also suggested that the Bulgars learn something of Roman customs.[252] John VIII warned the khan against following the footsteps of the Goths down the path to heresy, as had occurred in the time of Emperor Constantius II.[253] Even these few cases must have suggested to the unlettered Bulgars their need to absorb some of the history of this world so that they might grasp the ways of their God in determining the destiny of men. Their own tales of the past, which appear to have been recounted when they prepared for battle and when they celebrated marriage feasts,[254] may well have appeared inadequate.

We have some indications that the cultural vistas opened to the Bulgarians by the coming of Christianity prompted action even during the time of Boris. In composing his encomium to Clement, Theophylactus wrote:

> O good pastor, . . . you educated us in holy scripture which you interpreted in your tongue, and into ways of justice, and in the work of justice you have led us! Through you the whole kingdom of Bulgaria learned of God; you strengthened the churches with hymns and psalmody; through you the monks were led by the lives of the fathers to the ascetic life; through you the priests were taught to live according to the canons.[255]

This paean was prompted by the kind of work to which Clement devoted himself with the support of the khan. Finding himself among people "ignorant and beastly," Clement first undertook to introduce the

249. Nicholas, *Ep.*, No. 99, Chs. 6, 15, 64, pp. 572, 575–76, 590; *Iohannis VIII. Papae Epistolae*, No. 71, ed. Caspar, *MGH, Ep.*, VII, 66.

250. Photius, *Ep.*, No. 6, Chs. 6, 9, 11, 14, 16, 17, ed. Valetta, pp. 206, 209, 211, 212, 216.

251. *Ibid.*, Chs. 22, 92, pp. 222, 242.

252. Nicholas, *Ep.*, No. 99, Chs. 33, 92, 95, pp. 580–81, 597.

253. *Iohannis VIII. Papae Epistolae*, No. 66, ed. Caspar, *MGH, Ep.*, VII, 59–60.

254. Nicholas, *Ep.*, No. 99, Ch. 35, p. 581.

255. Theophylactus, *Vita s. Clementis*, Ch. 29, Migne, *PG*, CXXVI, col. 1237.

Bulgars to the simple tasks of learning to read and write.[256] Then, following the example of St. Methodius, he provided materials for the use of Bulgar priests, "many of whom found Greek difficult to understand."[257] In the Bulgar language, he prepared prayers, simple sermons for all occasions, compendia of miracle stories, the lives and journeys of the prophets and apostles, stories of the martyrs, saints' lives, and "in short all kinds of things pertaining to the church. . . ."[258] The monastery which Clement built at Ochrida was the center of this cultural activity, all of which was aimed at making available to the Bulgars some of that vast cultural heritage that other spokesmen for Christianity insisted the Bulgars must comprehend if they were to comprehend their new religion. Clement's work in Bulgaria was a symbol of the cultural impact of the new religion on the backward Bulgars. Its continuation by Nahum[259] and others led directly, and quickly, to the impressive achievements of the reign of Symeon, which assured that the impact of higher culture would have a permanent effect on Bulgaria.

It is almost impossible to estimate the immediate effects on Bulgar society of the sudden confrontation of that society with so vast a cultural challenge. It seems clear beyond dispute that the coming of Christianity dramatically posed a cultural problem for Bulgar leadership. We have seen that those who undertook the guidance of the conversion process took the position that the Bulgars were backward, and that they proceeded to set forth a number of areas where the new converts would have to achieve competence in order to be called good Christians. The Bulgars reacted by taking positive steps to narrow the gap between their inferior culture and the superior cultures beyond their boundaries. Until their efforts had borne fruit, in a generation or two, they must have lived in a cultural limbo of tensions and uneasiness.

Their old modes of thought and expression could hardly have been fully satisfactory. They had learned, in broad terms, that they must master theology, law, history, scriptural scholarship, poetry, music, and art in order to function as genuine Christians. Yet the specific content of these many areas of Christian learning was beyond them; it existed in languages they did not know. And their spiritual mentors had provided only broad clues to its existence, leaving for them the task of acquiring

256. *Ibid.*, Ch. 18, cols. 1224–25.
257. *Ibid.*, Ch. 22, col. 1229.
258. *Ibid.*
259. "Life of St. Nahum" (cited above, n. 226), pp. 143–44. For a good discussion of the activity at Nahum's monastery, see Sergheraert, *Syméon le Grand (893–927)*, pp. 49–53.

the appropriate specific materials. For the moment, they were at the mercy of outsiders for cultural guidance, outsiders who had suddenly become the élite in Bulgaria—and who had probably conducted themselves in a fashion appropriate to their role. Their presence must have engendered great dissatisfaction among the dispossessed élite of an earlier day.

All of this would again suggest that the coming of the new religion created serious strains upon the very roots of Bulgar society, that the very assumptions upon which Bulgar life was based were badly shaken by the somewhat vague but dynamic cultural forces that entered Bulgaria with the cross.

In reflecting on the events surrounding the initial stages of the conversion of the Bulgars, one is compelled to conclude that the introduction of Christianity marked a sharp division in Bulgarian history. Although the sources are far too inadequate to permit a full reconstruction of the situation, they strongly suggest that during the quarter century between Boris' decision to accept the new religion and his retreat to a monastery the accustomed pattern of life was seriously disturbed on many levels. New beliefs, practices, and ideas crowded into the land to create new standards against which the old ways had to be measured. Religious usages, political institutions and processes, legal practices, and moral customs that had enjoyed acceptance among the Bulgars from time beyond memory began to undergo modifications intended to adjust them to a new set of criteria of acceptability. The process of change was further accentuated by the introduction into the Bulgar social order of elements heretofore absent from the scene: a new élite group in the clergy, a new form or organization for that group, new intellectual, literary, and art forms, and even a new written language. The presence of so many forces of change makes it impossible to avoid the conclusion that all levels of Bulgar society felt the effects of conversion in a substantial way.

It would be illuminating if the historian could accurately measure the intensity and the tempo of change brought on by the appearance of Christianity in Bulgaria. Unfortunately, the surviving sources that deal with the internal history of Bulgaria preclude any adequate estimate on this score, but it seems safe to say that the forces of change did not proceed at a revolutionary pace: there was no concerted assault on an old order that aimed at entirely replacing it with an entirely new system. Indeed, the most informative sources—especially the letter of Nicholas I—strongly suggest that a spirit of timidity presided over the changes occurring in

Bulgaria. Boris' mood, as reflected in the questions he placed before Nicholas I, was conservative, restrained, almost reluctant to face the demands implicit in the new order. Yet Boris was certainly in the vanguard of the agents promoting modifications of the existing order, far more devoted to movement toward a new order than was a significant faction of *boyars*, who had for so long buttressed princely power with their support and helped provide leadership for Bulgar society.

Yet if the change was not revolutionary—in the sense that it did not involve a conscious assault on an old order with a view toward reconstituting a completely new order—it was intensive enough to disturb society deeply. The evidence suggests that change occurred in a rather patternless fashion, involving only particular usages and practices which were discovered to be incompatible with Christian usage. Boris was not interested in altering the Bulgar system of justice in its entirety so that it would conform to an abstract system with which he had become acquainted by virtue of Christian influences; rather, he felt compelled to modify the old manner of treating certain criminals and to search out a new basis for treating certain acts against the social and political order. He did not seek to impose a new moral code on his people but to discover whether, according to the new dispensation, it was morally proper to wear old-fashioned breeches, to copulate with one's wife on Saturday night, to prepare for battle in the accustomed way, and to pray for one's pagan ancestors.

Probably this order of change began at the moment of his baptism, and on an elemental level—where a mechanical conformance to directions was more clearly involved than a conscious realization of the implications of action. By the act of baptism the new convert was forced to change his manner of worshipping in a significant way. This first step into a new world created situations which called into question the propriety of ancient patterns of conduct. The new convert committed himself to attend mass, which immediately required that he dress differently, stand differently in the church building, desist from conversing with his neighbor while in the sacred precincts, and learn new formulas for addressing his deity. He partook of the sacrificial feast at holy communion as a part of his new religion, but only after he had made preparations which kept him away from the conjugal bed the night before and altered his eating habits on the day of communion. His baptism imposed on him the obligation to respect Sundays and holy days, but this requirement interfered with the execution of public justice, battle preparations, work patterns, and amusements. All of this necessitated changes in conduct.

Thus the most rudimentary practices of Christian worship, even when imposed upon a simple, unlettered populace, caused ripples of change to move across the existing patterns of life. Each ripple caused new disturbances, which were added to the existing turbulence, until the ripples became waves which swept away large portions of the old order. In this process there was neither pattern nor program, as is clearly reflected in the letter which Boris addressed to Pope Nicholas I, a letter composed of a confusing hodgepodge of questions, few of which appear to have any logical connection with any other. Boris' requests seem to represent the true measure or result of the introduction of Christianity into Bulgaria: the new religion generated a hectic, pell-mell, disruptive process of change that touched many aspects of life and called into question a wide variety of customary actions.

One is tempted to suggest that this kind of change creates more acute tension in a society than does a conscious, planned effort at revolution, but, regardless of one's response to this philosophical issue, it is beyond dispute that the appearance of the new religion in Bulgaria acted as an acid that ate at the texture of society to compel change. None of this change was planned or even conceived; all of it occurred in a confused way.

The evidence that Christianization bred change in Bulgaria prompts a new range of questions. What motivated Bulgars, as Christians, to try to change their accustomed ways? What was there about the introduction of a new religion—more specifically the Christian religion—that nourished an urge to move into new patterns of conduct? Why did not Christianity serve simply as a substitute for the old religion, without becoming a dynamic influence leading to change? One would like to say, with Photius and Nicholas I, that the new faith miraculously irradiated the stupid, beastly Bulgars with a new, divinely inspired wisdom that permitted them to comprehend clearly the folly of their old ways and that provided them with the will and the knowledge to act differently. However, there is little evidence to suggest that God spent his illuminating powers very generously on the Bulgars at the moment of their conversion. The quest for answers to these questions must turn in other directions.

In the manner of the modern modes of explaining human conduct, one is tempted to say that change occurred in Bulgaria because those who held power saw an opportunity to improve their positions as a consequence of the conversion of the Bulgars. *Cui bono?* It is difficult to escape the fact that the Bulgars stood to gain in the world of diplomacy by accepting the faith of their most dangerous adversaries and their most promising allies. In

Christianity Boris probably saw a source of greater authority for the khan, and therefore a mode of strengthening the monarchy in his land. The Bulgars' knowledge of the wealth, splendor, and power of Christian Byzantium (and perhaps, to a lesser degree, of Christian Rome and Christian Germany) undoubtedly bred an urge to share in those material benefits that appeared to come only to Christians. Christianity also certainly appeared as a potential binding force, capable of relieving the tension which existed between Bulgar masters and Slavic minions—the latter constituting the vast majority of the population of the Bulgar state. One can hardly escape the conclusion that baptism promised a rich harvest of tangible benefits that were as appealing as the spiritual fruits of which the great ecclesiastical authorities so often preached. It may well be, then, that change in Bulgar society was promoted by leaders who sought to gain positive advantages from the new religion which would improve their position as overlords in Bulgaria.

However, a thorough reading of the sources with a view to discovering what happened in Bulgaria and to the Bulgars during a crucial quarter of a century suggests another dimension to the problem of change. Religious inspiration was one of the many forces that prompted the new converts to alter their conduct and their attitudes. As best one can capture Boris' mentality, it appears certain that he was a religious man. He lived in a world where the power of the divine presided over every facet of human life: the administration of justice, diplomacy, daily conduct, preparation for battle, or the way one dressed. Every aspect of life involved acts which might please or displease the divine power, and thus shape the course of one's existence. Conversion involved a commitment to a new deity whose deportment toward men was fundamentally no different than that of the gods they had previously honored. The chief appeal for the new converts was their conviction that this new deity was more powerful than other gods, that he could work greater benefits and inflict more terrible disasters than the others. This belief imposed upon the new converts the absolute necessity of conforming to the law of the Christian God. They were compelled by the logic that ruled their basic religious outlook to discover and to abide by the rules imposed on men by the Christian God.

It is this quest that permeates Boris' requests to Nicholas and that appears to control his religious conduct in the few cases where there is evidence of that conduct. In short, conversion did not fundamentally change the religious outlook of the Bulgars; it involved the substitution of a new deity for old ones. The consequence of this fundamental fact was the need to adjust the outward conduct of life to a new law, to learn what pleased and displeased the new deity so as to assure the continued flow of divine bounty and to avoid the ever-present possibility of divine wrath. Basically, the urge to change Bulgar society flowed from a primitive, unsophisticated religious impulse. But that crude impulse was powerful enough to unleash forces that touched society at every level and in every aspect of human conduct.

The drive to transform existing cultural patterns that was generated within Bulgar society was clearly accentuated by the conduct of the missionaries who brought the new faith to Bulgaria. Their contempt for Bulgar patterns of behavior was manifest, as unmistakable as the condescension that pervaded the letters of Photius, Nicholas I, and John VIII.

The disdain of the missionaries for the pagan culture of the Bulgars was matched by their complete confidence that baptism would infuse the Bulgars with a new range of talents which would permit them to overcome their previous shortcomings. They believed that barbarism was a condition imposed by paganism and argued that the Bulgars were crude, ignorant, and savage because they worshipped inferior gods. The saving waters of baptism would wash away both sin and ignorance; the new convert would suddenly acquire a vast new range of intellectual and emotional powers which would make it possible for him to absorb all the essentials of the civilization enjoyed by those who worshipped the true God. Thus the missionaries, especially the Greeks, felt free to confront the Bulgars with the complete range of Christian civilization in the full expectation that the regenerated Bulgars could absorb it. They proceeded on the conviction that all the worldly aspects of their culture were inevitable consequences of the Christian faith. They never doubted that the splendid art, literature, theology, political institutions, wealth, and comforts of the civilized world were natural by-products of the benevolence of the Christian God. They made no distinction between culture and Christianity; to them there was only Christian culture, superior to all other cultures because it was Christian. Now that the Bulgars had become Christians, there was no reason why they could not absorb Christian culture in the fullest sense.

With a confidence that a modern historian—schooled to think of cultural patterns as derived from and dependent upon factors other than divine pleasure—finds almost unbelievable, the missionaries confronted the new converts with a demanding yet majestic goal. They argued, in effect, that all the Bulgars had to do was *will* to become civilized, and it would be so. Conversion itself gave the Bulgars the powers required for living like Christians; that is, to live as men did in Constantinople and

Rome. Buoyed by such assurances, which certainly must have softened the missionaries' deprecatory attitude toward ancient Bulgar culture, the Bulgars were encouraged to reach for a new mode of life. What their basic religious attitudes and their native aspirations for power, wealth, and acceptance drove them to undertake was reinforced by what their mentors urged them to undertake. And success had been assured them.

One is inclined to argue, then, that the most profound consequence of the conversion process was the creation in Bulgaria of a state of tension which could be released only by an effort to modify accustomed patterns of behavior. The coming of the new religion created fresh opportunities for the exercise of power and influence inside and outside Bulgaria. Christianity confronted each convert with the critical problem of making peace with a deity whose chief attribute was his greater power to control human destiny. The acceptance of Christianity let loose in Bulgaria persuasive spokesmen for the idea that the approach to the baptismal font had at one stroke created the need for a complete change of habits and had provided every convert with the full range of powers needed to acquire all the amenities of civilized life.

As these forces were generated in Bulgaria, they acted as a powerful reagent, casting doubts on the propriety of ancient ways, breeding new aspirations, and creating new norms for conduct. The only way to escape from these pressures was to alter conduct. And yet change itself was fraught with doubts: a lingering fear that abandonment of old ways could court danger, a constant uncertainty whether new patterns of behavior were being properly carried out, a sense of frustration when the new wisdom which allegedly came with baptism was not immediately and clearly operative when problems arose, and a feeling of inferiority in the presence of the proud minions of Christian civilization.

And what of the prince in this confusing world, at the vortex of all these forces? To him was promised the richest harvest of power, wealth, and influence—plus an especially exalted place in the world to come—if he could bring his subjects to a full acceptance of Christianity; no less an authority than Photius gave this assurance, and in the most inspired language. Against this sweet temptation was the threat of a terrible loss if his subjects refused to follow him into the Christian camp; the *boyars* who revolted in 865 dramatically posed the possible consequences of failure. As a man who was moved by powerful religious sentiments, the khan had to face the constant danger that a false move in dealing with the new God might unleash divine retribution so terrible that his nation would be ruined. In his role as the head of a people, he had to think constantly in terms of the displeasure the Christian God might feel if his subjects failed, in even the most minor matters, to act in a Christian way.

This terrible responsibility drove the khan to an incessant involvement in the particulars that surrounded the institution of the new religion. It was he who had to confront most directly the missionary forces, who haughtily belittled the past accomplishments of the Bulgars and who treated them as children. Moreover, he was compelled to contribute to this deflation of the Bulgars by humbly requesting guidance from the mighty guardians of the Christian faith and civilization on the most simple questions relating to religious matters, giving credence to the notion of the helplessness of the new-born children of the Christian God.

It is inescapable that the decision to lead a people to Christianity imposed a Herculean task on a prince, one that involved every aspect of his princely office. Perhaps this burden completely occupied a prince during the early years of the conversion period, leaving little time and less energy for the other considerations associated with his office. Yet it was equally true that the progress of a conversion process hinged absolutely on the prince's decisions and actions. Even though he was a prisoner of his decision, he became the decisive agent in enacting that decision.

In Bulgaria, Boris played a vital role in every major aspect of the Christianization process. He defined and enforced the new rules that governed the conduct of his Christian subjects. He decided from whence the missionaries would come. He chose the path which the organizational growth of Bulgaria would take. He determined the configuration of Bulgarian attachments to the rest of the Christian world. He controlled the ecclesiastical personnel who labored to Christianize his people. He took the harsh steps necessary for curbing the forces that opposed the conversion of Bulgaria. He made the ultimate decision which determined the adoption of a unique ritual, in the native tongue, for Bulgaria. The fate of Christianity in Bulgaria would have been perhaps radically different without the intimate involvement of the prince in the conversion process.

Having concluded that the introduction of Christianity exerted a profound influence on Bulgar society, one is then tempted to generalize upon the experiences of the other nations that were also drawn into the Christian orbit during the early middle ages. But such generalization is not valid because the situation in Bulgaria was unique; its conversion process was affected by factors that were not present in other areas into which Christianity spread. The bitter rivalry for jurisdiction between Rome and

Constantinople constantly influenced the progress of Bulgar Christianity. The penetration of foreign influences into Bulgaria was particularly strong prior to the actual conversion. The division between Bulgars and Slavs within the state was a special situation. The Byzantine world was at that moment sensitized to missionary problems to a degree that was never quite repeated, with the Byzantine government and church devoting special energy to the Bulgars. The personality of Boris was another unique ingredient in Bulgaria. All these factors created a situation which had no exact parallel elsewhere; and they make argument by analogy dubious or unsound.

However, the Bulgar case perhaps invites a new examination of the meager sources that pertain to the Christianization of Europe in the early middle ages with a view toward more firmly establishing the nature of the impact of the new religion on pagan, barbarian societies. The Bulgar experience may suggest or prompt a more careful screening of the kinds of sources that can be easily overlooked when the conversion process is examined primarily from the missionaries' point of view. Perhaps the sources that relate to the conversion of other peoples can yield additional evidence on the precise problems faced by a pagan society and its ruler in the early stages of the conversion process.

On the basis of the Bulgar case, it would appear that the religious mentality of the new converts was highly significant in determining the progress of Christianity. The attitudes of the new converts toward their missionary leaders and toward the culture represented by these missionaries appear to have been crucial factors in shaping the impact of Christianity and in determining the reaction of the converts to the religion. The interaction between local political conditions and the new ecclesiastical order cannot be slighted. The impact of particular Christian usages—liturgical, moral, disciplinary—on the ordinary conduct of daily life should be scrutinized more thoroughly, for the Bulgar experience strongly indicates it was in this area that conversion had the most profound and disturbing effect. Closer attention should be paid to the degree to which missionaries succeeded in impressing upon a newly converted society an awareness of its inferiority to the Christian, civilized world.

It is entirely possible that a new look at the entire range of missionary history in the early middle ages from these perspectives would not prove as informative in clarifying the impact of Christianization on a pagan society as it is in the Bulgar case. However, until such an investigation is made, with the Bulgar example firmly in mind, it seems permissible to presume that in a nation whose ruler had decided to Christianize his people a profound change had begun to affect all aspects of society from the moment that missionary work had begun. Although the new converts may not have become fully Christianized for many years, their lives were altered in a substantial way from the very beginning of the conversion process. Certainly Boris and his colleagues would affirm that this had been their experience in Bulgaria.

V

EARLY MEDIEVAL MISSIONARY ACTIVITY: A COMPARATIVE STUDY OF EASTERN AND WESTERN METHODS*

One of the more fascinating problems connected with the history of the early Middle Ages is the persistence of similarities and the emergence of differences in the ideas and institutions of the eastern and western remnants of the Roman Empire. Equally intriguing is the related problem of the origins and the nature of the differences which characterize the Slavic and Germanic groups that fell under the influence of the Greeks and the Latins during the early Middle Ages. This paper will attempt to throw some light on these problems by examining the field of missionary history. It will try to compare the methods employed by the eastern and western missionaries to convert the Slavic and Germanic groups living on the borders of Christendom in the period from about A.D. 600 to 900. Such a comparison might be revealing. It will permit one to see wherein the Greeks and the Latins acted alike or differently as each attacked the same problem. It will also allow one to detect some of the formative forces implanted in the Slavic and Germanic worlds as each underwent the fundamental experience of adopting a new religion.

A superficial reading of missionary history from about 600 to 900 leaves the impression that both eastern and western societies used the same methods of attack on paganism. In general, missionary practice consisted of employing political pressure, the lure of the superior civilization associated with Christian civilization, and religious arguments centering around the theme of the superiority of Christianity over pagan religions to persuade pagan groups to abandon their old religions. However, a deeper study suggests a wide difference in the practices of Greek and Latin missionaries. The expansion of Christianity from the Byzantine Empire shows little that is comparable to the pioneering efforts of western missionaries like Columban, Augustine, Boniface, or Anskar. Instead of the bold forays into the pagan world and the dramatic encounters with belligerent heathens which characterized western missionaries, the easterners won what seem to have been easy victories, involving little more than an honest endeavor to contact, instruct, and baptize the pagans. This paper will attempt to demonstrate that, in spite of the fact that eastern and western societies used the same general methods to persuade the pagans,

*Read, in substance, at the annual meeting of the American Historical Association at Chicago on December 28, 1953.

Reprinted from *Church History*, 23 (1954), 17-35, by permission of the publisher. Copyright © 1954 by the American Society of Church History.

the actual use of these methods differed considerably in the East and the West.

The outstanding feature of eastern missionary method was the elaborate preparations made prior to the appearance of Christianity in pagan lands. By the use of political pressure and cultural penetration Byzantine society sought to make Christianity desirable to the pagans before it was ever presented to them by missionaries. This conditioning was seldom the responsibility of the missionaries themselves. Lay society, and especially the imperial government, accepted this duty, calling upon the Greek church only to complete the formal process of conversion.

Political pressure was the chief weapon of Byzantine society in creating and exploiting missionary opportunities. An almost stereotyped procedure had been developed. The imperial government singled out for conversion pagan groups where a prince had already established his authority, a concept of Christianization that derived from the state-dominated religious establishment in Byzantine society. Then operating through war, diplomacy, economic concessions, and its own example of effective statecraft, the Byzantine government sought to convince or compel the pagan prince that it was advantageous to accept the new religion. It would be impossible to recount here the complicated political relationships between the imperial government and various Slavic groups prior to 900. However, a few cases, directly associated with the Christianization of certain groups, will illustrate the Byzantine technique of using political forces to encourage conversion.

According to some accounts Boris of Bulgaria accepted conversion at the hands of Greek missionaries in 864 as a means of halting the advance of victorious Greek armies.[1] The Greek emperor had apparently struck the Bulgars at a moment when they were especially vulnerable, being deeply involved in fulfilling their obligations toward their German allies and suffering a famine.[2] The Moravians appealed to Constantinople in 863 in hopes that the acceptance of Greek missionaries would cement a political alliance with Constantinople which would check German expansion into Moravia.[3] The Byzantines apparently tried to impress pagan princes with the idea that the acceptance of Christianity and the organization of a church would give them great power over their subjects. The patriarch Photius, for instance, in a letter to Boris of Bulgaria shortly after the latter's conversion, pointed out at some length that the power and prosperity of the king would increase now that he had accepted Christianity.[4] Pressures such as are illustrated by these few cases, if applied long enough, usually gained the desired end; the pagan prince petitioned for missionaries, having been persuaded that conversion was advantageous for himself and his state.

The Byzantine emperor assumed the full responsibility for organizing a mission to any pagan area that was prepared to receive it. The case involving the mission of Cyril and Methodius to Moravia illustrates the dominant role played by the emperor in sponsoring missionary ventures.[5] He selected the missionary personnel, apparently motivated as much by political considerations as by the piety and learning of his choices. Both Cyril and Methodius had grown up in Thessalonica and thus knew Slavic customs and language. Both were loyal imperial servants as had been their father. Methodius had served in a civil capacity in the Balkan area prior to his retirement to a monastery. Cyril had been educated under imperial auspices and had been destined to fill an important office before he voluntarily chose to devote his life to scholarship and teaching. He had already had prior diplomatic experience. Having chosen the missionaries, the emperor issued instructions concerning their conduct just as he would any other diplomatic mission. He provided the missionaries with a retinue, supplies, transportation, and safe conduct. Here his participation might end. However it was not unknown for emperors to continue to bring their resources to bear in support of missionaries. Basil I, for instance, as late as 885 made a special effort to purchase from the slave market at Venice some of the disciples of Methodius who had been sold into slavery in Moravia following the death of their master and to send these missionaries into Bulgaria.[6] He also did everything in his power to aid the Greek missionaries regain their position in Bulgaria after Boris had turned to Rome in 866.[7]

Upon his departure from Constantinople the Greek missionary was able to operate under nearly ideal conditions. He moved immediately under the protection of a native prince, from whose court he performed most of his work.[8] Backed by the power of a native ruler determined to Christianize his people, the missionary's success was almost assured. He could represent himself to the native population as a spokesman for that ruler. He needed to occupy himself very little with such mundane affairs as gaining a livelihood or protecting himself.[9] His only real concern was that of maintaining the favor of the prince under whom he worked, a task that was not always easy, as so resourceful an apostle as Methodius discovered in Pannonia and Moravia[10] or as the missionaries who first went to Bulgaria also learned when their protector turned to Rome.[11] However, if the prearranged political alignments could be maintained by the missionary and the Byzantine government, conversion was an uncomplicated matter.

Equally potent in preparing for the spread of Christianity, although much more difficult to evaluate briefly, was the powerful appeal of Greek culture and its steady penetration into the pagan world. Long before there was any thought of Christianizing Slavic peoples, Greek cultural penetration had made considerable progress, creating a growing desire on the part of the aristocracy among the barbarians for all things Greek. Rastislav of Moravia in his letter to Michael III requesting missionary assistance reflected the powerful pull exercised over the barbarians by Greek culture. He admitted the ignorance of his people and asked for a teacher, implying that none except the Greeks could overcome this ignorance.[12] A review of the rise of the new Bulgar state prior to its conversion offers even better proof of the expansive power of Greek culture and its appeal to the barbarians.[13] This cultural penetration was seldom connected with missionary activity or with the affairs of the Byzantine church. Greek armies, traders, diplomats, prisoners of war, and isolated settlements in the Balkans played the most significant role in acquainting the Slavic world with Greek civilization. There can be little doubt, however, that it was helpful to the missionary. He was accepted by the pagans as the finest product of a superior civilization. The barbarian Slavic groups were eager to gather around him for an education. They built monasteries to be used as centers of literary studies and set to work in these monasteries translating Greek literature into Slavic.[14] They migrated to Constantinople for further education.[15] Even the highest figures in barbarian society were powerfully impressed; Boris of Bulgaria, for instance, abdicated his throne in order to retire to a monastery for study.[16] There seems little doubt that the missionary's religion was looked upon and accepted as a part of that superior civilization which the barbarians sought so eagerly. Because the urge to imitate the Greeks pre-dated actual missionary work, the missionary himself had a captive audience, especially among the aristocratic elements in Slavic society.

Western missionaries likewise made use of political and cultural forces in their attack on paganism. However, their method offers some striking contrasts with the East. Usually the western missionary did not have his prospective converts prepared for him by other agencies of society. Such political aid as he might receive and the impression which the heathen might gain of western culture were both the results of the efforts of the missionary himself. For that reason neither was likely to be as decisive as was the case in the East.

The role of politics and of political figures in western missionary history illustrates this difference. There can be no doubt that western missionaries relied heavily upon and received the assistance of Christian princes and lay society. One might easily compile a long list of cases where political considerations entered into missionary affairs. This assistance assumed widely varied forms. Charlemagne, for instance, used his armies and his lawmaking power to achieve the conversion of the Saxons.[17] Pepin of Heristal and Charles Martel used military force to prepare a missionary field for Willibrord in southern Frisia.[18] Louis the Pious sought to insure the success of Anskar in Denmark by making the missionary's acceptance into Denmark one condition of an alliance between the Frankish emperor and Harald of Denmark, who badly needed assistance to gain the throne.[19] Newly converted kings and princes, as typified by Ethelbert of Kent and Edwin of Northumbria,[20] provided invaluable aid to missionaries in converting large masses of people in certain western areas. Almost every missionary who left a trace in western history received some sort of material aid from western lay society, usually in the form of land grants or gifts with which to impress potential converts or letters of commendation designed to assure hospitality and safe conduct for the missionary as he moved about his affairs.[21] In view of the numerous instances of the involvement of the state and lay society in western missionary activity, one is tempted to conclude that political factors played as great a role in the West as they did in the East.

However, all the support tendered to western missionaries had a different effect than it did in the East. The most notable difference lies in the fact that during most of the early Middle Ages the western missionaries themselves or the church had to solicit assistance from western governments and lay society. Whereas in the East the imperial government assumed the initiative in conceiving, inaugurating, and supporting missionary ventures, the western missionary himself selected his area of activity, recruited assistants, dealt with Christian rulers and nobles to gain whatever help they were willing or able to offer, and sought advice and direction wherever he might find it. A few cases stand out as illustrations of the burdens placed upon western missionaries in rallying support behind their efforts. Augustine, for instance, faced the pagan king of Kent armed with little more than his own faith; his success depended largely upon his own efforts to convince Ethelbert to aid him and his own ability to advise the king wisely on the policies to be adopted in order to convert Kent.[22] Willibrord in his appeals to kings Radbod of Frisia and Ongendus of Denmark[23] and Anskar in his attempt to persuade the Swedish king to permit him to carry on his work[24] likewise depended entirely upon their own ingenuity to gain political backing. Boniface spent a considerable part of his long missionary career traveling over much of western Europe attempting to secure promises of protection from Frankish princes, to recruit missionary personnel, to gain the means of supporting his missionary posts, and to secure permission to enter new areas.[25] One might well conclude that his success depended upon his own ability to perform these organizational tasks. The long history of the conversion of Frisia witnessed a heavy burden placed on the missionaries working there. Willibrord began the task in 690 by recruiting the aid and protection of Pepin of Heristal. He later sought to broaden his missionary field by personal appeals to the pagan kings of Frisia and Denmark.[26] Meanwhile he seems to have devoted considerable effort to the acquisition of the property necessary to support his work.[27] After his death in 739 his successors continued to direct the conversion of Frisia from the monastery at Utrecht.[28] Among their responsibilities was that of recruiting missionary personnel, a task accomplished by carrying on an educational program at Utrecht[29] and by enticing Englishmen to come to Frisia.[30] Neither did the missionaries who worked with the pagans in Frisia escape heavy burdens; one of them found it necessary to find his own food and lodgings as he traveled about northern Frisia trying to win converts.[31] On every hand, then, the western missionary of the early Middle Ages was required to solicit and inspire the assistance of the non-ecclesiastical world if he expected to bring political pressure to bear on the pagan world or to approach his missionary work with the necessary material backing. This responsibility clearly distinguishes his activity from that of the Greek missionary.

Only from Charlemagne's time onward did the West begin to use political pressures against paganism more after the fashion of the East. Charlemagne and his advisers were certainly moved by a keen sense of royal responsibility for spreading Christianity,[32] a conviction that clearly resembles the inspiration behind imperial management of eastern missionary activity. Their ideas perhaps found application in Charlemagne's Saxon policy. Even then western political efforts against paganism seem naive. Charlemagne's attempt to convert the Saxons was based on the premise that force alone would convert. Having defeated them in the field and having outlawed their religion under threat of severe punishment, he left them to the missionaries whom he trusted to make Christianity acceptable to the Saxons.[33] Time was to prove that his political actions had not created a desire on the part of many Saxons to become Christians. Perhaps, however, he eventually learned his lesson. When, after nearly twenty-five years of struggle in Saxony, Charlemagne undertook the conquest and conversion of the Avars, he took pains to call a council to plan a program for the peaceful conversion of his potential subjects; the decisions of this council emphasized persuasion instead of force.[34] Some of Charlemagne's successors showed a deeper insight into the use of political pressure as an instrument of conversion. The pressure exerted on the Slavic states by Louis the German, coupled with the aggressive missionary activity of the Bavarian bishoprics and extensive German colonization, offers perhaps the closest parallel to eastern practice that can be found in the history of the West in the early Middle Ages.[35]

Because western society was unable to execute effective political offensives against paganism, the missionary was seldom able to use political factors alone in securing success. Western missionary history contains a long record of missionary failures or setbacks resulting from too great dependence upon Frankish military support. As early as 714 and as late as 785[36] missionaries were driven out of Frisia and their work completely undone by Frisian attacks on territory recently conquered by the Franks; nothing that Pepin of Heristal, Charles Martel, and Charlemagne could do was sufficient to prevent these assaults. Obviously the many Frisian converts won during this period resulted from the play of forces other than the political backing given missionaries by the Frankish rulers. The case in Saxony up until at least 785 and probably even later was similar. Any missionary who followed armies into pagan areas was often confronted by the fact that the protecting armies soon left, having done little more than raise further opposition to Christianity. The pagans apparently had little respect for the attempts of western rulers to legislate their ancient religion out of existence. Charlemagne's *Capitulatio de partibus Saxoniae* apparently offered little assistance to missionaries working in Saxony. Revolts continued long after its enactment.[37] Charlemagne had eventually to resort to forced deportation to enforce his will.[38] As Alcuin pointed out in his criticisms of Charlemagne's policy, the work of missionaries was complicated by the provisions of this edict.[39] A reading of the law[40] convinces one that Charlemagne was incapable of setting up an administrative machinery capable of enforcing its provisions. Again one must conclude that the missionaries working in Saxony won converts by means other than political compulsion. Perhaps the majority of Saxons were converted by the efforts of missionaries like Willehad and Liudger, who certainly enjoyed Charlemagne's blessing but who also relied on other resources to carry on their work.[41] Cases such as these suggest that political pressure was never as reliable or as valuable a resource to the Latin missionary as it was to the Greek. If the missionary wished to assume the responsibility, he could usually recruit valuable aid from lay society, but upon him fell the burden of conceiving a way to use this aid and of putting it to use. Unless he assumed this responsibility and succeeded in implementing it, he could seldom depend upon the western world to pursue a consistent and comprehensive political program aimed at winning pagan assent to conversion.

The western missionary was as aware as the Greek of the appeal which Christian civilization had for the barbarian. He was, however, again called upon to exercise a different technique to use this appreciation. Western civilization had not made so strong an impression on surrounding barbarism as had Greek civilization. Consequently the missionary was obliged to demonstrate through his own labors the superiority of his culture. For instance, as soon as they entered pagan areas western missionaries began to dot the land with new churches which they themselves built.[42] Undoubtedly this was an impressive feat in the eyes of those whose places of worship largely consisted of open-air temples and secluded forest spots. The building of monasteries, a universally practiced part of western missionary procedure, was perhaps a more impressive demonstration of cultural superiority. The erection of an operating monastery involved a variety of talents. Land previously unusable was cleared and cultivated.[43] New crops were introduced, such as the vineyard planted at Boniface's monastery at Fritzlar.[44] Technical skills, such as metal working, milling, and stone construction, were introduced into pagan areas and pagan lives in conjunction with monastic life.[45] Along with the measures designed to support monastic life came the introduction of refinements. Formal schools, for instance, were opened in conjunction with missionary monasteries.[46] Books and learning began to make their appearance in the barbarian world, as the careers of Boniface[47] and Columban[48] would serve so well to illustrate. The western missionary in his role of farmer, builder, and technician was perhaps more impressive to the pagan than was the missionary as a preacher of a new religion. Monasteries like Fulda, Luxeuil, and Utrecht did as much as preaching to spread the fame of Christianity. The necessity of demonstrating the superiority of his civilization by his own labor put a greater burden on the western missionary than that borne by the easterner. It demanded a more versatile missionary. It gave the pagan a different version of Christianity than did the quiet teaching of the eastern apostle.

Whatever other kinds of forces might be used to aid in winning converts, early medieval missionaries still had to present Christianity as a religion to the pagans. Again the Greeks and the Latins followed different procedures.

The elaborate preparations prior to his arrival in a pagan area made it possible for the Greek missionary to present his religion in an orderly and systematic fashion. As a rule, he devoted himself

chiefly to the thorough training of certain apt disciples who then undertook the actual conversion of the bulk of the pagans. The careers
of Cyril and Methodius illustrate the large role which teaching played in Greek missionary activity. Cyril, who had established a reputation as a teacher before he began his missionary career, was given
a missionary task at least partly because of this reputation.[49] As soon
as the brothers arrived in Moravia they began to instruct groups of
young Moravians.[50] Methodius is said to have given daily instructions
to Rastislav of Moravia and Kocel of Pannonia[51]. Kocel and Svatopluk
of Moravia were both anxious to acquire the services of Methodius
as a teacher for their people.[52] The papacy was equally cognizant of
Methodius as a teacher; Hadrian II sent him to Pannonia with the
specific charge to teach.[53] John VIII, moved by what he had heard
of Methodius' teaching in Moravia, summoned the missionary to
Rome to ascertain his orthodoxy.[54] The Bavarian clergy, suspicious
of Methodius' activity in Pannonia, was alleged to have been especially fearful of his teaching.[55] There seems hardly to have been
an interval in the careers of Cyril and Methodius when they were
not actively involved in teaching. Photius, in a letter to the eastern
patriarchs bemoaning the corruption of the true religion in Bulgaria
due to the activities of Roman missionaries, likewise indicated the
importance of teaching in Greek missionary practice; he called upon
these leaders to assist him in correcting the situation in Bulgaria by a
new teaching effort.[56] The priest Clement, a disciple of Methodius
who sometime after 885 was assigned to proselytize in a remote area
of Bulgaria, set up a regular system of instruction in his territory.
He is said to have taught 3500 pupils and to have sent them to various
parts of his province.[57] Greek missionaries were seldom lauded as great
preachers in the sense of presenting the faith to the masses; that
task they left to their disciples.

Greek missionary teaching procedures are not clear. Apparently
schools were operated in connection with royal courts or in monasteries founded for that purpose.[58] Some sources suggest vaguely that
the educational program followed in these schools imitated that in
vogue in Constantinople, where the emphasis was placed on a wide
reading of sacred and profane literature. For instance, native Slavs
learned Greek.[59] The above-mentioned Clement is said to have instructed his Bulgarian students in writing, illustration, praying and
reading.[60] Some of Methodius' disciples were proficient enough in
literary skills to assist him in translating Greek literature into Slavic.[61]
The literary outburst that followed the introduction of Christianity
into Bulgaria suggests that missionary education had a literary slant.

Whatever their educational procedures might have been, the

Greeks had a definite purpose behind their teaching. They sought to transmit to the pagans a complicated and sophisticated version of Christianity. The convert was expected to accept the new religion in all its complexity; there were to be no simplifications of Christianity for pagan consumption. Perhaps the outstanding example of this attitude is contained in a letter sent by Photius to Boris of Bulgaria shortly after the latter's conversion. The purpose of the letter was to remind the king of his responsibility for maintaining orthodoxy in his kingdom.[62] He was informed that the orthodox Christian view was defined by the first seven ecumenical councils. Photius then plunged straight into an extensive discussion of each of these councils. In the process he involved Boris in such complicated issues as Arianism, Nestorianism, iconoclasm, and Christology.[63] Photius obviously expected the new convert to know these things already or to learn them immediately. One is not surprised to find Boris writing to Rome shortly thereafter asking advice on a whole series of practical problems,[64] including such mundane matters as whether it was properly Christian for the new converts to continue wearing their ancient pantaloons.[65] Other evidence suggests that Photius' complicated instructions to Boris were not exceptional in Greek missionary circles. The recriminations flung back and forth between Rome and Constantinople over control of Bulgaria and the quarrels generated in Moravia between Greeks and Germans indicate that such highly complicated matters as the *filioque* question, the theological problems involved in the marriage of the clergy, the nature of confirmation, and the question of proper fasting customs were all introduced into missionary areas.[66] These problems seem not to have been discussed merely in priestly circles. The Moravian prince, Svatopluk, is alleged to have become angry at the Greeks for their eternal theological disputes and their insistence that he become involved.[67] Occasionally there are hints that the Greeks went too far in theologizing among the pagans. Clement detected that the Greeks were talking over the heads of the pagans in the remote section of Bulgaria where he labored; he sought to remedy this condition by compiling simpler sermons and literature as a means of spreading Christianity.[68] The available evidence suggests, then, that the missionaries from Constantinople taught their religion in all its Byzantine nuances.

Moreover, the Greeks were willing to develop techniques to insure their success in transmitting such involved religious ideas. The presentation of the new faith in the native language is the chief evidence illustrating their concern that their religion be understood. Missionaries were expected to converse fluently in pagan languages. Their intimate knowledge of the Slavic tongue was the chief reason why Cyril and Methodius were sent to Moravia. The Slavic world knew they could expect missionaries who spoke their language. The Moravians, for example, requested Slavic speaking teachers from Constantinople because they were being confused by other foreigners who were unable to instruct them.[69] However, the most significant proof that the Greeks were willing to teach the pagans thoroughly was the decision to develop a written language and a liturgy in connection with the conversion of the Slavs. The familiar story of the successful efforts of Cyril and Methodius to develop a Slavic written language and to create a Slavic liturgy and the subsequent adoption of that liturgy over wide areas of the Slavic world cannot be retold here in all its details.[70] There is little doubt that Cyril and Methodius developed the new language and liturgy as a teaching device. Certainly the undertaking was not conceived as a concession to avert defeat by the pagans. Before their first trip to Moravia they had already developed the new written language and had set a minimum amount of Christian literature into the new language.[71] They devoted long years of labor to the further development of the Slavic liturgy.[72] Such resolute efforts indicate their serious intention of providing themselves with a tool for making Christianity comprehensible. What can be discovered concerning the kind of material eastern missionaries, and especially Cyril and Methodius,[73] translated from Greek into Slavic certainly indicates that the Greek intention was chiefly educational. Translation of scriptural selections, patristic selections, canonical collections, hagiography, and liturgical handbooks were especially prominent. Each of these types of literature had an instructive value. One must conclude, then, that the development of a native liturgy and literature was intended primarily as a way of presenting Christianity in all its complexity so that it would be understood by a pagan audience.

The employment of a native liturgy perhaps ought not be dismissed so simply. Taken in conjunction with the political and cultural aspects of eastern missionary method, it was the crucial factor by which the Greeks took advantage of all the forces operating in their favor. Christianity in a native language could well pass for a native religion; a pagan prince could Christianize his subjects with a minimum risk of seeming to submit to foreign domination. The adoption of a native liturgy and the development of a written language for liturgical and instructional purposes facilitated the progress of barbaric society toward filling its need for Greek culture. Its use reveals the inspiration moving Greek missionary thought and practice. Christianity was not to be presented as a religion foreign to the pagans, but as a means for the attainment of ends already desired. It was a Greek belief that Christianity was a religion for civilized and sophisticated men. When the pagans and barbarians had nearly accepted the Byzantine pattern of life, then they were privileged to become Christians. Having felt their own need for civilization and conversion, they were ready for the teachers of theology, literature, and philosophy, who could go among them, speaking a language that the pagans could understand and who could convert them to a well-rounded, comprehensive, and complete version of Christianity.

The presentation of Christianity in a convincing manner was the greatest task of the western missionary. Because his political and cultural support was not as effective as was that of his eastern counterpart, he had to rely heavily on persuasive religious appeals to win converts. Although he used many of the techniques familiar to the Greeks,[74] his religious approach to the pagans was different than that employed in the East.

The western missionary made very little attempt to instruct his pagan audience in Christian dogma. Western missionary sources contain very little evidence bearing on matters of theology and its presentation to pagans. This gap in the western approach is forcibly illustrated by the criticism occasionally aimed at missionary methods by different churchmen. Alcuin angrily maintained that the repeated apostasy of the Saxons was due to the failure of missionaries to teach these pagans anything about the real nature of Christianity. Yet when he attempted to recommend a program for overcoming this situation, he advised that only a minimum of doctrinal instruction be presented to the pagans.[75] The West apparently did not feel the obligation to present the pagans with a thorough knowledge of Christian doctrine nor did it trust such instruction to convince the pagans.

The technique most commonly used in the West was one of offering the pagans dramatic proof of the superiority of Christianity, such demonstrations often being staged so as to have the maximum emotional effect on the pagans. Western missionaries constantly destroyed pagan temples and idols in the presence of pagan audiences.[76] Interesting variations of this technique were worked out; for instance, a converted pagan priest in England mounted a stallion and took arms, both prohibited to priests by pagan practice, and went about Northumbria destroying temples.[77] Missionaries desecrated pagan temples by using them for Christian worship.[78] They boldly offered to trust their personal fate to the usual pagan procedures for reaching major decisions, like the casting of lots.[79] They incited Christian armies to march through pagan lands.[80] They staged awesome displays of Christian ritual.[81] They provoked pagan religious spokesmen into religious arguments[82]. What little can be recovered from their sermons reflects a like emphasis on dramatic and vivid contrasts between Christianity and paganism. Missionary preaching was chiefly concerned with highly colored harangues on the folly of pagan practices,[83] on the weaknesses of pagan gods,[84] on the contradictions in pagan mythology,[85] on the might of the Christian God,[86] and on the terrors of hell, especially for pagans.[87]

Behind this picture of western missionaries seeking to shock the pagan world into acceptance of Christianity lies the key to the western method of presenting Christianity. The missionaries bent every effort to fit their religion to the pattern of religious behavior and thinking which was already familiar to the pagans. Gregory the Great perhaps best illustrates this attempt to understand and make use of pagan mentality when he advised his English charges to retain pagan temples as centers of Christian worship because the pagans were accustomed to these places, to permit the use of the same rituals in celebrating the feasts of the saints as were used to celebrate pagan feasts, and to allow the slaying and eating of animals in honor of the Christian God just as the pagans had done in honor of their ancient gods.[88] It is amazing to note the close parallel between the aspects of Christianity especially stressed by the missionaries and the basic concepts of paganism. For example, the missionaries made use of the trust which the pagans put in their gods to take care of their material welfare by emphasizing constantly that the Christian God would take care of them better. For instance, Anskar's work in Sweden provoked some to argue that trade would be improved if the Swedes would accept Christianity.[89] Wilfrid of York is alleged to have won many converts in Frisia in 678-679 because the crops and the catch of fish were excellent during that year.[90] Eadbald of Kent is said to have been converted because he associated his ill-health with own apostasy.[91] Paulinus was careful to point out to Edwin of Northumbria that the latter's escape from assassination and the birth of his child on the same day were due to the Christian God. At the meeting of Edwin's council where the decision was taken to accept Christianity, a pagan priest argued that the Christian God was obviously better fitted to care for his adherents' material needs than were the pagan gods.[92] Since the pagans possessed an elaborate mythology explaining the origin of the universe and its inhabitants, the missionaries countered with simplified versions of the scriptural account of the same subject.[93] These are but two examples of the western attempt to make Christianity serve the needs of the pagans even more effectively than did their old religion.

It is this aspect of western missionary method that savors so strongly of the barbarization of Christianity. The western missionary would have denied such an accusation. His immediate goal was to convince the pagan to accept a new deity on the pagan's own grounds, which end was achieved when the pagan was baptized. The corrective for the new convert's ignorance of Christianity had still to be applied. Western missionary method envisaged a long period of education for the convert during which there was to be imposed on him a complete change of conduct designed to please the new God from whom he expected so much. This explains the deep concern of the western missionaries with such matters as dietary regulations, marriage customs, and standards of social conduct, all matters which loom large in the whole body of missionary literature, ecclesiastical legislation, papal directives, and law codes of the early Middle Ages. This also explains the preoccupation with organizational matters that accompanied the expansion of Christianity in the West. As soon as the pagans were converted all means were adopted to hold them to the Christian concept of good conduct and proper worship on the assumption that the pagan was bound to accept the dictates of the new God if he expected to benefit from his new religion. To the western pagan Christianity as presented by the missionaries must have seemed much more a new mode of living and worshipping than a theology and a system of doctrine.

The differences in eastern and western missionary methods described above certainly suggest some basic differences existing between eastern and western societies in the early Middle Ages. In missionary affairs the eastern church already demonstrates its subservience to the state, its willingness to serve the ends of the emperor, and its lack of interest in a position of leadership. The western church had achieved a much more independent and aggressive position in society; in missionary activity it demonstrated an ability and an inclination to order other elements of society to its interest. Perhaps this difference is explained by another contrasting condition which missionary history points up. Byzantine government operated on a higher level of efficiency than did western governments. The dependence of eastern society on political means to spread Christianity recalls the old Roman Empire with its supreme confidence that anything could be done to a barbarian people if only it were involved in the net of imperial political power. The West, although sometimes attempting to utilize its political resources to win converts, could not equal the performance of the Byzantine government. Missionary history also reveals that the East and the West were no longer in full agreement on what the true faith was. The differences in dogma, ritual, and concepts of the role of the faith in men's lives indicates a growing gap between East and West. The uncompromising attitude which each society assumed when the two missionary efforts met suggests that there was small hope of resolving these differences. Finally, and most difficult to sustain, missionary history suggests that a basic difference in outlook existed between East and West. The eastern world went about its missionary business with an air of having achieved perfection. It offered to the pagans a chance to join the already civilized world, the acceptance of Christianity being the final test of pagan preparedness. The West presented the aspect of a growing civilization, one that needed yet to be built both in its material and its spiritual and intellectual phases. Cyril, the highly educated theologian, the dialectician, the linguist, the incomparable teacher, the philosopher, the favorite of the mighty *basileus*, is the symbol that the proud Byzantine world presented to the pagan. Boniface, the clearer of forests, the builder, the chider of kings and popes, the reformer, the ecclesiastical politician, the martyr is the symbol of the youthful, struggling West.

However, these differences must not hide another consideration evident from missionary history. East and West drew their inspiration from a common source, namely, Christianity. The vigorous missionary campaigns of the early Middle Ages demonstrate that the same Christian ideas motivated both societies, provided them with a sense of direction and established for each the norms of success or failure. In their common religious orientation the East and the West possessed such a large area of agreement that one hesitates to speak of their differences. Nothing would perhaps better illustrate this bond than the magnificent welcome and the high praises extended Cyril and Methodius, Greeks sent abroad by the Greek emperor to win converts for the Greek church, when they arrived in Rome in 867.[94] Their success was praiseworthy in the eyes of all Christians.

Finally missionary history suggests some important factors for the Slavs and Germans converted during the early Middle Ages. The Slavs, as a result of the fashion in which Christianity was presented to them, were oriented toward a concept of caesaropapism, the new religion and its organization being thoroughly bound up with the destinies of certain princes. They received a religion with a strong intellectual tinge which perhaps had an application to only a minority, leaving the masses to make what they wanted or could of the new religion. They received a religious system which in its dependence upon the state, its complicated theology, and its native liturgies contained the seeds of particularism.

For the Germans all these factors were of less significance. Christianity as presented to them favored the development of an independent and aggressive church. The new religion placed a burden of moral and ethical reform on them much more than it did one of intellectualism. The missionaries, working within the framework of an organized church more often than within one of local political conditions, tied the new converts into a universalist organization which struggled to integrate the lives of these converts into the stream of western civilization instead of permitting them to enjoy their own churches and their own Christianized culture. It is difficult to escape the conclusion that such differences in the way Christianity was presented to these groups had an important bearing on their later history.

1. For example, Georgius Cedrenus, *Compendium Historiarum* (ed. I. Bekker, *Corpus Scriptores Historiae Byzantinae*, II [Bonn, 1838], pp. 151-153.

2. For a review of the background of the Greek war on the Bulgars see J. B. Bury, *A History of the Eastern Empire from the Fall of Irene to the Accession of Basil I (A.D. 802-867)* (London, 1912), pp. 381-386; F. Dvornik, *Les slaves, Byzance et Rome au IXe siècle* (Paris, 1926), pp. 184-189.

3. F. Dvornik, *Les legendes de Constantin et de Méthode vues de Byzance* (Prague, 1933), pp. 226-235.

4. *Photii Patriarchae Constantinopolitani Epistolarum Libri Tres*, #8, c. 22-24 Migne, *PG*, CII, 657-660) ; to be cited hereafter as Photius, *EP*. (Migne, *PG*, CII), with appropriate column numbers.

5. Chapters 2-14 of the Slavic biography of Cyril and chapters 2-5 of the Slavic biography of Methodius. For the text of these chapters in a French translation see Dvornik, *Les legendes de Constantin et de Méthode*, pp. 350-373, 384-386. These biographies will be cited hereafter as *Vie de Constantin* (tr. Dvornik) and *Vie de Méthode* (tr. Dvornik), with appropriate chapter and page numbers.

6. This story is told in a Slavic legend, entitled *Vita Naumi*, which was not available for this study ; for a review of its contents see Dvornik, *Les slaves, Byzance et Rome au IXe siècle*, pp. 298-301.

7. Anastasius Bibliothecarius, *Epistolae sive Praefationes*, #5 (ed. E. Perels and G. Laehr, *MGH*, *Epistolae*, VII, 403-415; this series of *MGH* will be cited hereafter as *Ep.*) ; *Vita Nicolae (Liber pontificalis*, ed. L. Duchesne, [Paris, 1886-1892], Vol. II, 164-167) ; *Vita Hadriani* (*ibid.*, pp. 180-185) ; Nicholas I, *Ep.* #100 (ed. E. Perels, *MGH*, *Ep.*, VI, 601-609) ; Hadrian II, *EP.* #41 (*ibid.*, p. 760).

8. *Vie de Constantin*, c. 15 (tr. Dvornik, pp. 373-375) ; *Vie de Méthode*, c. 5, 8-10 (tr. Dvornik, pp. 385-386, 387-389).

9. As illustrated in *Vita s. Clementis Bulgarorum archiepiscopi*, c. 14-17 (Migne, *PG*, CXXVI, 1217-1224).

10. For evidence of Methodius' difficulties stemming from his political connections

see *Vie de Méthode*, c. 9-10, 12 (tr. Dvornik, pp. 388-390) ; John VIII, *Fragmenti Registri*, #14-24 (ed. E. Caspar, *MGH*, *Ep.*, VII, 280-287) ; John VIII, *Ep.* #200-201, 255, 276 (*ibid.*, 160-161, 222-224, 243-244).

11. The sources cited in note 7, above, show that Boris' alliance with Rome caused the Greek missionaries to be driven out of Bulgaria.

12. *Vie de Méthode*, c. 5 (tr. Dvornik, pp. 385-386) ; *Vie de Constantin*, c. 14 (tr. Dvornik, pp. 372-373).

13. See Steven Runciman, *A History of the First Bulgar Empire* (London, 1930), pp. 25-70; William Miller in *Cambridge Medieval History*, IV (New York, 1923), pp. 230-245; Bury, *A History of the Eastern Roman Empire*, pp. 332-374.

14. Runciman, *op. cit.*, pp. 137-143; Matthew Spinka, *A History of Christianity in the Balkans* (Chicago, c. 1933), pp. 47-56.

15. Photius, Lib. II, #95 (Migne, *PG*, CII, 904-905).

16. Spinka, *op. cit.*, p. 49.

17. H. Wiedemann, *Die Sachsenbekehrung* (*Veröffentlichungen des international Instituts für missionswissenschaftliche Studien*, ed. J. Schmidlin, neue Reihe, V [Münster i. W., 1932] ; Louis Halphen, "La conquête de la Saxe" in *Études critiques sur l'histoire de Charlemagne* (Paris, 1921), pp. 145-218; Albert Hauck, *Kirchengeschichte Deutschlands*, II (3. and 4. Aufl., Leipzig, 1912), pp. 371-424.

18. The essential sources dealing with the assistance offered to Willibrord by these two rulers include *Chronicarum . . . Fredegarii . . . Libri IV cum Continuationibus*, c. 8, 17 (ed. B. Krusch, *MGH*, *Scriptores rerum Merovingicarum*, II, 172, 176; this series of *MGH* will be cited hereafter as *SS. rer. Merov.*) ; Alcuin, *Vita Willibrordi* (ed. W. Levison, *MGH*, *SS. rer. Merov.*, VII, 81-141) ; Bede, *Ecclesiastical History of England*, V. c. 10 (ed. J. A. Giles [London, 1903], pp. 249-250; this will be cited hereafter as Bede (ed. Giles), with appropriate book, chapter, and page numbers).

19. Hauck, *Kirchengeschichte Deutschlands*, II, 690-693.

20. Bede, I, c. 25, 26, 33; II, c. 2, 3, 14-17 (ed. Giles, pp. 36-40, 60-61, 68-74, 96-102).

21. To document this point with even a fair representation of cases illustrating the material support gained by western missionaries would involve much more space than is available in this article. Therefore, no attempt will be made to do so. Let it be said, however, that one can hardly turn a page of the rather voluminous hagiography connected with missionary activity without finding reference to this kind of assistance.

22. Bede, I, c. 25-26 (ed. Giles, pp. 36-40).

23. Alcuin, *Vita Willibrordi*, c. 9 (ed. W. Levison, *MGH, SS. rer. Merov.*, VII, 123-124).

24. Rimbert, *Vita Anskarii*, c. 26-27 (ed. G. Waitz, *MGH, Scriptores rerum Germanicarum in usum scholarum* [Hanover, 1884], pp. 55-59; this series of *MGH* will be cited as *SS. rer. Germ. in usum schol.*).

25. The essential sources referring to Boniface's heavy responsibility in organizing his own projects include *Bonifatii et Lulli Epistolae* (ed. Michael Tangl, *Die Briefe des heiligen Bonifatius und Lullus, MGH, Epistolae Selectae*, I [Berlin, 1916]; to be cited hereafter as Boniface, *Ep.* (ed. M. Tangl, *MGH, Ep. Select.*, I), with appropriate letter and page numbers); and Willibald, *Vita Bonifatii* (ed. W. Levison, *MGH, SS. rer, Germ. in usum schol.* [Hanover, 1905], pp. 1-58).

26. Bede, V., c. 10 (ed. Giles, pp. 249-251); Alcuin, *Vita Willibrordi*, c. 5, ff. (ed. W. Levison, *MGH, SS. rer. Merov.*, VII. 120, ff.).

27. *Diplomata maiorum domus e stirpe Arnulforum*, #5-9, 11-13 (ed. G. Pertz, *MGH, Diplomata Imperii*, I, 94-101); *MGH, Diplomata karolinorum*, #4 (ed. E. Mühlbacher, pp. 6-7); *Monumenta Epternacensia* (ed. L. Weiland, *MGH, Scriptores*, XXIII, 50-65); Albertus Poncelet, 'La "Testament" de Saint Willibrord,' *Analecta Bollandiana*, XXV (1906), 163-176.

28. Hauck, *Kirchengeschichte Deutschlands*, II, 354-371.

29. Liudger, *Vita Gregorii*, c. 11 (ed. O. Holder-Egger, *MGH, Scriptores*, XV, 76-79); Altfrid, *Vita Liudgeri*, Lib. I, c. 1-9 (ed. Wilhelm Diekamp, *Geschichtsquellen des Bisthums Münster*, IV. [Münster, 1881], pp. 6-14).

80. *Vita Lebuini antiqua* (ed. A. Hofmeister, *MGH, Scriptores*, XXX2, 789-795); Huebald, *Vita Sancti Lebwini* (Migne, *PL*, CXXXII, 875-894); *Vita Willehadi* (ed. A. Poncelet, *Acta Sanctorum*, Nov., III, 842-851).

31. Altfrid, *Vita Liudgeri*, Lib. I, c. 25, 29 (ed. W. Diekamp, pp. 30,34).

32. For examples, see *Codex Carolinus*, #6, 17, 24, 26, 35, 37, 39, 42, 50, 62 (ed. W. Gundlach, *MGH, Ep.*, III, 488-489,

514-517, 528-529, 530-531, 542-543, 547-550, 551-552, 554-555, 570, 589-590).

33. See the works cited in note 17, above.

34. *Concilia aevi karolini*, I, #20 (ed. A. Werminghoff, *MGH, Leges*, Sectio III, Tomus II1, pp. 172-176); Alcuin, *Ep.* #107, 110, 111, 113 (ed. E. Dümmler, *MGH, Ep.*, IV, 153-154, 156-166).

35. Hauck, *Kirchengeschichte Deutschlands*, II, 711-726; Ernst Dümmler, *Geschichte des Ostfränkischen Reiches*, 3 Bd. (2. Aufl., Leipzig, 1887-1888), *passim*.

36. Willibald, *Vita Bonifatii*, c. 4 (ed. W. Levison, *MGH, SS. rer. Germ. in usum schol.*, pp. 16-17); *Vita Willehadi*, c. 6 (ed. A. Poncelet, *Acta Sanctorum*, Nov., III, 844); Altfrid, *Vita Liudgeri*, Lib. I, c. 21 (ed. W. Diekamp, p. 25).

37. Sigurd Abel and Bernhard Simson, *Jahrbücher des fränkischen Reiches unter Karl dem Grossen*, I (2. Aufl., Leipzig, 1883), *passim*; II (Leipzig, 1883), *passim*, for a record of these wars.

38. *Annales regni Francorum*, a. 795, 797, 798, 804 (ed. F. Kurze, *MGH, SS. rer. Germ. in usum schol.* [Hanover, 1895], pp. 96, 100, 104, 118).

39. Alcuin, *Ep.* #112, 113, 174 (ed. E. Dümmler, *MGH, Ep.*, IV, 162-166, 289).

40. *MGH, Capitularia*, I, #26 (ed. A. Boretius, pp. 68-70).

41. Altfrid, *Vita Liudgeri*, Lib. I, c. 23-24 (ed. W. Diekamp, pp. 27-29); *Vita Willehadi*, c. 8-9 (ed. A. Poncelet, *Acta Sanctorum*, Nov., III, 845).

42. Among the missionaries famed as church builders under particularly difficult conditions were Willibrord (Alcuin, *Vita Willibrordi*, c. 12, ed. W. Levison, *MGH, SS. rer. Merov.*, VII, 126-127); Boniface in Hesse and Thuringia (Boniface, *Ep.* #24, 25, ed. M. Tangl, *MGH, Ep. Select.*, I, 42-44; Willibald, *Vita Bonifatii*, c. 5-6, ed. W. Levison, *MGH, SS. rer. Germ. in usum schol.*, pp. 18-36); Liudger in northern Frisia (Altfrid, *Vita Liudgeri*, Lib. I, c. 17-24, ed. W. Diekamp, pp. 21-29); Augustine and Paulinus in England (Bede, I, c. 33; II, c. 3, 14-16, ed. Giles, pp. 60-61, 72-74, 96-101); Willehad in Frisia and Saxony (*Vita Willehadi*, c. 5, ed. A. Poncelet, *Acta Sanctorum*, Nov., III, 844); Sturmi in southern Saxony (Eigilis, *Vita Sturmi*, c. 22, ed. G. Pertz, *MGH, Scriptores*, II, 376); the Bavarian missionaries sent into Carinthia (*De conversione Bagoariorum et Carantanorum libellus*, c. 5 (ed. W. Wattenbach, *MGH, Scriptores*, XI, 7-8).

43. Nun of Heidenheim, *Vita Wynnebaldi*, c. 7, ff. (ed. O. Holder-Egger, *MGH, Scriptores*, XV, 111, ff.); Eigilis, *Vita Sturmi*, c. 13 (ed. G. Pertz, *MGH, Scriptores*, II, 370-371); *Vita secunda s. Liudgeri*, Lib. I, c. 28-30 (ed. W. Diekamp, pp. 74-78).

44. Lupus, *Vita Wigberti*, c. 9 (ed. O. Holder-Egger, *MGH, Scriptores*, XV, 41).

45. Nun of Heidenheim, *Vita Wynnebaldi*,

c. 11-12 (ed. O. Holder-Egger, *MGH, Scriptores*, XV, 115); Eigilis, *Vita Sturmi*, c. 20 (ed. G. Pertz, *MGH, Scriptores*, II, 375).

46. Liudger, *Vita Gregorii*, c. 11 (ed. O. Holder-Egger, *MGH, Scriptores*, XV, 75-76); Lupus, *Vita Wigberti*, c. 5-6 (ed. O. Holder-Egger, *MGH, Scriptores*, XV, 39-40).

47. For examples of Boniface's interest in books and learning while he was engaged in missionary work see Boniface, *Ep.* #9, 27, 30, 34, 63, 76, 91, 96, 103 (ed. M. Tangl, *MGH, Ep. Select.*, I, 4-7, 47-49, 54, 58-59, 128-132, 158-159, 206-208, 216-217, 225-227).

48. Jonas, *Vita Columbani* (ed. B. Krusch, *MGH, SS. rer. Merov.*, IV, 65-108.

49. *Vie de Constantin*, c. 4-5, 13 (tr. Dvornik, pp. 352-354, 371-372).

50. *Ibid.*, c. 15, p. 373; *Vie de Méthode*, c. 5 (tr. Dvornik, pp. 385-386).

51. *Vita s. Clementis*, c. 4 (Migne, *PG*, CXXVI, 1200-1201).

52. *Vie de Méthode*, c. 8, 10 (tr. Dvornik, pp. 387, 389); *Vie de Constantin*, c. 15 (tr. Dvornik, pp. 374-375).

53. *Vie de Méthode*, c. 8 (tr. Dvornik, pp. 387-388).

54. John VIII, *Ep.* #200-201 (ed. E. Caspar, *MGH, Ep.*, VII, 160-161).

55. *Vie de Méthode*, c. 9 (tr. Dvornik, p. 388); *De conversione Bagoariorum et Carantanorum libellus*, c. 12-14 (ed. W. Wattenbach, *MGH, Scriptores*, XI, 13-14).

56. Migne, *PG*, CII, 722-737.

57. *Vita s. Clementis*, c. 18 (Migne, *PG*, CXXVI, 1224-1225).

58. Dvornik, *Les slaves, Byzance et Rome au IXe siècle*, pp. 312-322; Runciman, *A History of the First Bulgar Empire*, pp. 137-143.

59. *Vie de Méthode*, c. 17 (tr. Dvornik, p. 392); *Vita s. Clementis*, c. 12 (Migne, *PG*, CXXVI, 1216-1217).

60. *Ibid.*, c. 18, 1224-1225.

61. *Vie de Méthode*, c. 15 (tr. Dvornik, p. 391).

62. Photius, *Ep.*, Lib. I, #8, c. 1-3 (Migne, *PG*, CII, 628-629).

63. *Ibid.*, c. 4-21. 629-657.

64. Nicholas I, *Ep.* #99 (ed. E. Perels, *MGH, Ep.*, VI, 568-600).

65. *Ibid.*, c. 59, p. 588: "Femoralibus."

66. For some typical examples of these disputes see Photius, *Ep.* (Migne *PG*, CII, 725-736); *Vie de Méthode*, c. 12 (tr. Dvornik, p. 390); *Vita s. Clementis*, c. 5, 8, 9, 10 Migne, *PG*, CXXVI, 1201, 1204, 1208-1209, 1212-1213); Stephan V, *Epistolae passim Collectae, quotquot ad res Germanicas spectant*, #1 (ed. G. Laehr, *MGH, Ep.*, VII, 355-358); Stephan V, *Fragmenti Regestri*, #33 (ed. E. Caspar, *MGH, Ep.*, VII, 353); Nicholas I, *Ep.* #99, 100 (ed. E. Perels, *MGH, Ep.*, VI, 568-600, 603-604).

67. *Vita s. Clementis*, c. 10 (Migne, *PG*, CXXVI, 1213). Proof of Svatopluk's

involvement is clearly indicated in the papal letters concerning these disputes; see those of Stephan V, cited above in note 66, and John VIII, *Ep.* #200, 255 (ed. E. Caspar, *MGH, Ep.*, VII, 160, 222-224).

68. *Vita s. Clementis*, c. 10 (Migne, *PG*, CXXVI, 1228-1229).

69. *Vie de Constantin*, c. 14 (tr. Dvornik, pp. 372-373); *Vie de Méthode*, c. 5 (tr. Dvornik, 385-386).

70. The basic source for this point is *Vie de Constantin*, c. 14 (tr. Dvornik, pp. 372-373). The bibliography on the subject is too vast to provide even a representative selection here.

71. *Ibid.*, c. 14, pp. 372-373.

72. *Ibid.*, c. 15, p. 373; *Vie de Méthode*, c. 15 (tr. Dvornik, p. 391).

73. *Ibid.*, c. 15, p. 391; *Vie de Constantin*, c. 15 (tr. Dvornik, p. 373).

74. For instance, western missionaries were deeply concerned with teaching; see Alcuin, *Vita Willibrordi*, c. 9 (ed. W. Levison, *MGH, SS. rer. Merov.*, VII, 123-124); *De conversione Bagoariorum et Carantanorum libellus*, c. 4 (ed. W. Wattenbach, *MGH, Scriptores*, XI, 7); *Vita Willehadi*, c. 2 (ed. A. Poncelet, *Acta Sanctorum*, Nov., III, 843); Altfrid, *Vita Liudgeri*, Lib. I, c. 5, 9-12 ed. W. Diekamp, pp. 10, 14-17); Bede, I, c. 26 (ed. Giles, p. 39); Rimbert, *Vita Anskarii*, c. 8, 24 (ed. G. Waitz, *MGH, SS. rer. Germ. in usum schol.*, 30, 52-53); Liudger, *Vita Gregorii*, c. 11 (ed. O. Holder-Egger, *MGH, Scriptores*, XV, 75); Lupus, *Vita Wigberti*, c. 5-6 (*MGH, Scriptores*, XV, 39-40). They also educated native clergy; Altfrid, *Vita Liudgeri*, Lib. I, c. 1-12 (ed. W. Diekamp, pp. 6-17); Liudger, *Vita Gregorii*, c. 11 (ed. O. Holder-Egger, *MGH, Scriptores*, XV, 75-76); Eigilis, *Vita Sturmi*, c. 2 (ed. G. Pertz, *MGH, Scriptores*, II, 366); Rimbert, *Vita Anskarii*, c. 8 (ed. G. Waitz, *MGH, SS. rer. Germ. in usum schol.*, p. 30).

75. Alcuin, *Ep.* #110-113 (ed. E. Dümmler, *MGH, Ep.*, IV, 156-166).

76. For typical examples of the destruction of pagan temples and idols see *Vita Amandi*, I, c. 15 (ed. B. Krusch, *MGH, SS. rer. Merov.*, V, 439); *Vita Eligii*, Lib. II, c. 8 (ed. B. Krusch, *op. cit.*, IV, 700); *Vita Hugberti*, c. 3 (ed. W. Levison, *op. cit.*, VI, 484-485); Alcuin, *Vita Willibrordi*, c. 10. 14 (ed. W. Levison, *op. cit.*, VII, 124-125, 128); Willibald. *Vita Bonifatii*, c. 6, 8 (ed. W. Levison, *MGH, SS. rer. Germ. in usum schol.*, pp. 31-32, 47); *Vita Willehadi*, c. 4 (ed. A. Poncelet, *Acta Sanctorum*, Nov., III, 843); Altfrid, *Vita Liudgeri*, Lib. I, c. 16, 22 (ed. W. Diekamp, pp. 20, 26); Eigilis, *Vita Sturmi*, c. 22 (ed. G. Pertz, *MGH, Scriptores*, II, 376).

77. Bede, II, c. 13 (ed. Giles, pp. 95-96).

78. Alcuin, *Vita Willibrordi*, c. 10 (ed. W.

Levison, *MGH, SS. rer. Merov.*, VII,
124-125); Gregory I, *Reg.* XI, #56 (ed.
P. Ewald and L. Hartmann, *MGH, Ep.*,
II, 331).
79. *Vita Willehadi*, c. 3 (ed. A. Poncelet,
Acta Sanctorum, Nov., III, 843);
Alcuin, *Vita Willibrordi*, c. 10-11 (ed.
W. Levison, *MGH, SS. rer. Merov.*,
VII, 124-126).
80. For some sample appeals for Frankish
rulers to use military attacks on pagans
see Boniface, *Ep.* #120 (ed. M. Tangl,
MGH, Ep. Select., I, 256); Angilbertus,
De conversione Saxonum carmen. v.
27-29, 37-46, 48, 56-62 (ed. E. Dümmler,
MGH, Poetae latini aevi carolini, I,
380-381); *Codex Carolinus*, #17, 24, 26,
35. 37, 39, 42, 50. 62 (ed. W. Gundlach,
MGH, Ep., III, 514-517, 528-529, 531,
542-543, 547-550, 551-552, 554-555, 570,
589-590); Alcuin, *Ep.* #119, 171 (ed.
E. Dümmler, *MGH, Ep.*, IV, 174, 282).
81. Bede, I, c. 25; V. c. 10 (ed. Giles, pp. 38,
250); Altfrid, *Vita Liudgeri*, Lib. I, c.
22 (ed. W. Diekamp, p. 26).
82. *Vita Lebuini antiqua*, c. 4-6 (ed. A.
Hofmeister. *MGH, Scriptores*, XXX²,
793-794): Hucbald, *Vita Sancti Lebwini*,
c. 8-13 (Migne, *PL*, CXXXII. 884-890):
Vita Wulframni, c. 9 (ed. W. Levison,
MGH, SS. rer. Merov., V. 668).
83. For some samples of thinking on this
subject see Alcuin, *Ep.* #107 (ed. E.
Dümmler, *MGH. Ep.*, IV. 153-154):
Ratio de cathecizandis rudibus, c. iii
(ed. Joseph Michael Heer, *Ein karolingischer Missions-Katechismus*, [Frei-
burg im Breisgau, 1911], pp. 82-83);
Pirmin, *De singulis libris canonicis scarapsus* (Migne, *PL*, LXXXIX. 1041-
1042): Rudolph of Fulda, *Translatio
s. Alexandri*, c. 2-3 (ed. G. Pertz, *MGH,
Scriptores*, II, 675-676); *Vita Willehadi*, c. 3 (ed. A. Poncelet, *Acta Sanctorum*, Nov., III, 843); Boniface. *Ep.*
#26, 28, 32, 50, 51 (ed. M. Tangl.
MGH, Ep. Select., I, 44-47, 49-52, 55-
56, 80-92); Ermoldus Nigellus, *In
honorem Hludowici carmen*, Lib. IV, v.

1947-1957 (ed. E. Faral, *Les classiques
de l'histoire de France au Moyen Age*
[Paris, 1932], p. 148).
84. Boniface, *Ep.* #23 (ed. M. Tangl, *MGH,
Ep. Select.*, I, 38-41); *Ratio de cathecizandis rudibus*, c. vi (ed. J. Heer, pp.
87-88); Hucbald, *Vita Sancti Lebwini*, c.
12 (Migne, *PL*, CXXXII, 889); Pope
Boniface V's letter to Edwin of Northumbria in Bede, II, c. 10 (ed. Giles,
85-88).
85. Boniface, *Ep.* #23 (ed. M. Tangl, *MGH,
Ep. Select.*, I, 38-41); Ermoldus Nigellus, *In honorem Hludowici carmen*, Lib,
IV, v. 1911-1945 (ed. E. Faral, pp. 146,
148).
86. Boniface, *Ep.* #21 (ed. M. Tangl,
MGH, Ep. Select., I, 35-36); *Ratio de
cathecizandis rudibus*, c. vi (ed. J.
Heer, pp. 87-88); *Vita Willehadi*, c. 3
(ed. A. Poncelet, *Acta Sanctorum*, Nov.,
III, 843); Alcuin, *Vita Willibrordi*, c.
11 (ed. W. Levison, *MGH, SS. rer.
Merov.*, VII, 125).
87. Alcuin, *Ep.* #110 (ed. E. Dümmler,
MGH, Ep., IV, 158-159); *Vita Wulframni*, c. 9 (ed. W. Levison, *MGH,
SS. rer. Merov.*, V, 668); Boniface, *Ep.*
#10 (ed. M.Tangl, *MGH, Ep. Select.*,
I, 7-15).
88. Gregory I, *Reg.* XI, #56 (ed. P. Ewald
and L. Hartmann, *MGH, Ep.*, II, 331).
89. Rimbert, *Vita Anskarii*, c. 27 (ed. G.
Waitz, *MGH, SS. rer. Germ. in usum
schol.*, p. 58).
90. Eddius Stephanus, *The Life of Bishop
Wilfrid*, c. 26 (text, translation, and
notes by Bertram Colgrave [Cambridge,
England, 1927], p. 52).
91. Bede, II, c. 5-6 (ed. Giles, pp. 76-79).
92. *Ibid.*, II, c. 9, 13, pp. 84-85, 94-95.
93. See above, note 85, for references
illustrating how the Christian version
of the origin and development of the
world ought to be explained to pagans.
94. *Vie de Constantin*, c. 17-18 (tr. Dvornik,
pp. 378-380); *Vita (sancti Cyrilli) cum
translatione s. Clementis*, c. 8-12 (*Acta
Sanctorum*, Martius, II, 21-22).

VI

The Medieval Monk as Frontiersman

THIS CHAPTER IS intended to be suggestive rather than definitive, to raise questions rather than to offer answers. It will attempt to explore selected aspects of the medieval monastic experience in western Europe within a conceptual framework germane to the broad field of frontier history. Its objective will be to suggest that in significant ways various kinds of medieval monastic activities are remarkably similar to activities generally associated with the frontier phenomenon in history. My hope is that its argument will be sufficiently persuasive to encourage detailed investigations into the role of the medieval monk as a frontiersman. Such studies would certainly add significant new dimensions to the definition of the place of monasticism in medieval civilization. Perhaps such studies would also expand the general understanding of the frontier phenomenon in history and provide valuable data to the emerging area of inquiry designated as comparative frontier studies.

It must be acknowledged at the outset that there are serious difficulties attached to the argument that will be developed in the following pages. Not the least of these difficulties is the imprecision that surrounds the concepts that are basic to the argument, namely, "frontier" and "frontier experience."[1] The lack of clearly formulated and generally accepted definitions of these concepts is compounded when a medievalist attempts to utilize them. For he represents a subset of the historical profession whose conceptual vocabulary has not included serious consideration of the frontier phenomenon as a significant dimension of the millennium in human history that is the domain of medieval historians.[2] As a consequence medievalists (of whom I am one) are not particularly adept at translating the data of medieval history into the idiom of frontier history or at perceiving the interconnections between experiences in the medieval world and frontier history in general.[3] This ineptness of the medievalist in translating aspects of the medieval experience into the

Reprinted from *The Frontier: Comparative Studies*, Volume 2, edited by William W. Savage, Jr., and Stephen I. Thompson, published and copyrighted by the University of Oklahoma Press, 1979.

VI

conceptual framework relevant to the frontier is magnified when he tries
to enter the treacherous terrain of comparative frontier studies, where
the methodological approaches remain extremely fluid and the basic
vocabulary of discourse extremely imprecise.[4] A further difficulty
stems from the nature of monastic historical studies, where a long and
understandable tradition has emphasized the monastic experience as an
exercise in withdrawal from the world into a setting and a pattern of
activities isolated from and foreign to the mainstream of human endeavor. This approach to monasticism was perhaps validated during the
Middle Ages by a long succession of medieval monastic heroes who
urged the reform of monastic life by advocating detachment from the
world and its wicked ways. Steeped in a view of the monastic calling that
emphasized denial of the world, monastic historians have tended to
concentrate attention on those aspects of the *opus Dei* that separated
monks from the mainstream of medieval life, to highlight those aspects
of monastic history that internalized the search for godliness within the
cloister. Such an approach has tended to make the interface between the
monastery and the world of secondary importance in the reconstruction
of monastic history.[5] As a consequence, a considerable range of monastic activities has been given scant attention both by scholars interested in
monastic life per se and by those concerned with activities in the
medieval world occurring beyond the cloister walls. This neglect raises
problems for anyone who attempts to transpose monastic experience
into nonmonastic contexts. Needless to say, the medieval frontier constitutes a nonmonastic context.

   Conceptual and methodological problems of this order may assure the
failure of this effort from the beginning. But nothing too great can be
risked by an experimental effort to translate certain medieval monastic
experiences into a new idiom. The effort might be especially valuable if
it would provoke from frontier historians a judgment about whether
selected data from medieval monastic history seem relevant and poten-
tially useful to comparative frontier history. If the response from historians of the frontier is positive, it might encourage medievalists to add a
new dimension to their research into and interpretation of the Middle
Ages, one that would make that distant and often scorned age more
relevant to the total human experience.

   The material on which this essay is based has been drawn primarily
from the history of monasticism from its origins in the fourth century
A.D. down to the twelfth century.[6] This selectivity has been prompted in
part by my limited knowledge of monastic history in its post-Cistercian
phases. More importantly, it has been dictated by the fact that from the
twelfth century onward monastic energies were consciously redirected

toward involvement at the vital centers of established society — the cities, the universities, the royal courts, the cathedrals — thus radically changing the perceived societal role of monasticism and the fundamental orientation of the activities suited to monastic life.

The first point to be made in presenting the monk as a frontiersman is almost simplistically obvious. But it must be made to establish the fundamental connection between monasticism and the frontier phenomenon. The monastic experience of the early Middle Ages invariably involved physical displacement from one environment into a different environment; [those who partook of monastic life demonstrated their commitment at least in part by moving into a different physical setting.] The paradigm of the monk as mover to a foreign place, as emigrant, was dramatically established at the beginning of monastic history by the eponymous figure of Saint Anthony as mirrored in the seminal biography composed by Athanasius of Alexandria.[7] For centuries after Anthony's deliberate, considered departure in about 285 from the environs of Alexandria for the desert of the Thebaid, countless individuals displaced themselves geographically as the essential first act in taking up a new life.[8] Between the fourth and the twelfth centuries their peregrinations to "new" lands constituted one of the major components of human mobility in a society that otherwise was marked by a constricting absence of physical movement.[9]

It might be objected — and rightly so — that physical relocation alone does not qualify an emigrant as a frontiersman; the trek from County Cork to Boston or from Naples to New York or from Warsaw to Tel Aviv does not take an Irishman or an Italian or a Pole to a frontier or make him a frontiersman. What makes a frontiersman is movement to a unique kind of environment, a setting that is new and markedly different by comparison with the environment from which migration occurs chiefly by virtue of the fact that a new place is empty of most of what had existed in the setting left behind. I would submit that the movement associated with early medieval monasticism did involve displacement into a genuinely new and different environment, provided that one is willing to accept a medieval definition of a new and different environment. Certainly this movement cannot be so easily charted and described as can the migration characteristic of the classic American frontier, as a succession of movements across the Atlantic, the Appalachians, the Mississippi, the Great Plains, and so on. But the monastic migration was nonetheless one into new and different settings.

From a myriad of cases that come to mind, a typology of monastic frontiers might be tentatively sketched. Without pressing anyone's

VI

credibility too far by insisting that he or she take seriously as a part of
frontier history such aberrant examples of physical displacement into
"new" worlds as represented by the space ventures of Saint Simeon
Stylites atop his pillar or the outward-bound-only voyages of the early
Jules Verne produced in Ireland, I would suggest the following four
principal frontier settings to which the medieval monk as frontiersman
moved.[10]

There was first the uninhabited or barely habited environment,
dramatically contrasting with and considerably separated in distance
from the normal scenes of human existence: the deserts of Egypt and
Syria, the thick forests of early medieval western Europe, the barren
plains of central Spain.[11] Second, there were the uninhabited locations
discovered in near proximity to the inhabited world but still isolated
from normal human traffic: the lauras of Syria and Palestine; islands
such as Lerins and Reichenau and Iona; mountain fastholds such as
Monte Cassino and Mount Athos; barren spots such as Saint Gall and
Citeaux; caves such as Marmoutier and Subiaco.[12] Although the movement to these "frontier" settings was often short in distance, as the
careers of Benedict of Nursia or Bernard of Clairvaux illustrate, there
can be no doubt that the environment was dramatically different. Third,
there was the frontier of the foreign land inhabited by peoples with a
different culture and particularly a heathen religion, an environment, I
suspect, most nearly akin to the conventional concept of a frontier. This
was the frontier to which the monk-missionary was attracted to enact his
profession by winning souls for the true God: Ireland, Anglo-Saxon
England, Frisia, Saxony, the trans-Elbe world of the Slavs, Scandinavia, Iceland.[13] Finally — and here I risk appearing ridiculous —
there was the frontier created by the cloister enclave itself, undoubtedly
the smallest frontier that anyone will ever be called upon to scrutinize. It
is indeed a fact that, even after monastic establishments became a
regular part of the inhabited world of the Middle Ages, a serious effort
was constantly and persistently made to define the cloister as a place
physically apart from the known world, movement to which involved
departure to a place that was far removed, at least in a figurative sense. A
special vocabulary was developed in monastic literature to designate
these unique spots. They were called annexes to heaven, the foot of
Jacob's ladder, the new Jerusalem, stadia for training Christ's athletes,
"the house of God," "the center of angelic life" — in fact, everything
except the workaday, known world of the manor, the castle, the court, or
the town.[14] An objective view from the perspective of the twentieth
century might well conclude that the ordinary medieval cloister has
about as much to do with frontier history as does the Frontier Days

celebration in Cheyenne. I concede that point, reserving the right to choose which fiction best approximates reality. I would insist that this effort to depict the most conventional and common monastic establishment as a place apart to which men and women moved as if to a place foreign was indeed a vital symbolization of a fundamental aspect of the monastic tradition: the monastic life as an act of emigration from the known world to the unknown, from within the boundaries of the settled, established world beyond into the frontier.

Because some kind of physical displacement was implicit in the monastic commitment as a consequence of acceptance of that commitment, the medieval monk was always a frontiersman, at least to the degree that he betook himself to an environment apart from that inhabited by ordinary men. Perhaps by incorporating information pertaining to the kinds of frontiers created by medieval monks into a broader picture of the nature of frontiers, the comparative frontier historian can enlarge his understanding of the frontier phenomenon. And because the monastery was universally perceived as a place beyond the pale, early medieval society possessed an ultimate point of escape from whatever was unbearable. Perhaps the inclusion of this fact into his fomulation of the dynamics of early medieval history could provide the medievalist with some fresh understanding of the leavening forces that produced momentum where reason says it should not have existed in an age so demonstrably dark.

The instant one posits a dimension of the past involving relocation of men from one setting to another, a new theme germane to comparative frontier history is suggested: the definition of the forces that impelled movement and the exploration of the motives that prompted individuals to leave the known, settled situation for the unknown, unsettled location. If one poses these issues with respect to medieval monasticism, there emerge some themes that will, I believe, sound familiar to the frontier historian.[15] Movement to the ''new'' land of the monastery, to the monastic frontier, was often prompted by dissatisfaction with the existing order in society: disgust with a corrupt moral order, discontent with a too-worldly ecclesiastical establishment, pressures from an oppressive political, economic, and social order.[16] Migration took place in answer to an urge to extend the pale of civilized society. The ''white man's burden'' of the early Middle Ages was articulated in terms of converting and saving the pagan, but it was a no less challenging burden to bear to the frontier by virtue of being put in religious terms, especially since baptism to the new faith was interpreted to mean conversion to a totally new life.[17] A powerful utopianism was always at work prompting medieval men to leave behind one world for another. The configurations of the ideal existence as conceived by early medieval monks may appear somewhat bizarre to the modern frontier historian, who is not accustomed to giving serious consideration to institutionalized refuges where mature people practice perfect poverty or occupy themselves in perpetual prayer or engage the devil in warfare on his own turf or train as athletes of Christ. But these strange visions of utopia cannot veil the fact that medieval men and women were impelled to the frontier in order to create a perfect setting for the realization of a dream.[18] Although the statistical evidence is not available, there is some reason to believe that the number who moved to the monastic frontier to create a perfect order was matched by the number who fled to escape a serious debt they owed to the established order. The outlaw frontiersman is not a modern phenomenon. Monastic records are replete with renegades who sought more comfortable climes in cloisters far away from tax collectors, army recruiters, royal judges, established ecclesiastical authorities, and vengeful clansmen. More often than not their adjustment to the frontier was abetted by a merciful God who through a conversion process purged them of their crimes as they approached the frontier; the Middle Ages had its unique version of the American Civil War as a purificatory rite. Their miraculous reformation cannot, however, hide the fact that they departed for the unknown frontier under strong pressure from the established order; and the subsequent record often suggests that, despite conversion, such men ultimately reverted to type, to afflict their fellow frontiersmen with atavistic behavioral patterns that defied even divine attention.

All of which is to say that the history of medieval monasticism appears to put the frontier historian on familiar ground in terms of the forces that prompted men and women to depart for parts unknown. Here seems to be a fertile realm for illuminating comparisons of a factor threatening the stability of any society, namely, a many-faceted urge to depart for new places to achieve what is lacking in the established order or to escape from the corrupting influences of that order. Perhaps, obversely, the medieval experience would throw new light on the extent to which the frontier constitutes a safety valve for established societies — if indeed that is any longer an issue for frontier historians.

But as much as transplantation to new and strange places for certain special kinds of reasons is an important dimension of frontier history, it does not get to the heart of the matter. It would be agreed, I think, that more important to frontier history than the going to the new land for whatever number of good reasons is what happened in the new setting. Frontiers provide an ambience and a challenge that generate new institutions, new techniques, and new ideas palpably different from what had prevailed in the order from which frontiersmen had departed. Perhaps the frontier even generates improvement over the societal order that was left behind. It is obviously incumbent on anyone who would speak of a medieval monastic frontier and of the monk as frontiersman to demonstrate that the monastic environment was productive of new patterns of life in the fashion of other frontiers and frontiersmen.

There is certainly no lack of evidence that the medieval monastic establishment possessed a potential for creativity and innovation. Modern scholarship has, in fact, compiled a massive list of institutions, techniques, and ideas that originated in the monastic milieu. These monastic additions to, or variations on, the basic fabric of civilization range across the whole gamut of medieval culture from governance systems to art styles, leaving one with the impression that indeed early medieval civilization was the creation of the monks.[19]

As proof of the point under consideration, it is tempting to begin cataloguing the creative contributions of the monks to the shaping of the major components of early medieval civilization; the list is impressive enough to occupy us for a considerable interval. But that would be a diversionary tactic. The real question for this chapter is whether one can relate any significant part of the innovative process so evident in medieval monastic circles to what could be characterized as a frontier situation. Historians of medieval monasticism have not really addressed this question. But I believe that if they would look at the innovative process in the monastic world from a particular perspective it would become obvious that there was a close relationship between creative innovation and special kinds of monastic communities that can be characterized as frontier communities. The crucial question that has to be asked is this: What was the particular situation, circumstance, and context within which a particular monastic innovation emerged? If one proceeds across the entire rich and varied catalogue of monastic innovations in search of an answer to this question, an interesting result emerges. The most significant changes affected by monks came about rather consistently in those circumstances where the monastic milieu most nearly approximated what I conceive to be the frontier environment, that is, in situations where groups of monks found themselves for whatever reason separated from the mainstream of life in new physical locations where conventional modes of response to ordinary human situations were not available or not applicable and where new challenges

VI

generated by the environment threatened the very survival of the migrants. In short, the monks were most innovative when they were most unmistakably frontiersmen.

Let me, at least briefly, illustrate this facet of monastic history, heretofore singularly neglected. The great innovations in monastic governance occurred in situations demanding an immediate solution to critical political problems for which there were no obvious models.[20] Pachomius found himself faced in the Egyptian desert by a ragtag mob of uprooted social outcasts who had fled the established order for various reasons, whose conduct increasingly engendered an intolerable anarchy to which conventional society would have responded with jail sentences, and whose spiritual development lagged far below expectations. The Pachomian response was an act of unique political creativity: the delineation (with angelic assistance, to be sure) of a unique *regula* or constitution for the governance of an abnormal collectivity of men that imposed on them obligations and modes of social behavior theretofore unknown and that evoked from them a new style of behavior. It is true that the Pachomian rule was soon accepted as normative for the governance of monks, but that cannot hide the fact that its genesis lay in an existential situation created by the gathering of uprooted men in a new setting.[21] Close examination of the circumstances attending the establishment of the rule of Saint Benedict or the system of governance applied in the Irish clan-structured monasteries or the Cistercian Charta Charitatis strongly suggests a process comparable to the Pachomian case: creative political acts consummated under the pressures resulting from the congregation of men in special settings where none of the conventional modes of governance applied, primarily because these communities had moved away from the mainstream of society.[22] The evidence points convincingly to the conclusion that the major monastic political innovations reflected in monastic rules occurred as spontaneous responses to situations arising in what can without exaggeration be called frontier settings. Medieval historians have often overlooked this fact because of their passion to discover how something once begun evolved and their almost psychopathic obsession with discovering the earlier sources of what came later; these are a pair of conceptual postures that are deadly to what may be the essence of the historian's art, namely, the reconstruction of the decisive existential moment in human affairs, usually the instant when something new occurs.

A detailed examination of the specific circumstances that produced economic innovation in the monastic world again suggests that the impetus for change was most often provided by the location of a monastic establishment in a setting outside the normal environment where problems arose requiring a nonconventional response. The cele-brated Benedictine regularization of the application of human energies in a fashion that provided a legitimate place for manual labor in the pursuit of godliness, an innovation rightly characterized by Lewis Mum-ford as a milestone in economic history, was a response to a unique situation created when a mixed multitude of men, many of whom in their prior stations had known nothing of either regular schedules or manual labor, were faced with the exigencies of self-sustenance.[23] Perhaps the best proof of the creativeness of the Benedictine response to the existen-tial problem of economic self-sufficiency lies in a comparison of the history of Monte Cassino with other communities of well-intentioned holy men founded in the fifth, sixth, and seventh centuries that failed because no one found a formula that would apply the potential of the collectivity as a labor force to the immediate exigencies of physical survival in an isolated setting.[24] The particular circumstances that created the highly productive monastic conglomerates that first emerge in the historical record in the early Carolingian period are particularly intriguing.[25] These monastic communities, such as Fortenelle, Jumièges, Saint-Riquier, Saint-Bertin, Corbie, Farfa, and Saint Germain-des-Près, seem to have originated as rather conventional monastic frontier outposts in the sense that we have been using that term — small collectivities of holy men who isolated themselves in uninvit-ing settings to pursue holiness and who devised primitive means of supporting themselves at a minimal subsistence level. Then came the challenge that for some inexplicable reason seems to have constituted the madness of the seventh-century world: an unending shower of gifts flowing from every level of society to these inauspicious monastic establishments, gifts consisting of parcels of land that were situated hither and yon relative to ''frontier'' monasteries, had varied productive potential, and were in diverse states of exploitation. To put such gifts to the service of God and his holy servants required more than prayer and fasting. The record tells us disappointingly little about what happened, but enough to assure us that the response lay in the development of innovative managerial techniques aimed at orchestrating diverse and discordant physical and human resources into an integrated, productive system. Needless to say, the monastic establishments that responded to this challenge quickly lost their frontier characteristics as their wealth burgeoned from the fruits of innovative management. And their techniques were avidly imitated. But that should not hide the fact that success impinged on the unique response given to an economic chal-lenge posed to a frontier community existing outside the mainstream of seventh-century society. An even more dramatic example of economic innovation in a frontier setting is provided by the twelfth- and thirteenth-century Cistercian establishments as their inhabitants mastered the unique physical environment to which they were attracted in their efforts to realize perfection.[26]

Another area illustrative of the fecundity of the frontier monastic world as a source of innovation is in the realm of cultural history. This is a subject too vast to do justice to here. But it seems clear that a convincing case can be made for major monastic contributions to a revolutionary cultural transformation that occurred during the early Middle Ages. There is powerful evidence that the early monks who fled the world in Egypt, Syria, Palestine, Anatolia, and Gaul by the very act of flight helped subvert the basic ideology undergirding classical civilization, especially by repudiating the city as the sole meaningful arena of civilized existence. The impact of these radical "rebels" against civilization on the thinking of many educated, sophisticated, sensitive "citizens" of the great cities of the Roman Empire — Athanasius, Palladius, Jerome, Augustine, John Cassian, Cassiodorus, Gregory the Great — played a significant role in dissolving the connection in the late ancient world between constructive human existence and the city-state and in setting the stage for a new culture. That the danger posed by the monastic "frontiersmen" to the norms of civilized life was real is illustrated by fourth- and fifth-century imperial and ecclesiastical legislation against the outrageous behavior of the monks and by the fulminations of such defenders of civilization as Julian the Apostate, who railed against those who had "abandoned their fatherland, to wander as vagabonds about the earth . . . troublesome and insolent."[27] Within this same frontier environment came a dramatic assertion (or, perhaps better, enactment) of a pessimistic concept of human nature, stressing human debasement, corruption, weakness, and dependence on divine favor for redemption that contributed in a major way to destruction of the classical concept of heroic, Promethean man. That shift in the view of human nature was critical in establishing the cultural milieu of the early Middle Ages. There is persuasive evidence that the isolated monastic communities, concerned with articulating and justifying their new ways, played a decisive role in establishing the norms by which to judge what was acceptable from the classical philosophical and literary tradition and consequently in determining what of that rich inheritance would survive as a part of the cultural raw material available to the society of the early Middle Ages. The isolated monks voluntarily withdrawn from the mainstream of learning and education to their unique frontier had a major part in giving new meaning to the words and new content to the idea that they took over from the profane culture of the world they had abandoned. Their unique ways of doing the *opus Dei* resulted in new modes and forms of expression and in an entirely new educational system. In the face of these examples of the role of the monks in cultural life, it is difficult to escape the conclusion that the cultural framework that guided thought and creativity during the period from the fourth to the twelfth century was to a considerable extent a response to the special conditions that prevailed in a frontier setting.[28]

Other examples from nearly every facet of medieval life could be addressed to buttress my point. Let me rest the case without the benefit of this additional support. The evidence powerfully suggests that a major cutting edge of societal change in the early Middle Ages existed in a special environment. That environment involved collectivities of men and women who had consciously removed themselves from the established societal order to seek a new environment where a particular ideal could be realized. The act of separation and relocation immediately posed a wide range of problems that had to be met if the detached communities were to survive and progress toward the realization of their aspirations. It was in that unique, short-lived situation that new institutions, practices, and ideas were devised, many of which were replicated in subsequent detached communities and imitated in wide circles outside the monastic milieu, so that these innovations became basis components of what emerged as a newly established societal order. It is to those crucial episodes associated with migration to a new physical setting removed from the mainstream of society and to the remarkable processes of change that followed hard on the act of migration that I direct attention as a significant chapter in frontier history, one yet poorly described and analyzed, but one that I think would help all frontier historians understand more fully the creative dimensions of the frontier environment.

Let me now shift to another angle of vision in this attempt to relate the medieval monastic experience to frontier history. So far my suggestions have accentuated the frontier as a place apart and different, as a refuge to which escape could be made, and as a milieu productive of innovative change by virtue of its separateness. While these are legitimate aspects of frontier history, I suspect that they involve a limited approach to the frontier phenomenon that will not fully satisfy most experts on frontier history. For it seems to me that the frontier phenomenon always involves some ongoing interaction between an established order and a new settlement. There can be no frontier if there is a total separation of the old and the new. Rather, the essence of the frontier phenomenon involves a symbiosis between an established society and its frontier offshoot that in some significant way affects both.

If this is a valid characterization of the frontier, then I would submit that early medieval monastic history provides rich material for comparative studies of the interrelationships between frontier societies and the societies from which the frontier communities emerged. In fact, the possibilities are far too rich to permit even a preliminary survey here. There is, for example, the matter of what cultural baggage frontiersmen transport with them in their initial movement. There is also the matter of what physical items, techniques, and ideas continue to flow from the homeland to the frontier after it is established and what role those selected transhipped cultural artifacts have in shaping frontier society. I could amass a large body of evidence related to those issues to show that frontier monastic establishments were critically dependent on certain kinds of ties with the settled environment from which they emerged.[29] I strongly suspect that the material would provide significant assistance to the comparative frontier historian concerned with the nature of the dependence of frontier societies on the culture that produced them and with the processes by which elements vital to the implantation and development of frontier societies are moved from the homeland to the frontier.

But to give some concreteness to my contention that medieval monastic history provides enlightenment on the subject of the interrelationship between frontier and hinterland, let me take you to the arena where the frontier historian feels most at home, closest to the spirit of Frederick Jackson Turner. Let me speak to the influences flowing from the frontier back to the society that produced it. Since this is an aspect of frontier history that has not always nurtured restraint, I must proceed with caution here. The monastic influence on medieval society was so massive and so pervasive that it would be extremely easy for anyone who has planted the idea that monastic communities were sometimes frontier establishments to proceed with a line of argument suggesting that everything emanating from a monastery to influence society at large constituted a case of the frontier impacting on the homeland. The fact is that monastic influences had an impact on the nonmonastic world most often and most significantly in situations where the monastic establishment was a fully integrated part of the society it was influencing and not a frontier establishment. For example, the monasteries of Bede's England or the Carolingian and Ottonian royal monasteries or the Cluniae houses of the eleventh century were not frontier monasteries in the sense that I have been employing that term. Yet they were the kinds of monastic establishments that exercised a profound influence on contemporary society and put a monastic stamp on most aspects of the societal order.

With this caution against claiming too much for the role of the monastic frontier in influencing the hinterland firmly in mind, I believe that we can seriously entertain the idea that, in the Turnerian sense, the monks as frontiersmen did put their unique stamp on the early medieval society on whose frontier they existed. In reflecting on this matter, I am particularly struck by three vital forces that flowed back from the monastic frontier to affect established society decisively.

First, it seems to me that the monastic frontier provided a setting where there were forged leadership models that flowed out of the monasteries to play a major role in defining the qualities that allowed some men to exercise authority over others in the early medieval world. The role of the monastic frontier in this respect was particularly influential in the fifth, sixth, and seventh centuries, an era when monasticism most dramatically demonstrated its frontier characteristics and traditional leadership models, such as those provided by the senatorial aristocracy or the enlightened imperial bureaucracy or even the late imperial episcopacy, were badly confused and debilitated. It was not until the twelfth century that the monastic leadership model was challenged by other models being forged in the cathedral schools, the chivalric courts, the royal chanceries, and the mercantile establishments. The shape that the new hero of the monastic frontier took is contained in the saints' lives, a literary genre that presents such a supreme challenge to the modern historian that it is often neglected. It strikes me, however, that this hagiographical corpus contains some interesting parallels with modern cowboy literature in terms of delineating the qualities that made a hero and thereby defined leadership potential. At a considerable risk of oversimplification of the complex message contained in the saints' lives, I would suggest that the monastic frontier produced a leadership model that accentuated a capacity for action as the critical component of authority. The monastic frontier involved an ordinary mortal in a sequence of experiences that forged him into an "athlete of Christ," whose inner perfection allowed a special inflow of divine powers that were in turn manifested by a capacity to do things: put devils to flight, cure the sick, provide food for the starving, elucidate the meaning of God's word, correct the wicked, raise up the dead, defy the false gods of the pagans, and do all the other deeds recorded in the saints' lives. Inexorably the example of the new "hero" shaped on the monastic frontier began to reverberate throughout the settled world to suggest qualities suited to the good bishop, the good priest, the good warrior, the good worker, even the good king. The evidence seems to me conclusive that the charismatic man of action molded in the frontier monastery provided the prime archetype against which all types of leadership were measured in the early Middle Ages. If this is so, then indeed the frontier played a role in determining the shape of the settled world.[30]

Second, the frontier monastic establishment, as contrasted with the nonfrontier societal establishment, was a prime source of reform movements that were communicated back to the settled world to set afoot efforts to regenerate society there. The first monasteries in Egypt and Syria, in one sense the archetypal frontier establishments, were from one perspective established out of a reforming urge. Their tumultuous populations were not long in exporting the formulas for perfection discovered in the desert to such centers of inequity as Alexandria or Antioch or Constantinople. That pattern was repeated again and again in the early Middle Ages: a monastic establishment created by design away from the normal world as a frontier outpost to that world produced a reforming model that flowed back into society with notable impact. So convincing is the evidence that I believe one can argue that frontier monasteries constituted virtually the sole source of reform movements between the fifth and the twelfth centuries. The monk in the role of frontiersman was almost singlehandedly the provider of leaven in a society that suffered from massive inertia. In reflecting on the role played by frontier monasteries as producers of reform movements, I am struck by the fact that the frontier repeatedly generated a special kind of reform movement. These movements always focused on a program that would produce a change of heart among the wicked through a process that involved the simplication of life-styles. The frontier monks were protagonists of moral reform, which was to be achieved by abandoning wealth, luxury, frivolous intellectual pursuits, pleasures, power wielding, artistic creativity — in short, by retreating from civilized existence. The monastic reformers seldom addressed themselves to structural changes in society or to positive social-action programs or to new intellectual ventures as avenues through which the human condition could be improved. This repeated drive for moral regeneration originating in the frontier monastic setting and bearing interesting parallels with the prophetic movements of the Old Testament leads me to wonder whether frontiers in general are breeding grounds for a unique kind of puritanical moral fervor that flows back to the hinterlands as a call to achieve perfection by purging society of the burdens of civilization.[31]

Third, the frontier monasteries and their inhabitants played a basic role in shaping a vision of human nature that came to dominate early medieval society and to define the fundamental value system that colored the entire fabric of society. This is a complex issue that I broach here at considerable risk of confusing everyone. What is involved was that massive revolution that saw the classical concept of *humanitas* replaced by a pessimistic concept of human nature stressing man as sinful, debased, corrupt, powerless to free himself from his own corruption, and utterly dependent on grace from above to save him from his terrestial degradation. The participants in this great cultural revolution were legion. But I am powerfully impressed by the importance of frontier monastic life, especially in the period from about 350 to 600, in asserting in concrete terms the pessimistic concept of human nature and in conveying that message to ever-enlarging circles in the nonmonastic, nonfrontier world. In their daily practice the frontier monks made a cult of debasing the body, that vessel that the classical world took as the ultimate symbol of human power. The monks' endless round of prayer evidenced the conviction that man could find help only in God. A monk's whole existence was dedicated to the obliteration of rational power so as to prepare the soul for divine illumination. At least in legend those successful in debasing human nature were rewarded by a vision of the divine and by miraculous powers over nature. The monastic exemplification of the concept of human weakness and debasement was mediated by a remarkable succession of spiritual spokesmen of the fourth, fifth, and sixth centuries into a doctrine of human nature as totally corrupted that dominated thought and action at least to the scholastic age of the twelfth and thirteenth centuries. Although the evidence is not easy to interpret, it seems clear to me that, as a result of witnessing or hearing of the feats of the frontier monks, ordinary men and women found a reflection of and justification for what their experiences in a troubled world told them, namely, that man was weak, corruptible, sinful, condemned by nature to suffering, and utterly dependent on God. In short, the frontier monks made a vital contribution to creating and propagating the ethos of an entire age.[32]

While my characterization of what the monastic frontier gave back to the society the monkish frontiersman left behind may be somewhat oversimplified and certainly is not all-embracing, I would like to inject an observation that struck me as I developed this point. Is there not something almost classically Turnerian about a frontier that produces and feeds back into the old society new concepts of leadership, repeated calls for moral reform, and a radical view of human nature? Indeed, our medieval monk may have been a more conventional frontiersman than anyone imagined, especially in terms of his impact on the world on which he had turned his back. In any case it seems clear that more careful attention to the interactions between the medieval monastic frontier and the societal order out of which monastic frontier communities emerged could help to elucidate a broad problem generic to frontier history, namely, the symbiosis between frontier and hinterland.

Readers who have persevered to this point may be posing the question about it that frontier historians ultimately ask about the frontier: When does it end? I approach a conclusion reluctantly, for there remain several other aspects of medieval monastic history that seem to fit into the general context of frontier history. For instance, there is the fascinating subject of the medieval missionary monk who moved to a frontier setting to act as an agent for one culture in an encounter with another. This story, featuring the missionary monk as a masterful exploiter of the conversion process to effect on those foreigners whom he encountered on the frontier a major cultural transformation with a minimum of trauma to the victims, would provide illuminating comparative material to the frontier historian concerned with the frontier as the scene of cross-cultural encounters.[33] I would like to have suggested that monastic frontier life may have generated a special set of moral values and behavioral norms that ultimately exercised a considerable impact on medieval society.[34] I would like to have linked monastic history, frontier history, and psychohistory to suggest that the medieval monastic frontier produced some unique personality types whose chief characteristics were emulated in other circles in medieval society. I would like to have suggested that the medieval frontier monasteries created some special opportunities for medieval women and generated some unique attitudes toward them.

But even had I been able to explore all these avenues, I do not delude myself that I have fully established the credentials of the medieval monk as a frontiersman or convincingly demonstrated that medieval monastic history is rich in material relevant to comparative frontier history. I am experienced enough to know that scholarly papers seldom prove or demonstrate anything. Successful scholarly papers only pose the possibility of new approaches to old subjects and to familiar evidence. I hope that I have invited such a new approach by posing the outlandish proposition that Saint Martin of Tours and Daniel Boone or Saint Benedict of Nursia and Wyatt Earp or Saint Boniface of Crediton and General Custer or Saint Bernard of Clairvaux and Brigham Young shared comparable experiences by virtue of their involvement on the frontier. What is needed now is a way to get these frontiersmen to exchange views on their common experiences in an idiom that will instruct us as historians of the frontier phenomenon. For better or for worse, only the historian has the ability to re-create such discourse.*

Notes

* This chapter was read as a paper, essentially as here published, at the Second Oklahoma Symposium on Comparative Frontiers, sponsored by the University of Oklahoma on March 25–26, 1976.

1. For some suggestions on this problem see John C. Hudson, "Theory and Methodology in Comparative Frontier Studies," in David Harry Miller and Jerome O. Steffen, eds., *The Frontier: Comparative Studies*, vol. 1 (Norman, 1977), pp. 11–31.

2. It is fascinating to speculate on why the frontier phenomenon has failed to interest medieval historians. Perhaps this lacuna has been a consequence of the persistent tendency in medieval studies to concentrate on those aspects of medieval life that point toward a static, monolithic pattern of civilization prevailing over a millennium — an approach to the Middle Ages that has demonstrated a remarkable virulence in spite of massive evidence proving the dynamism of the medieval world. Even more significant in minimizing interest in the frontier phenomenon as a dimension of the medieval world has been the preoccupation of medievalists with the problem of establishing the medieval roots of the major facets of modern western European civilization — a civilization to which the frontier phenomenon has had very little relevance.

3. This is not to imply a total lack of interest in the medieval frontier. See the perceptive remarks of David Harry Miller, "The Early Middle Ages and Comparative Frontier Studies," *Comparative Frontier Studies: An Interdisciplinary Newsletter* 1 (Fall, 1975); and *ibid.* 2 (Spring, 1976). Illustrative of serious scholarship reflecting an interest in the medieval frontier are William C. Bark, *Origins of the Medieval World* (Stanford, Calif., 1958); Luis Weckmann, "The Middle Ages in the Conquest of America," *Speculum* 26 (1951): 130–41; C. J. Bishko, "The Castilian as Plainsman: The Medieval Ranching Frontier in La Mancha and Estremadura," in A. R. Lewis and T. F. McGann, eds., *The New World Looks at Its History* (Austin, 1963), pp. 47–69; Oscar Halecki, *Borderlands of Western Civilization* (New York, 1952); Oscar Halecki, *The Millennium of Europe* (South Bend, Ind., 1963), pp. 65–76; F. Graus et al., *Eastern and Western Europe in the Middle Ages* (New York, 1970); and Lynn White, Jr., "The Legacy of the Middle Ages in the American Wild West," *Speculum* 40 (1965): 191–202.

4. As is so well illustrated in the pioneering work in comparative frontier history entitled *The Frontier: Comparative Studies* (cited in note 2 above). Its editors make the point: "It is clear from the studies in this volume that no one definition of the frontier has emerged, just as it is apparent that no singular methodology will suffice for every frontier study" (p. 8).

5. The historian of monasticism interested in relating monasticism to the

42

mainstream of medieval history has not had his task made easier by an abiding prejudice common in intellectual circles that monasticism is basically an antisocial institution. This prejudice had its genesis in the later Middle Ages and was repeatedly reinforced by the value systems that emerged during the Renaissance, the Reformation, the Enlightenment, and the nineteenth century with its multitude of isms.

6. No attempt will be made to cite the massive body of evidence that could be accumulated from the monastic record covering eight centuries in support of the points made in this chapter. The documentation is highly selective and illustrative only.

7. *Saint Athanasius: The Life of Saint Anthony*, trans. Robert T. Meyer, Ancient Christian Writers, no. 10 (Westminster, Md., 1950), passim, but especially chaps. 1–13, pp. 19–31; chaps. 49–53, pp. 61–65. It has generally been accepted that Christian monasticism in the proper sense of the word originated when Christian ascetics, representing a tradition that dated back almost to the origins of Christianity, decided to separate themselves from the world *in locis* as well as *in actibus*. See Karl Heussi, *Die Ursprung des Mönchtums* (Tübingen, 1936), for the most cogent argument on this point.

8. The full catalogue of such cases is far too extensive to list here. Some exemplary cases that illustrate the point are provided by the careers of Saints Jerome, Patrick, Benedict of Nursia, Columban, Boniface, Anskar, and Bernard of Clairvaux.

9. For helpful insights on the matter of monastic peregrination see Hans von Campenhausen, *Die asketische Heimatlosigkeit im altkirchlichen und frühmittelalterlichen Mönchtum* (Tübingen, 1930); Chrysostomus Baur, "Die weltflüchtige und weltätige Gedanke in der Entwicklung des Mönchtums," *Bonner Zeitschrift für Theologie und Seelsorge* 8 (1930): 113–26; Jacques Winandy, "L'idée de fuite du monde dans la tradition monastique," in *Le message des moines à notre temps* (Paris, 1958), pp. 95–104; Jean Leclercq, "Monachisme et pérégrination" in *Aux sources de la spiritualité occidentale: Étapes et constantes* (Paris, 1964), pp. 35–90; Eleanor Duckett, *The Wandering Saints of the Early Middle Ages* (New York, 1959); and B. Kötting, *Peregrinatio religiosa: Wallfahrt und Pilgerwesen in Antike und alter Kirche* (Münster, 1950).

10. The most reliable edition of the materials relevant to Simeon Stylites is Hans Lietzmann, *Das Leben des heiligen Symeon Stylites* (Leipzig, 1904). Older editions of the biographies can be found in *Acta Sanctorum* (hereafter cited as *AASS*), January, vol. 1 (Paris, 1863), pp. 261–86; and J. P. Migne, *Patrologiae Cursus Completus, Series Graeca* (hereafter cited as Migne, *PG*), vol. 114 (Paris, 1903), cols. 335–92. See also Theodoret, *Religiosa Historia*, c. 26, Migne, *PG*, vol. 82 (Paris, 1864), cols. 1464–84. A French translation of Theodoret's work on Symeon can be found in René Draguet, ed., *Les pères du désert*, Bibliothèque spirituelle du chrétien lettre (Paris, 1949), pp. 182–96.

For the Irish see, for example, *Navigatio Sancti Brendani Abbatis*, ed. Carl Selmer (South Bend, Ind., 1959); for an English translation see *The Voyage of Saint Brendan: Journey to the Promised Land, The Navigatio Sancti Brendani Abbatis*, trans. John J. O'Meara (Atlantic Highlands, N.J., 1976). For commentary on such activity see G. A. Little, *Brendan the Navigator* (Dublin, 1945); and Geoffrey Ashe, *Land to the West: St. Brendan's Voyage to America* (New York, 1962).

11. Some feeling for this environment is provided by *Saint Athanasius: The Life of Saint Anthony*; Jerome, *Vita s. Pauli Theboei*, in *AASS*, January, vol. 1 (Paris, 1863), pp. 602–607, English translation in Helen Waddell, *The Desert Fathers* (New York, 1936), pp. 35–53; *The Lausiac History of Palladius*, ed. Cuthbert Butler, 2 vols. (Cambridge, England, 1898–1904), English translation by Robert T. Meyer, *Palladius: The Lausiac History*, Ancient Christian Writers, no. 34 (Westminster, Md., 1965);

Apophthegmata Patrum (alphabetical version) in Migne, *PG*, vol. 65 (Paris, 1864), cols. 71–440, English version as *The Sayings of the Desert Fathers: The Alphabetical Collection*, trans. Benedicta Ward (London and Kalamazoo, Mich., 1975); *Vitae Patrum* (systematic version) in J. P. Migne, *Patrologiae Cursus Completus: Series Latina* (hereafter cited as Migne, *PL*), vol. 73 (Paris, 1878), cols. 851–1022, English translation of part of this collection by Owen Chadwick, *Western Asceticism*, Library of Christian Classics, vol. 12 (London, 1958), pp. 33–189; a French translation of the complete collection by L. Regnault, J. Dion, and G. Oury, *Les sentences des Pères du désert: Les apophtegmes des Pères (recension de Pélage et Jean)*, (Solesmes, 1966); *Historia Monachorum in Aegypto*, ed. A. J. Festugière, Subsidia hagiographica, no. 34 (Brussels, 1961); *Sancti Pachomii Vitae Graeci*, ed. F. Halkin, Subsidia hagiographica, no. 19 (Bruxelles, 1932) a French translation of the so-called first Greek life, the most important one, in A. J. Festugière, *Les moines d'Orient*, vol. 4, part 2 (Paris, 1965); *Pachomiana Latina*, ed. Amand Boon (Louvain, 1932); *Les vies coptes de Saint Pachôme et de ses premiers successeurs*, French trans. L. Th. Lefort, Bibliothèque du Muséon, vol. 16 (Louvain, 1943); and Eigil, *Vita s. Sturmi*, ed. G. H. Pertz, in *Monumenta Germaniae Historica* (hereafter cited as *MGH*), *Scriptores*, vol. 2 (Hanover, 1829), pp. 365–77. Some secondary works illustrative of the point include Derwas J. Chitty, *The Desert a City: An Introduction to the Study of Egyptian and Palestinian Monasticism under the Christian Empire* (Oxford, 1966); Hugh G. Evelyn-White, *The Monasteries of the Wâdi 'n Natrûn*, 3 vols. (New York, 1926–33); Stephan Schiwietz, *Das morgenländische Mönchtum*, 3 vols. (Mainz and Mödling, 1904–38); L. Th. Lefort, "Les premiers monastères pachômiens: Explorations topographiques," *Muséon*, 52 (1939): 379–407; *España eremetica: Actas de la VI semana de estudios monasticos, Abadía de San Salvador de Leyre, 15–20 septiembre de 1963*, Analecta legerensia, 1 (Pamplona, 1970); and Antonio Linage Conde, *Los orígines del monacato beneidctimo en la península ibérica*, 3 vols., Fuentes y estudios di historia leonesa, 9–11 (Leon, 1973).

12. The laura settlements are exemplified in the foundations of Euthymius the Great and Sabas; see their vitae by Cyril of Scythopolis, published by Eduard Schwartz, *Kyrillos von Skythopolis* Texte und Untersuchungen, vol. 49, no. 2 (Leipzig, 1939); a French translation of these lives is provided by Festugière, *Les moines d' Orient*, vol. 4, parts 1, 3 (Paris, 1962). On the monastic locations in Syria and Palestine see also Arthur Vööbus, *History of Asceticism in the Syrian Orient: A Contribution to the History of Culture in the Near East*, 2 vols., Corpus scriptorum christianorum orientalium, vols. 184, 197 (Louvain, 1958–60); Virgilio Corbo, "L'ambiente materiale della vita dei monaci di Palestina nel periodo bizantino," in *Il Monachesimo orientale: Atti del convegno di studi orientali che sul predetto tema si tenne a Roma, sotto la direzione del Pontificio Instituto orientale, nei giorni 9, 10, 11 e 12 aprile 1958*, Orientalia christiana analecta, vol. 153 (Rome, 1958), pp. 235–57; and Simon Jargy, "Les premiers instituts monastiques et les principaux représentants du monachisme syrien au IVe siècle," *Proche-Orient chrétien* 4 (1954): 106–17. For examples of this kind of monastic establishment in the West see the following: for Lerins, *Vitae Sanctorum Honorati et Hilarii, episcoporum Arletensium* ed. S. Cavallin (Lund, 1952); there is an English translation of the life of Honoratus in F. R. Hoare, trans. and ed., *The Western Fathers* (New York, 1954), pp. 248–80; for Saint Gall, *Vita Galli confessoris triplex*, ed. Bruno Krusch, *MGH, Scriptores rerum Merovingicarum*, vol. 4 (Hanover and Leipzig, 1902), pp. 229–37; for Reichenau, *Vita et miracula Sancti Pirmini*, ed. O. Holder-Egger, *MGH, Scriptores*, vol. 15[1] (Hanover, 1887), pp. 21–35; for Iona, *Adomnan's Life of Columba*, trans. and ed. Alan Orr Anderson and Marjorie Ogilvie Anderson (London

44

and New York, 1961); for Monte Cassino, Gregory the Great, *Dialogi*, in Migne, *PL*, vol. 66 (Paris, 1866), cols. 125–204; for an English version, *The Dialogues of Gregory the Great: Book Two, Saint Benedict*, trans. Myra L. Uhlfelder (Indianapolis, Ind., 1967); for Ligugé and Marmoutier, Sulpicius Severus, *Vita s. Martini*, in Migne, *PL*, vol. 20 (Paris, 1845), cols. 159–76; an English translation in Hoare, trans. and ed., *The Western Fathers*, pp. 10–44. A massive array of secondary works could be cited to enlarge on the history of the foundations of these particular monasteries and others that are comparable; a guide to that literature can be found in Patrice Cousin, *Précis d'histoire monastique* (Paris, n.d.), pp. 115–55, 183–216.

13. The displacement involved in missionary effort is amply illustrated by the following: For Patrick, *Bethu Phátraic; the Tripartite Life of Patrick*, trans. and ed. Kathleen Mulchrone, 2 vols. (Dublin, 1939); *The Tripartite Life of Patrick, With Other Documents Relating to That Saint*, trans. and ed. Whitley Stokes, 2 vols., Rolls Series, vol. 89 (London, 1887) (this collection contains the biographical sketches by Muirchú and Tirechan); and *The Works of St. Patrick*, trans. Ludwig Bieler, Ancient Christian Writers, no. 17 (Westminster, Md., and London, 1953). For Augustine, *Bede's Ecclesiastical History of the English People*, ed. Bertram Colgrave and R. A. B. Mynors, Oxford Medieval Texts (Oxford, 1969), bk. 2, chaps. 23–33; bk. 2, chaps. 2–3, pp. 68–116, 134–44; and *Gregorii I Papae Registrum Epistolarum*, ed. Paul Ewald and Ludovic M. Hartmann, in *MGH, Epistolae*, vols. 1 and 2 (Berlin, 1891), vol. 1, reg. vi, 49–57, pp. 423–32; vol. 2, reg.-viii, 4, 29, pp 5–8, 30–31; reg. ix, 213, 222, pp. 198–200, 213–14; reg. xi, 34–42, 47–51, 56–56a, pp. 303–16, 319–24, 330–43. For Aidan, *Bede's Ecclesiastical History of the English People*, ed. Colgrave and Mynors, bk. 2, chaps. 3–5, 14–17, pp. 218–28, 254–66; and *AASS*, August, vol. 6 (Paris and Rome, 1868), pp. 688–94. For Cuthbert, *Two Lives of Saint Cuthbert: A Life by an Anonymous Monk of Lindisfarne and Bede's Prose Life*, trans. and ed. Bertram Colgrave (New York, 1969). For Columban, *Vitae Columbani abbatis discipulorumque eius libri duo auctore Iona*, ed. Bruno Krusch, *MGH, Scriptores rerum Merovingicarum*, vol. 4 (Hanover and Leipzig, 1902), pp. 61–152. For Willibrord, Alcuin, *Vitae s. Willibrordi*, ed. A. Poncelet, in *AASS*, November, Vol. 3[1] (Paris, 1910), pp. 435–57; an English translation of Alcuin's prose life is found in C. H. Talbot, *The Anglo-Saxon Missionaries in Germany* (New York, 1954), pp. 3–22; and *Bede's Ecclesiastical History of the English People*, ed. Colgrave and Mynors, bk. 5, chaps. 10–11, pp. 480–86. For Boniface, Willibald, *Vita s. Bonifacii archiepiscopi*, ed. G. H. Pertz, *MGH, Scriptores*, vol. 2 (Hanover, 1829), pp. 333–53, an English translation in *The Life of Saint Boniface, by Willibald*, trans. George W. Robinson (Cambridge, Mass., 1916); and *Die Briefe des heiligen Bonifatius und Lullus*, ed. Michael Tangl, *MGH, Epistolae selectae*, vol. 1 (Berlin, 1916), an English translation of the letters of Boniface in *The Letters of Saint Boniface*, trans. Ephraim Emerton (New York, 1940). For Anskar, Rimbert, *Vita Anskarii*, ed. G. Waitz, *MGH, Scriptores rerum germanicarum in usum scholarum* (Hanover, 1884), an English translation by Charles H. Robinson, *Anskar: The Apostle of the North, 801–865* (London, 1921). For Cyril and Methodius, F. Dvornik, *Les légendes de Constantin et de Méthode vues de Byzance* (Prague, 1933, a French translation from the Slavic of the lives of these missionaries; and F. Dvornik, *Byzantine Missions Among the Slavs: SS. Constantine-Cyril and Methodius* (New Brunswick, N.J., 1970).

14. The evidence illustrating this special vocabulary for monastic communities is scattered through a vast literature; an important contribution to monastic history could be made by collecting and analyzing such evidence to clarify how monks perceived their spatial relationship with the world — and the other world. Suggestive of the approach is

Jacques Lacarrière, *Men Possessed by God: The Story of the Desert Fathers of Ancient Christendom*, trans. Roy Monkcom (Garden City, N.Y., 1964); and Claude J. Peifer, *Monastic Spirituality* (New York, 1966). The latter work has an excellent bibliography.

15. It is extremely difficult to classify neatly the motives that inspired monastic profession during the Middle Ages, especially where such profession involved a move to the frontier. This subject needs systematic investigation. Suggestive of an approach to the problem is a remarkable study by Uta Ranke-Heinemann, *Das frühe Mönchtum: Seine Motive nach den Selbstzeugnissen* (Essen, 1964). Some general ideas on the forces motivating medieval monastic profession can be found in Peter F. Anson, *The Call of the Desert: The Solitary Life in the Christian Church*, 2d ed. (London, 1964); Walter Nigg, *Warriors of God: The Great Religious Orders and Their Founders*, trans. and ed. Mary Ilford (New York, 1959); Olivier Rousseau, *Monachisme et vie religieuse d'après l'ancienne tradition de l'église* (Chevetogne, 1957); Louis Boyer, *La spiritualité du Nouveau Testament et des Pères*, Histoire de la spiritualité chrétienne, vol. 1 (Paris, 1960); Jean Leclercq, François Vandenbroucke, and Louis Boyer, *La spiritualité du moyen âge*, Histoire de la spiritualité chrétienne, vol. 2 (Paris, 1961); Marie-Humbert Vicaire, *L'imitation des apôtres. Moines, chanoines et mendiants, IVe–XIIIe siècles*, Tradition et spiritualité, vol. 2 (Paris, 1963); Augustin Blazovich, *Soziologie des Mönchtums und der Benediktinerregel* (Vienna, 1954); and Peifer, *Monastic Spirituality*.

16. There is hardly a monk about whom we have a record who did not turn to monastic life at least in part out of dissatisfaction with his world — at least so said his admirers who recorded his feats. Helpful in understanding this posture in the medieval world is Robert Bultot, *Christianisme et valeurs humaines: La doctrine du mépris du monde, en Occident, de S. Ambroise à Innocent III*, 6 vols. (Louvain, 1963–).

17. The prime exemplar of this force as a factor in driving the monk to the frontier is Boniface; see note 13 above for the appropriate references. For certain ramifications of his "civilizing" role see Theodor Schieffer, *Winfrid-Bonifatius und die christliche Grundlegung Europas* (Freiburg im Breisgau 1954); and Wilhelm Levison, *England and the Continent in the Eighth Century* (Oxford, 1946). Irish monasticism in its expansionist aspects was not without a civilizing mission; see Ludwig Bieler, *Ireland: Harbinger of the Middle Ages* (New York, 1963); and Louis Gougaud, *Gallic Pioneers of Christianity: The Work and Influences of Irish Monks and Saints in Continental Europe (Sixth to Twelfth Century)* (Dublin, 1923).

18. While there are elements of utopianism in many monastic sources, this aspect of monastic life is best exemplified by certain early "theoreticians" on the monastic profession. Of immense importance in this respect were the widely circulated and utilized collections of sayings attributed to the early desert-dwelling *abbas*, known variously as the *Apophthegmata patrum* or *Verbi seniorum* or *Vitae patrum*; see note 12 above for references to this material. Among the theoreticians particularly important in western monasticism were Jerome, Basil, John Cassian, Augustine of Hippo, Gregory the Great, and Bernard of Clairvaux. A convenient guide to the sources outlining Jerome's often confusing but influential ideas on monasticism is provided by P. Antin, "Le monachisme selon saint Jérôme," in *Mélanges bénédictine publiées à la occasion du XIVe Centenaire de la mort de saint Benoit par les moines de l'abbaye de Saint Jérôme de Rome* (Abbey Saint Wandrille, 1947), who cites certain letters, conferences, and sermons, as well as saints' lives and polemical texts crucial to Jerome's teachings on monasticism; see also P. Antin, *Essai sur Saint Jérôme* (Paris, 1951). Basil's teachings on monasticism are scattered throughout his works, which can be found in Migne, *PG*, vols. 29–32 (Paris, 1857–86); for relative texts in an English translation see *Saint Basil:*

Ascetical Works, trans. Sister M. Monica Wagner, Fathers of the Church, vol. 9 (New York, 1950); and *St. Basil, Letters*, trans. Sister Agnes Clare Way, 2 vols., Fathers of the Church, vols. 13, 28 (New York, 1951, 1955); excellent discussions of Basil's ideas can be found in David Amand, *L'ascèse monastique de Saint Basil: Essai historique* (Maredsous, 1949); and Sister Margaret Gertrude Murphy, *St. Basil and Monasticism* (Washington, D.C., 1930). Augustine of Hippo's teachings on monasticism, scattered widely throughout his immense corpus of writings, have been summarized by Adolar Zumkeller, *Das Mönchtum des heiligen Augustus*, 2d ed., Cassiciacum, vol. 11 (Wurzburg, 1968); A. Manrique, *La vida monástica en San Agustin: Enchiridion historico-doctrinal y Regla* (El Escorial and Salamanca, 1959); and A. Sage, *La Règle de Saint Augustin commentée par ses écrits* (Paris, 1961). John Cassian speaks eloquently for himself in two works of immense significance in monastic history: *Conferences*, trans. and ed. E. Pichery, 2 vols. Sources chrétiennes, vols. 42 and 54 (Paris, 1955–58); and *Institutions cenobitiques*, trans and ed. Jean-Claude Guy, Sources chrétiennes, vol. 109 (Paris, 1965); see also Jean-Claude Guy, *Jean Cassien: Vie et doctrine spirituelle* (Paris, 1961); and L. Cristiani, *Jean Cassien: La spiritualité du désert*, 2 vols. (Abbey Saint-Wandrille, 1946). For Gregory the Great see Olegario M. Porcel, *La doctrina monastica de San Gregorio Magno y la "Regula monachorum"* (Madrid, 1950). Bernard of Clairvaux's ideas on the nature of monastic life penetrate the entire corpus of his writings; these are available in Migne, *PL*, vols. 182–85 (Paris, 1854–79); some of these works have appeared in a new edition, *Sancti Bernardi Opera*, ed. J. Leclercq et al., vols. 1–5 (Rome, 1957–68); for English translations of relevant works see *The Letters of St. Bernard of Clairvaux*, trans. Bruno Scott James (London, 1953); and *The Works of Bernard of Clairvaux*, vols. 1–3, 5, Cistercian Series, nos. 1, 4, 7, 13 (Spencer, Mass., 1970–74); see also L. Lekai, *The White Monks* (Okauchee, Wis., 1953); J. Leclercq, *Recueil d'études sur Saint Bernard et ses écrits*, 3 vols. (Rome, 1962, 1966, 1969); L. Bouyer, *The Cistercian Heritage* (London, 1958); and Etienne Gilson, *The Mystical Theology of Saint Bernard*, trans. A. H. C. Downes (London and New York, 1955). An important analysis of monastic thought from this perspective can be found in *Théologie de la vie monastique: Études sur la tradition patristique*, Théologie: Études publiées sous la direction de la faculté de théologie S. J. de Lyon-Fourviere, 49 (Paris, 1961). That monastic utopianism had its impact is suggested by Gerhart B. Ladner, *The Idea of Reform: Its Impact on Christian Thought and Action in the Age of the Fathers* (Cambridge, Mass., 1959), especially pp. 319–424; and Jeffrey Burton Russell, *Dissent and Reform in the Early Middle Ages* (Berkeley and Los Angeles, 1965).

19. There is no adequate synthesis treating the monastic contribution to medieval civilization. For the period treated in this paper see Charles Montalembert, *The Monks of the West from Saint Benedict to Saint Bernard*, 6 vols. (London, 1896). Also useful are Jean Décarreaux, *Monks and Civilization: From the Barbarian Invasions to the Reign of Charlemagne*, trans. Charlotte Haldane (London, 1964); Philibert Schmitz, *Histoire de l'Ordre de Saint-Benoît*, 7 vols., 2d ed. (Maredsous, 1948–56), vols. 1–2; Friedrich Prinz, *Frühes Mönchtum im Frankreich: Kultur und Gesellschaft in Gallien, den Rheinlanden und Bayern am Beispiel der monastischen Entwicklung (4. bis 8. Jahrhundert)* (Munich and Vienna, 1965); *Il monachesimo nell'alto medioevo e la formazione della civiltà occidentale*, Settimane di studio del Centro italiano di studi sell'alto medioevo, 4 (Spoleto, 1957); Joachim Wollasch, *Mönchtum des Mittelalters zwischen Kirche und Welt*, Münstersche Mittelalter-Schriften, 7 (Munich, 1973); Christopher Brooke, *The Monastic World, 1000–1300* (London, 1974); and Richard E. Sullivan,

''Some Influences of Monasticism on Fourth and Fifth Century Society,'' *Studies in Medieval Culture* 2 (1966): 19–34.

20. For general guidance on monastic governance see David Knowles, *From Pachomius to Ignatius: A Study of the Constitutional History of the Religious Orders* (Oxford, 1966); Terence P. McLaughlin, *Les très ancien droit monastique de l'Occident: Étude sur le développement général du monachisme et ses rapports avec l'église seculière et le monde laïque de Saint Benoît de Nursie à Saint Benoît d'Aniane* (Ligugé and Paris, 1935); and Gabriel LeBras, *Institutions ecclésiastiques de la chrétienté médiévale*, Histoire de l'Église dupuis les origines jusqu'à nos jours, vol. 12 (Paris, 1959), pp. 178–201, 443–78.

21. On the origins of the Pachomian rule see the Pachomian sources cited in note 12; in addition see *Oeuvres de Saint Pachôme et de ses disciples*, trans. and ed. L. Th. Lefort, Corpus Scriptorum Christianorum Orientalium, vols. 159–60: Scriptores Coptici, vols. 23–24 (Louvain, 1956); and *La vie latine de Saint Pachôme: Traduite du grec par Denys le Petit*, ed. H. van Craneburgh, Subsidia hagiographica, no. 46 (Brussels, 1969). Helpful in understanding Pachomian governance are Paulin Ladeuze, *Étude sur le cénobitisme pakhomien pendant le IVe siècle et la première moitié du Ve* (Louvain and Paris, 1898); and Fidelis Ruppert, *Das pachomianische Mönchtum und die Anfänge klösterlichen Gehorsams* (Münster-Schwarzach, 1971).

22. The literature on the origins and constitutional import of the Benedictine rule is immense; see Bernhard Jaspert, ''Regula Magistri — Regula Benedicti: Bibliographie ihrer historisch-kritischen Erforschung 1938–1970,'' *Studia Monastica* 13 (1971): 129–71. Also helpful are the extensive commentaries on the rule provided in the following works: *La règle de Saint Benoît*, trans. and ed. Adalbert de Vogüé and Jean Neufville, 6 vols., Sources chrétiennes, vols. 181–86 (Paris, 1971–72); Paul Delatte, *The Rule of Saint Benedict: A Commentary*, trans. Justin McCann (Latrobe, Pa., 1950); and *Commentationes in regulam Santo Benedicti*, ed. Basilius Steidle, Studia Anselmiana, no. 42 (Rome, 1957). See also Basilius Steidle, *Die Regel St. Benedikts* (Beuron, 1952); John Chapman, *Saint Benedict and the Sixth Century* (London, 1929); and Raymond Tschudy, *Les Bénédictins* (Paris, 1963), especially pp. 67–197. Helpful in identifying the basic sources relating to the governance of Irish monasteries are Kathleen Hughes, *Early Christian Ireland: Introduction to the Sources*, Sources of History: Studies in the Use of Historical Evidence (Ithaca, New York, 1972); and Louis Gougaud, ''Inventaire des règles monastiques irlandaises,'' *Revue Bénédictine* 25 (1908); 167–84, 321–33; 28 (1911): 86–89. Excellent discussions are in John Ryan, *Irish Monasticism: Origins and Early Development* (Dublin, 1931); Nora Chadwick, *The Age of the Saints in the Early Celtic Church* (London and New York, 1961); Kathleen Hughes, *The Church in Early Irish Society* (London, 1966); and John T. McNeill, *The Celtic Churches: A History A.D. 200 to 1200* (Chicago, 1974). For the sources relevant to the Cistercian system see Joseph M. Canivez, ed., *Statuta Capitulorum Generalium Ordinis Cisterciensis, ab anno 1116 ad annum 1786*, 8 vols. (Louvain, 1933–41); and Joseph Turk, *Cistercii Statuta Antiquissima*, Analecta Sacri Ordinis Cisterciensis (Rome, 1949). Also helpful are Gregor Müller, *Vom Cistercienser Orden* (Bregrenz, 1927); Jean-Berthold Mahm, *L'ordre cistercien et son gouvernement des origines au milieu du XIIIe siècle (1098–1265)*, Bibliothèque des Écoles françaises d'Athènes et Rome, vol. 161 (Paris, 1961); and C. Bock, *Les Codifications du droit cistercien* (Westmalle, 1955).

23. Lewis Mumford, *Techniques and Civilization* (New York, 1934), pp. 12–18; and Lewis Mumford, *The Condition of Man* (New York, 1944), pp. 92–97. For monastic

labor see Luis Redonet y López Dóriga, *El trabajo manual en las reglas monásticas* (Madrid, 1919); and Etienne Delaruelle, "La travail dans les règles monastiques occidentales du quartième au neuvième siècle," *Journal de psychologie normale et pathologique* 41 (1948): 51–62.

24. L. Tosti, *Storia della badia di Monte-Cassino*, 3 vols. (Naples, 1842–43). The histories of early medieval monastic communities that failed for economic reasons have yet to be told.

25. The following is suggested by Robert Latouche, *The Birth of the Western Economy: Economic Aspects of the Dark Ages*, trans. E. M. Wilkinson (New York, 1966), pp. 59–96.

26. An integrated assessment of the impact of the monasteries on the economy of the early Middle Ages still needs to be made. Suggestive are the following: J. A. Raftis, "Western Monasticism and Economic Organization," *Comparative Studies in Society and History* 3 (1961): 452–69; Giuseppi Salvioli, "Il monachismo occidentale e la sua storia economica," *Rivista italiana di sociologia* 15 (1911): 8–35; Latouche, *Birth of the Western Economy*; Bark, *Origins of the Medieval World*; Prinz, *Frühes Mönchtum im Frankreich*; Schmitz, *Histoire de l'ordre de Saint Benoît*, vol. II, pp. 11–52; Décarreaux, *Monks and Civilization*, pp. 355–64; Georges Duby, *The Early Growth of the European Economy: Warriors and Peasants from the Seventh to the Twelfth Century*, trans. Howard B. Clarke (London, 1974); Georges Duby, *Rural Economy and Country Life in the Medieval West*, trans. Cynthia Postan (Columbia, S.C., 1968); *Agricoltura e mondo rurale in occidente nell'alto medioevo*, Settimane di studio del Centro Italiano di studi sull'alto medioeva, 13 (Spoleto, 1966); and Renée Doehard, *Le haut moyen âge occidental: Economies et sociétés*, Nouvelle Clio, no. 13 (Paris, 1971).

27. Julian, "To the Cynic Heracleios," in *The Works of the Emperor Julian*, trans. Wilmer Cave Wright, Loeb Classical Library (Cambridge, Mass., and London, 1930–53), vol. 2, p. 123.

28. Despite all that has been written about the monastic contribution to early medieval cultural life, the issue addressed here has not been adequately studied. For a suggested approach see Sullivan, "Some Influences of Monasticism on Fourth and Fifth Century Society," *Studies in Medieval Culture* 2 (1966): 19–34, with the appended bibliography. Extremely helpful in providing an orientation to the later centuries of the early Middle Ages are Décarreaux, *Monks and Civilization*, especially pp. 320–64; Schmitz, *Histoire de l'ordre de Saint Benoît*, vol. 2, pp. 55–421; *Il monachesimo nell'alto medioevo e la formazaione della civiltà occidentale*, Settimane di studio del Centro Italiano di studi sull'alto medioevo, no. 4 (Spoleto, 1957); *Centri e vie di irradiazione della civiltà nell'alto medioevo*, Settimane di studio del Centro Italiano di studi sull'alto medioevo, no. 11 (Spoleto, 1964); Pierre Riché, *Education and Culture in the Barbarian West, Sixth Through Eighth Centuries*, trans. John J. Contreni (Columbia, S.C., 1976); and the remarkable study by Jean Leclercq, *The Love of Learning and the Desire for God: A Study of Monastic Culture*, trans. Catharine Mishrahi, 2d rev. ed. (New York, 1974). For the uniqueness of "monastic culture" in terms of what preceded and followed, see Charles Norris Cochrane, *Christianity and Classical Culture* (London, 1944); and Vincenzo Cilento, *Medio evo monastico e scholastico* (Milan and Naples, 1961).

29. The most dramatic example of the dependence of a frontier monastic establishment on a hinterland is provided by Boniface during his missionary efforts in Germany in the first half of the eighth century; see his *Letters* (note 13 above).

30. The concepts of leadership generated in "frontier" monasteries are best articulated in the evolving ideas about the office of abbot. They key sources are the

Apophthegmata patrum, the Pachomian corpus, the *Historica Lausica* of Palladius, Cassian's writings, Benedict of Nursia's rule, Gregory the Great's *Dialogues*, and Basil's writings; for editions of these works, see notes 11, 12, 18, 21, and 22 above. For some general points on the evolution of this office see Pierre Salmon, *The Abbot in Monastic Tradition: A Contribution to the History of the Perpetual Character of the Office of Religious Superiors in the West*, trans. Claire Lavoie (Washington, D.C., 1972); and Gregorio Penco, "La figura dell'abata nella tradizione spirituale del monachesimo," *Benedictina* 17 (1970): 1–12. For further references on the point see Sullivan, "Some Influences of Monasticism on Fourth and Fifth Century Society," *Studies in Medieval Culture* 2 (1966): 30–31. The impact of the saint-hero of the monastic world on the mentality of the secular clergy and the laity is an inadequately explored field; suggestive is the pioneering work of Hippolyte Delehaye, *The Legends of the Saints*, trans. Donald Attwater (New York, 1962).

31. For some works suggestive of the impact of monasticism on medieval reform movements see Russell, *Dissent and Reform in the Early Middle Ages;* Ladner, *The Idea of Reform*; Schieffer, *Winfrid-Bonifatius und die christliche Grundlegung Europas*; Suzanne Dulcy, *La règle de Saint Benoit d'Aniane et la réforme monastique à l'époque carolingienne* (Nimes, 1935); Herbert E. J. Cowdrey, *The Cluniacs and the Gregorian Reform* (Oxford, 1970); Kassius Hallinger, *Gorze-Kluny: Studien zu den monastischen Lebensformen und Gegensätzen in Hochmittelalter*, 2 vols. Studia Anselmiana, nos. 22–25 (Rome, 1950–51); Ernst Werner, *Pauperes Christi: Studien zu sozial-religiösen Bewegungen im Zeitalter des Reformpapsttums* (Leipzig, 1956); *Il monachesimo e la riforma ecclesiastica (1049–1122): Atti della quarta settimana internationale di studio, Mendola, 23–29 agosto 1968*, Pubblicazioni dell'Università cattolica del Sacro Cuore, Miscellanea del Centro di studi medioevali, no. 6 (Milan, 1971).

32. For this point see Sullivan, "Some Influences of Monasticism on Fourth and Fifth Century Society," *Studies in Medieval Culture* 2 (1966): 21–27.

33. Suggestive are Richard E. Sullivan, "The Carolingian Missionary and the Pagan," *Speculum*, 28 (1953): 705–40; and Richard E. Sullivan, "Khan Boris and the Conversion of Bulgaria: A Case Study of the Impact of Christianity on a Barbarian Society," in *Studies in Medieval and Renaissance History*, ed. William M. Bowsky, vol. 2 (Lincoln, Nebr., 1966), pp. 53–139.

34. See Richard E. Sullivan, "The Consequences of Retreat from the World: The Case of Medieval Monasticsm," *Indiana Social Studies Quarterly* 24 (1971–72): 17–19.

BIBLIOGRAPHICAL NOTE

The following works will provide a guide to the most significant recent works on missionary activity in the early Middle Ages.

Art., 'Bekehrung und Bekehrungsgeschichte', in *Reallexikon der germanischen Altertumskunde*, 2 (Berlin and New York, 1976), cols. 174–204

Art., 'Christentum der Bekehrungszeit', in *Reallexikon der germanischen Altertumskunde*, 4 (Berlin and New York, 1981), cols. 501–98

Cristianizzazione ed organizzazione ecclesiastica delle campagne nell'alto medioevo: Espansione e resiztenze, 2 vols. (Settimane di studio del Centro Italiano di studi sull'Alto Medioevo, 28 [Spoleto, 1982]).

La conversione al cristianesimo nell'Europa dell'alto medioevo (Settimane di studio del Centro Italiano di studi sull'Alto Medioevo, 14 [Spoleto, 1967]).

Haendler, Gert, *Die lateinische Kirche im Zeitalter der Karolinger* (Kirchengeschichte in Einzeldarstellungen, I, 7 [Berlin, 1985]).

Handbuch der Kirchengeschichte, ed. Hubert Jedin, vol 2: *Die Reichskirche nach Konstantin dem Grossen*, Part 2: *Die Kirche in Ost und West von Chalkedon biz zum Frümittelalter (451–700)*, by Karl Baus, Hans-Georg Beck, Eugen Ewig, and Herman Josef Vogt (Freiburg, Vienna, Basel, 1975); and vol. 3: *Die mittelalterliche Kirche*, Part 1: *Vom kirchlichen Frümittelalter zur gregorianischen Reform*, by Friedrich Kempf, Hans-Georg Beck, Eugen Ewig, and Josef Andreas Jungmann (Freiburg, Basel, and Vienna, 1966) (English translation as *Handbook of Church History*, ed. Hubert Jedin and John Dolan, vol. 2: *The Imperial Church from Constantine to the Early Middle Ages*, trans. Anselm Biggs [New York, 1980]; vol. 3: *The Church in the Age of Feudalism*, trans. Anselm Biggs [New York, 1969]).

Die Kirche in ihrer Geschichte. Ein Handbook, ed. K. D. Schmidt and E. Wolf, vol. 2, Part E: Gert Haendler, *Geschichte des Frühmittelalters und der Germanmission*, and G. Stökl, *Geschichte der Slavenmission*, 2nd ed. (Göttingen and Zurich, 1976).

Kirchengeschichte als Missionsgeschichte, ed. H. Frohnes et al, vol. 2, 1: *Die Kirche des frühen Mittelalters*, ed. Kurt Schäferdiek (Munich, 1978).

Morrison, Karl F., *Understanding Conversion* (Charlottesville and London, 1992).

INDEX

Abbreviations: ab.=archbishop; abb.=abbot; b.=bishop; d.=duke; k.=king; n.=footnote or endnote; q.=queen

Abbots, missionary: II 710–11
Acacius, patriarch Constantinople: IV 128
Adalgar, ab. Hamburg–Bremen: III 102
Adalwin, ab. Salzburg: III 100
Adelberga, Frisian noblewoman: II 738
Adoloald, Lombard prince: III 49
Agatho, pope: III 63, 64
Agilbert, b. Dorchester: III 62
Agrestius, monk: III 66
Aidan, monk: VI 28 n.13
Ailus, monk: III 66
Albericus, b. Utrecht: II 709, 720
Alchfrid, Northumbrian prince: III 64
Alcuin: I 277–8, 279–80, 281–3, 284;
  II 707, 716, 718, 719 n.96; III 47, 64,
  84; V 23, 28
Aldgisl, k. Frisia: III 70
Alemannia, Alemannians: I 287; II 716;
  III 65, 66, 77–8
Alexander the Great: IV 129
Alexandria: VI 27, 38
Amandus, b. Maastricht: III 65, 66, 67
Ambrose, b. Milan: IV 126
American Civil War: VI 30
American frontier: VI 27
Amöneberg: II 707, 727; III 75 n.44
Anastasius Bibliothecarius: IV 64
Anatolia: VI 34
Anglo-Saxon missionaries: I 279, 280–1; II
  714; III 68–80, 81
Angrarians: II 723
Anno, b. Friesing: III 100
Anskar (Ansgar), ab. Hamburg-Bremen:
  II 713, 714, 726–7, 731, 736, 739;
  III 80, 85–6, 87, 89, 89 n.1, 90–1, 102;
  IV 101; V 17, 21, 29; VI 27 n.8, 28
  n.13
Anthony, St: VI 27
Antioch: VI 38
Apophthegmata patrum: VI 30 n.18
Apostles' Creed: I 287
Appalachians: VI 27
Aquileia: III 84, 87

Archbishops, missionary: II 710–11
Arianism, Arians: III 49; IV 126; V 26
Arigius, patricius of Gaul: III 53
Arius: IV 126
Arles: III 53, 54
Armenia: III 49, 93
Arn, ab. Salzburg: I 279; III 84
Arnulf, k. East Franks: III 102
Asterius, ab. Milan: III 59
Athanasius, ab. Alexandria: IV 126; VI 27,
  34
Atherius, b. Lyons III 53 n.49
Atlantic Ocean: VI 27
Augustine, ab. Canterbury: III 53–7, 60; V
  17, 21, 24 n.42; VI 28 n.13
Augustine, b. Hippo: I 282–4; II 719 n.96;
  IV 126; VI 30 n.18, 34
Autharith, k. Lombards: III 49
Avars: I 277, 278, 279, 282, 283, 284;
  II 715, 718, 719 n.96; 724, 730, 733;
  III 46, 49, 80, 81, 83–4, 87; V 22

Balkans: III 49, 59: V 19, 20
Baptism: III 77, 79;
  of Bulgar converts: IV 76–8
Barbaricini: III 50, 51
Basil, ab. Caesarea: VI 30 n.18
Basil I, emperor: III 99, 99 n.49; IV 81, 97;
  V 19
Bavaria, Bavarians: I 287; II 710, 711, 715,
  724, 725; III 65, 66, 69, 72, 74, 77–80, 81
Bavarian clergy: II 725–6; III 87, 91,
  100–2; V 23, 25
Bede: II 722, 730n; III 47, 54, 56, 60, 60
  n.10, 61, 62 n.22, 63-4, 70, 71; VI 36
Belgrade: IV 97
Benedict III, pope: III 81
Benedict Biscop, abb.: III 64
Benedict of Nursia: VI 27 n.8, 28, 32, 40
Benedictine order: III 52, 58, 105; VI 33
Bernard, abb. Clairvaux: VI 27 n.8, 28, 30
  n.18, 40
Bernrad, abb.: II 708